The Sims 2 Pets

PRIMA Official Game Guide

Greg Kramer

Prima Games
A Division of Random House, Inc.
3000 Lava Ridge Court
Roseville, CA 95661
1-800-733-3000
www.primagames.com

Product Manager: Todd Manning
Editor: Alaina Yee
Design & Layout: Cathi Marsh

ISBN: 0-7615-5452-1
Library of Congress Catalog Card Number: 2006931183
Printed in the United States of America

06 07 08 09 GG 10 9 8 7 6 5 4 3 2

About the Author

Greg Kramer is a freelance writer residing in Washington DC. Since entering the game industry in 1993, Greg has written over forty strategy guides including *The Sims 2*, *Championship Manager 3*, *Command & Conquer Renegade*, *Icewind Dale 2*, *SimCity 4*, *Sid Meir's Pirates*, *The Movies*, *Ace Combat 4: Shattered Skies*, *The Sims Bustin' Out*, *Unreal Tournament 2: The Liandri Conflict*, *Rayman 3: Hoodlum Havoc*, *The Suffering*, and *American McGee's Alice*.

In prior lives, Greg was a foreign service spouse (with tours in Tel Aviv, Israel, and Calgary, Canada), a real estate attorney, an unhappy law student at the University of Maryland, an English/College Basketball major at Duke University, and the only Jewish student at a Catholic military high school.

TABLE OF CONTENTS

INTRODUCTION AND OVERVIEW

Welcome, ladies and gentlemen, boys and girls, kids of all ages, to the first ever multiplatform guide to *The Sims*™ 2. With the long-awaited addition of pets to *The Sims* 2, it seemed fitting that we collect all there is to know about these complex beasts in one tidy volume that covers:

◆ THE SIMS 2 PETS expansion pack for PC

◆ THE SIMS 2 PETS for PlayStation 2 and Nintendo GameCube

◆ THE SIMS 2 PETS for PSP handheld

> **note**
> THE SIMS 2 PETS is also available for the Nintendo Gameboy Advance and Nintendo DS, but these incarnations differ drastically from the games covered in this book; therefore, we had to omit them from this guide.

Though each of these games differs considerably, they share many fundamental elements and strategies. As such, this guide consists of two parts:

◆ Part I: An in-depth exploration of changes and new content introduced in the PC expansion pack. Part I also includes appendices containing unified tables of all objects, social interactions, and career tables from all prior expansion and stuff packs, and the original THE SIMS 2.

◆ Part II: A complete guide to the latest console version of THE SIMS 2 franchise (PlayStation 2 and Nintendo GameCube) as well as the nearly identical PSP incarnation. This guide includes information on the entire game from basic Sim life to the newly introduced pets. Finally, Part II highlights the minor differences between the console and PSP version so that handheld players can adjust their strategies to these small variations.

Commonalities

The PC and console versions of *The Sims 2 Pets* share many elements, though the details of each can differ in important ways.

Here are a few things these games have in common:

◆ Pet Simulator: Many of the fundamental mechanisms of Sim pet life are the same or very similar in all three versions of the game.

◆ Pet social relationships: Pets have special kinds of relationships that are the same or similar on all three platforms.

◆ Pet training: Pets can be trained to varying degrees and in different ways in each version, but the basic methods are the same.

◆ Create a Dog and Create a Cat: Though the level of detail and customization differ considerably between platforms, many of the same steps and principles guide the creation of your Sims' pets.

◆ Pet breeding and genetics: Pets reproduce in similar ways among the three versions, though what happens after birth is very different.

◆ Objects and socials: Several of the objects and social interactions found in the PC expansion are also found in identical (or nearly identical) form in the console and PSP versions.

The subtle differences in how each game works on each platform demands that they be treated separately, each in its proper place. Therefore, this book is structured so each part contains all the information you need for your version of the game.

Cross-Platform Unlocks

The clearest connection between the PC and console versions of the game is a shared, cross-platform system of unlockables. Unlocking these rewards generates alphanumeric codes that can be traded to either PC or console players to unlock content (though not necessarily the same content) for free.

Many of the unlockable rewards are the same for both platforms, but others differ; consequently, a code for one unlock on the console will release a very different reward on the PC (or vice versa). For example, if a console player unlocks the Orange Cat Hat and trades the code to a friend with the PC version, the friend will receive the Navy Hearts Collar for Cats. The following table shows the equivalent unlocks on each platform.

Console Unlocks	PC Unlocks
Pink Cat Bandana	Black Dot Collar for Cats
Green Dog Shirt	Blue Star Collar for Dogs
Pink Cat Glasses	Blue Camouflage Collar for Cats
Green Dog Cowboy Hat	Navy Hearts Collar for Dogs
Orange Cat Hat	Navy Hearts Collar for Cats
Pink Dog Bandana	Black Dot Collar for Dogs
Orange Dog Collar	White Zebra Stripe Collar for Dogs
Red Cat Fur Color	Deep Red Fur Color for Cats
Pink Dog Marking Color	Neon Green Fur Color for Dogs
Green Dog Fur Color	Green Fur Color for Dogs
Pink Cat Marking Color	Neon Green Fur Color for Cats
Orange Cat Shirt	Orange Diagonal Collar for Cats
Green Cat Bandana	Green Flower Collar for Cats

Console Unlocks	PC Unlocks
Blue Cat Fur Color	Blue Fur Color for Cats
Green Dog Catseye Glasses	Pink Vertical Stripes Collar for Dogs
Blue Cat Glasses	White Paws Collar for Cats
Purple Dog Marking Color	Light Green Fur Color for Dogs
Red Dog Fur Color	Deep Red Fur Color for Dogs
Purple Cat Marking Color	Light Green Fur Color for Cats
Green Cat Collar	Black Smiley Collar for Cats
Pink Dog Fur Color	Pink Fur Color for Dogs
Green Dog Bandana	Green Flower Collar for Dogs
Pink Dog Aviator Glasses	Blue Camouflage Collar for Dogs
Green Cat Glasses	Pink Vertical Stripes Collar for Cats
Green Dog Collar	Black Smiley Collar for Dogs
Red Dog Marking Color	Bandit Mask Coat Marking for Dogs
Blue Cat Marking Color	Neon Yellow Fur Color for Cats
Purple Cat Fur Color	Purple Fur Color for Cats
Red Cat Marking Color	Stars Coat Marking for Cats
Blue Cat Hat	Blue Bones Collar for Cats
Green Dog Marking Color	Goofy Fur Color for Dogs
Blue Dog Fur Color	Blue Fur Color for Dogs
Purple Dog Glasses	White Paws Collar for Dogs
Green Cat Marking Color	Goofy Fur Color for Cats
Orange Cat Collar	White Zebra Stripe Collar for Cats
Green Cat Shirt	Blue Star Collar for Cats
Orange Dog Shirt	Orange Diagonal Collar for Dogs
Pink Cat Fur Color	Pink Fur Color for Cats
Pink Dog Golf Hat	Blue Bones Collar for Dogs
Blue Dog Marking Color	Neon Yellow Fur Color for Dogs
Green Cat Fur Color	Green Fur Color for Cats
Panda Cat Marking	Panda Coat Marking for Cats
Zebra Dog Marking	Zebra Stripes Coat Marking for Dogs
Purple Dog Fur Color	Purple Fur Color for Dogs
Star Dog Marking	Stars Coat Marking for Dogs
Bandit Mask Cat Marking	Bandit Mask Coat Marking for Cats

note

Three PC unlocks release both a Create a Dog or Create a Cat element and a new breed in the Breed Bin. See the "Pet Life" chapter.

Unlocking Systems

The order and method of each platform's unlockables is different:

◆ PC: Unlockables are released when a pet on any lot gets a career promotion. Anytime a new promotion is achieved, an unlockable is randomly chosen and released. Thus, if you avoid playing the pet career game, your only source of unlocked content will be a console player or another PC player.

◆ Console: Unlockables are released in a specific order based on your entire town's cumulative earned Pet points (see the "Pet Life" chapter in Part II). Though these unlocks are set for certain point thresholds, using unlock codes before these points are earned will lower the point requirement for any future unlock. Thus, if unlock X requires 5,000 Pet points, unlock Y requires 8,000, and unlock Z requires 10,000 and you get Y via a code, unlock Z will instead release at 8,000 points and all other unreleased unlocks will drop one level. See the "Unlockables Summary" chapter in Part II for the full list and Pet point requirements.

Generating Codes for Sharing

Once you have an unlockable, you can share it by giving its code to another player. These codes are found and generated in different places on the two platforms:

PC

Go to Options, Game Options, and click on the key-shaped icon in the lower right.

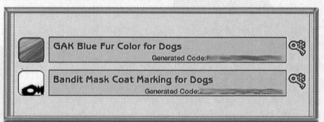

Each unlock shows its current sharable code.

Console

Locate the unlocked fashion item, fur color, marking color, or marking pattern in Create a Cat or Create a Dog and highlight it to display its current code. If you've unlocked something

and haven't yet personalized it, you must do so before you can generate a code.

note

Console players can also share breed mixes by entering genetic codes at the Pet Plaza pet store. We cover this in the "Unlockables Summary" chapter in Part II, since they can be traded only between consoles.

Personalizing Unlockables

When trading codes you've unlocked in the game, you can add a personal tag that will display when another player enters the code. Think of it as attaching a gift card to a nicely wrapped present.

note

On PC, codes are changed when you personalize them, so don't trade a code until after you've entered your personal message.

Personalized messages can be no longer than eight characters and can be applied to unlocks that you obtained through the game or from a shared code.

On PC, press the key-shaped button next to the unlocked item to add personalized gift messages. Change this message as many times as you like.

On console, locate an unlocked item, color, and so on, in Create a Cat or Create a Dog, highlight it, and press the Generate Sims Gift Code button. Add your personal tag and it's ready to send. Once generated, a code can't be changed.

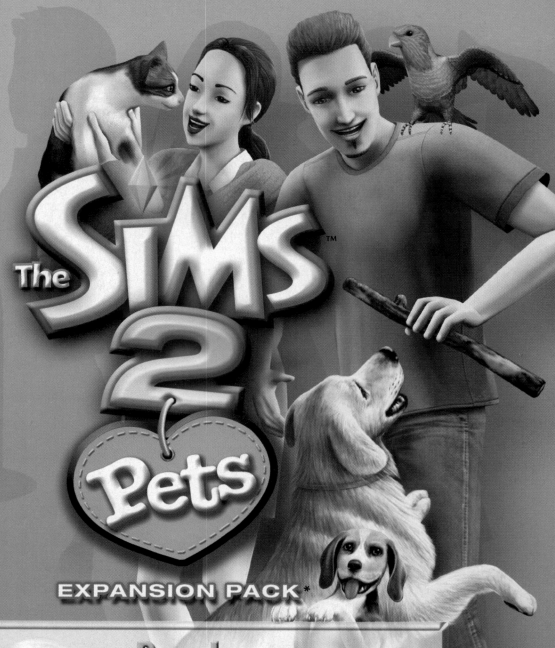

The Sims 2 Pets

EXPANSION PACK *

PART I
THE SIMS™ 2 PETS PC EXPANSION

In Part I, we dissect, inspect, scrutinize, and otherwise analyze every bit of *The Sims 2 Pets* expansion pack: the little things that make pets tick, the new Build mode tools that enable even more intricate structures, and the miscellaneous changes included in every expansion pack.

* Requires The Sims™ 2 or The Sims™ 2 Special DVD Edition to play.

Chapter 1

OVERVIEW AND MISCELLANEOUS NEW FEATURES

The Sims 2 Pets allows your Sims to have pets. Note that it doesn't allow *you* to have pets. The difference may seem minor, but with the over-abundance of pet games out there, it's important to understand exactly what you're getting.

Pets offer your Sims several benefits:

◆ Pets, at the most basic level, are living, breathing Fun and Social objects. Take care of them by providing for their Needs and make sure they're well trained. Your Sims will rarely hunt for entertainment or companionship.

◆ Pets are employable and earn money for the family funds. Getting jobs for your Sim's pets allows your Sim to tend to other matters; pets actually earn more than employed teens and elders.

◆ Pets bring new challenges. The powerful perks that pets provide don't come free, however. To have a pet that's more help than hassle, your Sims must divert attention from other obligations to ensure the pet is well trained. Sims may have to squeeze training and paying attention to pets between work, school, child care, running a business, and the various demands of their Wants and Needs. Keeping all these balls in the air can be tough, but it's a pretty fun juggling act with big rewards for your Sims.

◆ Pets make great stories. For those who like to use THE SIMS 2 as a canvas for their own imagination, pets open vast new possibilities. There is, for example, no rule that says you have to make a well-behaved pet. You can, in fact, train any pet to be a monstrous menace as long as you keep them contained or don't care what havoc they inflict on your Sims' home. With the powerful new Create a Dog and Create a Cat tools in Create A Family, and some out-there unlockable colors and markings, creative players can construct literal monsters.

These and more are possible thanks to a long slate of new features that are jammed into this cuddly new expansion pack. In *The Sims 2 Pets*, you get:

◆ Cats and dogs that, though not directly controllable, are living parts of your Sims' families with their own Needs, relationships, personalities, and abilities.

◆ Pet careers allow your pets to earn their keep by bringing home some bacon of their own.

◆ The new Create a Cat and Create a Dog sections of Create A Family let you mold, shape, and twist your pet in intriguing ways and design layered markings and coats of staggering complexity and beauty (or hideousness).

- Caged pets provide some of the fun of cat and dog ownership with a lower obligation for your Sims. If you do have cats and dogs, however, a caged pet can be a great source of pet entertainment.

- Pets can learn tricks and be taught to behave (or not) with two different kinds of training.

- A pet genetics system harnesses the power of the genome to shape your pets for generations.

- A revamp of the Collections system makes collections more accessible and powerful; collections are valid for both community and residential lots, and you can rename them, rearrange them, and more.

- Sims can be directed to create custom paintings from your own pictures.

- Build mode tools quickly create diagonal and octagonal rooms, diagonal roofs, fences, and half-walls; flatten a lot with one click; spin and cut floor tiles; destroy all objects and structures on a tile; and create flat fences for visual texture.

- Moving objects into and out of inventory is streamlined with a new Inventory hotkey.

- Invite over entire households (including pets) even if your Sims know only one family member.

- Let your Sims become more like their pets by turning them into werewolves.

- Many new Build and Buy mode objects and dozens of old objects changed to be useable (and we mean "useable") by pets.

- New service Sims, Sim Bin families, inhabited homes, pet-themed community lots, and unpredictable suburban wildlife.

- New cheats enable you to place formerly inaccessible accessories in your Sims' home for decorative or storytelling purposes, keep your puppies and kittens small forever, change the slope on individual parts of roofs, delete several build elements at once, make your pets controllable, deactivate pet free will, cancel actions from pets' queues, and show which game or expansion pack an objects belongs to.

- A new Game Tip Encyclopedia, found in the Options menu, provides easy access to all game tips (organized by game/ expansion pack), including ones that don't automatically arise in-game.

- Lot catalog can be made more useful by moving custom lots (marked with "*") to the front of the list and marking EA-created lots with the icon of the expansion pack that installed them.

Chapter 2
CREATE A CAT/DOG AND ACQUIRING PETS

The saying goes that great men are born, not made. The same can't be said of Sim pets; the great ones can be made, born, adopted, bought, or simply found. To be more specific, pets can be acquired by:

◆ Creating them in Create A Family using the Create a Dog or Create a Cat tools as part of a family (that includes Sims) and moving the whole family into an empty house or merging them with an existing household.

◆ Creating them in Create A Family in a household without Sims and merging them with a moved-in family.

◆ Adopting them by phone.

◆ Buying them from a community lot pet store.

◆ Getting them from another playable Sim.

◆ Befriending and taking in a stray.

This chapter examines all the possible ways that pets can be created or added to your Sims' households.

Create a Cat and Create a Dog

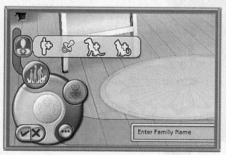

Create a Dog and Create a Cat buttons have been added to the Create-A-Sim menu.

The tools for Create a Dog and Create a Cat bear some resemblence to those for Create A Family, but many are new and work a bit differently than you may be used to.

Species

From the basic Create A Family screen, the Create-A-Sim button now leads to two new tools: Create a Dog and Create a Cat.

Your future pet's species is, therefore, the first of many choices you'll have to make.

note

The "Enter Family Name" box is optional at this point. If the family you create is composed entirely of pets, you'll never have to give them a family name in Create A Family. The resulting pet-only family will receive the temporary family moniker of "pets" until they're incorporated into an existing household.

Step 1: Name, Gender, Size, and Age

The process begins with a randomly generated pet of your chosen species that you can either use as is, use and modify, replace with another random breed, or swap for a specific breed in the next step (panel 2).

Panel 1 for dogs.

For cats, there's only one size choice.

Name

Name your pet whatever you want.

Sex

Pets can be either male or female, but this makes no difference in the pet's appearance. In fact, this choice affects only three things:

1. How the pet will relieve itself (leg up or squat)
2. With what sex they'll be able to breed
3. Whether they're still able to reproduce as elders (males only).

Pets of different sexes answer nature's call in different ways.

Age

Pets can be created in one of two ages: adult or elder. Pets spend a fixed number of days in each age, so this selection determines roughly how long this particular pet will be in the game.

The time (in days) in each age depends on both species and size:

Pet	Adult	Elder
Cat	25	5–10
Small Dog	25	5–10
Large Dog	21	5–10

 note

Adult or elder pets may have their current age extended by up to three days if they're commanded to eat from the Aspiration reward object, the Kibble of Life.

Adult pet.

Same pet as an elder.

note

Generally, if a Sim receives an adult pet as a child, the pet will die around the time the Sim becomes an elder. If the pet reproduces around the middle of its adult stage, the child Sim should live to see two or three generations of that pet's line.

Pug.

Giant Pug!

Elder pets get a gray fur layer and a more aged gait, and their Needs decay differently (see the "Pet Life" chapter). Elders' gray fur markings aren't editable or inheritable (if the pet breeds as an elder).

Size

You can, depending on the species, specify your pet's overall size.

Dogs

Dogs can be either large or small. Your choice of size will change the breeds available in the breed bin. For example, Jack Russell Terriers are only available from the Breed Bin if you choose small size, and Newfoundlands are only available after choosing large size.

Once you choose a breed, however, you can switch the size selector (in panel 1) to the other option and make larger versions of small dogs and smaller versions of large dogs.

note

Breeds that are already miniature versions of larger dogs (i.e., Shiba Inus vs. Akitas) will look very much like their larger version if you switch their size (and vice versa).

In addition to refining your initial breed choices, your size selection has a few repercussions. Large dogs have shorter life spans than smaller dogs, and there are a few object interactions that are exclusive to each size. For example, only large dogs may do the Chill interaction on bay windows (looking out the windows with paws on the sill).

Size makes no difference in whether two dogs may breed, though part of each pup's genome includes a size from either its mother or father.

Cats

Cats come in only one size.

Random

After you select a species and a size, you can randomly select a breed by pressing the Randomize button. Each time you press Randomize:

1. A breed from the Breed Bin is chosen. You'll only get breeds for your currently selected size, and the chosen pet could be from the shipping breeds, any breeds you've crafted and saved into the Breen Bin, and any player-designed breeds you've imported.

2. Personality traits are set to random positions (see panel 6).

Once a random pet is chosen, you can Randomize again or change any of the settings you like, including size (for dogs).

 note

If you delete all the breeds from the Breed Bin, Randomize will choose for you a body archetype, base coat color, and Personality.

Pet Bio

You can pen a bio for any pet to create a story about your new masterpiece.

Step 2: Choose a Breed

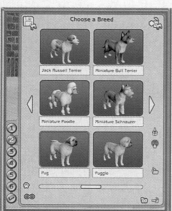

Panel 2, aka the Breed Bin.

In panel 2 of Create a Dog or Create a Cat, you can choose from saved breeds for the currently selected species and size.

A breed is a saved pet of a given species and size (for dogs). It can also include:

◆ Any number of coat and markings layers (see the "Step 3" section) and colors.

◆ Fur accessories (see the "Step 4" section)

◆ Coat shape (dogs only)

◆ Modifications to body, full face, brow and eyes, snout and jaw, ears, and tail.

A breed does *not* include:

◆ Sex   ◆ Collar

◆ Age   ◆ Personality

Your expansion pack includes several built-in breeds for each species/size. These breeds hew as closely as possible to the standards of each real-world breed or mix. The number of available breeds varies by species and size:

◆ Large dogs: 52 breeds   ◆ Cats: 31 breeds

◆ Small dogs: 25 breeds

 tip

The shipping breeds are artists' interpretations of what a "typical" pet of each breed looks like. Since individual cats and dogs vary in their features, you may have to change some things to mold a breed to your personal interpretation or resemblance to a specific pet in your life.

The blank slate Create a Dog.

Each bin also includes one blank-slate pet entitled "Create a Cat" or "Create a Dog." This "breed," with no markings or colors, is a good starting point for sculpting your own breed from scratch.

Save Breed

After you finish shaping a pet, you can save its finished form as a template for future pets; go to panel 2 and press the Save Breed button. This adds your custom breed to the bin, and you can select it either manually or when generating a random pet.

New breeds can also be added in-game by directing a Sim in the pet's household to use the telephone to Register Breed. This saves the specified pet's size, colors, markings, archetype, and modifiers as a new breed template for future selection. This is an excellent way to preserve and duplicate a pet created through in-game breeding.

Remove Breed

You can delete everything except the shipped breeds from the Breed Bin by pressing the Remove Breed button. This is permanent, so use this tool only if you're very sure.

Package Pet

Finished pets—including their gender, age, size, colors, markings, face and body shapes, collar, and Personality—can be saved and shared with others by packaging them. Packaging a pet works exactly like packaging a lot in the basic game.

Pets can be packed:

♦ To a file that can be imported via the Package Installer application. Press the Package Pet to a File button.

♦ To TheSims2.com to be shared with all players around the world. Press the Package Pet to TheSims2.com button.

Step 3: Coat Colors and Markings

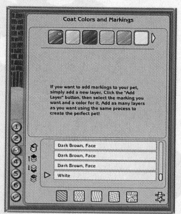

Panel 3.

Pets are as defined by their color and markings as they are by their overall shape. The combination of these factors that comprise a pet's appearance can range from the simple to the dazzlingly complex. With the Coat Colors and Markings tool in panel 3, you can reproduce a pet as nature intended or use your imagination to craft critters nature never considered.

note

This tool appears daunting at first, but with a bit of practice, you'll get surprisingly nice results. The best way to grasp the process of building a coat is to examine the layers of existing breeds and alter them to see how they interact with each other.

Coat Layers

Two parts define every pet's coat:

♦ Coat/marking layers and colors

♦ Coat texture

Layers and Colors

Layers are parts of a pet's coat that affect the appearance of part or all of the pet's body. For example, muzzle layer will color only the pet's muzzle area. Each layer consists of both a marking and a color.

This cat's face color is a layer that colors just the face region black. Change that layer's color and only the mask changes.

note

Unlock new markings and colors by earning pet career promotions or entering unlock codes from other players (see the "Overview and Miscellaneous New Features" chapter).

Every pet has at least one layer: the base coat. This layer is different from others since it's always at the bottom of the list (you can't move it) and it's defined solely by its color.

The base coat is always at the list's bottom, can't be moved, and is named only by its color.

Base Coat

The base coat is extremely important when designing pets. It defines the color of many dogs' fur accessories (ruffs, tufts, etc.). For example, if you want a dog to be black overall but have white fur accessories, use a white base coat and apply a black Full Body marking. Also, if a pet has a base coat and one or more Full Body marking, offspring will inherit them as a set. Cats take their accessory color from the outermost Full Body marking.

The layer list shows all the layers of a pet's coat, from top (or outermost) to bottom. The "higher" a layer, the more visible it will likely be. An opaque brown ear marking at the top of the list will be clearly visible over a black head patch (which includes the top of head and ear), but will be invisible if the order is reversed.

 Move layers up or down with these buttons.

The order of layers is controlled by the Move Layer Up and Move Layer Down buttons.

note

If two or more identical markings are applied to a pet, the pet's genetic code will contain both markings as a set rather than as separate markings. For example, if a pet has two belly markings of different colors and one of its offspring is selected to get that parent's belly marking, it'll always get BOTH belly markings rather than just one.

Just because one layer is below another, however, doesn't mean it has to be hidden. If layers mark different parts of the body (i.e., foot and tail), they'll both be clearly visible. Lower layers can also be visible if layers atop it are not entirely opaque.

The wolf marking is the top layer of this dog's coat, but the spots under it become more visible as the opacity is turned down (left).

This cat has three differently colored Full Body layers atop its base coat. Adjusting the opacity of any of them will change the body's overall hue.

You can adjust a layer's opacity with the Opacity slider below the layer list. The more opaque a layer, the less visible markings directly below it will be. As you reduce a layer's opacity, the color and shape of layers below it become increasingly visible.

Tinkering with layer opacity is a critical tool for creating blended colors or markings beyond the basic shapes and configurations. The more identical markings you stack atop each other, the more color shades will be possible and the larger and softer the marking's borders will become.

To make a marking more distinct or create a blended color, add two or more layers of the same marking. For distinct markings, make both markings the same color and full opacity. For blended colors, make the duplicate layers different colors and adjust each layer's Opacity sliders to change the overall hue.

Any layer can be duplicated except the very important base coat layer; every pet has only one and it can only be colored with the defined coat colors. If you want to create a full-body coat color that isn't of a standard hue, apply one or more Full Body markings and adjust the colors and opacity of each layer to get your desired color.

Coat Texture

Every pet coat can have one of five textures, depending on species:

Smooth.

Flowing.

Furry.

Curly (dogs only)

Shag (dogs only)

This texture only affects all visible layers, giving them the appearance of a short, long, shaggy, fluffy, or curly coat.

Activate the textures with the buttons at the bottom of panel 3.

Coat Templates

The Coat Template button (lower right in panel 3) contains several premade coats that you can apply to whatever pet you've chosen. If, for example, you've selected a Siamese cat but want a blue point (gray markings on the face, paws, ears, and tail) instead of the default seal point (brown markings), locate the blue point coat template and apply it to your pet.

 note
Although the Coat Template Bin looks much like the Breed Bin, selecting items within it has no effect on the pet's body or facial shape; it alters only the coat (but not the coat texture).

Changing coat template doesn't alter the pet's structure, fur accessories, coat texture, or coat shape.

Once you've applied a template, you can add, delete, or change any of the template's coat layers.

 note
After you design your coat in panel 3, save it for use on future pets by pressing the Coat Template button and saving via the Save Coat button (upper left). This saves all layers and colors but not the coat texture. Also, you can delete any saved or imported (but not shipped) coat with the Remove Coat button (upper right). Custom coats and breeds always appear at the start of the bin list and are marked with the asterisk-shaped Custom Content icon.

Step 4: Change Body and Face

All parts of your pet's body can be sculpted to your heart's content in the Archetype and Modifiers panel.

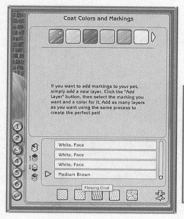

Panel 4.

note

The buttons in this panel differ a bit depending on the pet's species.

What's an Archetype?

Just as in Create A Sim, the modifier tools are based on collections of preset features that represent some typical or iconic appearance. These preset are called "archetypes," and they're displayed in each of the modifier panels.

The number of archetypes depends on the species you're building:

Cats

Cats have four basic archetypes:

Tapered (i.e., Abyssinian)

Pushed (i.e., Persian)

Balanced (i.e., American shorthair)

Heavy (i.e., Manx)

Dogs

Both small and large dogs have five archetypes:

Heavy Block (i.e., Rottweiler)

Hound (i.e., Golden Retriever)

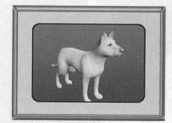

Wolf (i.e., Akita)

Sprinter (i.e., Greyhound)

Fighter (i.e., Boxer)

Using Archetypes

In each of the modifier panels, click on one of the archetypes to match your pet exactly to that archetype. Archetypes can also be used incrementally to create even more intricate shapes. By right-clicking on an archetype, the pet's features will move 10 percent of the distance from their current position toward the archetype's features.

Doing this also resets all the panel's modifiers to their center position. This may not seem important, but it allows you to create features that would be impossible otherwise. For example,

you can make a pet with a gigantic head by repeatedly right-clicking once on an archetype and moving the Head Size slider all the way to the right. After a few repetitions, you'll have this:

Giant-head dog!

Modifier Sliders

You can modify regions of your pet's body in each of the modifier panels. Regions include:

- Full Pet
- Body (dogs only)
- Full Face
- Brow and Eyes
- Snout and Jaw
- Ears
- Tails

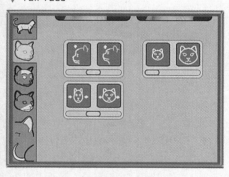

Sliders adjust specific pet features, leaving others unchanged.

Each panel has archetypes for its specific region, so Full Face archetypes alter all head features *en masse* while Ears archetypes will isolate the ears, leaving the rest of the head intact.

Along with regional archetypes, the modifier panels contain several fine-tuning sliders that modify the region's component parts in different ways.

note

You can use the sliders two ways: sliding the handle or clicking on the modifiers' thumbnails. If you slide the handle left, the pet becomes more like the thumbnail on the left. Alternatively, click on the left thumbnail and the feature moves one step closer to that extreme.

Full Pet

This panel holds the Full Body archetypes; clicking on an archetype alters the pet's entire physical shape. Additionally, you can incrementally change:

- Hindquarters thickness (cats only)
- Foreleg thickness (cats only)
- Back leg thickness (cats only)
- Midbody thickness (cats only)
- Chest thickness (cats only)
- Wolf shape (dogs only)
- Sprinter shape (dogs only)

note

When modifying regional archetypes, you can change the extremes of the sliders by first choosing a different archetype than the rest of the animal. Short ears (slider all the way left) on a Pushed archetype will, for example, be much shorter than Short ears on a Tapered archetype.

Body (Dogs Only)

Body archetypes change the dog's structure from the base of the skull to the tip of the tail. Modifiers control:

- Neck thickness
- Front paw size
- Foreleg thickness
- Midbody thickness
- Hindquarters thickness
- Rear paw size

Full Face

Full Face archetypes modify the pet's entire head and can more finely alter:

- Face height (cats and dogs)
- Skull thickness (cat only)
- Skull height (cat only)
- Face width (dogs only)
- Head size (dogs only)
- Skull crown height (dogs only)
- Skull crown width (dogs only)
- Cheek width (dogs only)

Brow and Eyes

Brow and Eye archetypes change only the pet's eye shape, layout, and depth. You may also change the color of both your pet's eyes or just one. To give your pet two different-colored eyes, select the Left Eye and Right Eye buttons and choose their colors separately.

Modifiers can also be applied to:

- Eye size
- Orbit height
- Orbit depth
- Eye spread
- Eye depth
- Brow depth (dogs only)

Snout and Jaw

Snout and Jaw archetypes change only the area around the pet's mouth and nose. More specifically, you can modify:

- Snout width
- Jaw width (dogs only)
- Bridge height (dogs only)
- Snout depth
- Nose height (dogs only)
- Nose depth (dogs only)
- Nose width (dogs only)
- Snout flatness (dogs only)
- Jowl height (dogs only)

Ears

Ear archetypes set the ears' length and general shape. The slider can make finer adjustments to ear length.

Ears up or ears down? The grayed-out sliders switch when you change this setting.

When building dogs, you'll have an additional choice to make: ears up or down. Your choice dictates which sliders are enabled, but in either case the sliders control:

- Ear height (dogs only)
- Ear width; clipped or tapered (dogs only)

Tails

Tails modify the shape and size of the pet's tail. Though you have six tails to choose from, the tails are not actually tied to the six dog archetypes.

Select which kind of tail you want and its thickness.

The Tail Thickness sliders increase or decrease the size and fluffiness of the chosen Tail archetype.

Fur Accessories

Fur accessories are tufts and hair arrangements that go beyond the shape of a pet's coat: beards, poodle tufts, ear tufts, and so on. Each pet can sport as many or as few accessories as you choose, though some combinations won't be possible. If two accessories conflict, the newer will be activated while the conflicting one will be turned off.

> **note**
>
> Fur accessories take on the color of the pet's base coat and are inherited as a group with the base coat and any full body markings.

Fur accessories can be applied along with layers and coat textures. For dogs, the accessories will take the color of the pet's base coat.

Sometimes, fur accessories will be disabled because they can only be used with, for example, certain kinds of tails.

Coat Shape (Dogs Only)

If you want a pet to fit the overall shape of a particular breed, you can alter the entire pet by changing its coat shape.

Changing coat shape, however, doesn't alter any modifiers you've already set, so applying a coat shape after other structural changes can yield very interesting results.

Adding a coat shape changes the pet's structure. The slider's far right determines the indicated breed's coat shape, while the far left is the converse of all settings—the anti-Collie, if you will.

You can set coat shape to match various classic breed coats:

- Airedale
- Collie
- Golden Retriever
- Bernese
- German Shepherd
- Malamute
- Chow

> **note**
>
> The coat modifiers are great shortcuts for some very difficult dog shapes. In particular, the Airedale is all but impossible to build with modifiers.

Of course, you can forgo this change by selecting "No Setting."

Within each coat shape, the Modify the Coat Shape slider alters the coat from its standard outline (the slider's rightmost position) to the opposite extreme (leftmost). The results can be either comical or just what you want.

Only one coat shape can be applied at a time.

Hey, who threw the Chow in the dryer?!

Step 5: Collars

Collars are entirely optional and can be added later through the mirror's Change Appearance of…interaction.

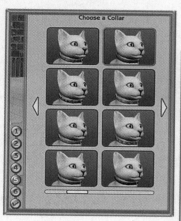

Panel 5.

To give a pet a collar once it's out of Create a Dog or Create a Cat, you must first buy collars from collar displays on community lots. It works just like buying clothes for your Sims.

Collars are mostly aesthetic additions to your pets, but they do serve one important functional role: if a pet runs away, their return is more likely if they have a collar.

Step 6: Personality

Pets, like Sims, have individual Personalities that greatly impact their choices and behavior. A pet's Personality will also affect its trainability. Pet traits are:

- ◆ Genius/Normal/Doofus
- ◆ Hyper/Normal/Lazy
- ◆ Independent/Normal/Friendly
- ◆ Aggressive/Normal/Cowardly
- ◆ Pigpen/Normal/Finicky

Unlike Sims, however, pets' Personality traits are simpler in two important ways. First, pet traits aren't scaled like Sim traits. In other words, a Sim can be a little bit Outgoing (Outgoing/Shy 6) or very Outgoing (Outgoing/Shy 10), but a pet is

Hyper, Normal, or Lazy; there's no "kind of Lazy." It's as if Sims could be given only 0, 5, or 10 for their traits.

Panel 6.

Change a trait and the pet will give you a sample of the change.

Second, pets have no Personality points that must be distributed between their traits. You're free to set each trait wherever you wish to make the pet you want.

Personality Impact

A pet's Personality is very important in determining how the pet behaves and what interactions it will choose. Because you can't directly control pets, the autonomous effects of its Personality are even more critical than for human Sims.

Specifically, Personality traits have three distinct effects:

♦ Affects what pets will do to satisfy their Needs or occupy their time when their Needs are not pressing. For example, an Aggressive cat will be more attracted to watching birds in a cage than a Normal or Cowardly cat.

♦ Determines what objects a pet will or won't interact with. Finicky pets, for example, won't eat out of a dirty food dish no matter how hungry they are. Pigpen pets, on the other hand, will eat out of even the filthiest food dish.

♦ Dictates how quickly the pet can be trained. Genius pets learn much more quickly than Normal or Doofus pets and will do trained behaviors more often without training.

♦ Traits are passed on genetically to a pet's offspring.

♦ Shapes a pet's reactions to objects, events, and Sims. For example, when the doorbell rings, an Independent dog will growl and a Friendly dog will bark cheerily.

♦ Impacts the outcome of social interactions.

note

The "Pet Training" chapter contains a full discussion of the various traits and their specific effects on training. Lists of the various Personality-driven pet reactions can be found in the "Pet Life" chapter.

tip

If you want to train your pets quickly, ALWAYS make them Genius. You'll lose out on some of the amusing behavior that comes with the Doofus trait, but that may be a small price to pay for a well-mannered pet.

Zodiac Presets

As in Create A Sim, pet Personalities are set and reflected by their Zodiac sign. If you're tuning a pet's Personality yourself, the sign will change as you change the traits' settings. Conversely, choosing a sign will set your pet's Personality to one of 12 preset types.

note

Zodiac signs have nothing to do with a pet's birthday; littermates will likely have different signs and, likewise, different Personalities.

Sign	Gifted/Doofus	Hyper/Lazy	Independent/Friendly	Aggressive/Cowardly	Pigpen/Finicky
Aquarius	Doofus	Normal	Friendly	Cowardly	Normal
Pisces	Normal	Hyper	Normal	Cowardly	Finicky
Aries	Gifted	Normal	Friendly	Aggressive	Normal
Taurus	Doofus	Lazy	Independent	Normal	Finicky
Gemini	Normal	Hyper	Normal	Aggressive	Pigpen
Cancer	Normal	Normal	Independent	Cowardly	Normal
Leo	Normal	Lazy	Friendly	Aggressive	Pigpen
Virgo	Gifted	Normal	Independent	Normal	Finicky
Libra	Doofus	Lazy	Friendly	Normal	Pigpen
Scorpio	Gifted	Hyper	Independent	Aggressive	Normal
Sagittarius	Doofus	Hyper	Normal	Cowardly	Pigpen
Capricorn	Gifted	Lazy	Normal	Normal	Finicky

Setting Relationships

When there is more than one pet in the family, you can set some relationships between them in the Family Relationship screen.

By default, pets are set to be Roomies. Pets of the same species can also be set to be Siblings (if the same age) or Parent (if different ages).

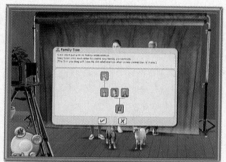

Pets can have preset relationships, too, but not with Sims.

To undo a Sibling relationship, drag one sibling pet back onto the other and choose "Roomie."

tip

Unless you're undoing a Sibling or Parent relationship, there's no need to manually set pets as Roomies.

A Sibling or Parent relationship has no other in-game significance except that family members are marked with the Pet Family icon in a pet's Relationship panel. For storytelling purposes, however, established pet-family relationships can be very important.

On the downside, pets set as Family cannot breed with each other (though it is done in real-world pet breeding). Therefore, if you want to create a breeding pair, don't set them as Siblings.

note

If you want the genetic effects of inbreeding, there's a way, but it's a bit inconvenient:

1. **Register one of the pet family members over the phone. This adds the pet to the Create a Dog or Create a Cat Breed Bin.**
2. **Create a family containing only this pet.**
3. **Add the duplicate pet to the original family.**
4. **Breed it with the pet you originally intended.**

Since Create-A-Family pets don't have any recessive genes, the offspring won't be a perfect inbreeding product, but the effect will be similar.

No Sim-to-Pet relationship can be set in Create A Family.

Household Limits

Create A Family still limits household size to any combination of eight members (no more than six of whom are pets)

Once the household is moved onto a lot, however, the limit increases:

◆ Household maximum: 10 Sims and pets

◆ No more than 8 Sims

◆ No more than 6 pets

Thus, a playable household could be six pets and four Sims or eight Sims and two pets, but never nine pets and one Sim or vice versa.

Other Ways to Acquire Pets

Maybe you don't want your new Sims to commit to a pet before they've established their careers. Or maybe you want to keep playing your old petless families. Either way, you needn't fear

a future without the companionship of pets; there are plenty of other ways to get them:

- Merging into a household
- Adoption by phone
- Befriending a stray
- Purchasing from a pet store
- Obtaining from another Sim

Merging Households

You can, space permitting, add pets (or Sims) into an existing household from the Neighborhood view. To merge households, select a household from the Family Bin and click on an inhabited household (the one with the green Plumbob overhead).

> **note**
>
> When merging households, the new higher household limit applies, rather than the traditional eight-Sim maximum. If the resulting household will have more than six pets, more than eight Sims, or more than ten total inhabitants, the merge won't be allowed.

When merging households, pick from the Family Bin and add them to an existing lot.

Pets acquired this way will be randomly assigned relationships—typically between 1–40 Daily and 1–20 Lifetime—with all existing inhabitants.

> **tip**
>
> Remember, you can create a pet-only family in Create A Family. You can save such families to the Family Bin with no last name, which you can't do with Sims. Once in the bin, the group of pets will hold the temporary family name of "Pets." When they are merged, they'll be shown by only their first name.

This method costs nothing, but all pets will be purebred adults or elders only, with no reinforced behaviors or commands. If you desire a puppy, a kitten, a trained pet, or one with a bit of genetic diversity, this may not be the best way.

Adoption by Phone

Sims may adopt puppies, kittens, adult, or elder pets by phone by calling the Pet Adoption Service (in the Service menu).

Give the Pet Adoption Service a call to bring home a bit of domesticated animal joy.

If there's room in the Sim's household, you can purchase a pet from the pool of adoptable pets. Pets are divided by species/size (Large Dogs, Small Dogs, and Cats) and sorted by price.

Price is determined by:

- Base Value: Totally untrained pets cost §399
- Reinforced Behaviors: Every reinforced behavior (positive or negative) can add up to §350 for dogs and §390 for cats (since they're harder to train) to a pet's adoption value. If a pet is partially trained, they get a proportional bonus.

◆ Commands: Every command a pet has been taught can increase its adoption value by up to §400 for dogs and §460 for cats (since they're harder to train). If the pet is partially taught a command, they get a proportional bonus.

note

Each pet's sex is shown in its thumbnail portrait. The arrow denotes male and the cross denotes female.

The more completely a pet has learned behaviors and commands, the more expensive it will be. You must decide if the time your Sims will require to train the pet is more valuable than the additional cost of a pretrained animal. If, for example, your Sims have very high Charisma—speeding training by 25 percent—and the pet has the Genius trait (another +25 percent), it may be worthwhile to save money by buying an untrained pet.

View adoptable pets' behaviors and commands in their separate panels in the right-hand window of the adoption screen. Personality and the adoption fee display below.

Adoptable pets in the adoption pool come from many sources:

◆ There are always at least two puppies or two kittens available for the base price of §399. As they're adopted, they're replaced by new puppies/ kittens. You can't determine a kitten or puppy's breed until it becomes an adult, so you never know what you're getting until it grows up.

◆ Several untrained pets are randomly drawn from the Create a Cat and Create a Dog Breed Bin. As these pets are adopted, they're randomly replaced by new random untrained pets.

◆ Each species is initially populated by several trained pets (of varying degrees). As these are adopted, they're replaced by randomly generated trained or untrained pets.

◆ When a pet is removed from a playable household by the Cop, it is added to the pool of adoptable pets.

Adopted pets are delivered to your door.

Once you select a pet, the Cop appears shortly with the new addition in tow. The pet is immediately added to the household (with relationships randomly set for all existing inhabitants), and the Cop congratulates and extracts the fee from Family Funds.

Sim-to-Sim Transfers

Sims (teen or older) can transfer pets to any playable or townie Sim (who is also teen or older) either in exchange for money or as a gift.

To sell a pet, click on the other Sim, use the Sales…Pet… interaction, and select the pet to be sold. If the relationship between the Sims and between the buyer and the pet are high enough, and the buyer has enough money to afford the pet's value (see the "Adoption by Phone" section above), the transfer takes place immediately. If the buyer rejects the sale, he or she will display a negative thought bubble of the Sim, the pet, or a § sign to indicate the reason they're rejecting.

To sell or give away a pet, both your Sim and the pet to be adopted must have a relationship with the buyer. If not, all the singing of a pet's praises will be for nothing.

When a buyer is convinced, they'll fork over the cash.

note

If the buyer is a townie, they'll never reject for lack of funds—townies have infinite cash.

tip

Even if you don't have the The Sims™ 2 Open for Business expansion pack or if your Sim only runs a home-based business, they can still make some good money selling pets. Pets obtained for free (from Create a Family, merged into the household, or bonded strays) can be sold at 100 percent profit. Selling purchased pets, on the other hand, is profitable only if your Sim has trained them beyond their purchased state. Thus, a Sim with high Charisma—and who's, perhaps, a werewolf—could train pets quickly enough to set up shop as a professional pet trainer, selling highly trained pets to others.

Alternatively, you can give the pet to another Sim for no money through the Propose…Give Pet… interaction. Choose the pet to be given away and the recipient will decide based on relationship with the seller and the pet to be given.

Either way, once the transfer is complete, the pet is removed from your Sim's household, though it'll stay on the lot as long as its new owner lingers. While the pet remains, you can no longer select it or see its information; it's just another visitor now.

Once a pet is transferred, the pet and all household pets and Sims maintain their Daily and Lifetime Relationship toward each other, but any Pack, Mine, or Master Relationships disappear (see the "New Socials" chapter).

Pet Stores

Stores can sell purebred untrained pets to your playable Sims.

note

If you have the THE SIMS 2 OPEN FOR BUSINESS expansion pack, your Sim business owners can sell pets with the new Pet Display object. You can also sell pet collars and caged pets. For full details about using these objects for your Sims' businesses, see the "New Objects" chapter.

Pets can be bought from Pet Displays on Community Lots.

Don't concern yourself with the actual pet in the display; you're not stuck with it or even its species. When, as a buyer, your Sim interacts with it, the case lets you specify the pet you want with miniaturized version of Create a Cat and Create a Dog. This slimmed-down system allows you to completely customize your Sim's new pet with one major exception: there is no collar selection. For that, you must find a store with a Collar Display, buy a collar, and put it on the pet through a mirror's Change Appearance… interaction.

Collars for any pets your Sims own can be purchased from Community Lot stores with this Collar Display object.

note

You also can't apply fur accessories or coat shape [dogs only] from the store display.

The base price for all pets from Community Lot stores is §399. If a playable Sim owns the store (if you have *The Sims 2 Open for Business*), the price may differ based on the price level the owner has assigned.

When you've finished designing your store-bought pet, press the checkmark and your Sim will be immediately charged the sale price; no visit to the cash register required. The Sim and their new pet can leave the lot whenever you choose.

When your Sim is the buyer, the actual pet in the bin is purely decorative; interacting with the case lets you pick any breed or species you want.

Adopting Strays

Sims can also acquire pets by befriending strays. To get a stray to join a household, one Sim must cultivate a high enough Daily and Lifetime Relationship with the stray and offer to adopt it.

note

If an owned stray is wearing a collar, your Sim can return it to its owner by calling them on the phone. You can't, however, direct your Sim to return an owned stray without a collar even if you know who the owner is. You can only return strays without collars when you're playing the original owner's lot. For full details on runaways, see the "Pet Life" chapter.

There are two kinds of strays:

- Unowned Strays: These pets are generated randomly and may have behaviors or commands or collars. Unowned strays initially have no Master or Mine Relationships with anyone. When a stray joins a family, it is replaced in the stray pool by a new random stray.

- Owned Runaway Pets: After about three days, pets that have run away from another playable lot in the neighborhood (see the "Pet Life" chapter) will become part of the stray pool until they are returned to their owners. These pets typically have a Sim with whom they have a Master/Mine Relationship. When these pets join a new household or return to their owner, they are not replaced in the pool.

note
Only adult or elder pets can be strays.

Stray Visits

Strays will visit a lot in much the same way as townies, but several rules determine how often they visit and how long they'll stay.

All strays can stay on a lot for a specific time (unless something else forces them to leave earlier) based on their Lifetime Relationship with any Sim on the lot. The higher the pet's greatest Lifetime Relationship with any Sim on the lot, the longer it'll stay.

A stray will leave if:

- Its visit time expires
- It loses too many collective Daily Relationship points with all Sims and pets in the household
- Its Needs drop too low
- It experiences the kind of events that would make an owned pet run away (see the "Pet Life" chapter).

Visit Frequency

The higher a stray's Lifetime Relationship with a Sim in a household, the more often it will visit.

Also, a stray will, regardless of relationship, be more likely to return if it's been fed on its previous visit.

note
Unlike walkby Sims, strays don't need to be greeted to partake of outdoor objects on a lot. They won't, however, enter houses until greeted. Before greeting, they won't scratch or chew anything or upend the trash can, and they won't initiate interactions with any pets or Sims. They will, however, interact with many outside objects as their Needs demand.

Dealing with Strays

There are several things you can and can't do with strays. No matter how many commands strays know, the only command you can give them is Call Over (and only if they've been taught it). However, a stray may, on its own initiative, perform a command it already knows.

Sims may do the Chase Off interaction to force strays to leave the lot immediately. This will, however, reduce the Daily Relationship between Sim and stray.

Strays can't be scolded or praised or trained in any way.

tip
Though it may seem like a good way to quickly build up relationship with a stray, don't fence it in on the lot. If a stray is unable to leave a lot, its Daily Relationship toward every Sim and pet on the lot drops by -2 every time it attempts to depart.

Bonding

When a pet has gained 60 Daily or 60 Lifetime Relationship toward one Sim on a lot, that Sim can adopt the stray via the Adopt interaction. If the interaction is available, the pet will always accept.

Get to know a stray and your Sim may make it her own. With your approval, of course.

If an adopted stray is a runaway, it's removed from the previous owner's household and can't be returned.

Getting Rid of a Pet

Sometimes it's necessary to get rid of a pet. There are several ways to do it:

◆ Put up for adoption: Use the phone, select Service...Pet Adoption Service—Give Up Pet..., and indicate the pet (or pets) to be adopted. The Cop will come shortly to take the pet away. All pets taken away are added to the Adoption Bin. From here they can be adopted by phone into any household.

◆ Give away/sell to another Sim: See the "Sim-to-Sim Transfers" section.

◆ Run Away: If a pet runs away, your Sim is not required to take it back. If the pet has no collar and the Sims don't report the pet lost, the pet will never return. If the pet did have a collar, your Sims might get a phone call asking if you wish the pet returned. If you don't, select "no" and the pet will be removed from the family. Also, if another playable Sim adopts the runaway (see the "Adopting Strays" section), it will also be removed from its former home.

◆ Removal: The Cop will come to remove ALL pets (including caged pets) from the household if any one cat, dog, puppy, or kitten's Hunger falls critically low or the last Sim in the house dies. All removed cats, dogs, kittens, and puppies become part of the adoption pool.

Chapter 3

PET LIFE

Pets in *The Sims 2* are actual—though limited—Sims. Understanding what makes them tick is critical to making them powerful members of your human Sims' households.

This chapter examines the various aspects of pet "Simology" (or "Petology") from their Needs and Moods, to their ages and deaths, and so much more.

Control

Unlike Sims, adult and elder cats and dogs, puppies and kittens, can't be directly controlled; you can't select a cat or dog and tell them where to go.

note

The level of control you have over pets is roughly equivalent to control of toddlers. Though pets can do far more than the youngest functional Sims, their viewable-but-not-directable status and the ability to control them via training makes the analogy pretty sound.

Pets can't be directly controlled, though you can select and view them. Their Action queue is grayed out because you can't cancel actions from it.

This doesn't, however, mean that pets are automatons that'll do what they will and can't be made to serve your will. While you can't direct pets, you can view their Action queue and their Needs, Moods, relationships, career info, and Petology. Also, pets can be indirectly controlled through effective training in learned behaviors and commands (see the "Training and Learned Behaviors" chapter). Because pets put interactions from your Sims ahead of all other actions, solid training can make them as responsive as other Sims so long as you keep them happy and well cared for.

You Sims can direct a well-trained pet to do almost anything.

It may take some time to adjust to playing a Sim that goes to work but can't be directed through a morning routine, but that's a matter of understanding what alternative tools are at hand (the next chapter) and what makes them tick (our concern here).

Needs and Mood

Like human Sims, pets have Needs and an overall Mood that function separately and in concert to shape the pet's behavior, actions, and willingness to interact and behave as trained. This system should be very familiar to any player of *The Sims 2*, so this section dwells only on the difference between pets and human Sims.

Pet Needs

Adult and elder cats and dogs have eight Needs:

- Hunger
- Energy
- Hygiene
- Comfort
- Fun
- Chew or Scratch (depending on species)
- Bladder
- Social

All but the last of these Needs are identical to Sim Needs, though the ways pets satisfy them can be very different.

Need Decay

Pets of different ages deplete their Needs at different rates. For example, an elder's Bladder Need decays 25 percent faster than for a puppy/kitten or adult. Likewise, Comfort decays 33 percent faster with each older age group. Faster decay means shorter time between having to deal with those Needs. As with human Sims, all decay is slowed when the pet is asleep.

Personality traits can also affect a Need's decay rate. Each Need's decay rate is discussed below.

Hunger

Pets satisfy Hunger by eating. Since they're animals, however, they're dependent on human Sims to provide their food. A simple food bowl, kept filled and clean, will take care of most pet's Hunger.

If pet food is not available, pets (depending on their Personality and training) will also satisfy Hunger by eating Sim food left on the floor (or, for cats, on counters). Through scolding and

praise, pets can be trained to eat exclusively from a pet bowl or human plates (wherever they can be found).

Keep food out, and to avoid inter-pet strife, have a bowl for each pet in the household.

 note
Finicky pets won't eat from a bowl in its dirty state no matter how Hungry they are. Regular pets won't refuse until the bowl gets VERY dirty (with flies and green stink cloud) and Pigpen pets don't care about their bowl's dirtiness.

Also, Finicky pets will be less likely to eat from the Good Value Pet Bowl.

Hunger can also be satisfied when Sims use the Give Love…Feed Treat interaction.

 note
Pigpen pets may eat until food is gone even if their Hunger is entirely satisfied. Whenever this happens, the pet might vomit.

Hunger decays more quickly in adults, puppies, and kittens because they're more active. Hyper pets deplete Hunger more quickly and Lazy pets more slowly.

When a pet's Hunger drops to critical levels, it'll begin to whine and you'll receive messages about the problem. If the Need hits bottom, the Cop arrives to remove the starving pet *and* all other cats, dogs, puppies, kittens, and caged pets from the household.

Bladder

When a pet has to go, their natural and trained options depend on their species.

You can impact where a pet does its business with proper house-breaking.

Generally, pets will satisfy their Bladder Need either inside or outside, without much preference for either.

Pets can be reinforced in either direction by praising for peeing in the correct place and scolding for peeing where they shouldn't. For most players, the correct place is outdoors, but sometimes players praise their pets for peeing inside, thus making them "yardbroken" instead of "housebroken."

Having a dog means cleaning up puddles.

Pets trained to pee outside will do so on the ground or a wide variety of objects: trees, flowers, bushes, flamingoes, gnomes, mailboxes, and so on. The result of Bladder satisfaction is a puddle that will bring down the Environment score and, if outside, sprout weeds. Puddles should be cleaned up regularly.

tip

If your Sims' pets pee outdoors, it might be a good investment to hire some help to keep up with the mess. A Gardener will pull the weeds that'll sprout from the puddles. A Maid will take care of any puddles he or she finds, regardless of the source.

note

Pets not reinforced in the Clean behavior may lick puddles of all kinds, including (shudder), puddles left by other pets and momentarily incontinent Sims. Scolding them for this or any other Clean/Dirty behaviors can squelch puddle-drinking.

Cats don't need to be housebroken if there's a useable litter box.

The situation changes, however, if the pet is a cat and there's a litter box in the house. If your Sim's house has a litter box, any cats or kittens in the house will use it automatically without any reinforcement. Cats can also be trained to pee in the toilet (Teach Command…Use Toilet). Once toilet-trained, a cat will use the toilet on command or by default if there's no litter box.

note

The presence of a litter box doesn't guarantee a puddleless floor in your cat-inhabited home. If a litter box gets too dirty, cats will refuse to use it and revert to whichever way they've been trained (i.e., a house-broken cat who won't use a dirty box will pee outside instead).

Older pets need to heed nature's call more often because elder pets' Bladder decays more rapidly than other ages. Bladder decays more quickly for pregnant pets as well.

When a pet's Bladder Need drops too low, dogs will have an "oops" guilty look and cats will meow. If it hits bottom, they'll pee where they stand.

Comfort

Pets satisfy Comfort by sitting or lying down. Where pets may do their relaxing depends on training and species.

Generally, pets will satisfy Comfort by using floors, the ground, bay windows (*The Sims 2 Open for Business*), or beds. Cats, due to their smaller size and extra agility, can also relax on sofas, love seats, counters, islands, chairs, and so on. Small dogs can also get on sofas, love seats, and chairs.

Cats can lounge in all sorts of places.

All pets can relax in pet beds and pet houses if they're available, and they prefer them to the ground/terrain.

Training lets you decide whether you want a pet to use furniture or the floor/ground/pet furniture to relax or sleep.

As a pet ages, Comfort becomes more important. Puppies and kittens decay the slowest, adults more quickly, and elders the fastest. Lazy pets of all ages deplete Comfort faster than regular pets and Hyper pets deplete Comfort more slowly.

When Comfort drops too low, pets will stretch a lot. When it hits bottom, they'll lie down anywhere.

Energy

Pets replenish their Energy by sleeping. As with Comfort, cats have more options for Energy satisfaction than dogs due to size and agility.

 note
As with Sims, a pet's Energy level DOES NOT impact a pet's Mood.

Both cats and dogs can sleep on the floor or ground, a sofa or love seat, or on a bed. Cats can also snooze on the Los Gatos Condominium cat condo, on counters or islands, and on chairs. Small dogs can also sleep on chairs.

Pet beds and houses provide faster Energy replenishment than the floor.

 note
Sleeping pets have dreams and nightmares (depending on Mood), just like Sims.

Since adult pets are larger than kittens/puppies and are more active than elders, their Energy decays slightly faster than the others. If a pet of any age is Lazy, the rate is quicker. Hyper pets need less sleep, so they decay more slowly.

When Pets get too low on Energy, they'll yawn more frequently. If it fails, they fall asleep where they stand.

Hygiene

Pet Hygiene is a very important Need but possibly more so to your Sims than for their pets. How pets react to and fulfill this Need depends on their species.

 note

Kittens and puppies don't have a Hygiene Need.

Dogs don't care if they're walking stink bombs.

Dogs don't care if they're clean or not. In fact, the level of their Hygiene has no impact on their overall Mood. However, *others* might care how dogs smell. Dogs with depleted Hygiene will bring down Environment score in their immediate vicinity (lowering your Sims' Moods) and may cause Sims to react with a nose-crinkling "Ewwww!"

Odoriferous dogs can be cleaned only with a good bath.

Cats, being naturally clean animals, are affected by the level of their Hygiene. Low Hygiene significantly brings down a cat's Mood.

A cat with low Hygiene—though unusual—will have the same effect on Environment and elicit the same response from passing Sims as smelly dogs.

The way each species can replenish their Hygiene is dramatically different. Dogs usually can't replenish Hygiene without your Sims' help.

 note

Sims will never bathe even the stinkiest dog autonomously; you must direct them to do it.

If a household has the Wet n' Wild Water Wiggler [THE SIMS 2 OPEN FOR BUSINESS], dogs will gain some Hygiene for autonomously playing in it.

Sims can bathe dogs in bathtubs or shower tubs (though not shower stalls). Dogs not fully trained in the Clean behavior (especially Hyper dogs) will often escape from the tub before the bath is complete. Stop this behavior by

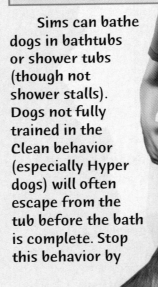

scolding them for leaving the tub and reinforcing any other actions that increase Clean behavior.

Cats, by contrast, are self-cleaning, so your Sims need not—in fact, cannot—give a cat a bath. When a cat's Hygiene is sufficiently depleted, they'll clean themselves by licking until Hygiene is replenished. The level at which a cat considers itself dirty enough to self-clean depends on whether it's Pigpen, Regular, or Finicky. Finicky cats will prioritize the activity more highly than other types, and Pigpens will put it near the bottom of their to-do list.

note
Occasionally, cats will clean...you know...down there. If Sims are nearby, they'll react rather overdramatically.

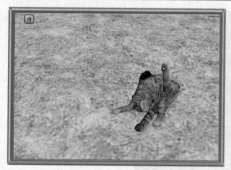
Unless you keep a cat constantly busy, it will never allow its Hygiene to get too low.

Only adult and elder pets have a Hygiene Need, and they deplete at identical rates. Pigpen pets decay more quickly while Finicky pets drop more slowly.

When Hygiene is too low, pets will emit an Environment-reducing stink cloud, dogs will shake their ears, and cats will lick their paws. In the event of failure, dogs will continue to shake their ears and cats will groom themselves until Hygiene is restored.

Fun

Pets desperately need to have lots of Fun, so replenish this Need by interactions with objects, other pets, or (primarily) Sims.

note
Fun interactions with pets go both ways, but Sims get more Fun from playing with dogs than with cats.

What gives a pet Fun depends on its species. For example, dogs gain Fun from:

- Playing with other pets
- Play...Razzle interaction
- Play...Fetch interaction
- Play...Toss in Air interaction (small dogs)
- Chew Toy object
- Digging holes
- Rolling in dirt piles
- Watching caged pets
- Watching TV

note
Kittens and puppies don't have a Fun Need. Sims can play with them, but only the Sim gets Fun from it.

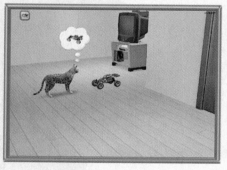
There are lots of ways for pets to have Fun.

Cats get Fun from:

- Playing with other pets
- Play...Cat Teaser interaction
- Play...Finger Wiggle interaction
- Play...Toss in Air interaction
- Kitty Kraze Katnip object
- Feline Birdie Stick object
- Scratching on the Scratch-O-Matic Scratching Post or Los Gatos Condominium objects
- Watching fish in aquariums or caged pets
- Watching TV

As previously stated, puppies and kittens don't have a Fun Need, but adults' Fun decays more quickly than elders'. Personality plays a big role too: Independent and Lazy pets have a slower decay, while Hyper and Friendly pets decay more quickly.

If Fun drops too low, dogs will sniff more often and cats will watch and bat at imaginary flies. When Fun hits bottom, pets will find a Sim and initiate Fun interactions.

Social

 note
Social interactions with pets go both ways, but Sims get more Social from playing with cats than with dogs.

Pets need to be around people and other pets to be happy. A good pet, however, gives back even more than it takes.

Pets need lots of social interaction to stay happy. Dogs in particular need lots of attention from Sims and other pets, as high Social plays a larger role in their Mood.

Social for pets is replenished by:

- Playing with other pets
- Give Love...Belly Rub interaction (dogs only)
- Give Love...Stroke interaction
- Give Love...Feed Treat interaction
- Give Love...Hug interaction (cats only)
- Play...Razzle interaction (dogs only)

- Play...Fetch interaction (dogs only)
- Play...Toss in Air interaction (small dogs and cats only)
- Play...Cat Teaser interaction (cats only)
- Play...Finger Wiggle interaction (cats only)

Socializing is most critical for kittens/puppies and elders, as their Social decays more quickly than adults'. Friendly pets need more socializing, so their Social drops more quickly while Independent pets can go longer without contact because of slower decay.

Critical levels and total failure of Social will drive pets to whine.

Chew/Scratch

Sims care about their surroundings, so they have the Environment Need. Cats and dogs could care less about Environment; instead, they have the Need to Chew (dogs) or Scratch (cats).

There goes the living room set.

Chew/Scratch is depleted gradually over time and is replenished by chewing on or scratching something. Pets will continue to chew on or scratch an object until one of the following happens:

- You direct a Sim to scold or praise the pet for chewing/scratching. This immediately stops the behavior as the pet awaits the Sim's arrival.
- The Chew/Scratch Need is fully satisfied.
- The object is destroyed.

Pets can chew or scratch many household objects (mostly furniture). Beds, sofas, and chairs are prime chewing/scratching material. Pets can also chew or scratch to destruction a child or teen Sims' homework that is left on the floor—and that is no excuse for not completing it; the Sim's school grade will be lowered for the missed assignment.

Consult the "New Objects" chapter to see which objects are chewable or scratchable. There are a few objects that pets can never destroy:

◆ The Chewinator by ChompCo (dogs only)
◆ Scratch-O-Matic Scratching Post (cats only)
◆ Los Gatos Condominiums (cats only)

Since there's no way to stop pets from fulfilling this Need, your Sims must teach their pets to chew or scratch these objects instead of the

furniture. Make sure every pet-inhabited house has a species-appropriate chewable/ scratchable object and reinforce proper satisfaction of the Need. If you praise pets for using their chew/ scratch objects and scold them for using the furniture, shredded objects will no longer cause you fits.

Good training and easy access to acceptable chew and scratch objects will solve the problem.

Elder pets have lived long enough to tire a bit of the pleasures of chewing and scratching, so their Need decays more slowly than that of adults. Aggressive pets' Needs decay more quickly than regular pets, and those of Cowardly pets drop more slowly. Puppies and kittens don't have a Chew/Scratch Need.

If Chew/Scratch reaches critical or failure levels, dogs will chew on their feet and cats will scratch their ear.

Mood

A pet's Mood is extremely important in making and keeping them positive assets to your Sims' households.

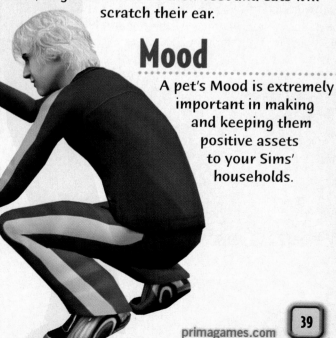

Mood Impacts

A pet's Mood will impact several things:

- Social Interaction Acceptance/Rejection: Along with relationship, most Sim-to-pet Social interactions are ruled by the pet's Mood. A happy pet with do anything a well-liked Sim wants it to do.

- Commands: A pet in a bad Mood won't obey the commands it's been taught.

- Training: Pets in a bad Mood won't accept command training from Sims.

- Job Attendance: Pets won't go to work if they're in a bad Mood.

- Job Performance: Just like Sims, pets' job performance is a function of the Mood they're in when they leave for work. High job performance accumulates to earn promotions.

- Promotion Bonus: When a pet is promoted, they receive a bonus of twice the daily salary of their new job.

> **note**
> Most Needs have different impacts on Mood, depending on their level. For example, a fully satisfied Bladder has no amplified effect on Mood, but a very low Bladder has a huge impact. Though there are small variations between cats, dogs, and kittens, the effect of each Need is approximately the same as for Sims.

Unhappy pets are disobedient pets.

Ages

Pets go through three ages:

- Puppy/kitten: 3 days
- Adult: 25 days for cats and small dogs and 21 days for large dogs
- Elder: 5–10 days. Actual duration is random.

> **note**
> Adult or elder pets can have their current age extended by up to three days if they eat from the Kibble of Life Aspiration reward object.

The pet Age meter is very similar to the Sim version.

As with human Sims, a pet's current age is indicated directly below its portrait. Pointing at the meter reveals how many days are left in the current age. If the pet is an elder, current age instead of days left are shown since the elder age spans are random.

Puppies and Kittens

When a mommy pet and a daddy pet love each other very much, they make puppies or kittens. They're cute, they're mischievous, and they're quite different from their forebears.

Most obviously, puppies and kittens are smaller than adult and elder pets. As such, there are many things puppies and kittens can't do and objects they can't climb on or use. For example, kittens can't even jump onto couches or chairs, let alone counters.

Puppies and kittens are simplified cats and dogs.

The other differences in the youngest pet set are more subtle.

Puppy and Kitten Needs

Puppies and Kittens have only five Needs:

- Energy: Puppies and kittens can sleep only on the floor or terrain, or in a pet bed or pet house.
- Social: Play or Chase with other puppies and kittens, Give Love interactions from Sims (Snuggle, Feed Treat), Play With interactions (Play With, Toss in Air, Finger Wiggle), Nuzzle from adult dogs and cats.
- Bladder: Pee on floor or terrain, or in litter box (kittens).
- Comfort: On floor or terrain, or on pet beds or houses.
- Hunger: Eat from pet food dish.

Birth and Development

When pets breed, they will have a litter of one to four puppies and kittens. The actual number in a litter is limited by the household pet (no more than 6 pets) and total household maximums (10 total Sims and pets).

The number of puppies or kittens added with each litter is unpredictable.

note

Puppies and kittens are born with random positive relationship to their parents. Their parents and littermates are marked in the Relationship panel with the Pet Family icon.

When first born, all puppies and kittens have their inherited coat color and generic tails; any inherited markings or tails will appear when they become adults.

During this three-day pet "childhood," they can be partially trained. You can teach these wee critters some reinforced behaviors and any commands that arise from them:

- Housebroken (Go Pee)
- Yardbroken (Go Pee)
- Playful (Play with..., Nuzzle Babies, Go Play)
- Eats Pet Food (Eat Food)
- Stays off Furniture (Go Lay Down, Go Sit Down)
- Stays off Sim Beds (Go to Bed)

These are the only commands you can teach them until they reach adulthood.

Adult pets are more useful and productive if you get a lot of their training done while they're young.

Well-trained puppies and kittens are an advantage because they'll be more controllable for more of their lives and will be worth more if you put them up for adoption.

Puppies and kittens grow to adults after three days.

Cans and Can'ts

It's important to understand your puppies' and kittens' limitations and abilities.

They can:

♦ Chase but only with other puppies and kittens.

♦ Be fed a treat.

♦ Play Finger Wiggle with Sims.

♦ Eat from bowls.

♦ Be picked up by Sims.

♦ Form Master and Pack (puppies) and Mine (kittens) relationships.

♦ Be adopted, put up for adoption, sold, or given to other Sims.

♦ Be hissed at/growled at by other puppies and kittens.

♦ Pounce (kittens).

♦ Be nuzzled, hissed at, or growled at by their parents.

They can't:

♦ Use stairs or elevators. They can move between floors but only when carried by Sims.

♦ Play with most toys. Kittens can, however, play with the Feline Birdie Stick toy.

♦ Get on furniture.

♦ Use the cat condo, scratching post, or chew toy.

♦ Be bathed (puppies).

♦ Own objects and won't be challenged if they use another pet's owned objects (see the "Ownership" section).

♦ Watch caged pets.

♦ Go with Sims to community lots.

Adults

Adult pets are more complex than kittens and puppies and are able to do more things, access more objects, and train more fully.

As described in the "Needs and Mood" section, adult pets have eight Needs:

♦ Hunger ♦ Bladder ♦ Energy ♦ Social

♦ Comfort ♦ Hygiene ♦ Fun ♦ Chew/Scratch

Above all, however, the three primary things adult pets can do are:

♦ Have a pet career

♦ Breed

♦ Go with Sims to community lots

Elder Pets

Elder pets are mostly identical to adult pets, with the same Needs and ability to access all possible objects and interactions. However, unlike adults, elders:

♦ Can't enter a new career.

♦ Can breed only if they're male.

♦ Can retire from a career and collect a pension.

Elders also look a bit different from their adult stage, with graying fur and a slower gait. On the inside, some Needs deplete at different speeds (i.e., Bladder depletes more quickly).

Careers

Adult and elder pets can work, and they contribute very good money to your Sims' households.

note

Elder pets can keep and be promoted in the jobs they had as adults, but they can't get new careers.

Pets get jobs from the newspaper, too, but Sims have to read it for them.

In most ways, pet careers work exactly like Sim careers:

◆ Job Listings: Listings for all three career tracks are available every day in the newspaper and on the computer. Any teen or older Sim in the household may use the Find Pet Job for... interaction to employ a pet.

◆ Hours/Days Off: Every job has a defined shift and at least two days off per week.

◆ Leave: Each day of work, pets accumulate paid days off that eventually add up to full paid vacation days.

◆ Needs Effects: A job takes its toll on a pet, so each shift removes a fixed amount from each of their Needs. This amount differs from job to job.

◆ Job Performance: Every time a pet goes to work, their Mood each day proportionally increases (by half the level of the Mood) their job performance. The higher the pet's cumulative job performance, the greater the odds they'll be promoted (if they know the required commands for the next level). Since pets won't go to work in a bad Mood, the only way to decrease job performance is to miss work.

◆ Missing Work: if a pet misses a day of work, their job performance declines. If they miss two days in a row, they'll be fired.

◆ Calling in Sick: Pets can't get sick, so their owners can't call in sick for them. However, owners can call a pet's job—up to one hour after work begins—to keep the pet home for the day, but only if the pet has at least one full vacation day. Doing this when a pet has no vacation days will mean an immediate dismissal.

◆ Carpool: The carpool for pets arrives one hour before their shift starts and returns when it ends. If a pet shares a shift start time with another Sim or pet in the house, they'll share a carpool.

◆ Chance Cards: Pets have a random chance of receiving chance cards for bonuses or penalties when they return from work each day.

note

Since Mood, not individual Needs, impact job performance, it's important to remember which Needs factor into a pet's Mood. Energy does not affect Mood for either species, and Hygiene is irrelevant for dogs (they can stink but still be in a great Mood).

There are several important ways pet careers differ from Sim careers:

◆ Pets can't get sick, so you can't get free sick days.

◆ If a pet leaves a career or is fired from a track, they can rejoin that track only at Level 1, regardless of their previous job level. However, since they'll already know the requisite commands, it shouldn't take long to restore them to their previous status.

◆ There are no pet career reward objects.

note

Pets can only get into certain vehicles, so if a pet and Sim leave at the same time, they'll go in the pet's assigned vehicle if the Sim's vehicle is inaccessible.

Pets and Their Needs

With Sims, playing the career game well requires skillful time management to get each Sim's Needs highly satisfied before the carpool leaves. However, since you can't directly control pets, it may feel like you have very little power over their Mood when they head to work.

tip

Remember that Energy does not affect any pet's Mood, and Hygiene isn't a Mood factor for dogs. Therefore, you don't have to make sure pets have a good rest or a bath (for dogs) before work.

For untrained pets, there's only so much you can do to prepare them for work. Make sure pets are well provided for with food, proper scratch/chew objects, a pet bed for Comfort, and some quality time for playing and socializing before the carpool comes.

A game of fetch before work can really boost a pet's job performance.

However, once the pet fully learns some reinforced behaviors, your Sims can command pets to tend to their Needs. For example, you can command a housebroken pet to "Go Pee." Unless the pet is in a *very* bad Mood, it will immediately comply regardless of the level of its Needs.

Fully trained pets get extra commands.

To attain full control over your pet's Needs, they must completely learn the following commands:

- Clean: Get Clean (Cats)
- Destructive: Chew/Scratch Stuff
- Eats Pet Food: Eat Food
- Eats Sim Food: Eat Food
- Goes On: Get on Furniture
- Housebroken: Go Pee (outside or litter box)
- Playful: Play with...(pet or Sim), Go Play
- Respectful: Use Chew Toy, Use Scratching Post
- Stays off Furniture: Go Lay Down/Go Sit Down
- Yardbroken: Go Pee (inside)

Mood and Going to Work

As long as their Mood is positive (green on the Mood bar), pets will go to work automatically when the carpool arrives (one hour before their shift starts). If their Mood bar is red, they won't autonomously go to work and will refuse if commanded.

When a pet misses two consecutive days, they'll be fired.

note

If a pet is deeply involved in an interaction and an in danger of missing their carpool, Sims can use the "Go to Work" command to send them on their way. However, if the pet is in a bad Mood, they'll refuse.

A grumpy pet just won't go to work. Cheer them up by the next shift or you may have to put your Sims on an austere mac-and-cheese diet.

Retirement

When pets become elders, they can retire from their job. Once retired, elder pets can't get new jobs but will receive a daily pension of 50% of their wage at retirement for the rest of their lives.

Promotions and Unlocks

Whenever a pet receives a promotion, you'll receive an added bonus: an unlocked color, collar, or marking for Create a Dog or Create a Cat.

note

This unlock system is cross-platform, allowing codes to be traded between PC users and between PC and PlayStation 2/GameCube players. The "Overview and Miscellaneous New Features" chapter outlines the steps to enter and share these codes and the equivalencies for what each unlock activates on each platform.

Promotions mean more options for creating or modifying your Sim's pets.

On the PC version of *The Sims 2 Pets*, unlock codes are selected randomly every time a pet on any lot in any neighborhood is promoted. Unlike on console, they aren't revealed in any particular order. With each promotion, you could receive:

- Bandit Mask Coat Marking for Cats
- Bandit Mask Coat Marking for Dogs
- Black Dot Collar for Cats
- Black Dot Collar for Dogs
- Black Smiley Collar for Cats
- Black Smiley Collar for Dogs
- Blue Bones Collar for Cats
- Blue Bones Collar for Dogs
- Blue Camouflage Collar for Cats
- Blue Camouflage Collar for Dogs
- Blue Fur Color for Cats
- Blue Fur Color for Dogs
- Blue Star Collar for Cats
- Blue Star Collar for Dogs
- Deep Red Fur Color for Cats
- Deep Red Fur Color for Dogs
- Goofy Fur Color for Cats
- Goofy Fur Color for Dogs
- Green Flower Collar for Cats
- Green Flower Collar for Dogs
- Green Fur Color for Cats
- Green Fur Color for Dogs
- Light Green Fur Color for Cats
- Light Green Fur Color for Dogs
- Navy Hearts Collar for Cats
- Navy Hearts Collar for Dogs
- Neon Green Fur Color for Cats
- Neon Green Fur Color for Dogs

- Neon Yellow Fur Color for Cats
- Neon Yellow Fur Color for Dogs
- Orange Diagonal Collar for Cats
- Orange Diagonal Collar for Dogs
- Panda Coat Marking for Cats
- Pink Fur Color for Cats
- Pink Fur Color for Dogs
- Pink Vertical Stripes Collar for Cats
- Pink Vertical Stripes Collar for Dogs
- Purple Fur Color for Cats
- Purple Fur Color for Dogs
- Stars Coat Marking for Cats
- Stars Coat Marking for Dogs

- White Paws Collar for Cats
- White Paws Collar for Dogs
- White Zebra Stripe Collar for Cats
- White Zebra Stripe Collar for Dogs
- Zebra Stripes Coat Marking for Dogs

note

You don't really need to earn promotions to gain unlock codes. If another PC or console player provides you their unlock code, you can enter it into your game to extract its prize. Since codes may unlock different assets on PC and console, you may get something different than your console friend received with the same code.

note

Cats are paid more than dogs because they're more difficult to train (see the "Pet Training" chapter).

Jobs by Career Level

Level 1 Pet Jobs

Career	Job Name	Commands Required	Hours	Days Off	# Work Days	Daily Salary (Dog)	Daily Salary (Cats)
Security	Snooper Department	None	7p–2a	Sun & Sat	5	§113	§130
Service	Vermin Chaser	None	6p–1a	Sun & Tues	5	§107	§123
Showbiz	Extra	None	9a–4p	Mon & Fri	5	§125	§144

Unlocked Breeds

Three unlocks contain an additional bonus: a special unlocked breed in the Breed Bin. Once you unlock the color or marking, the breed is (without any announcement) simultaneously added for your use and adaptation.

Bandit Mask Coat Marking for Cats also unlocks the Bandit Mask Cat.

Purple Fur Color for Dogs unlocks the Purple Pug (small dogs).

Stars Coat Marking for Dogs unlocks the Star Dalmatian (large dogs).

note

Unlocked breeds are marked with the Open Lock icon and sorted at the top of the list.

Weekly Average (Dog)	Weekly Average (Cat)	Energy	Bladder	Hygiene	Social	Hunger	Fun	Comfort	Chew/Scratch
§565	§650	-2	-3	-1	-1	-5	-2	-3	-1
§535	§615	-2	-3	-2	-1	-3	-2	-3	1
§625	§720	-2	-3	-1	1	-5	-2	-3	-1

Level 2 Pet Jobs

Career	Job Name	Commands Required	Hours	Days Off	# Work Days	Daily Salary (Dog)	Daily Salary (Cats)
Security	Guard Pet	Stay	5p–12a	Sun & Sat	5	§200	§230
Service	Therapy Pet	Shake	8a–3p	Sun & Sat	5	§190	§218
Showbiz	Understudy	Speak	10a–4p	Tues & Fri	5	§220	§253

Level 3 Pet Jobs

Career	Job Name	Commands Required	Hours	Days Off	# Work Days	Daily Salary (Dog)	Daily Salary (Cats)
Security	Contraband Sniffer	Speak	12p–6p	Wed, Sat, Sun	4	§353	§406
Service	Seeing-Eye Pet	Come	8a–2p	Thu, Fri, Sat	4	§335	§385
Showbiz	Stunt Double	Roll Over	8a–1p	Mon, Tue, Wed	4	§388	§446

Level 4 Pet Jobs

Career	Job Name	Commands Required	Hours	Days Off	# Work Days	Daily Salary (Dog)	Daily Salary (Cats)
Security	Pet Corps	Play Dead	8a–1p	Sun, Tue, Thu, Sat	3	§670	§770
Service	Rescue Pet	Roll Over	8p–1a	Mon, Tue, Wed, Thu	3	§636	§731
Showbiz	Star	Play Dead	12p–4p	Sun, Wed, Fri, Sat	3	§737	§847

Ownership

Pets, somewhat like Sims and their beds, feel a sense of ownership over certain objects, preferring them over all others and using them exclusively unless unavailable. Unlike Sims, however, they tend to be very protective of things they've deemed to belong to them alone, even fighting to scare off an impinging rival.

To avoid fights, make sure every pet has his own bed.

Pets can claim ownership over:

- Pet bowls
- Pet beds
- Pet houses
- Sim beds
- Couches
- Chairs
- Bay window
- Scratching posts
- Feline Birdie Stick
- Chewinator by ChompCo

note

A pet can claim ownership over only one of each kind of item (the one with his highest Ownership score). In other words, one dog will own only one bowl.

Here's how it works. Every time a pet uses an object, it gains Ownership points over it. Once a pet has Ownership points toward an object, it will increasingly go to that object exclusively to satisfy its Need.

Weekly Average (Dog)	Weekly Average (Cat)	Energy	Bladder	Hygiene	Social	Hunger	Fun	Comfort	Chew/Scratch
§1,000	§1,150	-2	-3	-1	-1	-5	-3	-3	-1
§950	§1,090	-2	-3	-1	1	-5	1	-3	-1
§1,100	§1,265	-2	-3	-1	-1	-5	-2	-3	-1

Weekly Average (Dog)	Weekly Average (Cat)	Energy	Bladder	Hygiene	Social	Hunger	Fun	Comfort	Chew/Scratch
§1,412	§1,624	-2	-3	-1	-1	-5	-2	-3	-1
§1,340	§1,540	-2	-3	-1	1	-5	-2	-3	-1
§1,552	§1,784	-2	-3	-2	-1	-5	2	-3	-1

Weekly Average (Dog)	Weekly Average (Cat)	Energy	Bladder	Hygiene	Social	Hunger	Fun	Comfort	Chew/Scratch
§2,010	§2,310	-2	-3	-1	2	-5	-2	-3	1
§1,908	§2,193	-3	-3	-1	-1	-5	1	-3	1
§2,211	§2,541	-2	-3	-1	-1	-5	-2	3	-1

note

Any number of pets can amass Ownership points for an object at the same time. It's possible for every pet in a house to feel it "owns" a pet dish. Who owns a dish more is really the issue; when two pets have Ownership points over an object, challenges ensure.

Ownership battles may seem petty, but they're critical for pets.

When one pet witnesses another pet using an object for which it has gained significant Ownership points, it can Challenge the other pet. Challenge is an interaction in which each pet's Ownership points are compared—the pet with the most points further cements its dominance over the object. The pet with the higher Ownership points gains a bonus number of Ownership points, and the loser surrenders some of its points.

You can tell when a challenge is occurring when one pet hisses or growls at another that's using an object. The challenging pet's negative thought bubble also shows the object in dispute. The pet using the object will stop interacting with it and will engage in the challenge.

Whether or not a pet mounts an ownership challenge can depend on:

◆ Relationship: If the challenger has a Pack or Mine Relationship with the challengee, they may decide to forgo a challenge. Conversely, an Enemy Relationship will increase the odds of a challenge.

◆ Relationship Level: The challenger's level of Daily and Lifetime Relationships can increase or decrease the likelihood of a challenge.

◆ Furious: If the challenger is Furious with the challengee, a challenge is more likely.

◆ Aggressive Trait: If the challenger has the Aggressive trait, it's more likely to mount a challenge.

How a pet reacts to or forces a challenge depends on its Personality. Given the combination of traits, the result is usually one of the following:

◆ The loser leaves

◆ The loser leaves and the winner begins using the object

◆ Both pets interact to dramatize the conflict—barking/hissing, chasing, fighting. Which of these occurs also depends on Personality. In the end, the loser leaves and the winner may or may not use the object.

note
Kittens and puppies don't gain ownership and don't participate or inspire challenges.

Pet Behavior

Much of the joy in pets is observing what they do with their time. In *The Sims 2 Pets*, that joy comes from seeing them act as you'd expect from their species or Personality. There are several things that drive dogs to be dogs and cats to be cats, and (for example) Hyper pets to be Hyper.

note
Pets may try to sleep near a Sim or another pet with whom they have a Master, Pack, or Mine Relationship with.

Food Behaviors

Pets are keenly interested in food. You'll see this in several ways:

◆ If their Hunger is low and the food bowl is empty, pets may appeal to a Sim to fill the bowl (with the Ask for Food interaction).

◆ If a Sim is preparing any kind of food, pets may stop what they're doing to observe.

◆ If a Sim is eating, pets may approach and watch them eat or even beg for food. If the Sim shares their food, pets remember and are more likely to beg from Sims who have shared before.

◆ If a Sim drops a plate of Sim food on the floor, a pet may eat it. This behavior can be discouraged or encouraged with scolding or praising.

◆ Pets become protective of the bowl they've used most often, even fending off other pets that try to use it. (See the "Ownership" section.)

Unpredictability

Cats and dogs will frequently do things for reasons we will never understand. Many of these behaviors are tied to Personality traits, but most just happen because pets are pets:

◆ Dogs bark for no reason.

◆ Dogs and cats run back and forth.

◆ Nighttime howling or yowling.

◆ Tail-chasing. This is more likely if the pet is Doofus and less likely if Genius.

◆ Cats running around performing random acrobatics ("Cat Crazies").

Reacting to Events

Pets often react to things that Sims are too busy or too unaware to notice:

◆ Approaching Sims, pets, strays, or wild animals when they visit the lot.

◆ Looking at Sims or pets when they pass.

◆ Barking or yowling when they hear distant pets (ambient off-lot pet noises).

◆ Fascination with stinky or unpleasant things (trash piles or dirt).

Pets frequently become agitated or interested when noisy or exciting things happen around them. For example:

◆ TV, stereos, or karaoke machines that are playing
◆ Sims or pets fighting
◆ Burglar
◆ Alien abductions
◆ DJ booths
◆ Sims dancing
◆ Sims working out
◆ Cars or other vehicles
◆ Microwave running
◆ Food processor running

note
Some of these events or objects are limited to certain previous expansion packs.

Trait-Based Behaviors

Some events trigger different responses in different pets, based on their traits and species. They may, for example, be more likely to growl at the Mail Carrier if Aggressive, or flee from a doorbell if Cowardly.

note
When a pet's traits qualify it for more than one reaction to a stimulus, the first one to arise is the one that'll happen.

Cat Crazies

Beyond the trait-based behaviors, adult and elder cats exhibit an additional array of random weird behaviors collectively termed "Cat Crazies." These oddball and seemingly pointless frenzies usually revolve around the catnip and other cat toys but can also happen any time without warning.

Who's got the "Cat Crazies?!" Who does?!

Memories

Like Sims, cats and dogs collect memories of significant moments. These are displayed in the pet's Petology/Memories panel. When they dream, they frequently dream about their memories.

Pet Death

Pets can die only of old age. When the random and/or Kibble of Life-extended number of elder days are up, the Grim Reaper comes to take the pet to the great dirt pile/catnip patch in the sky. The Sims who knew the pet may be sad, but the pets seem quite pleased.

Go get the stick in the afterlife, boy. Go get it!

A dead pet is replaced with a tombstone or urn—depending on where it shuffled off the mortal coil—that functions exactly like a normal Sim tombstone or grave. They even produce ghosts of departed pets.

Pet Ghosts

Pet ghosts arise and are colored like Sims who died of old age. Pet ghosts can interact only with other ghosts (pets and Sims).

Run Away

Most pets are loyal to the core, but there may come a time when they feel it's necessary to run away into the cold cruel world of stray pets. Chances are, this will happen to you at some point, so it's important to understand why and how it happens and what you can do.

note

Since pets can die only of old age, inspiring them to run away is one method for getting rid of a pet; you can also put it up for adoption or transfer it to another Sim.

Why Pets Run Away

Running away can be triggered by several events, many of which depend on a particular pet's traits. Pet may run away when:

◆ They're chased by another pet. This is more likely for Cowardly pets.

◆ They're chased by a wolf.

◆ They lose a fight with another pet.

- They amass four or more Enemy Relationships with pets and Sims in their household.

- A fire breaks out.

- The Sim with whom a dog has a Master Relationship dies.

- The last Sim with whom a cat has a Mine Relationship dies.

- A relationship is so damaged that a Master or Mine Relationship is lost.

- They're so starved for attention that their Social Need drops below -85.

tip

You can prevent pets from ever running away by surrounding the lot with an uninterrupted fence and a gate set to exclude pet use.

The chances of a pet running away in any of these circumstances is affected by their collective Daily and Lifetime Relationships with all other pets and Sims in the household; the better their collective relationships, the less likely they'll run away.

When a Pet Runs Away

If one of your Sims' pets hightails it off the lot, it needn't be forever…unless you want it to be.

Runaway pets are still part of your Sims' household, but their portrait shows that they're lost.

A runaway pet's portrait along the screen's left side will be marked with a Runaway icon. You can't select it until the runaway returns.

note

There is no time limit for reporting an uncollared pet lost as long as another household doesn't adopt it. However, since that can happen only when you're playing the other household, you have control of that possibility.

Recovering a pet can happen in several ways:

- Send a Sim to the phone and use the Report Lost Pet interaction. Regardless of whether or not the pet has a collar, your Sims will eventually receive a phone call asking if you want the pet returned. If you select Yes, the pet is returned by the Cop and is restored to the household. If you select No, the pet is permanently removed from the household and added to the neighborhood's adoption pool.

- If the pet has a collar, you don't need to report the pet lost. Each day, there's a random but declining chance that another Sim or the Cop will phone to say they found the lost pet and ask if you want it back. If you select Yes, the pet is returned by the Cop and restored to the household. If you select No, the pet is permanently removed from the household and added to the neighborhood's adoption pool. The chance of this call declines each day; after a while, no call will come.

- If a pet runs away from a lot and it appears as a stray when you're playing another lot, Sims in the current household can use the Call Pet's Owner interaction to contact the owner—if the pet has a collar OR if the pet is collarless but someone in the current household has a Daily relationship above 0 with the pet. The owner will visit shortly to retrieve the lost pet, giving thanks and getting a Daily relationship boost towards the Sim that called, and may offer a monetary reward.

 note
If a Sim calls to report a found pet during hours when off-lot Sims are asleep, you'll get the standard nighttime response. Try again in the morning.

 note
If you move a household to a new lot while one of its pets is lost, the pet will be automatically removed from the household and added to the adoption pool.

Caged Pets

In addition to cats, dogs, puppies, and kittens, your Sims can also own caged pets. These pets aren't as complex as cats and dogs, but they do require some responsibility from your Sims and offer some of the more complex pets' Social and Fun benefits.

Some of the joy and only a bit of the work make caged pet ownership an attractive option.

 note
There's also a new saltwater aquarium found in Buy Mode catalog in the Decorative > Miscellaneous sort.

Caged pets come in two varieties:

- Womrats: small hamsterlike mammals that can be bought for the FMCU 3000 habitat.
- Bird: tropical birds can be bought for the Tropico Avian Sanctuary birdcage.

Though they can do different things, these pets are fundamentally the same:

- You purchase the pet's empty cage from the Buy Mode catalog (Miscellaneous: Pets). The pet is added by using the cage's Restock interaction.
- A caged pet's Mood is based on whether its cage is clean and it's been recently fed. Feeding costs money.

- If a pet's Mood drops, it becomes foul-tempered, biting anyone who tries to interact with it.

- If a pet isn't fed, it eventually dies of starvation. Very hungry pets will squeak frequently when hungry and flash food scream bubbles.

- If the cage isn't cleaned, it gets dirtier and dirtier, lowering the pet's Mood and making it effectively unavailable to interact with.

- Sims can watch a caged pet for Fun.

- Caged pets can only be disposed of if they die or if a Sim does the Set Free interaction.

- A dirty cage or dead pet lowers the Environment score in the room and attracts flies.

- Both kinds of pets can be taken out and played with for Fun.

- Cats and dogs can watch a caged pet. If the cat or dog is Aggressive or has a depleted Hunger Need, there's a chance the pet will die of fright.

note

Aggressive reactions to caged pets can be trained away or reinforced with praise or scolding.

Teaching birds to talk makes them valuable and always available sources of Social satisfaction.

There are also some important differences to keep in mind:

- Cost: Womrats cost §70 to stock while birds cost §400.

- Birds can perch on Sims' shoulders with the Carry interaction.

- Birds can be taught to talk. This training is identical to teaching a toddler to talk but is, like all pet training, sped by the Sim's Charisma level (up to 25 percent faster for Charisma 10). Sims can thereafter talk to the bird to gain Social in addition to Fun.

- You can open the bird's cage and let it fly around the lot; anyone watching the bird fly will gain Fun. Birds won't leave the lot and can't be caught by watching cats and dogs.

Chapter 4

PET TRAINING

Ideally, a pet is a boon to a Sim's life. It offers interesting new things to do, no-charge Fun satisfaction, an additional household income stream, and a ready and reliable source of Social satisfaction. For a humble pet to fulfill this heady role, however, the pet must be well trained.

note
Sims who live alone or Shy Sims who have difficulty making friends will benefit most from a pet. The ample Fun and Social satisfaction a pet provides keeps these usually troublesome Needs well under control for even the most insular Sims.

This chapter covers the intricacies of training pets to behave better and perform commands that bring them under your indirect control.

Why Train?

Investing time in training pets benefits you and your Sims. The early time commitment pays off handsomely because a trained pet is more self-regulating and more controllable. More self-regulation means the pet distracts your Sims less from their obligations (serving only as a positive presence), and more control means you can reliably get pets to do what you want (meaning less micromanagement for you).

Of course, there's another reason to train that has nothing to do with easing anyone else's burden. You can train a pet in negative behaviors as well. This makes them more Destructive (for example), but if that's what you want, you probably aren't concerned with your Sims' efficient time management anyway. It's all about the pain!

Untrained pets force your Sims to take time out from their jobs, relationships, and other obligations. Invest time early and pets will take care of themselves.

There are two distinct types of training:

◆ Reinforced Behavior
◆ Commands

Reinforced Behavior

Untrained pets do, mostly, whatever their Needs and Personality compel them to do. An untrained dog won't distinguish between relieving itself inside or outside, but a Finicky dog may naturally prefer the former. To overcome or buttress the pets' natural tendencies, you can reinforce (positively or negatively) the things they do so they'll autonomously behave as you desire.

note
Reinforced behaviors increase the adoption value of a pet by up to §400 (dogs) or §460 (cats) per behavior.

Praising and Scolding

Behavior is reinforced by either the Praise for… or Scold for… interactions. Praising teaches the pet to do the kind of thing for which it was praised and not do the opposite. Scolding, conversely, instructs them to stop doing the kind of thing they were doing and do the opposite.

note

Giving a pet a treat when it has the teachable moment icon on its picture has the same result as praising, encouraging the pet to behave in the same way in the future.

Praising and scolding guide your pets into whatever behavior you want them to perform autonomously.

tip

Daily Relationship is affected by Praise for… and Scold for… interactions, so try to train by praise whenever possible. If you have to scold, follow it up with a Give Love… interaction before your Sim moves on.

Skillful use of praising and scolding will quickly transform your Sim's pets into low-maintenance members of the household, readily able to improve the lives of their Sim family.

Teachable Moments

When your pet is doing something that can be reinforced, a circular arrow icon appears on the pet's portrait on the left side of the screen.

Pets showing this icon have done something that can be reinforced. Praise or scold them before the icon disappears to seize the teachable moment.

This icon—along with the opportunity it represents—is fleeting. Once it's gone, the Praise for… and Scold for… interactions become unavailable. Note that a teachable moment's clock stops when you *initiate* the Praise for…/Scold for…, so even if your Sim is clear across the lot, he or she won't lose the opportunity to reinforce just because it's a long walk.

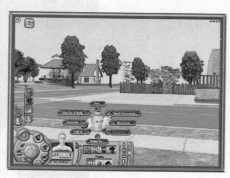

When a pet is doing something reinforceable, the Praise for… and Scold for… menus become available to your Sims.

Praise for… and Scold for… are available only for the most recent action. If you don't initiate a Praise for…/Scold for… before the pet moves on to another reinforceable action, the prior action disappears; pets have very short memories.

Reinforceable Behaviors

Pets can be trained in up to eight reinforceable behaviors. Each behavior has a positive and a negative extreme. Praising for positive actions or scolding for negative actions trains the pet toward the positive end. Praising for negative actions and scolding for positive ones trains the pet toward the negative end.

note
Learned behaviors for each pet are displayed in its Petology panel under Learned Behaviors. Pointing at the top of the icon displays a description of the positive behavior. Pointing at the bottom of the icon shows a description of the negative behavior.

Learned Behaviors

A pet's Learned Behavior panel shows every behavior it has had reinforced. A mostly green bar indicates that current behavior training is positive, and mostly red means current behavior is negative.

Positive Behavior	Negative Behavior	Icon
Calm	Disruptive	
Clean	Filthy	
Eats Pet Food	Eats Sim Food	
Housebroken	Yardbroken	
Playful	Hostile	
Respectful	Destructive	
Stays off Furniture	Goes on Furniture	
Stays off Sim Beds	Goes on Sim Beds	

Learned Behavior Actions

To see what action can be reinforced, select the Praise for… or Scold for… interaction menu.

Each of the eight behaviors is associated with several specific actions for which a pet can be praised or scolded. Reinforcing *any* actions for a behavior will train the pet in all of them.

For example, scolding a dog for eating trash will train it toward the positive behavior of Clean and, therefore, also make it less likely to jump out of the bath.

Reinforceable Actions

Action	Train by Praising	Train by Scolding	Who
Ask for Treat	Playful	Hostile	All
Chase (pet-to-pet)	Hostile	Playful	Cats, Dogs
Chase (pet-to-Sim)	Hostile	Playful	Cats, Dogs
Chewing Chew Toy	Respectful	Destructive	Dogs
Chewing Flowers	Destructive	Respectful	Cats, Dogs
Chewing Objects	Destructive	Respectful	Dogs
Chewing/Scratching Homework	Destructive	Respectful	Cats, Dogs
Digging in the Lawn	Filthy	Clean	Dogs
Dig through Trash	Filthy	Clean	Dogs
Drinking from Puddles	Filthy	Clean	Cats, Dogs
Eat Food off Counters	Eats Sim Food	Eats Pet Food	Cats
Eating Food off Plates	Eats Sim Food	Eats Pet Food	All
Eating Pet Food	Eats Pet Food	Eats Sim Food	All
Eating Trash	Filthy	Clean	Dogs
Escaping from a Bath	Filthy	Clean	Dogs
Fight	Hostile	Playful	Cats, Dogs
Finishing a Bath without Escaping	Clean	Filthy	Dogs
Getting Up on Chairs/Couches	Gets on Sim Furniture	Stays off Sim Furniture	Cats, Dogs
Getting Up on Counters	Gets on Sim Furniture	Stays off Sim Furniture	Cats
Groom Self	Clean	Filthy	Cats
Growl/Hiss at Puppies/Kittens	Hostile	Playful	Cats, Dogs
Bark/Growl/Hiss (pet-to-pet)	Hostile	Playful	Cats, Dogs
Bark/Growl/Hiss (pet-to-Sim)	Hostile	Playful	Cats, Dogs
Hiss/Bark at Contained Pet	Hostile	Playful	Dogs

Action	Train by Praising	Train by Scolding	Who
Hug (pet-to-Sim)	Playful	Hostile	Cats, Kittens
Lick Toddler	Playful	Hostile	Large Dogs
Nuzzle Puppies, Kittens	Playful	Hostile	Cats, Dogs
Pee in Litter Box	Housebroken	Yardbroken	Cats, Kittens
Pee on Bushes, Flowers, or Trees	Housebroken	Yardbroken	All
Pee on Flamingo or Gnome	Housebroken	Yardbroken	All
Pee on Floor	Yardbroken	Housebroken	All
Pee Outside	Housebroken	Yardbroken	All
Pet Play	Playful	Hostile	All
Play Cat Teaser (pet-to-Sim)	Playful	Hostile	Cats, Kittens
Play Fetch (pet-to-Sim)	Playful	Hostile	Dogs
Play Finger Wiggle (pet-to-Sim)	Playful	Hostile	Cats, Kittens, Puppies
Play in Water Wiggler	Clean	Filthy	Dogs
Play Razzle (pet-to-Sim)	Playful	Hostile	Dogs
Play Toss in Air	Playful	Hostile	Cats, Kittens, Puppies
Relax on Sim Bed	Goes on Sim Beds	Stays off Sim Beds	Cats, Dogs
Roll in Flowers	Filthy	Clean	Dogs
Roll in Puddle	Filthy	Clean	Dogs
Rolling in Dirt	Filthy	Clean	Dogs
Rolling in Trash/Ashes	Filthy	Clean	Dogs
Rub Belly (pet-to-Sim)	Playful	Hostile	Dogs
Running Around Crazily	Disruptive	Calm	Cats, Dogs
Scratch Cat Condo	Respectful	Destructive	Cats
Scratching Objects	Destructive	Respectful	Cats
Scratching Scratching Post	Respectful	Destructive	Cats
Sit/Lie in Bay Window	Stays off Sim Furniture	Gets on Sim Furniture	Cats, Dogs
Sit/Lie in Pet Bed	Stays off Sim Furniture	Gets on Sim Furniture	All

Reinforceable Actions continued

Action	Train by Praising	Train by Scolding	Who
Sit/Lie in Pet House	Stays off Sim Furniture	Gets on Sim Furniture	All
Sit/Lie on Cat Condo	Stays off Sim Furniture	Gets on Sim Furniture	Cats
Sit/Lie on Ground	Stays off Sim Furniture	Gets on Sim Furniture	All
Sleep in Bay Window	Stays off Sim Beds	Goes on Sim Beds	Cats, Dogs
Sleep in Pet Bed	Stays off Sim Beds	Goes on Sim Beds	All
Sleep in Pet House	Stays off Sim Beds	Goes on Sim Beds	All
Sleep on Cat Condo	Stays off Sim Beds	Goes on Sim Beds	Cats
Sleep on Chair	Gets on Sim Furniture	Stays off Sim Furniture	Cats
Sleep on Couch	Gets on Sim Furniture	Stays off Sim Furniture	Cats, Dogs
Sleep on Ground	Stays off Sim Beds	Goes on Sim Beds	All
Sleep on Sim Bed	Goes on Sim Beds	Stays off Sim Beds	Cats, Dogs
Sniff Ground	Calm	Disruptive	Dogs
Sniff Other Pets	Calm	Disruptive	Dogs
Stroke (pet-to-Sim)	Playful	Hostile	All
Use Catnip Toy	Playful	Hostile	Cats
Use Chew Toy	Playful	Hostile	Dogs
Use Feline Birdie Stick	Playful	Hostile	Cats, Kittens
Watch TV	Calm	Disruptive	Cats, Dogs
Yowling/Howling	Disruptive	Calm	Cats, Dogs

Calm

Calm pets are quiet.

Train by praising:

- Sniff Ground
- Sniff Other Pets
- Watch TV

Train by scolding:

- Running Around Crazily
- Yowling/Howling

Clean

Clean dogs put up with their baths.

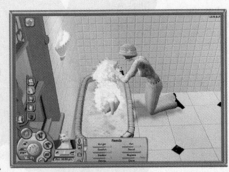

Train by praising:

- Finishing a Bath without Escaping
- Groom Self
- Play in Water Wiggler

Train by scolding:

- Digging in the Lawn
- Dig through Trash
- Drinking from Puddles
- Eating Trash
- Escaping from a Bath
- Roll in Flowers
- Roll in Puddle
- Rolling in Dirt
- Rolling in Trash/Ashes

Destructive

Destructive pets are a major distraction; break these habits early.

Train by praising:

- Chewing Flowers
- Chewing Homework
- Chewing Objects
- Scratching Objects

Train by scolding:

- Chewing Chew Toy
- Scratch Cat Condo
- Scratching Scratching Post

Disruptive

Disruptive pets wake Sims by howling or yowling.

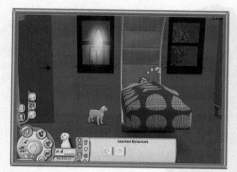

Train by praising:

♦ Running Around Crazily   ♦ Yowling/Howling

Train by scolding:

♦ Sniff Ground   ♦ Watch TV

♦ Sniff Other Pets

Eats Pet Food

Pets trained to eat only pet food will eat exclusively from their bowl.

Train by praising:

♦ Eating Pet Food

Train by scolding:

♦ Eat Food off Counters   ♦ Eating Food off Plates

Eats Sim Food

Pets trained to eat Sim food will eat from dirty dishes and beg at the table.

Train by praising:

♦ Eat Food off Counters   ♦ Eating Food off Plates

Train by scolding:

♦ Eats Pet Food

Filthy

If you like holes in the yard, train pets to be Filthy.

Train by praising:

♦ Digging in the Lawn   ♦ Roll in Flowers

♦ Dig through Trash   ♦ Roll in Puddle

♦ Drinking from Puddles   ♦ Rolling in Dirt

♦ Eating Trash   ♦ Rolling in Trash/Ashes

♦ Escaping from a Bath

> ## note
> To pets, puddles are puddles, whether they're made of yummy chocolate, overflowing water, or...um...anything else. If having to watch pets drink from their own, other pets', or Sims'...um...you know, isn't reason enough to train pets to be Clean (scold for drinking from puddles), we don't know what is.

Train by scolding:

♦ Finishing a Bath without Escaping

♦ Groom Self

♦ Play in Water Wiggler

Gets on Sim Furniture

Pets on the furniture can be a problem, but if you train them out of it, Sims can't snuggle with cats on the couch.

Train by praising:

- Getting Up on Chairs/Couches
- Getting Up on Counters
- Sleep on Chair
- Sleep on Couch

Train by scolding:

- Sit/Lie in Bay Window
- Sit/Lie in Pet Bed
- Sit/Lie in Pet House
- Sit/Lie on Cat Condo
- Sit/Lie on Ground

Goes on Sim Beds

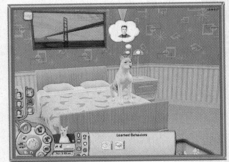

Sim beds give pets lots of new places to sleep.

Train by praising:

- Relax on Sim Bed
- Sleep on Sim Bed

Train by scolding:

- Sleep in Bay Window
- Sleep in Pet Bed
- Sleep in Pet House
- Sleep on Cat Condo
- Sleep on Ground

Hostile

Hostile pets will act out their most aggressive tendencies.

Train by praising:

- Chase (pet-to-pet)
- Chase (pet-to-Sim)
- Fight
- Growl/Hiss at Puppies/Kittens
- Bark/Growl/Hiss (pet-to-pet)
- Bark/Growl/Hiss (pet-to-Sim)
- Hiss/Bark at Contained Pet

Train by scolding:

- Ask for Treat
- Hug (pet-to-Sim)
- Lick Toddler
- Nuzzle Puppies, Kittens
- Pet Play
- Play Cat Teaser (pet-to-Sim)
- Play Fetch (pet-to-Sim)
- Play Finger Wiggle (pet-to-Sim)
- Play Razzle (pet-to-Sim)
- Play Toss in Air
- Rub Belly (pet-to-Sim)
- Stroke (pet-to-Sim)
- Use Catnip Toy
- Use Chew Toy
- Use Feline Birdie Stick

Housebroken

Housebroken pets will only pee outside or in litter boxes.

Train by praising:

- Pee in Litter Box
- Pee on Bushes, Flowers, or Trees
- Pee on Flamingo or Gnome
- Pee Outside

Train by scolding:

- Pee on Floor

Playful

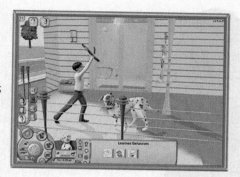

Playful pets are always ready to have fun with your Sims.

Train by praising:

- Ask for Treat
- Hug (pet-to-Sim)
- Lick Toddler
- Nuzzle Puppies, Kittens
- Pet Play
- Play Cat Teaser (pet-to-Sim)
- Play Fetch (pet-to-Sim)
- Play Finger Wiggle (pet-to-Sim)
- Play Razzle (pet-to-Sim)
- Play Toss in Air
- Rub Belly (pet-to-Sim)
- Stroke (pet-to-Sim)
- Use Catnip Toy
- Use Chew Toy
- Use Feline Birdie Stick

Train by scolding:

- Chase (pet-to-pet)
- Chase (pet-to-Sim)
- Fight
- Growl/Hiss at Puppies/Kittens
- Bark/Growl/Hiss (pet-to-pet)
- Bark/Growl/Hiss (pet-to-Sim)
- Hiss/Bark at Contained Pet

Respectful

Cats'll scratch, Dogs'll chew, but Respectful pets won't touch the furniture.

Train by praising:

- Chewing Chew Toy
- Scratch Cat Condo
- Scratching Scratching Post

Train by scolding:

- Chewing Flowers
- Chewing Objects
- Chewing/Scratching Homework
- Scratching Objects

Stays off Sim Beds

Keep Sims' beds free by teaching pets to stay off.

Train by praising:

- Sleep in Bay Window
- Sleep in Pet Bed
- Sleep in Pet House
- Sleep on Cat Condo
- Sleep on Ground

Train by scolding:

- Relax on Sim bed
- Sleep on Sim bed

Stays off Sim Furniture

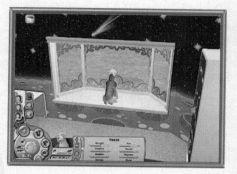

Pets won't climb on the furniture, but they'll find other interesting places to relax.

Train by praising:

- Sit/Lie in Bay Window
- Sit/Lie in Pet Bed
- Sit/Lie in Pet House
- Sit/Lie on Cat Condo
- Sit/Lie on Ground

Train by scolding:

- Getting Up on Chairs/Couches
- Getting Up on Counters
- Sleep on Chair
- Sleep on Couch

Yardbroken

To Yardbroken pets, the outside is a place to run around, but anywhere inside is their toilet.

Train by praising:

- Pee on Floor

Train by scolding:

- Pee in Litter Box
- Pee on Bushes, Flowers, or Trees
- Pee on Flamingo or Gnome
- Pee Outside

How Behaviors are Learned

All Create A Family, store-bought, and bred in-game pets and some adopted pets begin with no learned behaviors. More precisely, they begin with *neutral* learned behaviors. Reinforcement will move them away from this neutral state toward one behavioral extreme or another.

note

Pets with certain traits are naturally more or less likely to engage in certain reinforceable actions. Aggressive pets, for example, are more likely to growl or hiss. This natural state has no effect on how easy or difficult a pet is to train: although the pet's "natural" behavior tends more toward one of the extremes, it's still considered neutral for training purposes. Only the Genius or Doofus traits affect training, and that's a matter of speed rather than difficulty (see the "Training Speed" section).

Learned Behaviors Training Meter

When your Sims praise or scold a pet, a training bar appears above the pet's head to reflect the progress of the training. Unlike conventional skill progress bars, however, these bars reflect both positive and negative states (think of it as -100–100 with all pets starting at 0). When the bar is green, training is currently toward the positive end (for example, Clean). When it's red, training is currently toward the negative end (Dirty).

When pets are being scolded or praised, a two-way progress bar shows whether the pet is learning the positive or negative behavior.

Every Praise for… or Scold for… interaction moves the pet's training a certain amount toward one extreme or the other. When training is moving down (toward the negative), the bar shows downward moving red circles. When it's going up (toward the positive), green circles move toward the top.

Learned Behaviors Panel

The Learned Behaviors panel (found in the pet's Petology panel) shows the current state of all behaviors for which the pet has received reinforcement. Any not shown are neutral; for them, the pet will act according to its Personality and natural tendencies.

The line in each behavior's meter shows the current training level. The dominant color also represents this state: If it's more green than red, training is positive, and vice versa.

Completed Training

When a pet is fully trained—either positively or negatively—the training bar flashes sparks. The behavior's bar on the Learned Behavior panel will reflect this success as well, filling either all green or all red.

When the bar is full green or full red, the behavior is fully learned.

Once a pet is completely trained, it will *always* act according to its training. A dog trained to be Respectful will chew *only* on a chew toy and *never* on the furniture. As long there's a chew toy on the lot, it will resist the instinct to chew furniture. If, however, a Need dwindles low enough and the only way a pet can satisfy it is to act against its

training (for example, if there's no chew toy), it'll have no choice but to chew furniture despite its training.

note

Learned behaviors do not decay.

The only way to "untrain" a fully trained pet is to either scold it for the fully trained behavior's actions or praise it for the opposite actions. For example, if a cat is fully trained to stay off furniture and you direct your Sim to scold it for relaxing on the pet bed, its training in that behavior will drop. No longer fully trained, the pet becomes slightly more likely to do the unwanted behavior but will still act mostly as trained. Further scolding against training changes the probabilities further, making the pet increasingly likely to behave in the other direction.

note

If you scold or praise a fully trained pet away from its training, any learned behavior commands (see the "Learned Behavior Commands" section) will be lost until full training to the previous extreme is restored. Thus, if a Housebroken dog is scolded for peeing outside, the Go Pee command will be lost until 100 percent Housebroken training is restored.

Learned Behavior Commands

Not only can a fully trained pet be trusted to act as you wish, it also becomes indirectly player-controllable for any fully trained behavior. Even though you still can't tell a trained pet what to do, you can tell your Sims to tell it what to do and the pet will, mostly, obey.

Fully learned behavior adds powerful new commands to your pet's Command menu.

Both the positive and negative forms of each behavior unlock one or more commands that tell your pet to immediately do something related to that behavior.

- Calm: Go Investigate, Sniff...pet
- Clean: Get Clean (cats only)
- Destructive: Chew Stuff/Scratch Stuff
- Dirty: Get Dirty (dogs only)
- Disruptive: Sing, Run Around Crazily
- Eats Pet Food: Eat Food
- Eats Sim Food: Eat Food
- Goes on Furniture: Get on Furniture
- Goes on Sim Beds: Go to Bed
- Hostile: Bark/Hiss at...pet or Sim, Fight with...pet, Chase...pet or Sim, Growl/Hiss at baby
- Housebroken: Go Pee
- Playful: Play with...pet or Sim, Nuzzle Baby, Go Play
- Respectful: Use Chew Toy, Use Scratching Post
- Stays off Furniture: Go Lay Down, Go Sit Down
- Stays off Sim Beds: Go to Bed
- Yardbroken: Go Pee

These commands are available only if the pet remains fully trained in the command's behavior. Any drop below 100 percent trained (positive or negative) disables the command.

Pets will obey learned behavior commands immediately and ahead of anything it's chosen to do itself unless its Mood is less than -50. Above

-50, obedience will depend on Relationship type and level toward the Sim and the pet's Personality.

note

The specifics of what would make a pet reject a command are listed in the "New Socials" chapter.

Commands

Commands are tricks your Sims can teach their pets to perform. Learning commands makes pets more valuable for sale, helps them get job promotions, and provides more opportunities for Fun and Social satisfaction for pets and Sims alike.

note

Commands enhance a pet's adoption and sale value by up to §350 (dogs) or §390 (cats) per command.

Teaching Commands

Pets don't naturally know any commands; a Sim must teach them. This process takes time, but the benefits are hard to beat. There's no need to teach your pets *every* command available, but you will want to dedicate your time to the ones that'll have a direct impact on the household and your ability to control it.

Teaching pet commands is more like standard skill training or teaching toddlers to walk.

Pets learn commands from Sims though the Teach Command... interaction. A Sim can only teach a command to a pet if the Sim is part of the pet's household and the pet's Mood is high enough relative to its relationship with the Sim. The greater the pet's relationship to the Sim, the worse its Mood can be while still accepting training.

note

Teach Command... resembles the process of teaching a toddler to walk, talk, and potty train. In fact, it works almost exactly the same.

See the "New Socials" chapter for the full details on how a pet decides to accept training.

To accept command training, a pet must be in a positive Mood. If it's not, it'll reject training much like Sims reject skill building when their Mood or critical Needs are dragging.

If the pet has a good enough relationship with a Sim, only an abysmal Mood will preclude training.

note

Sims and pets will exit command training early for the usual Mood- or Need-related reasons for which Sims will quit skill building. The pet's progress is preserved, so training can resume right where you left off.

During training, pets show a progress bar above their heads. As the command is learned, the bar rises. When it reaches the top, the command is permanently and unshakably learned.

note

Learned commands are listed in a pet's Skills and Career panel.

Command training builds Daily Relationship between pet and Sim and satisfies both Fun and Social Needs. Training depletes pets' Energy.

Fun gain and Energy loss occur over time, but Social and Relationship changes are based on the interactions during training. Watch command training and you'll see the repeated process:

◆ Sim demonstrates.

◆ Pet attempts to reproduce and either succeeds or fails.

The lower the pet's learning bar, the more likely its attempt at imitation will fail.

Social satisfaction and Daily Relationship changes occur at each step, and the size and direction of the change depend on the pet's success or failure.

Training Event	Pet Social	Pet Daily Rel.	Sim Social	Sim Daily Rel.
Sim Demonstrates	3	0	3	0
Pet Success	3	1	3	1
Pet Failure	3	-1	3	-1

Performing Commands

Mastered commands appear in the pet's Command... interactions.

Once a command is mastered, the pet can be commanded to perform it any time through the Command... interaction. Pets will accept commands from any Sim (including non-household Sims) according to the same Mood-based rules as

for learning commands. Both the pet and the commanding Sim will get Fun and Social boosts from the interaction, and their relationship will improve.

note

Pets may perform commands on their own initiative if they choose.

Both pet and Sim gain Fun satisfaction, and pets expend Energy while performing commands.

Teachable Commands

Pets may be taught to:

◆ Come Here (Go Inside, Go Outside) ◆ Sit Up
◆ Play Dead ◆ Speak
◆ Roll Over ◆ Stay
◆ Shake ◆ Use Toilet (cats only)

Most commands serve primarily as Fun and Social vehicles and as job promotion requirements. Three, however, have other purposes.

Stay and Come Here (which also unlocks Go Outside and Go Inside) are required for promotions but are useful tools for controlling the movement of your Sims' pets, giving you approximately the same power you have over Sims. These should, therefore, be the first commands you teach.

note

Other commands may appear in the Command menu. These are unlocked by a pet's mastery of a learned behavior and can't be learned by teaching.

Cats can be taught Use Toilet. Though it may seem like an amusing but unnecessary trick (and it *is* amusing), this can be a very important and efficient command to have at your disposal. Not only will cats trained to use the toilet do so on command, but they'll use it autonomously if there's no litter box on the lot or all litter boxes are unavailable because they're too dirty or in use. Thus, cats can be trained to be *completely* mess free; no puddles to clean up outside and no litter boxes to sift.

Funny and useful!

note

If you simply don't want to be bothered with teaching commands, you can hire the services of the Obedience Trainer. For a fee, this service NPC will teach your pets commands at blinding speed. The Obedience Trainer doesn't, however, train in reinforced behaviors. See the "New NPCs & Lycanthropy" chapter for full details.

Commands and Pet Jobs

Pets can advance in their jobs only if they have the requisite commands for the next level. No matter how good their job performance or how regular their attendance, they'll never get promoted if they don't have the tricks for the next job in the career.

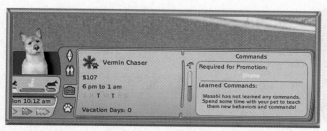

Commands required for the next promotion are also displayed in the pet's Skills and Career menu.

Commands and the Careers That Require Them

Command	Careers (Job Level)
Come Here	Service (3)
Play Dead	Security (4), Showbiz (4)
Roll Over	Service (4), Showbiz (3)
Shake	Service (2)
Speak	Security (3), Showbiz (2)
Stay	Security (2)

Training Speed

Werewolves, especially Charismatic ones, are the best pet trainers.

The speed of a pet's training (in both learned behaviors and commands) is affected by several factors:

◆ Personality: Whether the pet has either the Genius or Doofus trait (pets set for Normal in this trait will train at the base rate). Genius speeds training by 25 percent and Doofus slows it by 25 percent. In other words, it'll take twice as long to train a Doofus as it would a Genius.

◆ Species: Cats are more willful and, therefore, more difficult (by 25 percent) to train. It takes 25 percent longer to train a cat than a dog. This is compensated for, however, by the fact that employed pets are paid more and their commands and reinforced behaviors add more to their sale value.

◆ Sim Personality: Charismatic Sims make better trainers, accelerating training by up to 25 percent of the base rate (scaled to the level of the Sim's Charisma skill). A Charisma 5 Sim would, therefore, train pets 12.5 percent faster than a Charisma 0 and 12.5 percent slower than a Charisma 10.

◆ Lycanthropy: Werewolves are natural pet trainers, speeding training by 25 percent. This effect occurs only when the Sim is actually in the werewolf state. See the "Lycanthropy" section in the "New NPCs & Lycanthropy" chapter for more detail.

These various training bonuses/penalties are added together to determine what percentage of the base training time will be needed to fully train the pet. If it would take 10 hours (to pick a random but round number) for a Charisma 0, non-werewolf Sim to train a Normal (non-Genius, non-Doofus) dog from its neutral state, it'd take a Charisma 10 (-25 percent) werewolf (-25 percent) training a Genius (-25 percent) dog only 25 percent of that time or 2.5 hours. Conversely, it'd take a Charisma 0 non-werewolf training a Doofus (+25 percent) cat (+25 percent) 150 percent of that time or 15 hours.

Chapter 5

Pet Birth and Genetics

Sure, sculpting your own pets in Create a Cat and Create a Dog is fun, but the real challenge comes from rolling the genetic dice by breeding pets in-game. To hear the pitter-patter of tiny paws, build a pet family, replace an aging pet, or attempt to engineer an ideal super-pet, become familiar with how pets are bred and born and how their genome determines what the next bundle of joy will look like.

Pet Breeding

Pets breed only on command—via the Try for Puppy/Kitten with… interaction—from your Sims and only if:

- There's a useable pet house (such as Pets' Desires House) on the lot.
- There's another pet of the same species, opposite sex, not blood related, and of breedable age in the household.
- Both pets have high Relationship scores with the commanding Sim (Daily Relationship > 25, Lifetime Relationship > 0).
- Both pets have high Relationship scores toward each other (Daily Relationship > 25, Lifetime Relationship > 0).

A pet house must exist on the lot, and it must not be filthy or occupied, otherwise pets won't be willing or able to use it.

note

Among dogs, size is not an issue in breeding. Large and small dogs can breed as if they were the same size.

note

Male pets can continue to breed once they become elders, but female pets can't. Thus, adult females may breed with either adult or elder males, but males may breed only with adult females.

First your Sim commands the pet to breed.

Then the pet sees if the other pet is willing.

Finally, they both retire to the nearest pet house for a little "alone time."

The Try for Puppy/Kitten with… interaction will only be available if there's a breedable mate in the household and present on the lot and a pet house can be used for the breeding.

When the interaction is available, there are two points at which the breeding command can be rejected. The first pet the Sim commands to breed may reject the interaction if its relationship with the Sim is too low. If the first pet accepts, it goes and asks the other pet, which decides based on its relationship with the first pet. If they like each other enough, puppies or kittens will be due very soon.

 tip

Since relationships vary, be sure to match up a Sim with a pet it knows very well, especially if the Sim lacks a sufficient Relationship score with the other pet in the breeding pair. Also, since relationships can be uneven, be sure to ask the pet with the higher Lifetime Relationship toward the other.

Two pets raring to breed slip into the nearest available pet house and WooHoo with the customary pyrotechnics and bystander reactions.

Pet breeding is always successful, and the gestation period for all pets is two days.

Litter Size

When the blessed day arrives, the birth process begins. The number of puppies/kittens in the litter is determined at random (up to four) but limited by the household size limits. If, for example, you already have five pets, no litter can be bigger than one since more would push the household over the six-pet ceiling. Likewise, if the household has seven Sims and two pets already, the litter can only be one due to the total household limit of ten inhabitants.

Litter size is random.

Since no litter of any size can be born into a full household, the Try for Puppy/Kitten with… interaction will be unavailable in that situation.

Pet Genetics

Like Sims, pets have a genetic system that dictates how a puppy or kitten born in-game will look and behave. Understanding how this system works and what it can (and can't) do enables you to control this seemingly random process, harnessing the power of pet DNA.

Eggs and Genomes

At conception, the genetics simulator decides how many offspring the litter will yield and from how many eggs the litter will draw.

note

The number of eggs in a litter (as opposed to the number of offspring) determines how many possible genetic outcomes the litter will reveal. For example, you may have seen a litter of puppies or kittens in which all but one look the same and the other is a genetic oddball.

This system simulates that outcome by distributing the number in the litter among a smaller number of eggs. In many cases, there will be only one egg and all the offspring will emerge with the same expressed and recessive genes, but now you'll know why when that doesn't happen.

Three offspring of the same parents, from two eggs. Two are similar…

…but not the same…

…and one is quite different.

Each egg is assigned a genome, a complexly selected slate of traits from the parents that will rule how the offspring look and what kind of progeny they can later generate.

A genome is a collection of genetic traits that a pet built from it will show on the outside (called "expressed" traits) and carry as dormant traits that can arise in future generations (called "recessive" traits).

In pet reproduction, each egg is randomly assigned a genome generated from the combination of the parents' expressed and recessive traits. If there's only one egg, then all offspring will match and carry the same version of their parents' traits as their own genetic code. If more than one egg is produced, two or more combinations of the parents' genes will produce offspring.

To get to the bottom of this process, let's explore how the traits are selected to form a genome.

A Note on Purebreds

In *The Sims™ 2 Pets*, a purebred pet is one with identical expressed and recessive genes. All pets made in Create a Cat and Create a Dog, and those bought from community lot pet store, are purebred. In other words, if you breed two identical pets from these sources (for example, two Persian cats with the same color, etc.), you'll always get kittens that are identical to their parents.

It is possible to produce a purebred in the game by very skillful breeding over generations.

You can also convert one of your in-game pets into a template in the Breed Bin by using the phone's Pet Registry interaction. Any pets constructed from that model (but not the registered pets themselves) will be genetically purebred.

Genome Traits

For pets, a genome consists of six traits that can be inherited:

- Coat
- Eye Color(s)
- Body Size (dogs only)
- Tails and Ears
- Body and Face Shape
- Personality

Genetic Definitions

- **Allele:** An allele is a pair of genes that together define a single trait. Each allele contains an expressed gene and a recessive gene.
- **Genome:** All the alleles that make up a pet's genetic code.
- **Expressed Gene:** The expressed gene contains how an allele's trait will affect the pet's appearance or Personality. If a pet has brown fur, brown fur is the expressed gene on the fur color allele.
- **Recessive Gene:** The recessive gene is a dormant version of the allele's trait that does not affect how the pet looks or acts but that can be passed on to affect the appearance or Personality of the pet's future offspring. A pet with brown fur may produce white-furred offspring because white fur is the recessive gene on the fur color allele.

Coat

A pet's coat consists of:

- Marking Layers (including base coat)
- Fur Accessories
- Coat Shape (dogs only)
- Fur Texture

When pets breed, the first step in genome creation is combining their expressed coats into a potential expressed coat for their offspring and, likewise, combining their recessive coats to form the potential recessive offspring coat.

Layers

First, layers are compared to determine how many unique coat layers the parents have between them. For example:

Dad	Mom
Base Coat	Base Coat
Spots	Stripes
Colored Paw	Colored Left Ear
—	Colored Right Ear
—	Colored Paw

Between them, they have six unique layers (base coat and colored paw are common). Thus, the resulting coat will begin with six potential layers.

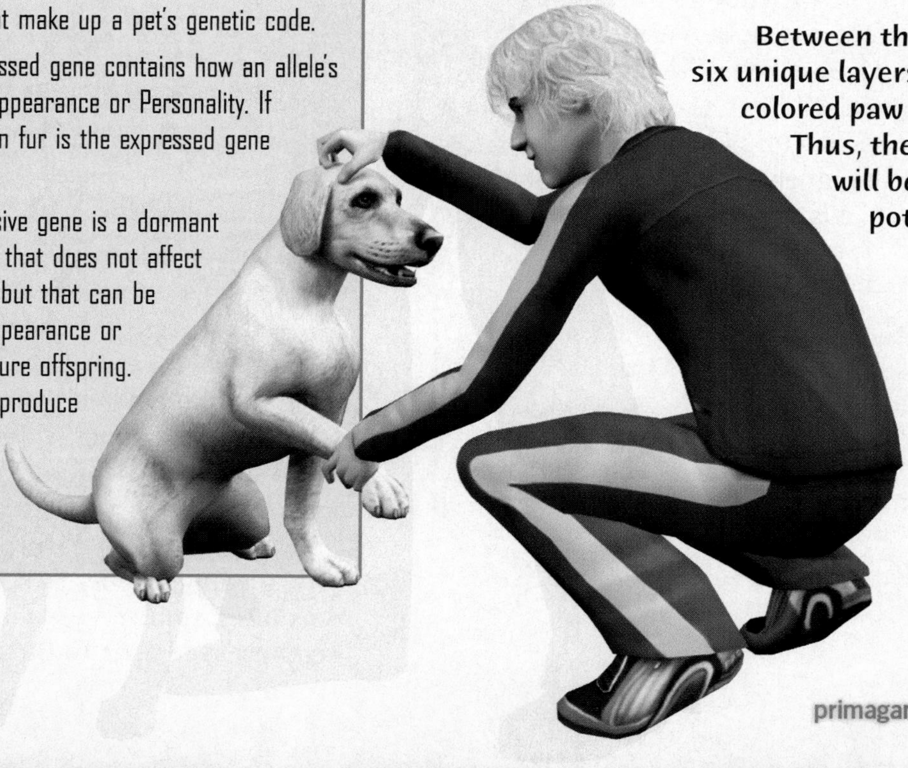

The number of layers a pet will have depends on how many each parent had.

note

For this step, the layer colors don't yet matter. This is just going to determine which layers get used; selecting which parents' version of the layer to use is the next step.

The layers are then ordered from bottom to top, reconciling any duplications and conflicts to arrive at six layers of coat, ordered to reflect both parents' own order.

Next, each layer has a chance of going into the final coat, but the probability of a layer's inheritance is different if both parents share the layer. If both parents have the layer, it has a 90 percent chance it'll be inherited. If only one parent has the layer, it's less likely (25 percent probability) that the layer will part of the final coat. If not chosen, a layer is tossed out of the final coat.

note

If multiple markings of the identical type (such as three back markings) are in a pet's coat, all (including order, color, and opacity) are passed down together even if only one is selected for inheritance.

Once each layer has been either inherited or thrown out, the color and opacity of each marking are selected randomly between the parents. If Mom's base coat is white and Dad's is black, the inherited coat could be either.

Coat Texture, Fur Accessories, and Coat Shape

Next, coat texture (curly, smooth, etc.), fur accessories (beards, ruffs, etc.), and coat shape (Collie, Malamute, etc.) are selected randomly from the parents.

All fur accessories are inherited as a group; you get one or none.

To illustrate, an offspring coat could end up like this:

Coat Part	Mom	Dad	Offspring
Coat Texture	Smooth	Shag	Shag
Fur Accessories	None	Beard, Poodle Tufts	Beard, Poodle Tufts
Coat Shape	Chow	Collie	Chow

The Final Coats

The result of this process is a set of two coats: an expressed coat derived from the parents' expressed coats and a recessive coat derived from the parents' recessive coats.

To produce some genetic variation, there's a chance these coats will be swapped to make the expressed coat the genome's recessive coat and vice versa.

Next, to match nature's tendency to let some traits disappear only to reemerge a few generations later, some layers may randomly switch from the expressed coat to the recessive.

Additionally, if the recessive coat has more layers than the expressed coat, there's a random chance the last layer in the recessive coat will simply be deleted, never to appear in the pets' genetic line again.

note

This last step allows you to eventually breed a pet with identical expressed and recessive coats. In other words, you can, by breeding the same kinds of pets over and over, eventually produce a purebred pet in the game itself. There's no prize for this achievement, but you can be sure it's quite a feat.

Eye Color

Like coats, eye color is inherited through alleles from a pet's mother and father.

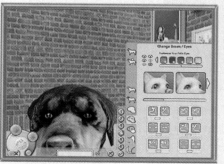

Pets can be born with two different color eyes.

A pet's expressed eye color can be either of its parent's expressed or recessive eye colors, but the probability is much higher for a parental expressed color to be chosen as either the offspring's expressed or recessive color.

If the pet has two different eye colors and this combination is selected to be the offspring's expressed eye colors, the location of each color will be random. For example, if Mom has a blue right eye and a green left eye and her eye trait is chosen to be her offspring's expressed eye color, it could have a blue left eye and a green right eye or vice versa.

Body Size (Dogs Only)

Dogs naturally favor their mother's body size, so puppies in *The Sims 2 Pets* will inherit their mother's size (large or small) 70 percent of the time.

Tails and Ears

Tails will be from one parent or the other.

Tails and ears work exactly like eye color: they can draw from either parent's expressed or recessive tail and ear traits, but expressed traits are more likely than recessive traits to be chosen. The odds of getting one parent's tail or ears over the other is an even split.

Body and Face Shape

Inherited face and body shape work similarly as for Sims: offspring get either the father or the mother's shape or some degree in between.

Face and body shape of a bred pet will be some geometric point between its parents' shapes. You can use Create a Cat/Dog to see how this works by selecting one archetype…

…and right-clicking on a different archetype. With each click, the features of the pet will shift 10 percent toward the clicked archetype.

An offspring's shape will be selected from some point along the line between the two parental shapes.

Pets are divided into four independently editable regions:

◆ Body   ◆ Brow and Eyes

◆ Full Face   ◆ Snout and Jaw

Each region is separately inherited either exactly from one parent or the other or from a point somewhere between their features.

Personality

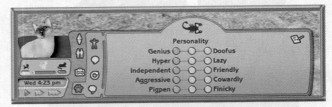

Mom's Personality.

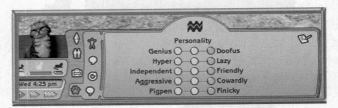

Dad's Personality.

Offspring's Personality.

Every puppy and kitten born into the game takes its Personality at random, trait by trait, from one parent or the other. If, for example, one parent is Genius and one is Doofus, any offspring will be either one or the other. These parents could never, however, produce a Normal offspring for that trait since neither of them is Normal.

 tip
To take a close look at an offspring's trait details, use the phone to register the pet and locate it in the Breed Bin. All the information you need is viewable in Create a Dog or Create a Cat.

Chapter 6

NEW OBJECTS

Pets are like no other expansion pack feature; they're a different life form. It's fitting, therefore, that they require a very special collection of new objects to take care of their Needs and become more integrated in your Sims' lives. Perhaps even more significant, many familiar objects have subtly changed to reflect the new possibilities and differences in physical structure brought on with pets.

This chapter introduces you to all these new objects along with some very snazzy new features that will make working with objects even easier.

Chewable/Scratchable Objects

Your pets can chew or scratch many existing objects:

- Dining Chairs
- Living Chairs
- Sofas/Loveseats
- Easel
- Recliners
- Homework/Assignments
- Floor Sculptures
- Bookshelves
- Floor Potted Plants
- Sectional Sofas
- Toy Box Toys
- Teddy Bear
- Dollhouse
- Indoor Catalog Trash Cans
- Floor Lamps
- Beds
- Coffin
- Grandfather Clock
- Potty Chair
- Crib Cheap
- Chess Tables
- Toy Oven
- "It's MYSHUNO!" (The Fabulously Zany Party Game)
- Barstools

Item					Category
FMCU 3000	$250	$37	$25	$100	Surfaces
Formicium Counter by Astro-Tops Design	$770	$115	$77	$308	Surfaces
Futur-Nu by Vidioblast	$800	$20	$80	$320	Electronics
Galactix Animal Home	$1,500	$225	$150	$600	Miscellaneous
Good Value Pet Bowl	$45	$6	$4	$18	Miscellaneous
Hydrocyanic Cat No. 7	$165	$74	$16	$66	Decorative
In Memory of Johnny Gnome	$120	$18	$12	$48	Decorative
Inner Atmos End Table	$260	$39	$26	$104	Surfaces
Johnny the Pump	$325	$48	$32	$130	Decorative
Junior Cosmonauts Bedside Table	$115	$17	$11	$46	Surfaces
King Kricket Klobberin' Klub	$75	$11	$7	$30	Decorative
Kitten vs. Yarn: Season 1 Print	$130	$19	$13	$52	Decorative
Kitty Kraze Katnip	$35	$5	$3	$14	Miscellaneous
Leash Racque by DeFarge	$145	$21	$14	$58	Miscellaneous
Little Space Rangers Chair	$175	$26	$17	$70	Comfort
Los Gatos Condominiums	$450	$67	$45	$180	Miscellaneous
Lounge-O-Rama by Nucular Novelties	$850	$127	$85	$340	Comfort
Marbleplex Island Counter by Astro-Tops Design	$770	$115	$77	$308	Surfaces
Mentionable Plastic Litter Box	$150	$22	$15	$60	Miscellaneous
Mixed Flowers Planter by BowerFlux	$175	$26	$17	$70	Decorative
Moon Hopper Sink by Atmos Furnishings	$340	$51	$34	$136	Plumbing
Moonshot Thruster Clock	$230	$34	$23	$92	Electronics
Mr. Maritime	$3,000	$450	$300	$1,200	Decorative
Neo Lighto by Glucolux	$200	$30	$20	$80	Lighting
Neo-Quartzo by Astro-Tops	$770	$115	$77	$308	Surfaces
Neukum Systems "Yee Haw" Country Wall Speaker	$400	$60	$40	$160	Electronics
Nova Jazz by Saturn McGee	$2,750	$412	$275	$1,100	Decorative
Nuclear Family Dining Chair by Nucular Novelties	$450	$67	$45	$180	Comfort

New Object Directory

Object	Price	Initial Depreciation	Daily Depreciation	Depreciation Limit	Hunger	Comfort	Hygiene	Bladder	Energy	Fun	Environment	Cleaning	Study	Charisma	Creativity	Body	Logic	Mechanical	Cooking	Function	Kids	Study	Dining Room	Outside	Living Room	Bathroom	Bedroom	Kitchen	Miscellaneous	Street	Outdoor	Shopping	Food
A Cat Haiku by D. Marga	$325	$48	$32	$130	0	0	0	0	0	0	3									Decorative		X			X		X		X				
A Dog Haiku by D. Marga	$325	$48	$32	$130	0	0	0	0	0	0	3									Decorative		X			X		X		X				
A Portrait of Fuzzy Babies	$415	$62	$41	$166	0	0	0	0	0	0	3									Decorative		X	X		X		X		X				
Affluent Animal Dinner Dish	$125	$18	$12	$50	8	0	0	0	0	0	0									Miscellaneous								X	X				X
Andromeda Far Out Dresser	$485	$72	$48	$194	0	0	0	0	0	0	2									Miscellaneous							X		X			X	
Andromeda Li'l Astronaut Desk	$550	$82	$55	$220	0	0	0	0	0	0	4									Surfaces	X	X							X				
Aqueduct of the Future!	$475	$71	$47	$190	0	0	0	0	0	0	5									Decorative				X	X				X		X		
Asayake MZ-3D: Soothing Sun Device	$195	$29	$19	$78	0	8	0	0	2	0	5									Comfort					X				X				
Asteroid Bowl Lamp	$300	$45	$30	$120	0	0	0	0	0	0	3									Lighting		X			X	X	X		X		X	X	
Asteroid Standing Lamp	$300	$45	$30	$120	0	0	0	0	0	0	3									Lighting	X	X		X	X				X		X		
Atom Bench by Nucular Novelties	$600	$90	$60	$240	0	4	0	0	0	0	2									Comfort				X					X				
Atomic Clothing Manager by Streamlined Industries	$950	$142	$95	$380	0	0	0	0	0	0	0									Miscellaneous							X		X				
Atomicles Loveseat by Nucular Novelties	$1,000	$150	$100	$400	0	7	0	0	2	0	5									Comfort					X				X				
Atomatoybot by Galactica	$55	$8	$5	$22	0	0	0	0	0	7	0		X							Comfort	X								X				
Average Paws Bedding	$550	$82	$55	$220	0	5	0	0	7	0	1									Miscellaneous							X		X		X	X	
Barstool by Simulated Comfort	$690	$103	$69	$276	0	4	0	0	0	0	0									Comfort			X	X				X	X				
Beta Fomicron Dining Table	$260	$39	$26	$104	0	0	0	0	0	0	5									Surfaces	X		X	X	X				X		X		
Beware of Pet Sign	$70	$10	$7	$28	0	0	0	0	0	0	3									Decorative				X					X	X	X		
Bone Rug by Bonafide Luxury	$100	$15	$10	$40	0	0	0	0	0	0	1									Decorative					X				X				
Boronica by d'Lange	$625	$93	$62	$250	0	0	0	0	0	0	3									Miscellaneous		X	X	X	X	X			X		X		
Cat-Crazy Pet Display	$625	$93	$62	$250	0	0	0	0	0	4	0									Miscellaneous									X			X	
Collar Connection Display	$1,000	$150	$100	$400	0	0	0	0	0	3	5									Miscellaneous									X			X	
Comfy Pet Pillow	$1,500	$225	$150	$600	0	6	0	0	6	0	4									Miscellaneous							X		X			X	
Discombobulated Mirrortron from Galactica	$160	$24	$16	$64	0	0	0	0	0	0	3			X						Decorative					X		X		X				
Doggonit Pet Display	$500	$75	$50	$200	0	0	0	0	0	3	0									Miscellaneous									X			X	
EcoPure Park Sign	$50	$7	$5	$20	0	0	0	0	0	0	1									Decorative				X					X	X	X		
Elemental Balance	$375	$56	$37	$150	0	0	0	0	0	0	3									Decorative		X			X				X				
E-to-the-Z Chair	$875	$131	$87	$350	0	8	0	0	0	0	2									Comfort		X	X	X	X		X		X		X		
Feline Birdie Stick	$60	$9	$6	$24	0	0	0	0	0	6	0									Miscellaneous									X			X	
Fierce Gargoyle—Home Edition	$4,500	$675	$450	$1,800	0	0	0	0	0	0	10									Decorative			X	X	X		X		X			X	X

Object	Price				Category
Organically Atomic Rug	$850	$142	$95	$380	Decorative
Paws-A-Plenty Rug by Bonafide Luxury	$360	$54	$36	$144	Decorative
Pet Pillow Fantastic	$825	$83	$62	$250	Miscellaneous
Pet Sculpture Solution	$100	$15	$10	$40	Decorative
Pet Store Sign by Super Signguys	$99	$14	$9	$39	Miscellaneous
Pet's Desires House	$300	$45	$30	$120	Decorative
Planetoid Explorer Rug	$200	$30	$20	$80	Decorative
Pot of Roses by Pot-a-Ree	$175	$26	$17	$70	Decorative
Ring-O-Posies Commercial Planter	$75	$18	$12	$48	Decorative
Rings of Saturn Light by Galactico	$250	$37	$25	$100	Lighting
Saturnacity Lighting from Galactico	$275	$41	$27	$110	Lighting
Scientifically Superior Pet Dish	$80	$12	$8	$32	Miscellaneous
Scratch-O-Matic Scratching Post	$100	$15	$10	$40	Miscellaneous
Scratchpaw Manor Pet House	$2,500	$375	$250	$1,000	Miscellaneous
Scruffies the Quilted Dog	$100	$15	$10	$40	Decorative
Shapes in Space	$200	$45	$30	$120	Decorative
Sirloin Shuffle Screenshot	$90	$28	$19	$76	Decorative
Sleepwave 42 by Streamlined Industries	$2,500	$375	$250	$1,000	Comfort
Snoozing Enemies Comic	$850	$142	$85	$380	Decorative
Solo Neutrino by Astro-Tops Design	$1,800	$270	$180	$720	Miscellaneous
SpaceKid Sim's Atomic Armoire	$850	$127	$85	$340	Miscellaneous
SpaceKid Sims Sonic Sleeper	$500	$75	$50	$200	Comfort
Spacious Spaces	$295	$44	$29	$118	Decorative
Stumped Hound—Reprint	$30	$19	$13	$52	Decorative
Sumo!! Kite	$750	$112	$75	$300	Decorative
Super Settee by Sputnix Furnishings	$1,375	$206	$137	$550	Comfort
Talkatron 9000C by AEC Techtronics	$125	$7	$5	$20	Electronics
Talkatron 9000D by AEC Techtronics	$175	$11	$7	$30	Electronics
Talkatron 9000W by AEC Techtronics	$770	$40	$27	$108	Miscellaneous
The Basket Experience					

New Object Directory

Object	Price	Initial Depreciation	Daily Depreciation	Depreciation Limit	Hunger	Comfort	Hygiene	Bladder	Energy	Fun	Environment	Cleaning	Study	Charisma	Creativity	Body	Logic	Mechanical	Cooking	Function	Kids	Study	Dining Room	Outside	Living Room	Bathroom	Bedroom	Kitchen	Miscellaneous	Street	Outdoor	Shopping	Food
The Beckoning Cat from Worldly Stuff Inc.	$70	$10	$7	$28	0	0	0	0	0	0	1									Decorative		X	X		X		X		X			X	
The Chewinator by ChompCo	$10	$8	$5	$22	0	0	0	0	0	4	0									Miscellaneous							X		X				
The Children's Fusion Lamp by Galactico	$55	$8	$5	$22	0	0	0	0	0	0	1									Lighting	X	X	X		X		X					X	
The Comfy Critter Pallet	$220	$33	$22	$88	0	6	0	0	8	0	0									Miscellaneous	X	X	X		X	X	X	X	X			X	
The House Pets Comic	$375	$56	$37	$150	0	0	0	0	0	6	2									Decorative							X		X				
The Imposing Falcon	$50	$7	$5	$20	0	0	0	0	0	0	2									Decorative		X	X		X	X	X	X	X			X	
The Luna Torch by Glucolux	$200	$30	$20	$80	0	0	0	0	0	0	2									Lighting			X		X	X	X					X	
The Perfect Cat	$85	$12	$8	$34	0	0	0	0	0	0	3									Decorative		X	X		X	X	X		X				
The Photonic Ha'Sphere by Glucolux	$245	$36	$24	$98	0	0	0	0	0	0	2									Lighting		X	X		X	X	X	X	X			X	
The Prototype X94 "Angstronaut" Robosuit	$250	$37	$25	$100	0	0	0	0	0	0	1									Decorative	X	X	X		X		X		X			X	
The Stodgy Badger Family Portrait	$150	$22	$15	$60	0	0	0	0	0	0	1									Decorative		X			X		X		X			X	
The Stodgy Badger Family Portrait	$130	$19	$13	$52	0	0	0	0	0	0	1									Decorative	X	X			X	X	X	X	X			X	
Tropico Avian Sanctuary	$500	$75	$50	$200	0	0	0	0	0	8	3			X						Decorative		X		X	X		X		X		X	X	
Tropico Birds in the Wild	$325	$48	$32	$130	0	0	0	0	0	0	1									Decorative	X	X	X	X	X	X	X	X	X	X		X	X
Yummers in My Tummers! Poster	$40	$6	$4	$16	0	0	0	0	0	0	1									Decorative	X	X	X					X	X			X	X
Zero-G Dresser	$500	$75	$50	$200	0	0	0	0	0	0	10									Miscellaneous		X	X		X		X		X			X	
Zip Zap! Coffee Table	$300	$45	$30	$120	0	0	0	0	0	0	2									Surfaces		X							X				

Object Catalog

Comfort

Dining Chairs

Little Space Rangers Chair

- Price: §175
- Need Effects: Comfort 3

Nuclar Family Dining Chair by Nuclar Novelties

- Price: §450
- Need Effects: Comfort 6

Living Chairs

E-to-the-Z Chair

- Price: §875
- Need Effects: Comfort 8, Environment 2

Recliners

Lounge-O-Rama by Nucular Novelties

- Price: §850
- Need Effects: Comfort 8, Energy 2 (Nap), Environment 2
- Need Max: Energy up to 25 (Nap)

Sofas

Atomicles Loveseat by Nucular Novelties

- Price: §1,000
- Need Effects: Comfort 7 (Sit/Nap), Comfort 8 (Lounge), Energy 2 (Nap), Fun 4 (Play)
- Need Max: Energy up to 70 (Nap)

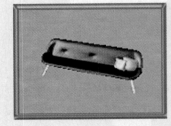

Super Settee by Sputnix Furnishings

- Price: §1,375
- Need Effects: Comfort 7, Comfort 8 (Lounge), Energy 2 (Nap), Fun 4 (Play)
- Need Max: Energy up to 70 (Nap)

Beds

SpaceKid Sims Sonic Sleeper

- Price: §500
- Need Effects: Comfort 3, Energy 3

Sleepwave 42 by Streamlined Industries

- Price: §2,500
- Need Effects: Comfort 6, Energy 6, Fun 4 (Jump), Environment 5
- Need Max: Fun up to 80 (Jump)

Miscellaneous

Atom Bench by Nucular Novelties

- Price: §600
- Need Effects: Comfort 8 (Sit/Nap), Comfort 9 (Lounge), Energy 2 (Nap), Fun 4 (Play), Environment 10
- Need Max: Energy up to 70 (Nap)

Barstool by Simulated Comfort

- Price: §690
- Need Effects: Comfort 7, Environment 2

Surfaces

Counters

Neo-Quartzo by Astro-Tops

- Price: §770
- Need Effects: Environment 2

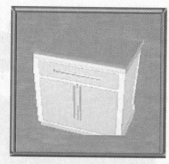

Marbleplex Island Counter by Astro-Tops Design

- Price: §770
- Need Effects: Environment 2

Dining Tables

Beta Fomicron Dining Table

- Price: §260

End Tables

Junior Cosmonauts Bedside Table

- Price: §115

Inner Atmos End Table

- Price: §260

Coffee Tables

Zip Zap! Coffee Table

◆ Price: §300

◆ Need Effects: Environment 2

Desks

Andromeda Li'l Astronaut Desk

◆ Price: §550

Decorative

Plants

Pot of Roses by Pot-a-Ree

◆ Price: §120

◆ Need Effects: Environment 2

Mixed Flowers Planter by BowerFlox

◆ Price: §175

◆ Need Effects: Environment 1

Ring-O-Posies Commercial Planter

◆ Price: §175

◆ Need Effects: Environment 3

Sculptures

The Beckoning Cat from Worldly Stuff Inc.

◆ Price: §70

◆ Need Effects: Fun 4 (View), Environment 1

◆ Need Max: Fun up to 95 (View)

The Prototype X94 "Angsternaut" Robosuit

◆ Price: §150

◆ Need Effects: Environment 1

Hydrocyanic Cat No. 7

◆ Price: §165

◆ Need Effects: Environment 1

The Imposing Falcon

◆ Price: §200

◆ Need Effects: Environment 2

Shapes in Space

◆ Price: §300

◆ Need Effects: Environment 3

A Cat Haiku by D. Marga

- ◆ Price: §325
- ◆ Need Effects: Environment 3

A Dog Haiku by D. Marga

- ◆ Price: §325
- ◆ Need Effects: Environment 3

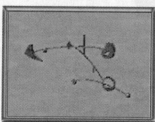

Johnny the Pump

- ◆ Price: §325
- ◆ Need Effects: Environment 3

Elemental Balance

- ◆ Price: §375
- ◆ Need Effects: Environment 3

Aqueduct of the Future!

- ◆ Price: §475
- ◆ Need Effects: Environment 4

Wall Hangings

Yummers in My Tummers! Poster

- ◆ Price: §40
- ◆ Need Effects: Environment 1

The House Pets Comic

- ◆ Price: §50
- ◆ Need Effects: Environment 1

King Kricket Klobberin' Klub

- ◆ Price: §75
- ◆ Need Effects: Environment 1

Scruffles the Quilted Dog

- ◆ Price: §100
- ◆ Need Effects: Environment 1

In Memory of Johnny Gnome

◆ Price: §120

◆ Need Effects: Environment 1

Kitten vs. Yarn: Season 1 Print

◆ Price: §130

◆ Need Effects: Environment 1

Stumped Hound—Reprint

◆ Price: §130

◆ Need Effects: Environment 1

The Stodgy Badger Family Portrait

◆ Price: §130

◆ Need Effects: Environment 1

 note

Two versions of The Stodgy Badger Family Portrait exist—a female one and a male one. This is the female one.

The Stodgy Badger Family Portrait

◆ Price: §130

◆ Need Effects: Environment 1

 note

Two versions of The Stodgy Badger Family Portrait exist—a female one and a male one. This is the male one.

Leash Racque by DeFarge

◆ Price: §145

◆ Need Effects: Environment 1

Sirloin Shuffle Screenshot

◆ Price: §190

◆ Need Effects: Environment 2

The Perfect Cat

◆ Price: §245

◆ Need Effects: Environment 2

Spacious Spaces

- Price: §295
- Need Effects: Environment 2

Tropico Birds in the Wild

- Price: §325
- Need Effects: Environment 3

A Portrait of Fuzzy Babies

- Price: §415
- Need Effects: Environment 3

Boronica by d'Lange

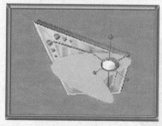

- Price: §625
- Need Effects: Environment 5

Sumo!!! Kite

- Price: §750
- Need Effects: Environment 6

Snoozing Enemies Comic

- Price: §950
- Need Effects: Environment 7

Nova Jazz by Saturn McGee

- Price: §2,750
- Need Effects: Environment 10

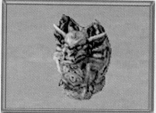

Fierce Gargoyle—Home Edition

- Price: §4,500
- Need Effects: Environment 10

Mirrors

Discombobulated Mirrortron from Galactico

- Price: §525
- Skill: Charisma (Practice Romance or Practice Speech)
- Need Effects: Hygiene 2 (Gussy Up), Environment 3

Rugs

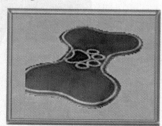

Bone Rug by Bonafide Luxury

- Price: §100

Planetoid Explorer Rug

- Price: §200

Paws-A-Plenty Rug by Bonafide Luxury

◆ Price: §360

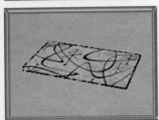

Organically Atomic Rug

◆ Price: §950

Miscellaneous

EcoPure Park Sign

◆ Price: §50
◆ Need Effects: Environment 1

Beware of Pet Sign

◆ Price: §70
◆ Need Effects: Environment 1

Pet Store Sign by Super SignGuys

◆ Price: §99
◆ Need Effects: Environment 1

Pet Sculpture Solution

◆ Price: §100
◆ Need Effects: Environment 1

Mr. Maritime

◆ Price: §3,000
◆ Skill: Cleaning (Clean Tank)
◆ Need Effects: Fun 10 (Watch), Fun 5 (Feed), Fun 4 (Restocking), Environment 6
◆ Need Max: Fun up to 70 (Watch) or 50 (Feed)

This saltwater aquarium functions identically to the original AquaBox Five-Gallon Aquarium. Like the Sims with the older version, cats may now Watch for Fun. (Aggressive cats are very attracted to this interaction, and Cowardly cats are less attracted.)

Plumbing

Sinks

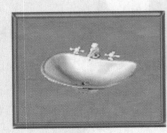

Moon Hopper Sink by Atmos Furnishings

◆ Price: §340
◆ Type: Countertop
◆ Skill: Cleaning (Clean), Mechanical (Repair)
◆ Need Effects: Hygiene 5 (Wash), Hygiene 7 (Sponge Bath), Hunger 1 (Drink)
◆ Need Max: Hygiene up to 90 (Wash), Hygiene up to 25 (Sponge Bath), Hygiene up to 70 (Bathe Baby).

Electronics

TVs & Computers

Futur-Vu by Vidioblast

◆ Price: §800

◆ Skill: Cooking (Watch Yummy Channel), Body (Work Out), Mechanical (Repair)

◆ Need Effects: Fun 7 (varies by Sim's reaction to the channel), Energy -3, Comfort -3, Hygiene -7 (Work Out), Environment 3

◆ Need Max: Depends on Sim's reaction to channel.

The Futur-Vu functions identically to older TVs.

Small Electronics

Talkatron 9000C by AEC Techtronics

◆ Price: §125

Talkatron 9000W by AEC Techtronics

◆ Price: §175

Functions identically to original telephones.

Moonshot Thruster Clock

◆ Price: §230

◆ Need Effects: Fun (View)

◆ Need Max: Fun up to 95 (View)

Lighting

Table Lamps

Neo Lighto by Glucolux

◆ Price: §200

◆ Need Effects: Environment 3

The Children's Fusion Lamp by Galactico

◆ Price: §220

◆ Need Effects: Environment 2

Floor Lamps

Rings of Saturn Light by Galactico

◆ Price: §250

◆ Need Effects: Environment 2

Asteroid Standing Lamp

◆ Price: §300

◆ Need Effects: Environment 3

Wall Lamps

The Photonic Ha'Sphere by Glucolux

◆ Price: §250

◆ Need Effects: Environment 2

Ceiling Lamps

Saturnocity Lighting from Galactico

◆ Price: §275

◆ Need Effects: Environment 3

Asteroid Bowl Lamp

◆ Price: §300

◆ Need Effects: Environment 3

Outdoor Lamps

Asayake MZ-30: Soothing Sun Device

◆ Price: §195

◆ Need Effects: Environment 2

Miscellaneous

The Luna Torch by Glucolux

◆ Price: §85

◆ Need Effects: Environment 3

Miscellaneous

Dressers

Andromeda Far Out Dresser

◆ Price: §485

◆ Need Effects: Environment 10

Zero-G Dresser

◆ Price: §500

◆ Need Effects: Environment 10

SpaceKid Sim's Atomic Armoire

◆ Price: §850

◆ Need Effects: Environment 4

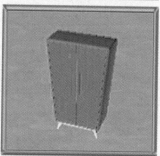

Atomic Clothing Manager by Streamlined Industries

◆ Price: §950

◆ Need Effects: Environment 5

Children

Atomotoybot by Galactico

◆ Price: §55

◆ Need Effects: Fun 7

◆ Need Max: Fun up to 85

This toy box functions exactly like the Rip Co. Toy Bin.

Party

Solo Neutrino by Astro-Tops Design

◆ Price: §1,800

◆ Need Effects: Fun 3

◆ Need Max: Fun up to 50 (Juggle) or 80 (Make Drinks) or 50 (Consume Drinks) or 70–90 (Drink from Bottle, depends on Playful/Serious).

All island bars connect with matching island counters and, when placed on a community lot, spawn an NPC Bartender. When on a home lot, they function just like normal juice bars (such as Bachman Busbar).

 note

If you place identical bars side-by-side, they'll connect.

Interactions:

◆ Order Drink: Community lot only. Order a Blended (§15) or Poured (§10) drink from the NPC Bartender. Drinking satisfies Fun.

◆ Tend Bar: Community lot only. Young adult or older can replace the NPC Bartender at the machine and serve any Sims who order drinks. Earn simoleons for time spent working job, awarded when you cancel interaction.

◆ Drink from Bottle: Home lot only. Satisfies Hunger and Fun. Playful Sims get a higher maximum Fun than Serious Sims.

◆ Make a Drink: Home lot only. Satisfies Fun. Prepares single drink.

◆ Make Drinks: Home lot only. Prepares multiple drinks.

◆ Juggle Tumblers: Home lot only. Satisfies Fun.

◆ Join: Home lot only. Join Juggling. Satisfies Fun.

Pets

Kitty Kraze Katnip

◆ Price: §35

◆ Need Effects: Fun 6, Energy –1

Interactions:

◆ Play With: Toy can be used only by cats (not kittens) and will be used more by Hyper cats. After a bit of play, the cat starts acting, well, weird, running around crazily, scratching things, batting at imaginary bugs, chasing its tail, yowling, or getting the jitters (à la Sims with coffee). Cats get Fun satisfaction but

decreased Energy. They can be praised/scolded toward Playful/Hostile. After a while, toy will be used up and turn into a trash pile that will bring down the Environment score until cleaned up.

◆ Watch: When cat is playing or "nipping," Sims may gather to Watch; they'll get Fun and Social (group chat) and may laugh at the cat's herb-addled antics.

Good Value Pet Bowl

◆ Price: §45

◆ Skill: Cleaning (Clean)

◆ Need Effects: Hunger 6

◆ Need Max: Hygiene down to -75 (Toddler Eat), Fun up to 90 (Toddler Eat)

> **note**
> Pets will remember which Sim most often fills a dish. If the pet is hungry and the dish is empty, it'll go to the "giver of food" and ask to be fed.
> Dishes can be owned by pets with repeated use, and pets with enough ownership points over a bowl may challenge other pets for using it.

> **note**
> Finicky pets will be less likely to eat from this cheapest bowl.

Interactions:

◆ Fill: Sims can be directed to fill an empty bowl or will do so autonomously if asked by a pet. Refilling a dish costs §10.

◆ Call to Eat: Summons specific pet to come eat at the bowl. If the pet knows the Come command, it'll always obey. If not, it may sometimes reject, but there's no relationship decrease. This is a good way to avoid ownership squabbles by indirectly telling different pets to eat from different bowls.

◆ Eat: Cats, dogs, puppies, and kittens will eat from a bowl when hungry. Finicky and Normal pets will eat until full, but Pigpen pets may continue eating even after Hunger is fully satisfied;

occasionally, this makes the pet throw up (depleting Hunger and Hygiene and creating a mess that reduces Environment until cleaned). Finicky pets won't eat from a dirty dish until their Hunger drops below -75. Pets can be praised or scolded for eating from pet bowls to train them in Eats Pet Food/Eats Sim Food behavior.

◆ Eat (Toddler): Toddlers can be directed or may autonomously eat from pet food bowls, satisfying Fun and Hunger but depleting Hygiene.

◆ Clean: The pet bowl gets dirty with use. Once it becomes dirty, Sims can clean it (earning Cleaning skill). When it becomes filthy, it emits flies and green stink, which brings down Environment and makes the bowl unavailable to Normal or Finicky pets; Pigpen pets will eat even from a filthy bowl (but will NOT become sick). If the bowl has food in it when cleaned, the remaining food will be wasted and the bowl must be refilled. Maids and Servos will autonomously clean pet bowls.

The Dirt Pile

One of the favorite canine pastimes centers around an object, but it's not one that you can buy from the catalog; it's one dogs make by themselves. The dirt pile is created when a dog digs in the yard, and it provides endless hours of entertainment.

When a dog digs, it creates a dirt pile. The longer the dog digs, the larger the dirt pile gets. The smaller a dirt pile is, the more attractive it will be to other dogs to make it bigger by digging more.

For Sims, dirt piles are nuisances, pulling down outdoor Environment score until the holes are filled in. Filling in a dirt hole builds Cleaning skill but lowers Hygiene.

For dogs, however, dirt piles are the best toys ever. Digging satisfies Fun and depletes Hygiene. Lazy dogs will be less likely to dig and Hyper dogs more likely.

Once a pile is created, dogs can roll in it for even more Fun and even lower Hygiene. Pigpen dogs will be more likely to do this and Finicky dogs less likely.

Digging and rolling can be praised/scolded to reinforce Clean/Filthy behavior.

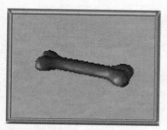

The Chewinator by ChompCo

- Price: §55
- Need Effects: Fun 6, Chew 4 (dogs only)

Interactions:

- Chew: Dogs will chew this toy to satisfy both Fun and Chew. Dogs can be praised or scolded for this interaction toward training Respectful/Destructive behavior.

Feline Birdie Stick

- Price: §60
- Need Effects: Fun 6, Energy -1

note

This is the only toy that kittens can play with. Since, however, they don't have a Fun Need, they can do just fine without it.

Interactions:

- Play With: Cats may play with this wall-mountable object for Fun (and a small depletion of Energy). Hyper pets are more likely to choose this object than Normal or Lazy pets. If the toy is used near a sleeping Sim, the Sim will wake up. Cats can build ownership over this toy, challenging other cats (not kittens) that try to use it. Cats can be praised or scolded for using this object to train in the Playful/Hostile behavior.

- Watch: Sims may watch a cat or kitten play with this toy, pointing and laughing, satisfying Fun and (if in a group) Social. Other cats may also watch for Fun.

Scientifically Superior Pet Dish

- Price: §80
- Skill: Cleaning (Clean)
- Need Effects: Hunger 6
- Need Max: Hygiene down to -75 (Toddler Eat), Fun up to 90 (Toddler Eat)

This bowl is mostly identical to the Good Value Pet Bowl but provides faster Hunger satisfaction and is more appealing to Finicky pets.

Scratch-O-Matic Scratching Post

- Price: §100
- Need Effects: Scratch 8

Interaction:

- Scratch: Satisfies cats' Scratch Need. Cats can be praised/scolded for this interaction to train in the Respectful/Destructive behavior.

Affluent Animal Dinner Dish

- Price: §125
- Skill: Cleaning (Clean)
- Need Effects: Hunger 8
- Need Max: Hygiene down to -75 (Toddler Eat), Fun up to 90 (Toddler Eat)

This bowl is mostly identical to the Good Value Pet Bowl but provides faster Hunger satisfaction and is more appealing to Finicky pets.

Mentionable Plastic Litter Box

- Price: §150
- Skill: Cleaning
- Need Effects: Bladder 10, Hygiene -2 (Clean), Hunger 5 (Munch Out), Hygiene -5 (Munch Out)

Interactions:

- Use: Cats and kittens who enter the box relieve their Bladder need. After several uses, the box becomes dirty, bringing down Environment score. With more usage, the box becomes super dirty, emitting flies and green stink. Finicky cats will be less likely to use a dirty litter box. Only Pigpen pets will reliably use a super dirty litter box; Finicky will refuse to use it and Normal will be more likely to pee elsewhere. If a litter box is unusable, Finicky and Normal pets will pee inside or outside according to their Housebroken/Yardbroken training. Praising/scolding cats and kittens for using the litter box reinforces Housebroken/Yardbroken training.

- Clean: Sims get Cleaning skill when they restore the litter box to its clean state but take a hit to their Hygiene. Pregnant Sims will not be able to clean the litter box. Maids and Servos will clean the litter box as part of their duties.

- Munch Out: Hungry Pigpen dogs may eat out of a super dirty litter box. This nasty habit satisfies Hunger, depletes Hygiene, and may cause the dog to throw up.

Comfy Pet Pillow

- Price: §160
- Skill: Cleaning
- Need Effects: Comfort 4, Energy 6, Hygiene -5 (Clean)

> ## note
> The Comfy Pet Pillow will be unusable if placed with the wrong side against the wall. Unfortunately, it's hard to tell which is the wrong side just by looking at it. When placing this bed, be mindful of the green arrow on the placement tool and be sure it's pointing to an accessible place.

Interactions:

- Relax: Pets will use pet beds instead of the floor to replenish Comfort. They can be praised/scolded to reinforce the Stays Off the Furniture/Goes on the Furniture.

- Sleep: Pets will use to replenish Energy and Comfort and can be praised/scolded to reinforce the Stays Off Sim Beds/Goes on Sim Beds behavior.

- Clean: With repeated use, the pet bed gets dirty, emitting flies and a green stink cloud, depressing Environment score, and making Finicky pets less likely to use it. Sims can clean it to restore Environment score and make it available to pets that refuse to use it. Cleaning builds Cleaning skill but reduces Hygiene. Maids and Servos will clean pet beds as part of their duties.

Cat-Crazy Pet Display

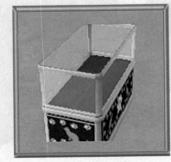

- Price: §222
- Need Effects: Fun 3, Environment 4

note

This display functions differently depending on whether you have THE SIMS™ 2 OPEN FOR BUSINESS expansion pack.

In THE SIMS™ 2 PETS, the display can only be placed on community lot businesses.

note

If you don't have THE SIMS 2 OPEN FOR BUSINESS, the case will be filled with a randomly generated pet of the case's specified breed with no behaviors or commands. No other display on the same lot can have this breed of pet so there'll be some variety in the store's selection.

Interactions without *The Sims 2 Open for Business*:

◆ Browse: Autonomously or by user direction, Sims will watch the pets inside. Satisfies Fun.

◆ Purchase: Autonomously (visitors or townies) or by user direction, Sims can buy a pet. If the Sim lacks room for a household pet, the attempt will be rejected. If there is room, a streamlined version of Create a Cat/Create a Dog (see "Pet Stores" in the "Create a Cat/Dog and Acquiring Pets" chapter) allows you to design whatever pet you want from either species, regardless of the kind of display or the pet shown in it. The finished pet appears next to your Sim, and money is automatically deducted from the Sim's household funds. When you direct the Sim to leave the lot, the pet follows. If the purchaser is an uncontrollable townie or a visiting Sim, the displayed pet is put into a bag and the Sim pays for it at the cash register. The display pet is replaced by a new random pet of the case's species. Townies don't keep pets; the transaction is imaginary.

note

Whether you have THE SIMS 2 OPEN FOR BUSINESS or not, if a playable Sim purchases a pet (or pets) as an autonomous visitor to a community lot, the next time you play that Sim's household, you'll be asked if you want to keep the pet. Pets purchased this way are not designable, and you get whatever was in the case when the Sim made the purchase.

Interactions with *The Sims 2™ Open for Business*:

◆ Browse: Autonomous Sims (townies and visitors) will browse the display with the standard Buy bar function and can be a target for sales Socials.

◆ Purchase: Autonomous or controllable Sims can interact with stocked displays. The purchase process is identical to the Purchase interaction for those without THE SIMS 2 OPEN FOR BUSINESS.

◆ Set Price: Business owners can set the price level of any pet purchased from the display.

◆ Change Breed for Sale: The business owner can choose from a random selection of pre-generated pets to specify the breed that will appear in the bin and that autonomous Sims will get when they buy.

◆ Restock: If a pet has been bought from the bin, restocking allows the owner to restore a pet of the chosen breed to the case.

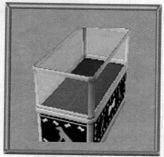

Doggonit Pet Display

◆ Price: §222
◆ Need Effects: Fun 3, Environment 4

This is identical to the Cat-Crazy Pet Display except display pets will be small and large dogs instead of cats. Controllable Sims can buy any species of pet from this bin, but autonomous Sims can only buy the species and breed on display.

FMCU 3000

- Price: §250
- Skill: Cleaning
- Need Effects: Fun 7, Social (Play With)
- Need Max: Fun up to 90 (Play With), Fun up to 80 (Watch, Sims and Aggressive pets), Fun up to 60 (Watch, non-Aggressive pets)

note

For full details on caged pets' Needs and Mood, see the "Pet Life" chapter.

tip

Don't put this object in the same room as a Sim's bed; when the womrat runs in the wheel, it'll wake up sleeping Sim.

Interactions:

- **Stock:** Child or older Sims can purchase a womrat for an empty and cleaned cage. Womrats cost §70.
- **Play With:** Children or older Sims can pick up the pet and play with it for Fun and Social satisfaction. If the pet is in a bad mood due to hunger or a dirty cage, it may bite the Sim.
- **Fill Food Dish:** For §10 per feeding, Sims can be directed to refill the caged pet's food dish. Keeping it well fed is important because hungry caged pets bite, making them less useful as sources of Fun for Sims. Hungry womrats squeak, climb into their empty dish and up their water bottle, and flash food scream balloons when hungry. Fail to feed them and they'll eventually die. Sims never feed caged pets autonomously, so they're YOUR responsibility.
- **Clean Cage:** Cages get dirty with time, eventually drawing flies, emitting a green stink cloud, and bringing down Environment. A dirty cage also brings down the pet's Mood, increasing the odds of it biting. When a Sim cleans the cage, the cage stops bringing down Environment, the pet's mood improves, and the Sim gets some Cleaning skill.

- **Watch:** Sims or pets can watch the pet for Fun. All cats and dogs will be more likely to watch if their Hunger is low. Aggressive pets will watch longer than other pets (due to higher Fun max). When an Aggressive pet watches, it barks/hisses/growls at the cage, possibly causing the caged pet to die of fright. Watching peacefully or stalking the cage can be praised/scolded toward the Playful/Hostile behavior.
- **Set Free:** If the pet is in the cage, a Sim can release the pet to the bittersweet freedom of the suburban jungle.
- **Mourn the Loss:** A Sim can have a good cry over the loss of the little beast.

tip

The rodent plague has been cured, so no Sim will ever get sick from playing with the womrat.

The Basket Experience

- Price: §270
- Skill: Cleaning
- Need Effects: Comfort 5, Energy 7, Hygiene -5 (Clean)

The Basket Experience functions identically to the Comfy Pet Pillow.

Pets' Desires House

- **Price: §300**
- Skill: Cleaning
- Need Effects: Comfort 4, Energy 6, Hygiene -5 (Clean)

Pet houses are the only places pets can conceive puppies or kittens, through the Sim-to-pet Try for Puppy/Kitten with… interaction. If there's no pet bed on the lot, the interaction will be unavailable. Note that this interaction is available on pets, not on the house itself.

Interactions:

◆ Relax: Pets will use the house instead of the floor to replenish Comfort. They can be praised/scolded to reinforce the Stays off Furniture/Goes on Furniture behavior.

◆ Sleep: Pets will use pet houses to replenish Energy and Comfort and can be praised/scolded to reinforce the Stays off Sim Beds/Goes on Sim Beds behavior.

◆ Clean: With repeated use, the pet house gets dirty, emitting flies and a green stink cloud, depressing Environment score, and making Finicky pets less likely to use it. Sims can clean it to restore Environment score and make it available to pets that refuse to use it. Cleaning builds Cleaning skill but reduces Hygiene. Maids and Servos will clean pet houses as part of their duties.

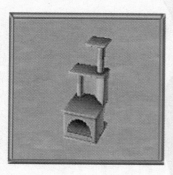

The Comfy Critter Pallet

◆ Price: §375
◆ Skill: Cleaning
◆ Need Effects: Comfort 6, Energy 8, Hygiene -5 (Clean)

This pallet functions identically to the Comfy Pet Pillow.

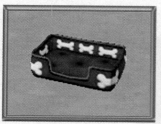

Los Gatos Condominiums

◆ Price: §450
◆ Need Effects: Comfort 5 (Sleep/ Survey), Energy 7 (Sleep), Fun 4 (Scratch/Survey), Scratch 8
◆ Need Max: Fun up to 90 (Scratch/Survey), Scratch up to 90

Up to eight cats can use this object at once from positions on four different levels:

◆ Level 4: Small platform at the top, useable for Survey or Sleep only

◆ Level 3: Medium platform with roped scratching point on vertical post.

◆ Level 2: Large platform with roped scratching point on vertical post.

◆ Level 1: Enclosed space at the bottom can be used for Sleep only. If the post is positioned away from the wall, there are two scratching places on the rear vertical posts that can accommodate two cats per post at one time.

Kittens can't use any part of this object.

tip

This object is a good investment for a Sim with several cats. Unlike pet beds and houses, this object sleeps four at once, can't give rise to ownership challenges, and requires no cleaning. The only thing it can't do that a pet house can is play host to the making of kittens.

Interactions:

◆ Scratch: Cats can use any of the four available rope-wrapped scratching posts to satisfy their Scratch need. Hyper cats will be particularly attracted to this use. Pets may be praised/ scolded for doing this interaction to reinforce Respectful/ Destructive behavior.

◆ Sleep: Cats can sleep on any of the three available platforms (with Comfort and Energy about equivalent to the midrange pet beds and houses). Cowardly cats will favor sleeping in the enclosed bottom platform, and Lazy cats will be more attracted to this interaction than most.

◆ Survey: Cats can relax and check out the view from the top three platforms to satisfy Fun and Comfort.

note

Unlike the basic scratching post, this object can't be owned by any cat.

Tropico Avian Sanctuary

- Price: §500
- Skill: Cleaning, Charisma (Teach to Talk)
- Need Effects: Fun 8, Social (Play With)
- Need Max: Fun up to 90 (Play With), Fun up to 80 (Watch, Aggressive pets), Fun up to 70 (Watch, non-Aggressive pets), Fun up to 60 (Sims)

note

For full details on caged pets' Needs and Mood, see the "Pet Life" chapter.

tip

Don't put this object in the same room with a bed; the bird's squawking will wake sleeping Sims.

This object functions very similarly to the FMCU 3000 (womrat cage), but with more possible interactions with the caged pet. The bird is more expensive: §400. The bird's Mood also affects its willingness to be trained to talk.

In addition to the interactions listed for the FMCU 3000, the birdcage offers:

- Carry: Children or older Sims can take the bird out and carry it on a shoulder. Sims can walk or run with the bird on a shoulder, but they'll return it to the cage if they decide or are directed to do anything else.

- Teach to Talk: Sim can teach birds to talk to build their own Charisma skill and make the bird a greater source of Fun and a source of Social satisfaction. During training, the bird will show a progress bar. Training is hard work, depleting the Sim's Energy and the bird's Hunger. If the bird is in a bad mood due to hunger or a dirty cage, it may reject training or exit before it's complete.

- Talk With: Once a bird has been taught to talk, Sims can talk to it for Fun and Social boosts.

- Open Cage: Opening the cage allows the bird to fly freely around the lot, gaining Fun for the Sim while the bird is flying. It won't ever escape, however, and can't be caught by cats or dogs. The bird will fly around for a time and eventually return to the cage. The cage can't be sold or closed as long as the bird is in flight.

- Close Cage: Sim closes the cage when bird has returned.

Average Paws Bedding

- Price: §550
- Skill: Cleaning
- Need Effects: Comfort 5, Energy 6, Hygiene -5 (Clean)

This bedding functions identically to the Pets' Desires House.

Pet Pillow Fantastic

- Price: §625
- Skill: Cleaning
- Need Effects: Comfort 7, Energy 9, Hygiene -5 (Clean), Environment 1

Functions just like the Comfy Pet Pillow.

Galactix Animal Home

- Price: §1,500
- Skill: Cleaning
- Need Effects: Comfort 6, Energy 8, Hygiene -5 (Clean), Environment 3

This pet house functions identically to the Pets' Desires House.

Scratchpaw Manor Pet House

- Price: §2,500
- Skill: Cleaning
- Need Effects: Comfort 7, Energy 9, Hygiene -5 (Clean), Environment 5

Scratchpaw Manor works just like the Pets' Desires House.

Community Lot-Only Objects

Surfaces

Counters

Formicium Counter by Astro-Tops Design

- Price: §770
- Need Effects: Environment 2

Electronics

Audio

Neukum Systems "Yee Haw" Country Wall Speaker

- Price: §400
- Need Effects: Fun 2

Miscellaneous

Pets

Collar Connection Display

- Price: §1,500
- Need Effects: Fun 4 (Browse), Environment 6
- Need Max: Fun up to 80 (Browse)

note
Collars are important if your Sims' pets ever run away: the collars make their return much more likely.

How this countertop object works depends on whether you have *The Sims 2 Open for Business* expansion pack. In either case, from the buyer's point of view, the display is a cross between a video game stand and a clothing rack.

Interactions without *The Sims 2 Open for Business*:

- Buy Collar: Your Sim can view the available collars via thumbnails of generic large and small dogs and cats. Select collars, add them to your cart, and confirm to purchase. Your Sim will take the collar(s) to the cash register to pay for the purchase. When

the Sim returns home, the object can be put on a pet via the Change Appearance of... interaction on any mirror. Go to panel 3 and you'll see all purchased collars.

> **note**
>
> New collars are unlocked and become available from this stand when pets earn job promotions.

With *The Sims 2 Open for Business*, the display works the same for buyers. For business owners, it functions just like a clothing rack but without the Try On interaction.

Objects Modified for Pets

> **note**
>
> For all the new pee interactions, pets remember favorite spots and will favor them in the future.

Pets can use many existing objects, including:

- Aquarium: Cats watch for Fun.
- Band Objects: Cats and dogs may howl or yowl at Sims performing or practicing on band instruments (regardless of the Sim's Creativity). They can be praised/scolded to reinforce Calm/Disruptive behavior. Hyper pets are more likely and Lazy pets less likely to do this.
- Bay Windows: Dogs and cats can climb onto the bay window ledge and sleep or look out for Energy, Comfort, or Fun. Lazy pets are more likely to sit in the bay window. Pets will gain ownership points over this object and may challenge

other pets for use of it. Large dogs can chill in the bay window for Fun, standing with hindpaws on the floor and forepaws on the window.

- Beds: Pets can sleep or relax on beds; they can be praised/scolded to reinforce Stays off Sim Beds/Goes on Sim Beds behavior.
- Cars: Pets can get in all Sim-owned cars and many carpool vehicles. If a Sim and pet go to work at the same time and the Sim's vehicle is inaccessible, the pet's job vehicle will come instead. Sorry, no pets in helicopters. SAA rules!
- Chairs: Cats can sit and sleep on chairs; small dogs can only sit. Large dogs can't do either. Pets can be praised/scolded to reinforce Stays off Furniture/Goes on Furniture behavior.
- Counters: Cats can jump onto counters to relax/sleep or eat off plates. The former can be praised/scolded to reinforce Stays off Furniture/Goes on Furniture behavior and the latter for Eats Pet Food/Eats Sim Food behavior.
- Doors and Gates: Sims can now lock doors and gates to "Disallow Pets" or "Allow Pets" to control which rooms pets can enter.
- Eclectic and Enigmatic Energizer Aspiration Reward Object: Pets will bark/yowl/hiss when a Sim uses the object. They can be praised/scolded to reinforce Calm/Disruptive behavior.
- Elevators: Cats and dogs can use elevators. Puppies and kittens can't ride in elevators, but, like toddlers, they can be carried by a Sim into the elevator. Pets, like toddlers, are immune to the effects of falling elevators.
- Flamingo/Gnome: Cats and dogs may pee on these yard decorations. Aggressive pets will be more likely and Cowardly pets less likely to do this. Pets can be praised/scolded to reinforce Housebroken/Yardbroken behavior.

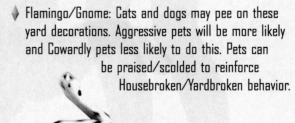

◆ **Flower Beds:** Dogs and cats can pee in flower beds for Fun and Bladder satisfaction. Aggressive pets are more likely and Cowardly pets less likely to do so; all can be praised/scolded to reinforce Housebroken/Yardbroken behavior. Dogs can roll in flower beds for Fun (reducing Hygiene); this can be praised/scolded to reinforce Filthy/Clean behavior. Pets can also eat flower beds to satisfy Hunger, though they may throw up afterward. They can be praised/scolded to reinforce Respectful/Destructive behavior. If the rolling or eating isn't interrupted, the flowers will be destroyed and must be replanted.

◆ **Food:** Pets can eat Sim food to satisfy Hunger. Finicky pets won't even consider it until their Hunger has dropped farther than that of other kinds of pets. Pigpen pets will be the most attracted to Sim food. Sim food can be the subject of ownership challenges. Pets can be praised/scolded to reinforce Eats Pet Food/Eats Sim Food behavior. All but Finicky pets will eat spoiled food.

◆ **Hoverbots/Roverbots:** Pets react to moving robots based on their Aggressive/Cowardly trait. They can be praised/scolded to reinforce Playful/Hostile behavior. Pets can scratch or chew turned off Hoverbots/Roverbots, breaking (but not destroying) them. They can be praised/scolded to reinforce Respectful/Destructive behavior. Pets don't react to Servos as robots; to them they're normal Sims.

◆ **Karaoke:** Cats and dogs will yowl/howl when someone uses the karaoke machine. The lower the Sim's Creativity, the more likely pets will react. Lazy pets react less and Hyper pets react more. Pets get Fun and can be praised/scolded to reinforce Calm/Disruptive behavior.

◆ **Mailbox:** Cats and dogs may pee on mailboxes. Aggressive pets are more likely and Cowardly pets are less likely to do this. Pets can be praised/scolded to reinforce Housebroken/Yardbroken behavior.

◆ **Mirrors:** Pets will react to their own reflection according to Personality. Genius pets are more likely to do this and Doofus pets less likely. They can be praised/scolded to reinforce Calm/Disruptive behavior. Sims can change pets' coats (from the Coat Template Bin), coat layers, and collars via mirrors' Change Appearance of... interaction. Changes to coat do not affect genetics.

◆ **Puddles:** Dogs can play in and both cats and dogs will drink from puddles of any origin (ANY origin at all...eww) for Fun and Hunger satisfaction (and a drop in Hygiene). Playful and Pigpen pets are more likely to do this. Pets can be praised/scolded to reinforce Clean/Filthy behavior.

◆ **Radio-Controlled Car:** Dogs and cats can bark, hiss, and chase the RC car for Fun. Dogs, especially Aggressive dogs, might chew on the RC car when it's not running.

◆ **Resurrect-O-Nomitron:** Pets can be resurrected but always come back fully restored (never partially restored or as a zombie). If a Sim is resurrected, nearby pets may react according to Personality and can be praised/scolded to reinforce Calm/Disruptive. Hyper pets are more likely to react, Lazy pets less so.

◆ **Sofas:** Sofas can hold multiple pets, and Sims seated on them can cuddle a cat seated near them. Sofas can inspire ownership challenges between pets. Pets can be praised/scolded to reinforce Stays off Furniture/Goes on Furniture behavior.

◆ **Stairs:** Cats and dogs can use stairs. Puppies and kittens can't climb stairs but, like toddlers, can be carried by a Sim.

◆ **Stereos:** Cats and dogs may howl and yowl at the stereo for Fun. Hyper pets are more likely and Lazy less likely to do so. When Sims are dancing, pets may run around and react. Hyper and Friendly pets will do this more, Lazy and Independent pets less. They can be praised/scolded to reinforce Calm/Disruptive behavior.

◆ **Teddy Bears:** Cats and dogs can chew or scratch and can be praised/scolded to reinforce Respectful/Destructive behavior.

◆ **Telescope:** If a Sim using a telescope is about to be abducted by aliens, pets will approach the telescope before the abduction (showing a thought balloon of aliens) and react according to their Personality.

◆ **Toybox Toys:** If toybox toys are left on the lot, dogs and cats will chew/scratch them for Fun and Chew/Scratch satisfaction. Praising or scolding reinforces Respectful/Destructive behavior.

◆ **Trash Cans:** Dogs can knock over outdoor trash cans and eat, dig, and roll in trash for Fun and Hunger satisfaction. They can be praised/scolded to reinforce Clean/Filthy behavior.

- Trees, Bushes: Pets can pee on them. Aggressive pets do it more often and Cowardly pets do it less. Pets remember their favorite spot to do their business. Praise/scold to reinforce Housebroken/Yardbroken behavior.

- Tubs: Dogs can be bathed in tubs and shower/tubs for Hygiene satisfaction. Sims doing the bathing get a drop in Hygiene and Energy (but no Cleaning skill). Dogs may escape from the bath before it's done. Hyper dogs are more likely and Lazy dogs less likely to do this. Any dog can be praised/scolded to reinforce Clean/Filthy behavior.

- TVs: Pets bark/hiss, etc. at TVs when they're on. If a Sim is working out to the TV or stereo, pets will react. They can be praised/scolded to reinforce Calm/Disruptive behavior. Friendly and Hyper pets do this more, Lazy pets less so. Pets may also watch TV for Fun (more likely if Genius, less likely if Doofus).

- Wet n' Wild Water Wiggler: Dogs will play in the spray for Fun and Hygiene. Cowardly and Lazy dogs may run away; Hyper dogs are more likely to play in the water. Cats will always flee the water wiggler. Pets can also watch pets or Sims in the toy for Fun. Dogs can be praised/scolded for playing in the water wiggler to reinforce Clean/Filthy behavior.

New Aspiration Object

Your Sims can now earn an Aspiration reward object that benefits your pets. For a mere 12,000 Aspiration points,

your Sims can have the Kibble of Life, a bowl of magical food that can prolong a pet's life (and it satisfies Hunger).

The Kibble of Life comes with five "charges," each of which can extend by three days the current age of any pet (adult or elder) that eats from it.

A pet can only receive this effect once per age (that is, once as an adult and once as an elder) but may use it twice over a full lifespan.

Munching the Kibble of Life grants a pet longevity.

Pets eat the Kibble of Life only when commanded to by a Sim, never autonomously. Sims can command a pet to eat from the dish more than once per age, but it will have no effect except to waste one of the bowl's five charges.

Unlike other Aspiration reward objects, the Kibble of Life won't ever fail.

 note
The bowl is adorned with five green jewels. As each charge is used, one of the jewels turns red. When all the jewels are red, you can delete the object.

Collections Enhancements

Collections have always been powerful but awkward tools. The ability to bring together your favorite Buy and Build mode objects and architectural elements in one easy-to-find place is undeniably useful, but several limitations made collections impossible to modify once created and available only on either residential or community lots.

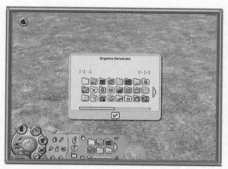

When creating a new collection, you can specify if it will be available on community lots only, residential lots only, or on both.

tip

In the Organize Items or Organize Collections panels, you can move a highlighted item by dragging it or by pressing your keyboard's arrow buttons. [← → ↑ ↓] The left and right arrow keys move the collection or item one position in the list. The up and down arrow buttons move to the top and bottom of the list, respectively.

You can now sort collections; the arrow buttons move a selected collection toward the front or end of the list. The highlighting tells you which are residential lots, community lots, or both.

Thanks to a major overhaul, collections become the flexible tools they were always destined to be. Collections are now:

◆ Rearrangeable: Collections can be manually rearranged so that your most used collections are sure to be immediately available in the Collections panel.

◆ Modifiable: You can now change an existing collection's name or icon and specify the order of the objects/elements in it.

◆ Universally Available: New and existing collections can be configured and color-coded to appear in the Collections panel in residential lots only (orange outline), community lots only (purple outline), or in both (no outline). Any objects/elements in a collection that can't be placed on your current lot type will be listed in the collection but will be grayed-out and unplaceable.

Objects and elements within a collection can also be organized.

note

Only collections set for your current lot type or both lot types will be shown in the Collections panel. If, however, you activate the Organize Collections panel, ALL collections will appear. Residential collections are outlined in orange, community collections are outlined in purple, and collections available in both have no outline.

Inventory Hotkey

The Sims 2 Pets features a new hotkey to simplify moving objects into your Sim's inventory. While a Sim's inventory panel is open, grab the object and press [I] to move it directly to inventory rather than having to drag each item.

Chapter 7

NEW SOCIALS

Pets and the Sims who love them are very sociable and fun-loving creatures, and so, of course, you'll have a rich slate of new social interactions between your Sims and their pets.

This chapter covers all the new social interactions between Sims and pets, pets and other pets, and between other wild and woolly creatures and Sims and pets.

Social Interaction Directory

Interaction	Menu	Availability Daily A to B Above	Availability Daily A to B Below	And/Or	Availability Lifetime A to B Above	Availability Lifetime A to B Below	Crush	Love or Go Steady	Autonomous Personality	User Directed
Adopt a Stray	Main	60	100	Or	60	100	—	—	—	Yes
Ask to be Fed	Pet	-100	100	And	-100	100	—	—	— (Finicky)	No
Bark/Growl/Hiss (to pet)	Pet	-100	10	And	-100	5	—	—	Aggressive	No
Bark/Growl Hiss (to Sim)—Cower	Pet	-100	10	And	-100	5	—	—	Aggressive	No
Bark/Growl Hiss (to Sim)—Ignore	Pet	-100	10	And	-100	5	—	—	Aggressive	No
Bark/Growl Hiss (to Sim)—Yell At	Pet	-100	10	And	-100	5	—	—	Aggressive	No
Beg for Food	Pet	0	100	And	0	100	—	—	— (Finicky)	No
Cat Teaser	Play	-100	100	Or	-100	100	—	—	Playful (Hyper)	Yes
Chase	Pet	-100	-5	And	-100	0	—	—	Aggressive	No
Chase Off	Main	-100	100	And	-100	100	—	—	—	Yes
Check Collar	Main	-100	100	And	-100	100	—	—	—	Yes
Cuddle	Give Love	-100	100	Or	-100	100	—	—	Nice	Yes
Feed Treat	Give Love	-100	100	Or	-100	100	—	—	Nice (Pigpen)	Yes
Fetch	Play	-100	100	Or	-100	100	—	—	Lazy (Hyper)	Yes
Fetch (Wolf)	Play	20	100	Or	20	100	—	—	Lazy (Hyper)	Yes
Fight	Main	-100	-30	Or	-100	-30	—	—	Aggressive	No
Finger Wiggle	Play	-100	100	Or	-100	100	—	—	Playful (Hyper)	Yes
Give Pet to...	Propose	-100	100	Or	-100	100	—	—	—	Yes

Autonomous	If Accept, A's Social	If Accept, A's Daily	If Accept, A's Lifetime	If Accept, B's Social	If Accept, B's Daily	If Accept, B's Lifetime	If Reject, A's Social	If Reject, A's Daily	If Reject, A's Lifetime	If Reject, B's Social	If Reject, B's Daily	If Reject, B's Lifetime
No	10	5	1	10	5	1	0	-5	-1	0	-5	-1
Yes	8	4	1	8	4	1	0	-5	-1	0	-5	-1
Yes	10	-7	-2	10	-7	-2	—	—	—	—	—	—
Yes	10	-5	-1	0	-5	-1	—	—	—	—	—	—
Yes	0	-3	0	0	-3	0	—	—	—	—	—	—
Yes	10	-7	-1	10	-7	-1	—	—	—	—	—	—
Yes	4	4	0	3	2	0	4	-3	0	0	-4	0
Yes	5	4	1	5	5	1	0	-5	-1	0	-5	-1
Yes	10	-5	-1	10	-5	-1	—	—	—	—	—	—
No	10	-5	-1	10	-5	-1	0	0	0	0	0	0
No	10	3	0	10	3	0	0	-2	0	0	-2	0
Yes	5	7	2	5	6	1	0	-5	-1	0	-5	-1
Yes	8	4	0	8	4	0	0	-3	0	0	-3	0
Yes	5	5	1	5	5	1	0	-5	-1	0	-5	-1
Yes	5	5	1	5	5	1	0	-5	-1	0	-5	-1
Yes	15	-10	-4	15	-12	-6	15	-12	-6	15	-10	-4
Yes	8	4	1	8	4	1	0	-4	-1	0	-4	-1
No	8	5	1	8	5	1	0	-5	-1	0	-3	-1

Social Interaction Directory continued

Interaction	Menu	Availability Daily A to B Above	Availability Daily A to B Below	And/Or	Availability Lifetime A to B Above	Availability Lifetime A to B Below	Crush	Love or Go Steady	Autonomous Personality	User Directed
Go to Work	Main	-100	-30	Or	-100	-30	—	—	—	Yes
Grr!	Irritate	-100	100	Or	-100	100	—	—	Grouchy	Yes
Hug	Give Love	20	100	And	20	100	—	—	Nice (Friendly)	Yes
Lick Toddler	Pet	-100	100	Or	-100	100	—	—	— (Friendly)	No
Nibble	Wolf	50	100	And	50	100	—	—	—	No
Nuzzle	Pet	-100	100	And	-100	100	—	—	— (Friendly)	No
Ownership Challenge	Pet	-100	100	Or	-100	100	—	—	Active (Hyper)	No
Perform Command	Main	-100	100	And	-100	100	—	—	—	Yes
Pet	Sales	-100	100	Or	-100	100	—	—	—	Yes
Pet	Skunk	-50	100	And	-50	100	—	—	Playful	Yes
Pick Up	Main	-100	100	And	-100	100	—	—	—	Yes
Play	Pet	-100	100	Or	-100	100	—	—	— (Hyper)	No
Play With	Play	-100	100	And	-100	100	—	—	Playful	Yes
Pounce	Pet	-100	100	Or	-100	100	—	—	— (Hyper)	No
Praise for...	Main	-100	100	Or	-100	100	—	—	—	Yes
Razzle	Play	-100	100	Or	-100	100	—	—	Active (Hyper)	Yes
Razzle (Wolf)	Play	25	100	Or	25	100	—	—	Active (Hyper)	Yes
Rub Belly	Give Love	20	100	Or	20	100	—	—	Nice (Friendly)	Yes
Savage	Werewolf	-100	100	Or	-100	100	—	—	—	Yes
Scold for...	Main	-100	100	Or	-100	100	—	—	—	Yes
Set Down	Main	-100	100	Or	-100	100	—	—	—	Yes
Sniff	Pet	-100	100	And	-100	100	—	—	— (Genius)	No
Snuggle	Give Love	-100	100	Or	-100	100	—	—	Nice	Yes
Spray	Skunk	-100	100	Or	-100	100	—	—	—	No
Stroke	Give Love	-50	100	And	-50	100	—	—	Nice (Friendly)	Yes
Take for a Walk	Main	-100	100	And	-100	100	—	—	—	Yes
Teach Command	Main	-100	100	And	-100	100	—	—	—	Yes

Autonomous	If Accept, A's Social	If Accept, A's Daily	If Accept, A's Lifetime	If Accept, B's Social	If Accept, B's Daily	If Accept, B's Lifetime	If Reject, A's Social	If Reject, A's Daily	If Reject, A's Lifetime	If Reject, B's Social	If Reject, B's Daily	If Reject, B's Lifetime
No	8	4	0	8	4	0	0	-3	0	0	-3	0
Yes	0	0	0	0	0	0	0	0	0	0	0	0
Yes	12	5	1	12	5	1	0	-5	-1	0	-5	-1
Yes	10	5	2	10	7	2	0	-6	-1	0	-5	-1
Yes	0	-4	-1	-10	-4	-1	0	-2	0	0	-2	0
Yes	10	5	1	10	5	1	0	0	0	0	0	0
Yes	—	—	—	—	—	—	—	—	—	—	—	—
No	8	5	1	8	5	1	0	-4	0	0	-4	0
No	8	5	1	8	5	1	0	-3	-1	0	-3	-1
Yes	8	8	2	8	8	2	0	-5	-1	0	-5	-1
Yes	—	—	—	—	—	—	—	—	—	—	—	—
Yes	0	10	2	0	10	2	0	-5	-1	0	-5	-4
Yes	10	5	2	10	5	2	—	—	—	—	—	—
Yes	—	—	—	—	—	—	—	—	—	—	—	—
No	0	1	0	0	1	0	—	—	—	—	—	—
Yes	8	5	2	8	4	2	0	-5	-1	0	-4	-1
Yes	8	5	2	8	4	2	0	-5	-1	0	-4	-1
Yes	12	6	1	12	7	1	0	-4	-1	0	-5	-1
No	15	4	1	15	-6	-2	—	—	—	—	—	—
No	0	-1	0	0	-1	0	—	—	—	—	—	—
Yes	0	0	0	0	0	0	0	0	0	0	0	0
Yes	10	5	1	10	5	1	0	-3	0	0	-3	0
Yes	10	5	2	10	5	2	—	—	—	—	—	—
Yes	12	0	0	12	0	0	0	-5	-1	0	-5	-1
Yes	8	4	1	8	5	1	0	-4	-1	0	-5	-1
No	5	1	0	5	1	0	0	-4	0	0	-4	0
No	8	5	1	8	5	1	0	-4	0	0	-4	0

Social Interaction Directory continued

Interaction	Menu	Availability Daily A to B Above	Availability Daily A to B Below	And/Or	Availability Lifetime A to B Above	Availability Lifetime A to B Below	Crush	Love or Go Steady	Autonomous Personality	User Directed
Toss in Air	Play	-100	100	And	-100	100	—	—	Active (Hyper)	Yes
Try for Puppy/Kitten (pet-to-pet)	Pet	N/A	N/A	N/A	N/A	N/A	—	—	—	No
Try for Puppy/Kitten with... (Sim-to-pet)	Main	-100	100	Or	-100	100	—	—	—	Yes
Yell At	Main	-100	100	And	-100	100	—	—	—	Yes

Sim-to-Pet/Pet-to-Sim Interactions

For most of the pet-to-Sim and Sim-to-pet interactions, the decision to accept or reject is based on the recipient's Mood. The required level of the Mood, however, depends on the kind of relationship it has with the initiator (Master, Pack, or Mine), the Daily Relationship toward the initiator, and the recipient's Personality traits (Playful for Sims, Friendly and Independent for pets). The more positive factors there are (Independent makes acceptance harder), the worse the recipient's Mood can be. For example, a pet will accept a given social from its Master at Mood 0, but not from an acquaintance until 50.

Very low Social and/or Fun Need can, however, take precedence to allow a Sim or pet to accept regardless of relationship or Personality. In many (but not all) interactions, as long as Mood is above -50, acceptance is ensured if either Social or Fun is below -50.

note
If the recipient is a Sim, low Fun will never ensure acceptance.

To be honest, the process is extremely complicated, and no one in their right mind would noodle through this every time they want their pet to play a game of Fetch. Still, if you crave more detail, here it is (see "Pet-to Sim" and "Sim-to-Pet" sidebars).

The social interaction catalog deviates a bit from our usual format. Socials with their own decision trees follow the customary format, but ones based on the two models above will make reference to these standard models.

Among these standardized socials, some include the automatic acceptance for low Social and/or Fun but others do not. The capsules note this in each case.

Autonomous	If Accept, A's Social	If Accept, A's Daily	If Accept, A's Lifetime	If Accept, B's Social	If Accept, B's Daily	If Accept, B's Lifetime	If Reject, A's Social	If Reject, A's Daily	If Reject, A's Lifetime	If Reject, B's Social	If Reject, B's Daily	If Reject, B's Lifetime
Yes	12	5	0	12	5	0	0	-4	0	0	-4	0
Yes	25	8	2	25	8	2	0	-5	-1	0	-5	-1
No	8	5	0	8	5	0	0	-5	0	0	-5	0
No	8	-4	-1	-8	-5	-1	8	-4	-1	-8	-5	-1

Pet-to-Sim

If the Sim's Mood is above -50 and Social Need is below -50, the Sim always accepts. If Sim's Mood is below -50, he or she always rejects.

If, regardless of the kind of relationship (Master, Mine, Pack), the Sim's Mood is greater than 50, acceptance is a given.

If the Sim is the pet's Master and Daily Relationship to the pet is above -40, the Sim always accepts if Mood is above 0. If Daily Relationship is below -40, pets always accept interactions from their Master if their Mood is above 20.

If the Sim has a Pack or Mine Relationship with the pet and Daily Relationship is above -40, the Sim always accepts if Mood is above 30. If Daily Relationship is below -40 and there's a Pack or Mine Relationship, Sims always accept if their Mood is above 50.

If the Sim can't meet any of these standards, he or she will accept if:

1. Daily Relationship > 0, Playful 8 or more, Mood > -15; or

2. Daily Relationship > 0, Playful 5–7, Mood > 5; or

3. Daily Relationship > 0, Playful < 5, Mood > 25; or

4. Daily Relationship < 0, Playful 8 or more, Mood > -40; or

5. Daily Relationship < 0, Playful 5–7, Mood > 0; or

6. Daily Relationship < 0, Playful < 5, Mood > 20.

Sim-to-Pet

If the pet's Fun Need is less than -50 or Fun Need is above -50 but Social Need is less than -50, the pet always accepts. If the pet's Mood is less than -50, it always rejects.

If, regardless of the kind of relationship (Master, Mine, Pack), the pet's Mood is greater than 50, it always accepts.

If the Sim is the pet's Master and Daily Relationship to the pet is above -40, the pet always accepts if Mood is above 0. If Daily Relationship with a Master is below -40, pets always accept if Mood is above 20.

If the pet has a Pack or Mine Relationship with the Sim and Daily Relationship is above -40, it'll always accept if Mood is above 30. If Daily Relationship is below -40 and there's a Pack or Mine Relationship, pets always accept if Mood is above 50.

If the pet can't meet any of these standards, it'll accept if:

1. Daily Relationship > 0, Pet is Friendly, and Mood > -15; or

2. Daily Relationship > 0, Pet is not Friendly but is Independent, and Mood > 25; or

3. Daily Relationship > 0, Pet is neither Friendly nor Independent, and Mood > 5; or

4. Daily Relationship < 0, Pet is Friendly, and Mood > 0; or

5. Daily Relationship < 0, Pet is not Friendly but is Independent, and Mood > 40; or

6. Daily Relationship < 0, Pet is neither Friendly nor Independent, and Mood > 20.

Top Menu Interactions

Adopt a Stray

⬥ Who: teen/young adult/adult/elder to adult cat/elder cat/adult dog/elder dog

 note

For more information, see "Adopting Strays" in the "Create a Cat/Dog and Acquiring Pets" chapter.

This interaction is always accepted.

Chase Off

⬥ Who: child/teen/ young adult/adult/ elder to adult cat/elder cat/adult dog/elder dog/ wolf/skunk

Chase Off is always accepted.

Check Collar

⬥ Who: child/teen/ young adult/adult/ elder to adult cat/elder cat/adult dog/elder dog

Checking the collar on a stray enables your Sim to return a runaway pet to another of your playable Sims. See the "Create a Cat/Dog and Acquiring Pets" chapter for full details.

Accepted if pet's Daily Relationship to Sim is > 0.

Go to Work

- Who: child/teen/young adult/adult/elder to adult cat/elder cat/adult dog/elder dog

If a pet's carpool is waiting and it's engaged in an interaction, Sims can command it to stop what it's doing and go to work. It will not, however, make a pet Go to Work when it's in a bad Mood.

Accepted if pet's Mood is > 0.

Perform Command...

- Who: child/teen/young adult/adult/elder to adult cat/elder cat/adult dog/elder dog/kitten/puppy

Accepted based on the standard rules unless Fun or Social Need is critically low. If either Fun or Social Need is below -50 and Mood is above -50, pets always accept.

Pick Up

- Who: child/teen/young adult/adult/elder to kitten/puppy

Puppies and kittens won't ask to be picked up, but many puppy/kitten-initiated interactions first make the Sim do Pick Up.

Young pets always accept Pick Up.

Praise for...

- Who: child/teen/young adult/adult/elder to adult cat/elder cat/adult dog/elder dog/kitten/puppy

This interaction is accepted based on the standard rules unless Fun or Social Need is critically low. If either Fun or Social Need is below -50 and Mood is above -50, pets always accept.

Scold for...

- Who: child/teen/young adult/adult/elder to adult cat/elder cat/adult dog/elder dog/kitten/puppy

Acceptance is based on the standard rules unless Fun or Social Need is critically low. If either Fun or Social Need is below -50 and Mood is above -50, pets always accept.

Set Down

- Who: child/teen/young adult/adult/elder to kitten/puppy

When Sims are carrying a kitten/puppy, they may Set Down autonomously if they elect to do something else. Set Down is always accepted.

Take for a Walk

- ◆ Who: child/teen/ young adult/adult/ elder to adult cat/elder cat/adult dog/elder dog

Need	Pet	Sim
Fun (per hour)	50	50
Energy (per hour)	-20	-20

Walks last 40–60 minutes, and Sim and pet get the Social and relationship effects every 5 minutes during the walk.

Acceptance is based on the standard rules unless the recipient's Social Need is critically low. If Social Need is below -50 and Mood is above -50, the recipient always accepts.

Teach Command...

- ◆ Who: child/teen/ young adult/adult/ elder to adult cat/elder cat/adult dog/elder dog/ kitten/puppy

Acceptance is based on the standard rules unless Fun or Social Need is critically low. If either Fun or Social Need is below -50 and Mood is above -50, pets always accept.

Try for Puppy/Kitten with...

- ◆ Who: teen/young adult/adult/ elder to adult cat/ elder cat/adult dog/elder dog

The breeding process is initiated with the Sim-to-pet interaction. The pet then goes to the indicated breeding pet and uses the Try for Puppy/Kitten (pet-to-pet) interaction. See the "Pet Interactions" section.

 note
Full details on pet breeding can be found in the "Pet Life" chapter.

The interaction is accepted if Pet B's Mood > -25, Daily Relationship to Sim A > 25, Lifetime Relationship to Sim A > 0, Daily Relationship to Pet C > 25, and Lifetime Relationship to Pet C > 0.

Yell At

- ◆ Who: child/teen/ young adult/adult/ elder to adult cat/ elder cat/adult dog/elder dog

If you want to actively drive down relationship with a pet, use the Yell At interaction. Dogs may pee in fear in response if their Bladder Need is low; Cowardly dogs are more likely to do it.

Yell At is always accepted.

Give Love Interactions

Feed Treat

◆ Who: child/teen/
young adult/adult/
elder to adult cat/
elder cat/adult dog/
elder dog or adult
cat/elder cat/adult
dog/elder dog to
child/teen/young
adult/adult/elder

Accepted if Sim B's:

1. Hunger < -50; or

2. Hunger > -50, Daily Relationship > -80, and Pigpen; or

3. Daily Relationship > -80, Finicky, and Hunger > 80; or

4. Daily Relationship > -80, not Pigpen or Finicky, and Hunger > 90.

Need	Adult Pet	Puppy/Kitten
Hunger	20	40

note

If a treat is given while a pet shows the teachable moment icon, the treat will affect training as if it were praise.

Many things can happen after feeding a treat:

◆ If a pet has full Hunger satisfaction, it might throw up.

◆ If another pet sees a pet given a treat, there's a chance it'll beg for a treat.

◆ A pet given a treat may beg for another.

Hug

◆ Who: child/teen/
young adult/adult/
elder to adult cat/
elder cat or adult
cat/elder cat to
child/teen/young
adult/adult/elder

Acceptance is based on the standard rules unless the recipient's Social Need is critically low. If Social Need is below -50 and Mood is above -50, the recipient always accepts.

Rub Belly

◆ Who: child/teen/
young adult/adult/
elder to adult dog/
elder dog or adult
dog/elder dog to
child/teen/young
adult/adult/elder

Acceptance is based on the standard rules unless the recipient's Social Need is critically low. If Social Need is below -50 and Mood is above -50, the recipient always accepts.

Snuggle

◆ Who: child/teen/
young adult/
adult/elder to
kitten/puppy

Puppies and kittens never reject.

Stroke

♦ Who: child/teen/young adult/adult/elder to adult cat/elder cat/adult dog/elder dog or adult cat/elder cat/adult dog/elder dog to child/teen/young adult/adult/elder

Acceptance is based on the standard rules unless the recipient's Social Need is critically low. If Social Need is below -50 and Mood is above -50, the recipient always accepts.

Need	Pet	Sim
Fun	6	6

Cuddle

♦ Who: toddler to adult cat/elder cat/adult dog/elder dog or adult cat/elder cat/adult dog/elder dog to toddler

Acceptance is based on the standard rules unless the recipient's Social Need is critically low. If Social Need is below -50 and Mood is above -50, the recipient always accepts.

Need	Pet	Sim
Comfort (per hour)	-40	40
Social (per hour)	60	40
Energy (per hour)	-10	-10

Irritate Interactions

Grr!

♦ Who: teen/young adult/adult/elder werewolf to child/teen/young adult/adult/elder

Need	Werewolf	Sim
Fun	12	-5
Customer Loyalty	—	-100

Grr! is always accepted.

Pet Interactions

 note
These actions can only be initiated by pets. Since you can't control pets, there are no interaction menus.

Ask to be Fed

♦ Who: adult cat/elder cat/adult dog/elder dog to child/teen/young adult/adult/elder

The interaction is accepted if the Sim's Mood is > -20.

Bark/Growl/Hiss (to pets)

▶ Who: adult cat/ elder cat/adult dog/ elder dog to adult cat/elder cat/ adult dog/elder dog/kitten/puppy

note
This can only be done toward kittens or puppies if pet's Mood is below 0. Pets respond according to their Personality.

This interaction can't be rejected, but reaction comes, in part, from Personality-based probabilities:

Trait	Cower	Growl/Bark	Fight
Cowardly	+50%	-15%	0
Aggressive	-20%	+20%	+20%
Lazy	-10%	-15%	-10%

An additional 20 percent is added to Fight probability if Pet B's Daily Relationship to Pet A is < -20.

Bark/Growl/Hiss (to Sims)

▶ Who: adult cat/elder cat/adult dog/elder dog to child/teen/young adult/adult/elder

note
The target Sim can react by yelling at the pet, cowering from the pet, or ignoring the pet. Each result has a different impact on the pet's and the Sim's Social Needs and relationship toward each other.

This can't be rejected, but reaction comes, in part, from Personality-based probabilities:

Trait	Cower	Yell At
Outgoing/Shy < 5	+50%	-15%
Nice/Grouchy < 5	-20%	+30%
Active/Lazy	-10%	-10%

An additional 20 percent is added to Fight probability if Pet B's Daily Relationship to Pet A is < -20.

Beg for Food

▶ Who: adult cat/ elder cat/adult dog/elder dog to child/teen/young adult/adult/elder

Acceptance is based on the standard rules unless the recipient's Social Need is critically low. If Social Need is below -50 and Mood is above -50, the recipient always accepts.

Chase

◆ Who: adult cat/
elder cat/adult
dog/elder dog to
child/teen/young
adult/adult/elder/
adult cat/elder cat/
adult dog/elder dog
or kitten/puppy to
kitten/puppy

 note

Kittens and puppies may chase or be chased only by each other.

Need	Pet	Sim
Energy	-10	-10

Chase can't be rejected.

Fight

◆ Who: adult cat/
elder cat/adult
dog/elder dog to
adult cat/elder
cat/adult dog/
elder dog

Fight can't be rejected, so accept/reject effects in the social interactions table represent changes if A is the winner (Accept) or if B is the winner (Accept).

Fight works very much like the Sim-to-Sim Attack. The winner is random, but the odds are affected by which pet has the greater training toward Hostile.

Winners may follow Fight with Chase, and losers may be inspired to run away (see the "Pet Life" chapter).

Lick Toddler

◆ Who: adult large
dog/elder large
dog to toddler

Need	Pet	Sim
Fun (Accept)	12	12
Hygiene (per hour)	—	-5

Acceptance is based on the standard rules.

Nuzzle

◆ Who: adult cat/
elder cat/adult
dog/elder dog to
kitten/puppy

Parents of a puppy or kitten are more likely to do this than other pets.

Acceptance is based on the standard rules unless the recipient's Social Need is critically low. If Social Need is below -50 and Mood is above -50, the recipient always accepts.

Ownership Challenge

♦ Who: adult cat/ elder cat/adult dog/elder dog to adult cat/elder cat/adult dog/ elder dog

This is always accepted. Effects are determined by the outcome of the challenge:

Effect	Lose	Win	Big Win
A Daily Relationship	-10	-6	-1
A Lifetime	-1	-1	-1
A Social	-10	5	3
B Daily Relationship	-3	-10	-5
B Lifetime	-3	-3	-5
B Social	5	-3	-6

Play

♦ Who: adult cat/elder cat/adult dog/elder dog to adult cat/elder cat/adult dog/elder dog or kitten/puppy to kitten/puppy

Need	Pet
Fun	65
Social	65

Acceptance is based on the standard rules unless the recipient's Social Need is critically low. If Social Need is below -50 and Mood is above -50, the recipient always accepts.

Pounce

♦ Who: adult cat/elder cat to child/teen/ young adult/adult/ elder/adult cat/ elder cat/adult dog/elder dog

note
Aggressive pets react to a pounce with a hiss/bark, and Cowardly pets respond with a cower.

Need (per hour)	Pet	Sim
Fun	100	—

Pounce is always accepted.

Sniff

♦ Who: adult dog/ elder dog to child/teen/young adult/adult/elder/ adult cat/elder cat/adult dog/ elder dog

Acceptance is based on the standard rules unless the recipient's Social Need is critically low. If Social Need is below -50 and Mood is above -50, the recipient always accepts.

Try for Puppy/Kitten

◆ **Who:** adult cat to adult cat, elder male cat to adult female cat, adult dog to adult dog, elder male dog to adult female dog

Once a pet accepts the Sim-to-pet Try for Puppy/Kitten with… interaction, it approaches the specified pet to run this interaction. If the other pet accepts, pets adjourn to an available pet house to consummate the union and spawn the next generation.

 note
For full details on pet breeding, see the "Pet Life" chapter.

It's accepted if Pet C's Mood > -25, Daily Relationship > 25, and Lifetime > 0.

Play Interactions

Cat Teaser

◆ **Who:** child/teen/young adult/adult/elder to adult cat/elder cat/kitten or adult cat/elder cat/kitten to child/teen/young adult/adult/elder

Need (per hour)	Pet	Sim
Fun	50	40
Social	50	40
Energy	-10	-10

If a pet is the recipient, acceptance is based on the standard rules unless the recipient's Fun or Social Need is critically low. If either Fun or Social Need is below -50 and Mood is above -50, the recipient always accepts.

If a Sim is the recipient, acceptance is based on the standard rules unless the recipient's Social Need is critically low. If Social Need is below -50 and Mood is above -50, the recipient always accepts.

Fetch

◆ **Who:** child/teen/young adult/adult/elder to adult dog/elder dog/wolf or adult dog/elder dog to child/teen/young adult/adult/elder

 note
Sims can play Fetch with a wolf (see the "New NPCs & Lycanthropy" chapter) but the interaction won't be available until the wolf gains Daily 20 or Lifetime 25 Relationship score with the Sim. Wolves can't initiate Fetch.

If a pet is the recipient, acceptance is based on the standard rules unless the recipient's Fun or Social Need is critically low. If either Fun or Social Need is below -50 and Mood is above -50, the recipient always accepts.

If a Sim is the recipient, acceptance is based on the standard rules unless the recipient's Social Need is critically low. If Social Need is below -50 and Mood is above -50, the recipient always accepts.

 note
If there isn't a large enough area outside for either a long or short Fetch, the Sim will give up.

Need	Pet	Sim
Fun	40	40
Social	40	40
Energy	-10	-10

Finger Wiggle

- Who: child/teen/ young adult/adult/ elder to adult cat/ elder cat/kitten or adult cat/elder cat/kitten to child/teen/young adult/adult/elder

note
If the Sim is accidentally scratched, Daily Relationship toward cat drops by 2.

Need (per hour)	Pet	Sim
Fun (per hour)	40	30
Social (per hour)	40	40
Energy (per hour)	-10	-10

If a pet is the recipient, acceptance is based on the standard rules unless the recipient's Fun or Social Need is critically low. If either Fun or Social Need is below -50 and Mood is above -50, the recipient always accepts.

If a Sim is the recipient, acceptance is based on the standard rules unless the recipient's Social Need is critically low. If Social Need is below -50 and Mood is above -50, the recipient always accepts.

Play With

- Who: child/teen/ young adult/ adult/ elder to kitten/puppy

Need	Pet	Sim
Comfort	4	4
Social	4	4

This interaction is always accepted.

Razzle

- Who: child/teen/ young adult/adult/ elder to adult dog/elder dog/ wolf or adult dog/elder dog to child/teen/young adult/adult/elder

note
Sims can play Razzle with a wolf (see the "New NPCs & Lycanthropy" chapter), but it won't be available until the wolf gains a Daily or Lifetime Relationship of 25 with the Sim. Wolves can't initiate Razzle.

Need	Pet	Sim
Fun	40	40
Social	40	40
Energy	-10	-10

If a pet is the recipient, acceptance is based on the standard rules unless the recipient's Fun or Social Need is critically low. If either Fun or Social Need is below -50 and Mood is above -50, the recipient always accepts.

If a Sim is the recipient, acceptance is based on the standard rules unless the recipient's Social Need is critically low. If Social Need is below -50 and Mood is above -50, the recipient always accepts.

Toss in Air

♦ Who: teen/young adult/adult/elder to adult cat/elder cat/kitten/puppy or adult cat/elder cat/adult dog/elder dog to teen/young adult/adult/elder

Puppies and kittens never reject.

For adults, if a pet is the recipient, acceptance is based on the standard rules unless the recipient's Fun or Social Need is critically low. If either Fun or Social Need is below -50 and Mood is above -50, the recipient always accepts.

If a Sim is the recipient, acceptance is based on the standard rules unless the recipient's Social Need is critically low. If Social Need is below -50 and Mood is above -50, the recipient always accepts.

There's a chance cats will throw up after being tossed.

Need	Pet	Sim
Fun (per hour)	50	50
Energy (per hour)	-10	-20

Propose Interactions

Give Pet to...

♦ Who: teen/young adult/adult/elder to teen/young adult/adult/elder

note

See the "Pet Life" chapter for details.

Sales Interactions

Pet

♦ Who: teen/young adult/adult/elder to teen/young adult/adult/elder

Accepted if B's:

1. Lifetime and Daily are positive; or

2. Lifetime is positive, Daily is negative, and Nice/Grouchy > 2; or

3. Lifetime is negative, Daily is positive, and Nice/Grouchy > 4; or

4. Lifetime and Daily are negative.

Once Sim B purchases the pet, the pet's relationship toward the buyer is reduced by Daily -10/Lifetime -10.

Skunk Interactions

Pet

◆ Who: child/teen/ young adult/adult/ elder to Skunk

Need	Sim
Hygiene	Set to -99
Fun	-30
Comfort	-40

Mostly, this foolish attempt fails and the Sim gets sprayed. Sometimes, however, the Sim gets lucky and the skunk deigns to be petted (5 percent chance for Sims but 60 percent chance for werewolves).

Memories of being sprayed lower the chance of the Sim doing this autonomously in the future. Sims with high Logic are even less likely to try it again.

Spray

◆ Who: Skunk to child/teen/young adult/adult/elder to adult cat/elder cat/adult dog/elder dog/kitten/puppy

Need	Sim
Hygiene	Set to -99
Fun	-30
Comfort	-40

Spray is always accepted.

Werewolf Interactions

Savage

◆ Who: teen to teen or young adult/ adult/elder to young adult/ adult/elder

While a Sim is a werewolf, it can bite any age-appropriate Sim to turn him or her into a werewolf. The interaction is accepted if Sim B's Mood > 0 and always results in a lycanthropic infection.

Sims won't take kindly to being bitten, becoming Furious at the werewolf.

This interaction can be used on Servos.

note

Details on life as a werewolf and how to cure the affliction can be found in the "Werewolves" chapter.

Nibble

◆ Who: Leader of the Pack NPC to teen/young adult/adult/elder

Nibble is accepted if Sim B's Mood > 0.

Relationships

Pets have their own kinds of relationships that have a strong effect on how they relate to Sims and other pets. The kinds of relationships available to a pet depend on its species.

Dogs

Dogs have two kinds of special relationships:

◆ Pack ◆ Master

Pack

The Pack Relationship is roughly equivalent to Friend for Sims but is available only to Sims and pets in their own household.

Once a dog or puppy reaches 50 Lifetime Relationship and has known a Sim or pet for 24 hours, it decides that that creature is part of its pack. Sims with the Pack Relationship with a dog get a larger increase in Fun and Social when interacting with the dog.

A dog or puppy's relationship to pack Sims and pets will never naturally decay if it's above zero. As long as the relationship is positive, decay does not take place. If the relationship falls below zero through negative interactions, it will trend toward zero at the normal rate.

The Pack Relationship is destroyed if Lifetime Relationship of the dog toward the other pet/Sim drops below -10.

Master

Dogs need to know their place in the hierarchy of the household, so they'll eventually get to know a Sim so well that they'll declare him or her their "Master." Master is roughly equivalent to the "Best Friend" for Sims.

The first Sim to gain 70 Lifetime Relationship from the pet, to know the pet for 24 hours, and to do one more relationship-building social, becomes the dog's one and only Master. A Sim can be Master to more than one dog, but each dog can have only one Master.

The primary benefit of the Master Relationship is a change of Daily Relationship decay. Unlike all other relationships, which naturally decay to zero, dog-to-Master relationships do not decay if Daily Relationship is greater than 25. If the relationship is below 25 due to negative interactions, Daily Relationship will trend up toward 25 (instead of zero) faster than normal.

Dogs also get the friend-of-my-Master bonus. If a dog's Master is interacting with another Sim while the dog is nearby, the dog passively gains or loses Daily Relationship toward that Sim along with the Master. Thus, if the Master does a social interaction to Sim B that gains 4 Daily Relationship points, the dog standing at his or her side gets 2 points toward Sim B without interacting with Sim B. The size of this effect, positive and negative, grows with the size of the Master's changes in relationship to Sim B.

Master to Sim B Daily Relationship Change	Pet to Sim B Daily Relationship Change
7+	4
4–6	2
1–3	1
-1	-3– -1
-4	-6– -2
-7+	-4

Finally, a dog's Master gets an even bigger Fun boost than normal or for Pack when playing with the dog.

Once dogs have decided upon a Master, they're very reluctant to break that relationship. Even if the dog achieves a higher relationship with another Sim, the first Sim to become Master stays Master. A Sim would have to decimate a dog's relationship (below -80) to him to break a Master Relationship.

tip

If you're trying to break a dog's Master Relationship to a Sim, direct the Sim to repeatedly use the Yell At interaction.

Losing a Master to either relationship drops or death can cause a dog to run away.

Cats

Instead of Friend and Best Friend, cats have one nonexclusive kind of signature relationship: Mine.

Mine

Cats, feeling that they own others, rather than the other way around, wouldn't insult themselves by considering anyone their "master." Moreover, they don't have the collective mentality of dogs that could lead to a Pack Relationship (though dogs can consider cats to be part of their pack).

Instead, cats claim those they know well as their very own with the Mine Relationship. This special status is given to any Sim or pet in the household who develops a relationship of 60 Lifetime with the cat and whom the cat has known for at least 24 hours.

Any Sim or pet that a cat considers Mine gets special treatment. The cat is more likely to accept social interactions from a Mine Relationship even when its Mood would normally cause it to reject. Cats are much more inclined to interact with their Mine Relationships than with others, favoring the familiar to the less well known.

Finally, the cat's relationship to Mine Sims and pets will not decay if Daily Relationship is above 15. If the relationship falls below 15 through negative interactions, it will trend toward 15 (rather than zero) faster than normal.

All Pets

Pets can have a few other relationships pets, but they function identically to their Sim equivalents.

- Pets can have Enemies.
- Pets can get Furious at another pet.
- Pets have Family Relationships.
- Non-household pets can be a Sim's "Pet Friend" if they have a Daily Relationship with the Sim greater than 50.

Other New Social Features

The advent of pets has inspired some new social features or changes to existing systems that integrate pets into traditional functions but also expand non-pet possibilities as well.

Invite Household

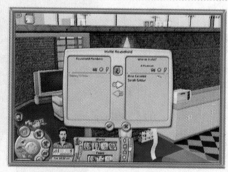

Now you can invite over multiple Sims from a household, even if your Sim has only met one of them.

Previously, your Sim could invite over only Sims they had met. Sure, sometimes they'd bring a friend, but mostly, expanding your social circle required leaving home.

Now, you can have your Sims call any Sim they know and specify which members of their household (including pets) you'd like them to bring along.

Chapter 8

New NPCs & Lycanthropy

Life with pets can be wild, but since animals are the subject at hand, we shouldn't forget the wildlife that now inhabits your Sims' neighborhoods. *The Sims 2 Pets* comes complete with a slate of new nonplayer characters including two kinds of suburban fauna, a new service provider, and a fearsome creature that can turn your Sim into a super animal trainer (and, well, a werewolf).

This chapter unpacks all these new players along with copious changes to existing NPCs, the new houses and Sims you'll find in the neighborhood bins, and the facts of werewolf life.

Service NPCs

Obedience Trainer

♦ Call Hours: Anytime

♦ Shift: 8 am to 9 pm

♦ Fee: §25 per visit and §75 per hour

♦ Service: One-time

If training your pets is just too time-consuming, help is only a phone call away thanks to the Obedience Trainer. This elder female will come to your Sims' homes and teach commands (not learned behaviors) to any pet for a hefty but reasonable hourly fee.

For an upfront fee of §25 plus §75 per hour she spends on the lot, the Obedience Trainer will train any pets that have commands to learn.

As soon as the Trainer arrives, set her to work or you'll be paying her to play with the pets rather than train them.

When the Obedience Trainer arrives, she wanders the lot, meeting all the pets and awaiting your instructions on whom to train. She's on the clock from the moment she arrives, so point her to the pet to be trained as soon as she arrives. Any child or older Sim on the lot can use the Purchase Training for... interaction on the Trainer to begin command training.

The Trainer is an accomplished professional, teaching with the speed of a high-Charisma Sim (though not as fast as a werewolf). Though the Trainer is fast, a pet will exit training if its Mood or critical Needs drop too low, so make sure the pets to be trained are well cared for before she arrives.

Once put on the case, the Trainer works with the indicated pet until:

♦ Her shift day ends at 9 pm.

♦ The pet kicks out for standard skill training exits (for example, low Needs).

♦ You direct your Sims to interact with her.

The Obedience Trainer makes pets more manageable and increases their earning potential while leaving your Sims free to tend to other matters.

When a pet has fully learned a command or the pet exits early, the Obedience Trainer is available to assign to another pet or to linger (on the clock, of course) for socializing with Sims. She will also wait for a pet to tend to its Needs, then resume training.

If all pets on the lot are unavailable for training or fully trained in all commands, the Obedience Trainer will take her leave (after the customary waiting-to-socialize opportunity).

note

If you assign the Obedience Trainer to a pet but she doesn't immediately engage the pet, it's probably because the pet is taking care of its Needs and not ready to train. See what the pet is up to and give it some time; when it's ready, it'll go to the Trainer to begin learning.

Got werewolf? The Obedience Trainer can hook you up with the cure.

The Obedience Trainer is also a source for the werewolf cure, Lycanthropic-B. To purchase this cure for your Sim, or to give to another, direct the Sim to do the Buy Potion...Lycanthropic-B interaction on the Obedience Trainer, and select the quantity you wish to buy (at §60 per bottle).

note

If you have THE SIMS™ 2 NIGHTLIFE expansion pack, you can also purchase Lycanthropic-B from the Gypsy Matchmaker NPC.

The bottles are placed in your Sim's inventory. If your Sim is a werewolf (transformed or not), the self-interaction Drink Lycanthropic-B instantly administers the cure.

Alternatively, you can place the bottle on the ground for another Sim to pick up and put in his or her inventory.

The Obedience Trainer can be interacted with like all other service NPCs. This means she is potentially marriageable/joinable, retaining her Charisma 10. Once an Obedience Trainer becomes part of a household, however, she no longer sells potions or training services.

Cop (Animal Control)

The Cop has a new job. In addition to his or her various other duties, the officer of the law now acts as the town animal control officer.

New functions include:

- Delivering adopted pets or returning runaway pets.
- Removing all household pets when one cat, dog, kitten, or puppy's Hunger Need falls critically low. There is, however, no fine imposed for this removal.
- Removing all household pets if the last teen or older Sim on the lot dies.

New Functions for Old NPCs

There are several small but important changes for your familiar slate of NPCs.

The Mail Carrier proves critical to a dog's daily routine.

- Cops: See above.
- Gardeners: Will fill in holes dug by dogs.

- Gypsy Matchmaker: Now sells the Lycanthropic-B potion to cure werewolves.
- Maid: Will clean litter boxes, pet beds, and pet houses as part of her duties.
- Mail Carrier: Only a dog's Master is more important than the Mail Carrier. So important is this force in a dog's life that the arrival of this civil servant triggers several special behaviors. Dogs know the Mail Carrier is arriving before he or she appears, and they'll wait by the box, thinking of the Mail Carrier. When the Mail Carrier does appear, the dog reacts according to Personality. There is a chance the Mail Carrier will attempt to Greet the dog; a positive relationship between postal worker and dog will cause the dog to stop chasing, mean barking, and growling.

Wildlife

Suburbia is a bit wilder with two kinds of wildlife that can wander onto your Sims' lots. One of these feral beasts can even be adopted as your own.

Skunk

Skunks occasionally wander onto your Sims' lots, creating a nuisance and possibly spraying your pets and Sims.

The skunk is particularly attracted to dirty items, and the chances of it showing up are heavily influenced by the presence of:

- Ash Piles
- Dead Flowers
- Debris Piles
- Dirty Diapers
- Puddles
- Trash Piles

Skunks will, if provoked, spray pets and Sims. Skunk spray flattens a Sim or pet's Hygiene Need—bringing it down to absolute bottom—and lowers the Fun and Comfort Needs. The Sim or pet also gets a memory of the event that affects its future autonomous behavior toward the skunk. Pets—even Doofus pets—do learn from their mistakes.

Pets may follow the skunk when it's on the lot. Initially, the skunk won't notice any pets following behind it. But it will, over time, become increasingly agitated. When the skunk has been followed too long, it threatens to spray, turning its rear to face the following pet, snuffling, and kicking its rear paws. For the pet, it's decision time. Once the skunk threatens, the pet may either leave or continue to follow. This decision is based on:

This might be the time to find something else to do.

◆ Genius Trait: Smarter pets usually realize the threat and take the opportunity to move on. Doofus pets are more likely than Normal pets to keep following. The Genius and Doofus traits affect only the pet's chance of picking the interaction, not the chance of getting sprayed. Genius pets also have a 30 percent chance of avoiding a spray.

◆ Memories: Every time a pet is sprayed, it gets a memory of being sprayed. Each spray memory a pet has increases the chances (by 20 percent) that it'll disengage once threatened.

Your Sim may stop the pet from following the skunk if the pet has been trained in the Come Here command.

Oh, well. Live and learn.

Cats and dogs, especially Aggressive ones, may chase the skunk. If the skunk doesn't immediately spray the pet, it'll eventually be chased off the lot, and the pet will get a boost to its Fun Need.

Sims can Watch the Skunk, but this too eventually agitates the skunk. If the skunk threatens, the Sim's autonomous decision to keep watching or move on is affected by his or her level of Logic skill; the higher Logic is, the more likely the Sim will go about his or her business.

Sims can be directed to or may autonomously (based on Logic skill and previous spray memories) try to pet the skunk. This almost always results in getting sprayed, but there's a very slim chance (5 percent) your Sim may get the rare treat of petting the skunk.

note
Werewolves, being one with the animal kingdom, have a much higher chance (60 percent) of being able to successfully pet skunks.

To get rid of a skunk, use the Chase Off interaction. Though it usually works, there is a chance the skunk will remain. If it doesn't leave as commanded, the skunk will spray.

Wolves

Wolves may randomly wander onto your lots, but they're more likely to come sniffing around if the lot contains:

- Trees/Bushes: Each four trees on a lot raises the chance of a wolf visit by 1 percent.
- Babies/Toddlers: Though having these kinds of Sims on your lot attracts wolves, they don't particularly seek out the little ones or do them any harm.
- Other Wolves: If there's a wolf already on the lot as a visitor or as part of the household, other wolves are more likely to show up.

All wolves have a fixed Personality profile:

- Genius
- Aggressive
- Hyper
- Pigpen
- Independent

Functionally, wolves are large dogs, but they do have some important differences:

- Wolves can develop Master Relationships, but the required Lifetime Relationship is higher (Lifetime 85).
- Wolves can develop Pack Relationships, but the required Lifetime Relationship is higher (Lifetime 65).
- Wolves' Daily Relationship decay is slower (only 2 per day rather than the dog's 3 per day) unless a Master or Pack Relationship exists. If either of these relationships is in place, a wolf's relationship decay is identical to that of a dog's with the same relationship (3 for Pack, 5 for Master).
- Wolves can dig holes, eat flowers, knock over trash cans, etc. in Sims' yards without being greeted. Normal dogs can't dig unless greeted.

note

You can make wolves come to your lot if your Sim is a werewolf. Direct the transformed werewolf outside and do the Summon Wolves self-interaction. One or more wolves will appear on the lot shortly.

Wolves make challenging pets, but they're worth the effort.

If a pet gets into a fight with a wolf and loses, there's a high chance that the pet will run away (see the "Pet Life" chapter).

To get rid of a visiting wolf (or to try to, at least), direct any child or older Sim to do the Chase Off interaction on the wolf. If it works, the wolf leaves (with lowered Daily Relationship to the Sim). If it fails, however, the wolf chases the Sim who tried to banish it.

It is possible to build a relationship so high that a wolf agrees to be domesticated (adopted). Its particular quirks, however, make it a difficult task.

Once adopted, wolves brought into your Sim's household remain wolves in their behavior and their genetics. A wolf bred with a wolf produces another wolf, but a wolf bred with a dog *always* produces a dog (ending the genetic wolf line).

note
Wolves living on the lot also increase the chances of a visit from the Leader of the Pack.

Howling is one of the pitfalls of life with wolves. A bit of training will take care of that.

Domesticated wolves are likely to howl during the night and wake any sleeping Sims regardless of their location (usually waking only happens if a sound is in the same room).

note
Sleeping transformed werewolf Sims won't be awakened by wolf howls.

Sims can train wolves out of howling by scolding. This builds the Calm behavior that will eventually eliminate howling.

Leader of the Pack

Behaviorally, this black wolf with its shining yellow eyes is almost exactly like any other wolf.

The differences are:

- He can't be brought into your Sims' household.
- Once he develops a substantial relationship with a Sim, he can do the Nibble interaction to turn him or her into a werewolf.
- He's drawn to your Sims' lots by the same factors that draw wolves in general, but he will only come at night.

Lycanthropy (Werewolves)

It's been whispered for some time that the woods around these neighborhoods hide a strange kind of wolf, but it hasn't had reason to venture into town until now. With the sunny side streets now teeming with pets, however, this dark force has stepped into the light. They say its bite can turn a Sim into a howling werewolf. We say they're right. And we can prove it.

Becoming a Werewolf

Any teen-or-older Sim can become a werewolf. Only two things can infect a Sim with lycanthropy:

- Receiving the Nibble interaction from the Leader of the Pack NPC.
- Receiving the Savage interaction from a werewolf Sim.

Being a Werewolf

The 8 pm transformation is a dramatic event for the Sim and all bystanders.

The most obvious fallout from lycanthropic infection is what happens every night at 8 pm.

tip

Since the transformation can frighten or realize werewolf-related fears of Sims in the same room, it's best to have your soon-to-be werewolf in an enclosed (and locked) room just before 8 pm.

During the day (6 am–8 pm), a lycanthropic Sim is perfectly normal. When the appointed hour strikes, however, the Sim changes into a hairy beast. Though the most obvious changes are on the outside—the fur and all—becoming a werewolf causes many important transformations:

Grr! Argh!

- Upon transformation, the Sim's Hunger Need drops to -50, driving him or her to find food immediately.

- Also, transforming drives the Sim's Energy Need to the top, meaning sleep in unnecessary for a while.

- Over time, the werewolf Sim's Personality shifts toward the "werewolf" Personality. These changes remain even when the Sim is not furry.

- Over time, the werewolf Sim's Body skill shifts toward Body 10.

- Werewolves can infect other Sims with whom they have a high relationship by doing the Savage interaction. Note that doing this substantially damages the relationship and causes the bitten Sim to be Furious at the biter.

- Werewolves have a special walk—the werewolf lope.

- Werewolves get a special Irritate social: Grr! This social frightens the recipients so much they lose Fun and might wet themselves.

- Werewolves can do the self-interaction Howl. Non-werewolf Sims in the room will suffer a Bladder and Comfort hit, may wet themselves, and could take a loss of Aspiration points if they fear hearing the other Sim howl. If Sims are sleeping in the same room, the howl will awaken them. Another werewolf present in the room might lope over and howl back.

- Werewolves are excellent pet trainers; the pet will learn an extra 25 percent faster than normal. This bonus is added to any bonus for the teaching Sim's Charisma. So, a Charisma 10 werewolf is the best trainer you can get.

- If you have a burglary, all items stolen before the attack (which the werewolf will always win) are transferred into the werewolf's inventory.

- Werewolves can't be made over. Thus, they can't use any mirror's Change Appearance of... interaction, Dr. Vu's Automated Cosmetic Surgeon, or the Ug-No-More Makeover Station.

- Werewolves can bring wolves (though not the Leader of the Pack) to the lot with the Summon Wolves self-interaction. The werewolf must be outside to perform this interaction.

- Werewolves are not immortal; they can be killed in all the conventional ways.

- Werewolves can also be vampires, zombies, or all three at once.

- Servos can be werewolves.

- Werewolves can produce children normally, but lycanthropy is not hereditary. The baby will be normal.

Behold the smooth moves of the zombie vampire werewolf.

The Slow Transformation

The longer a Sim is a werewolf, the more their Personality traits and Body skill grow to match the werewolf Personality:

- Outgoing (Outgoing/Shy 10)
- Sloppy (Neat/Sloppy 0)
- Grouchy (Nice/Grouchy 0)
- Playful (Playful/Serious 10)
- Active (Active/Lazy 10)

Likewise, if the Sim remains a werewolf long enough, Body skill during the day will eventually max out without having to do any Body skill training. Even if the Sim is cured of lycanthropy, these changes remain intact unless changed by other forces.

> **note**
>
> Werewolves, once their Body skill begins to shift toward 10, will excel in any career that requires Body skill. Get your werewolf involved in the Athletic, Criminal, Law Enforcement, Military, Natural Scientist, or Show Business career tracks.

This altered Personality may or may not be desirable. For some, this may provide ample incentive to live life as a werewolf, with all its drawbacks and oddities. For others, it might be a reason to be cured as soon as possible.

Curing Lycanthropy

Lycanthropy can be cured with the Lycanthropic-B potion. This potion can be purchased from the Obedience Trainer or, if you have *The Sims™ 2 Nightlife*, from the Gypsy Matchmaker for §60.

Drinking it ends the nightly transformations, but your Sim will keep any Personality changes received during the infection.

Neighborhood Bin

For the first time, a *The Sims 2* expansion pack contains not only new Family Bin families and unoccupied lots and houses, but also two occupied houses.

Family Bin Families

Crittur

◆ Danny: Large male dog (Doofus, Lazy, Friendly, Pigpen) that has learned Goes On Furniture, Eats Sim Food, Filthy, Shake, and Speak

◆ Sarah: Large female dog (Hyper, Aggressive, Pigpen) that has learned Goes on Furniture and Eats Sim Food

note

Merge this pet-only household into any existing household.

Roseland

◆ Funds: §11,337

◆ Cyd: Adult, Knowledge Aspiration

◆ Porthos: Male small dog (Genius, Hyper, Friendly, Finicky) who has learned Housebroken, Eats Pet Food, Playful, Come Here, and Play Dead

Lot Bin Occupied Lots

Katt (Cozy Kitten Condo)

◆ Bedrooms: 1

◆ Funds: §31,933

◆ Tara Katt: Adult, Family Aspiration

◆ Mickey: Adult male cat (Lazy, Friendly) that has learned Housebroken, Playful, Come Here, and Speak

◆ Samantha: Adult cat (Hyper, Independent, Finicky) that has learned Disruptive, Housebroken, Eats Sim Food, and Come Here

◆ Faline: Male kitten (Hyper, Friendly)

Kim (Nuclear Nest)

◆ Bedrooms: 2

◆ Funds: §106,758

◆ Cynthia Kim: Adult, Popularity Aspiration

◆ Robert Kim: Adult, Fortune Aspiration

◆ Justin Kim: Child, Grow Up Aspiration

◆ Cheech: Adult male cat (Genius, Independent, Finicky) that has learned Housebroken, Eats Pet Food, Respectful, Come Here, and Stay

◆ Gabby: Adult female large dog (Genius, Friendly) that has learned Housebroken, Eats Pet Food, Playful, Come Here, Play Dead, and Stay

Unoccupied Lots

Planetary Pet Store

♦ Purchase Price: §54,528

♦ Business Type: Shop (pets, pet supplies, caged pets, collars)

Pepe's Pets

♦ Purchase Price: §34,473

♦ Business Type: Shop (pets, pet supplies, caged pets, collars)

Planetary Pet Park

♦ Purchase Price: §43,380

Pettina's Pet Retreat

♦ Purchase Price: §31,795

Neighborhood Lot Catalog Changes

The Lots and Houses Bin has gotten a bit of an overhaul:

From now on, lots and houses added by expansion packs will be marked with their pack's icon.

♦ From THE SIMS 2 PETS forward, new lots introduced in expansion packs will have the icon of their pack and will be sorted to the front of the list (after any custom lots).

♦ Custom and downloaded lots will appear at the front of the list.

note

Lots and houses from previous expansion packs won't bear their pack's mark, but all future ones will.

Chapter 9

Build Mode Additions

Diagonal Rooms

The Diagonal Room tool simplifies the process of making diagonally oriented rooms.

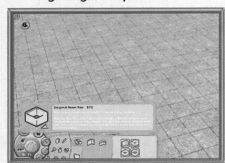

You'll find the Diagonal Room tool in the Wall tool panel.

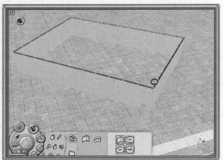

Simply click and drag to construct a nifty diagonal room.

note
Previously, the only way to draw a diagonal room was to manually draw out four diagonal walls.

tip
When using the regular Room tool, hold Ctrl D to toggle to the Diagonal Room tool.

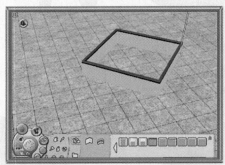

The Diagonal Room hotkey (Ctrl D) lets you quickly build walls…

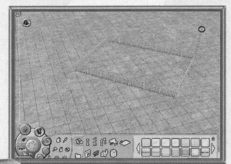

…and fences.

Diagonal Roofs

Now you can build properly aligned roofs over diagonal rooms without corner overhangs (and their supporting columns).

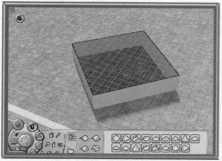

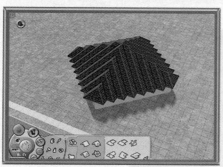

Previously, to cover a simple, square diagonal room, you'd have had to use the Auto Roofs tool or meticulously cobble together something like this.

With the Diagonal Roofs tool, it's as simple as this.

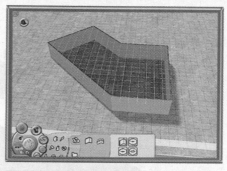

Combination spaces aren't much more difficult.

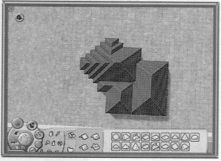

This elaborate covering would have been the way to roof this house.

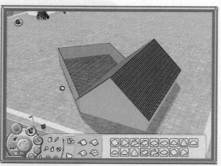

The diagonal roof, however, makes it clean and neat, especially at the corners.

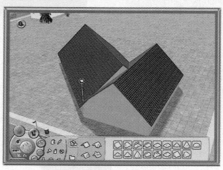

You'll find diagonal roofs in the Roof Types panel, marked with an angle icon.

Diagonal roofs come in all the same varieties as normal, nonconical/octagonal roof varieties, *except* Mansard:

- Long Gabled
- Short Gabled
- Hipped
- Shed Gabled
- Shed Hipped

Individual Roof Pitch Cheat

The roof slope cheat from *The Sims 2 Nightlife* enabled you to change the slope of every roof on the lot. Now you can change the slope of individual roofs.

To use the individual roof slope cheat, open the Cheat console ([Ctrl][Shift][C]) and enter *individualroofslopeangle* and a number between 15 and 75.

For example, entering *individualroofslopeangle* 50 will change a roof to a 50-degree angle.

Once the cheat is entered, activate the Roof Types panel and select the roof to be changed by holding [Ctrl][Alt] and clicking on the desired roof.

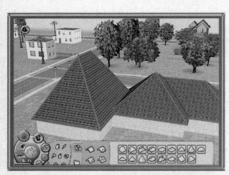

After entering *individualroofslopeangle* 60 in the console, the left roof can be changed by [Ctrl][Alt] and clicking on it.

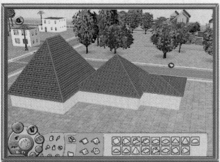

The rightmost roof has now been changed to a 20-degree angle.

Octagonal Room Tools

Instead of dragging individual walls to make octagonal spaces, the new Octagonal Room tool lets you drop and adjust an octagonal room to suit your whims.

The Octagonal Room tool is in the Wall tool panel.

This tool works differently from other room tools in that you don't drag the room but rather drop it. Resizing and rotating are done with the keyboard before the room is placed.

tip

With the Wall tool you can plop down a basic octagonal room without switching to the Octagonal Room tool by holding [Ctrl][E].

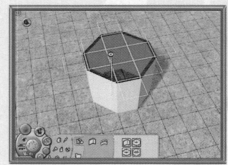

Selecting the Octagonal Room tool and clicking on the lot yields a nice, tidy three-by-three octagonal room.

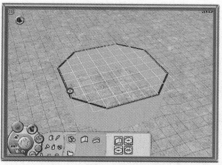

If, however, you want to go a little bigger, keep holding the left mouse button and press + or − to enlarge and shrink the room.

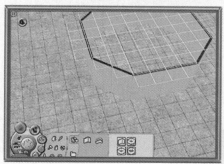

Note that with each alternating change, the diagonals are shorter than the straight walls (four on the straight and two on the diagonals here). Since the room's position in its footprint is offset, you can rotate nonsymmetrical rooms by pressing < and >.

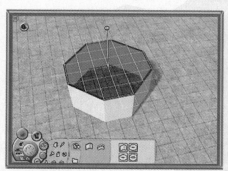

To build on top of an octagonal wall, press the Go Up a Floor button (Page Up) and point the tool at the center of the room grid.

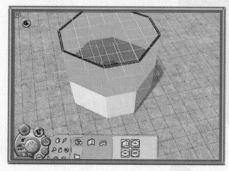

Click and the room will be placed to match the size of the floor below it.

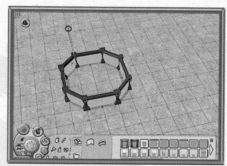

Though you can't stack them, holding Ctrl E (and adjusting for size and orientation) lets you make octagonal rooms with half walls...

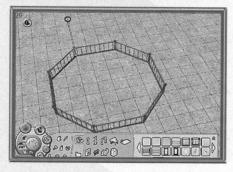

...or fences.

Flatten Lot

The Flatten Lot tool changes the elevation of the entire lot to match the elevation of the mailbox/trash can.

Change from this...

...to this.

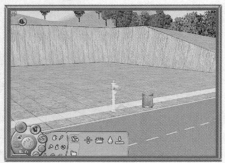

Note that terrain around the borders of the lot will remain the same, so you may get a lot surrounded by sheer walls. You may be able remedy this by going into adjacent lots and flattening them, too.

If there's a structure on the lot, the Flatten Lot tool will leave alone any tiles supporting it, creating an effect like this.

Sledgehammer Tool

The Sledgehammer tool. You can also activate it by pressing [J].

Yearn to destroy stuff in new ways? Then the Sledgehammer tool is for you. Nestled in the Build (and Buy) mode tool panels, next to the Design mode button, the Sledgehammer tool is the Swiss Army knife of Build mode deletion.

Select the Sledgehammer tool to delete any kind of object and anything on or attached to that object. For example:

Clicking on a wall with a window and drapes will delete all three at once.

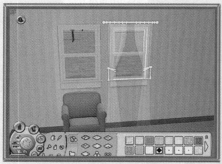

Clicking on the drapes deletes only the drapes.

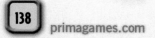

Clicking on a table with a lamp deletes both the table and the lamp.

> ## note
> Sledgehammer destructions can be Undone.

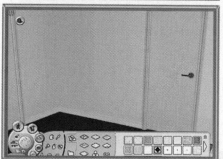

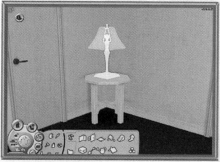

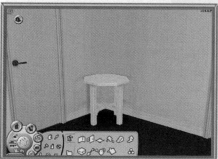

Clicking on the lamp deletes only the lamp.

> ## note
> You can't sledgehammer contained pets, so don't even think about it, sicko!

The tool highlights the object it's going to delete, not the tile on which it sits, so be sure you've selected the right element before you click. If you want to delete a chair that's sitting on a rug, for example, pointing at the tile will delete the rug and leave the chair undisturbed.

One of the handiest uses for the Sledgehammer tool is deleting objects that contain other objects. This store display can't be deleted in the traditional way, but the Sledgehammer does it all in one click.

When you delete an item with the Sledgehammer tool, you receive a refund of the object's current depreciated value. Selling a Buy mode object, therefore, now takes only one click instead of a click, a drag, and another click.

Mass Delete Cheats

If you wish your destruction to be more widespread, several targeted but object- or element-specific cheats will save lots of labor.

To use them, bring up the Cheat console and enter *deleteall* followed by the kind of object you want to delete.

deleteall will instantly and simultaneously destroy all:

- Awnings
- Half-Walls
- Fences
- Walls

caution

Not all of these actions are Undo-able, so save before entering these codes.

Now there are walls…

…Now there are no walls. That was easy!

So, entering *deleteallwalls* will—surprise—delete all the lot's walls.

The cheat can also be used with certain kinds of objects. Type *deleteallobjects* followed by one of the following:

- Doors
- Stairs
- Windows

note

Deleteallobjects will not be able to delete objects in use. For example, if a Sim is walking through a door, the cheat will leave that door while deleting all others).

Floor Tool Enhancements

Several changes to the Floor-Covering tool add some sweet new functionality, especially for patterned floor tiles.

Rotating Floor Tiles

Floors lay out naturally in a specific direction that was, until now, unchangeable.

Select the floor covering you want and press <kbd><</kbd> or <kbd>></kbd> to rotate the tile. When the orientation is to your liking, click on the tile.

Even tiles that have already been placed can be rotated. Select the same floor tile from the catalog, point to the spot you want to change, and repeat the rotation process.

Quarter Tiles

With a new hotkey toggle, you can now place only quarter segments of any floor tile. This new tool streamlines flooring diagonal areas and provides a major creative opportunity.

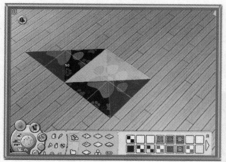

Press Ctrl F to activate the Quarter-Tile tool to, for example, make new tiles from duplicated tiles of different colors.

Use this tool to create wild floor patterns of your own imagining. Since quarter tiles can also be rotated, the possibilities are vast.

The tool will remain on even if you switch to another floor tile or floor-tile category.

To switch out of Quarter-Tile mode, press Ctrl F again, exit Build mode, switch to another Build mode panel, or click and drag. Doing any of these will automatically revert you to Full-Tile mode.

tip

While in Quarter-Tile mode, hold Ctrl to delete a quarter of a laid-out tile.

Edger Fences

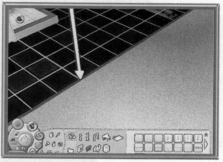

The Fence tool (Miscellaneous > Fence Tool) now includes six edgers that can be used to delineate where two kinds of floor tiles meet.

note

Though they are fences, these edgers don't divide rooms for Environment score purposes and can be walked over. In fact, your Sims and pets won't even notice them.

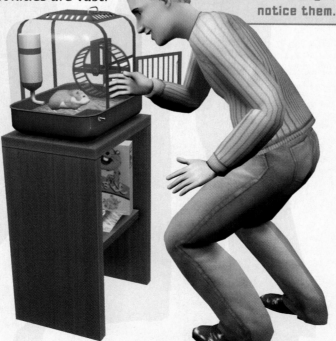

Chapter 10
CHEATS

To summon the Cheat window, press [C] [S] [C].

tip

To make pets controllable AND be able to cancel their interactions, you must enter both the BOOLPROP CONTROLPETS and BOOLPROP PETACTIONCANCEL cheats.

Console Cheats

◆ BOOLPROP CONTROLPETS [on/off]: Makes pets fully controllable. You can't, however, cancel actions from their queue.

◆ BOOLPROP DISABLEPUPPYKITTENAGING [true/false]: Turns off aging for kittens and puppies.

◆ BOOLPROP PETACTIONCANCEL [true/false]: Normally, you can't cancel actions in a pet's interaction queue; they're grayed out. This cheat makes these actions accessible so you can cancel anything your pet has chosen to do. This does not, however, make your pets controllable.

◆ BOOLPROP PETSFREEWILL [true/false]: Turns off pet free will. They won't do anything unless you tell them to, and you can only tell them to with the other pet cheats.

◆ BOOLPROP SHOWCATALOGEPFLAGS [true/false]: Activates labels in the detail view of each Buy mode and Build mode object (except floor or wall coverings) to show from which product they came.

◆ DELETEALLAWNINGS: Deletes all awnings on a lot.

◆ DELETEALLFENCES: Deletes all fences on a lot.

◆ DELETEALLHALFWALLS: Deletes all half walls on a lot.

◆ DELETEALLOBJECTS [Doors/Windows/Stairs]: Deletes all doors, windows, or stairs on a lot.

◆ DELETEALLWALLS: Deletes all walls on a lot.

note

See the "Build Mode Additions" chapter for more information on mass delete cheats and the roof slope cheat.

◆ INDIVIDUALROOFSLOPEANGLE [15–75]: Activates a tool to change the roof slopes of individual roofs on a lot.

Bonus Materials from The Sims™ 2

The following three chapters have been provided as a reference guide—they cover all the pertinent info on careers, objects, and socials from the base game and all expansion packs prior to *The Sims 2 Pets*.

Chapter 11   JOBS BY CAREER LEVEL

Adult Careers

Level 1 Careers

Career	Job Name	Logic	Body	Creativity	Mechanical	Charisma	Cooking	Cleaning	Friends	Hours
Artist	Canvas Stretcher	0	0	0	0	0	0	0	0	7a–2p
Athletic	Team Mascot	0	0	0	0	0	0	0	0	3p–9p
Business	Mailroom Technician	0	0	0	0	0	0	0	0	9a–3p
Criminal	Pickpocket	0	0	0	0	0	0	0	0	11a–5p
Culinary	Dishwasher	0	0	0	0	0	0	0	0	2p–10p
Law Enforcement	Security Guard	0	0	0	0	0	0	0	0	8p–2a
Medical	Emergency Medical Technician	0	0	0	0	0	0	0	0	8a–2p
Military	Recruit	0	0	0	0	0	0	0	0	7a–1p
Natural Scientist	Ratkeeper	0	0	0	0	0	0	0	0	9a–4p
Paranormal	Psychic Phone Pal	0	0	0	0	0	0	0	0	8p–3a
Politics	Campaign Worker	0	0	0	0	0	0	0	0	9a–6p
Science	Test Subject	0	0	0	0	0	0	0	0	11a–5p
Show Business	Screen Test Stand-In	0	0	0	0	0	0	0	0	10a–5p
Slacker	Golf Caddy	0	0	0	0	0	0	0	0	5a–10a

Level 2 Careers

Career	Job Name	Logic	Body	Creativity	Mechanical	Charisma	Cooking	Cleaning	Friends	Hours
Artist	Canvas Stretcher	0	0	0	0	0	0	0	0	7a–2p
Athletic	Minor Leaguer	0	1	0	0	0	0	0	0	9a–3p
Business	Executive Assistant	0	0	0	0	1	0	0	0	9a–4p
Criminal	Bagman	0	0	0	0	0	0	0	0	5p–1a
Culinary	Drive Through Clerk	0	0	0	0	0	0	0	0	5p–9p
Law Enforcement	Cadet	0	1	0	0	0	0	0	0	9a–3p
Medical	Paramedic	0	0	0	0	0	0	1	0	8p–2a
Military	Elite Forces	0	0	0	0	0	0	0	0	7a–1p
Natural Scientist	Ratkeeper	0	0	0	0	0	0	0	0	9a–4p
Paranormal	Psychic Phone Pal	0	0	0	0	0	0	0	0	8p–3a
Politics	Intern	0	0	0	0	0	0	0	0	9a–3p
Science	Lab Assistant	0	0	0	0	0	1	1	0	4p–10p
Show Business	Screen Test Stand-In	0	0	0	0	0	0	0	0	10a–5p
Slacker	Gas Station Attendant	0	0	0	0	0	0	0	0	10p–3a

Days Off	# Work Days	Daily Salary	Weekly Average	Energy	Bladder	Hygiene	Social	Hunger	Fun	Comfort	Game
Mon & Wed	5	§231	§1,155	-8	-8	-10	-3	-4	-10	-3	University
Mon & Thu	5	§154	§770	-48	-48	-60	0	-60	18	-60	The Sims™ 2
Sun & Fri	5	§168	§840	-48	-48	-18	24	-24	-18	-48	The Sims™ 2
Mon & Thu	5	§196	§980	-48	0	-60	-30	-60	30	-30	The Sims™ 2
Mon & Fri	5	§126	§630	-64	-40	-80	-32	-80	-24	-24	The Sims™ 2
Mon & Fri	5	§336	§1,680	-48	-60	-6	-30	-12	-6	-6	The Sims™ 2
Mon & Sat	5	§280	§1,400	-48	-48	-18	24	-24	-18	-48	The Sims™ 2
Mon & Wed	5	§350	§1,750	-60	-30	-60	0	-60	-30	-30	The Sims™ 2
Sun & Fri	5	§325	§1,625	-8	-8	-10	-3	-4	-10	-3	University
Sun & Wed	5	§252	§1,260	-8	-8	-10	-3	4	-10	-3	University
Mon & Wed	5	§308	§1,540	-72	-72	-27	36	-36	-27	-72	The Sims™ 2
Sun & Fri	5	§217	§1,085	-48	-30	-60	-24	-60	-12	-42	The Sims™ 2
Mon & Sat	5	§420	§2,100	-8	-8	-10	-3	4	-10	3	University
Mon & Sat	5	§126	§630	-40	-40	-15	20	-20	-15	-40	The Sims™ 2

Days Off	# Work Days	Daily Salary	Weekly Average	Energy	Bladder	Hygiene	Social	Hunger	Fun	Comfort	Game
Mon & Wed	5	§231	§1,155	-8	-8	-10	-3	-4	-10	-3	University
Tue & Thu	5	§238	§1,190	-48	-48	-60	0	-42	18	-48	The Sims™ 2
Mon & Sat	5	§252	§1,260	-56	-56	-21	28	-28	-21	-56	The Sims™ 2
Mon & Wed	5	§280	§1,400	-64	0	-80	-16	-56	24	-24	The Sims™ 2
Mon & Wed	5	§168	§840	-32	-16	-40	4	-28	-4	-20	The Sims™ 2
Mon & Sat	5	§448	§2,240	-48	-30	-60	24	-42	18	-60	The Sims™ 2
Wed & Fri	5	§385	§1,925	-48	-48	-18	24	-24	-18	-48	The Sims™ 2
Wed & Fri	5	§455	§2,275	-48	-30	-60	0	-42	-18	-24	The Sims™ 2
Sun & Fri	5	§325	§1,625	-8	-8	-10	-3	-4	-10	-3	University
Sun & Wed	5	§252	§1,260	-8	-8	-10	-3	4	-10	-3	University
Sun & Fri	5	§420	§2,100	-48	-48	-18	24	-24	-18	-48	The Sims™ 2
Mon & Sat	5	§322	§1,610	-36	-42	-30	12	-42	12	12	The Sims™ 2
Mon & Sat	5	§420	§2,100	-8	-8	-10	-3	4	-10	3	University
Mon & Thu	5	§154	§770	-40	-40	-15	20	-20	-15	-40	The Sims™ 2

Level 3 Careers

Career	Job Name	Logic	Body	Creativity	Mechanical	Charisma	Cooking	Cleaning	Friends	Hours
Artist	Canvas Stretcher	0	0	0	0	0	0	0	0	7a–2p
Athletic	Rookie	0	2	0	0	0	0	0	0	9a–3p
Business	Field Sales Rep	0	0	0	0	2	0	0	0	9a–4p
Criminal	Bookie	0	0	1	0	0	0	0	0	11a–6p
Culinary	Fast Food Shift Manager	0	0	1	0	0	0	0	0	5p–10p
Law Enforcement	Patrol Officer	0	2	0	0	0	0	0	0	3p–11p
Medical	Nurse	1	0	0	0	0	0	2	0	7a–2p
Military	Drill Instructor	0	1	0	1	0	0	0	0	7a–1p
Natural Scientist	Ratkeeper	0	0	0	0	0	0	0	0	9a–4p
Paranormal	Psychic Phone Pal	0	0	0	0	0	0	0	0	8p–3a
Politics	Lobbyist	0	0	0	0	0	0	0	0	8a–2p
Science	Field Researcher	1	0	0	0	0	1	3	0	9a–3p
Show Business	Screen Test Stand-In	0	0	0	0	0	0	0	0	10a–5p
Slacker	Convenience Store Clerk	0	0	0	1	0	0	0	0	9a–3p

Level 4 Careers

Career	Job Name	Logic	Body	Creativity	Mechanical	Charisma	Cooking	Cleaning	Friends	Hours
Artist	Comic Book Penciller	0	0	4	3	0	1	0	2	10a–5p
Athletic	Starter	0	3	0	0	1	0	0	1	9a–3p
Business	Junior Executive	0	0	1	0	2	0	0	1	9a–4p
Criminal	Con Artist	0	0	3	0	0	0	0	1	9a–3p
Culinary	Host/Hostess	1	0	2	0	0	0	0	1	10a–4p
Law Enforcement	Desk Sgt	1	2	0	0	0	0	0	1	9a–3p
Medical	Intern	2	0	0	2	0	0	4	1	9a–6p
Military	Junior Officer	0	1	0	2	1	0	0	0	7a–1p
Natural Scientist	Scatmaster	0	4	0	3	0	0	3	1	11a–6p
Paranormal	Hypnotist	0	0	5	0	3	0	0	2	11a–6p
Politics	Campaign Manager	1	0	1	0	0	0	0	1	8a–5p
Science	Science Teacher	1	0	0	0	0	2	5	1	8a–3p
Show Business	Commercial Actor/Actress	0	3	0	0	3	0	0	1	8a–5p
Slacker	Record Store Clerk	0	0	0	1	1	0	0	0	10a–3p

Days Off	# Work Days	Daily Salary	Weekly Average	Energy	Bladder	Hygiene	Social	Hunger	Fun	Comfort	Game
Mon & Wed	5	§231	§1,155	-8	-8	-10	-3	-4	-10	-3	University
Tue & Wed	5	§322	§1,610	-48	-48	-48	0	-36	30	-48	The Sims™ 2
Tue & Thu	5	§350	§1,750	-56	-56	-21	28	-28	-21	-56	The Sims™ 2
Tue & Wed	5	§385	§1,925	-56	-35	-56	28	-42	35	35	The Sims™ 2
Wed & Thu	5	§182	§910	-40	-30	-40	20	-30	15	15	The Sims™ 2
Wed & Fri	5	§552	§2,760	-64	0	-64	80	-48	8	-64	The Sims™ 2
Mon & Thu	5	§476	§2,380	-56	-56	-21	28	-28	-21	-56	The Sims™ 2
Mon & Tue	5	§560	§2,800	-48	-30	-24	0	-36	30	-18	The Sims™ 2
Sun & Fri	5	§325	§1,625	-8	-8	-10	-3	-4	-10	-3	University
Sun & Wed	5	§252	§1,260	-8	-8	-10	-3	4	-10	-3	University
Sun & Sat	5	§504	§2,520	-48	-48	-18	24	-24	-18	-48	The Sims™ 2
Wed & Fri	5	§448	§2,240	-48	-36	-48	-18	-36	18	-24	The Sims™ 2
Mon & Sat	5	§420	§2,100	-8	-8	-10	-3	4	-10	3	University
Mon & Tue	5	§210	§1,050	-48	-48	-18	24	-24	-18	-48	The Sims™ 2

Days Off	# Work Days	Daily Salary	Weekly Average	Energy	Bladder	Hygiene	Social	Hunger	Fun	Comfort	Game
Sun & Fri	5	§630	§3,150	-8	-8	-3	-3	-5	-4	-5	University
Tue & Thu	5	§420	§2,100	-48	-48	-18	0	-24	30	-24	The Sims™ 2
Wed & Sun	5	§448	§2,240	-56	-56	-21	35	-28	-21	-28	The Sims™ 2
Sun & Sat	5	§490	§2,450	-36	-18	-6	60	-24	30	36	The Sims™ 2
Mon & Tue	5	§242	§1,210	-48	-30	-12	30	-24	18	-12	The Sims™ 2
Sun & Sat	5	§616	§3,080	-30	-36	-18	30	-24	30	-18	The Sims™ 2
Tue & Fri	5	§574	§2,870	-81	-72	-27	45	-36	-27	-45	The Sims™ 2
Sun & Sat	5	§630	§3,150	-48	-36	-18	0	-24	18	18	The Sims™ 2
Sun & Sat	5	§787	§3,935	-8	-8	-10	-3	-5	-4	-5	University
Sun & Wed	5	§672	§3,360	-8	-8	-3	-3	-5	-4	5	University
Tue & Wed	5	§602	§3,010	-64	-64	-24	40	-32	-24	-32	The Sims™ 2
Sun & Sat	5	§525	§2,625	-56	-42	-14	35	-28	35	42	The Sims™ 2
Sun & Mon	5	§861	§4,305	-8	-8	-3	-3	5	-4	5	University
Tue & Thu	5	§252	§1,260	-40	-40	-15	25	-20	-15	-20	The Sims™ 2

Level 5 Careers

Career	Job Name	Logic	Body	Creativity	Mechanical	Charisma	Cooking	Cleaning	Friends	Hours
Artist	Wedding Photographer	0	0	5	4	3	2	0	4	8a–3p
Athletic	All Star	0	6	0	0	2	0	0	2	9a–3p
Business	Executive	2	0	1	0	4	0	0	1	8a–3p
Criminal	Getaway Driver	0	1	4	2	0	0	0	2	10p–6a
Culinary	Waiter/Waitress	3	0	2	0	0	0	0	2	2p–7p
Law Enforcement	Vice Squad	1	3	0	0	0	0	0	2	10a–4p
Medical	Resident	3	0	0	3	0	0	5	2	6p–1a
Military	Counter Intelligence	0	4	0	2	2	0	0	0	8a–2p
Natural Scientist	Soil Identifier	1	5	0	4	0	0	5	2	9a–4p
Paranormal	Hypnotist	0	0	5	0	3	0	0	2	11a–6p
Politics	City Council Member	2	0	2	0	2	0	0	2	9a–3p
Science	Inventor	4	0	0	0	0	4	6	3	10a–7p
Show Business	Cartoon Voice	1	3	2	0	4	0	0	3	1p–8p
Slacker	Projectionist	0	0	1	3	2	0	0	4	6p–1a

Level 6 Careers

Career	Job Name	Logic	Body	Creativity	Mechanical	Charisma	Cooking	Cleaning	Friends	Hours
Artist	Art Forger	0	0	5	5	4	3	0	5	2p–9p
Athletic	MVP	0	8	0	1	3	0	0	3	9a–3p
Business	Senior Manager	3	0	3	0	4	0	0	2	8a–3p
Criminal	Bank Robber	0	2	5	4	0	0	0	3	3p–11p
Culinary	Prep Cook	3	0	2	0	0	3	0	2	9a–3p
Law Enforcement	Detective	4	3	0	0	0	0	2	3	9a–3p
Medical	General Practitioner	4	0	0	4	0	0	6	3	10a–6p
Military	Flight Officer	0	5	0	4	3	0	0	1	9a–3p
Natural Scientist	Rogue Botanist	3	5	0	6	0	0	6	4	10a–5p
Paranormal	Douser	0	0	6	0	3	3	3	6	5p–12a
Politics	State Assemblyperson	3	0	2	0	4	0	0	3	9a–4p
Science	Inventor	4	0	0	0	0	4	6	3	10a–7p
Show Business	Supporting Player	2	5	3	0	5	0	0	5	6p–1a
Slacker	Projectionist	0	0	1	3	2	0	0	4	6p–1a

Days Off	# Work Days	Daily Salary	Weekly Average	Energy	Bladder	Hygiene	Social	Hunger	Fun	Comfort	Game
Sun & Tue	5	§808	§4,040	-6	-8	-8	-2	5	-4	6	University
Tue & Wed	5	§539	§2,695	-36	-48	-48	0	-24	36	-12	The Sims™ 2
Sun & Sat	5	§560	§2,800	-42	-56	-14	35	-28	-14	-14	The Sims™ 2
Sun & Sat	5	§595	§2,975	-48	-40	-64	-24	-32	16	64	The Sims™ 2
Tue & Wed	5	§308	§1,540	-45	-25	-25	35	-25	30	-40	The Sims™ 2
Tue & Wed	5	§686	§3,430	-36	-30	-30	30	-24	36	-30	The Sims™ 2
Wed & Thu	5	§672	§3,360	-42	-56	-14	35	-28	-14	-35	The Sims™ 2
Wed & Thu	5	§700	§3,500	-36	-36	-12	0	-24	48	-12	The Sims™ 2
Mon & Thu	5	§945	§4,725	-6	-8	-10	-2	-5	-4	-6	University
Sun & Wed	5	§672	§3,360	-8	-8	-3	-3	-5	-4	5	University
Sun & Sat	5	§679	§3,395	-36	-48	-12	30	-24	-12	-12	The Sims™ 2
Tue & Thu	5	§756	§3,780	-36	-36	-9	-27	-45	99	54	The Sims™ 2
Sun & Sat	5	§1,008	§5,040	-6	-8	-8	-2	5	-4	6	University
Wed & Thu	5	§392	§1,960	-42	-56	-14	35	-28	-14	-14	The Sims™ 2

Days Off	# Work Days	Daily Salary	Weekly Average	Energy	Bladder	Hygiene	Social	Hunger	Fun	Comfort	Game
Sun, Fri, Sat	4	§1,339	§5,356	-4	-8	-5	-2	-5	-5	-3	University
Tue, Wed, Thu	4	§893	§3,572	-24	-48	-30	0	-30	18	-12	The Sims™ 2
Sun & Sat	5	§728	§3,640	-42	-56	-14	35	-28	-14	-14	The Sims™ 2
Sun & Sat	5	§742	§3,710	-32	-40	-40	-40	-40	24	-64	The Sims™ 2
Mon & Tue	5	§469	§2,345	-36	-30	-54	-6	3	18	-30	The Sims™ 2
Mon & Tue	5	§756	§3,780	-24	0	-24	30	-30	18	-24	The Sims™ 2
Sun & Sat	5	§770	§3,850	-48	-64	-16	40	-32	-16	-16	The Sims™ 2
Sun & Sat	5	§770	§3,850	-24	-6	-30	0	-30	18	18	The Sims™ 2
Tue & Thu	5	§1,134	§5,670	-4	-8	-5	-2	-5	-5	3	University
Sun & Tue	5	§1,092	§5,460	-4	-8	-5	-2	-5	-5	-3	University
Sun & Sat	5	§756	§3,780	-42	-56	-14	35	-28	-14	-14	The Sims™ 2
Tue & Thu	5	§756	§3,780	-36	-36	-9	-27	-45	99	54	The Sims™ 2
Sun & Fri	5	§1,155	§5,775	-4	-8	-5	-2	5	-5	3	University
Wed & Thu	5	§392	§1,960	-42	-56	-14	35	-28	-14	-14	The Sims™ 2

Level 7 Careers

Career	Job Name	Logic	Body	Creativity	Mechanical	Charisma	Cooking	Cleaning	Friends	Hours
Artist	Fashion Photographer	0	0	6	6	6	3	0	8	10a–5p
Athletic	Superstar	0	10	0	2	4	0	0	4	9a–4p
Business	Vice President	4	0	3	0	5	0	0	1	8a–4p
Criminal	Cat Burglar	0	5	7	4	0	0	0	3	9p–3a
Culinary	Sous Chef	4	0	4	0	0	4	0	3	2p–9p
Law Enforcement	Lieutenant	5	4	0	0	0	0	4	5	9a–3p
Medical	Specialist	5	0	0	7	0	0	7	4	10a–4p
Military	Senior Officer	0	6	0	5	3	0	0	3	8a–2p
Natural Scientist	Animal Linguist	6	5	0	6	0	0	6	6	10a–5p
Paranormal	Police Psychic	0	0	7	0	4	4	6	8	1p–7p
Politics	Congressperson	4	0	3	0	6	0	0	5	9a–3p
Science	Scholar	5	0	0	0	0	5	7	3	8a–1p
Show Business	Broadway Star	3	7	4	0	6	0	0	7	6p–1a
Slacker	Home Video Editor	0	0	2	4	2	0	0	5	11a–5p

Level 8 Careers

Career	Job Name	Logic	Body	Creativity	Mechanical	Charisma	Cooking	Cleaning	Friends	Hours
Artist	Acclaimed Muralist	0	0	7	7	7	4	0	9	12p–7p
Athletic	Assistant Coach	0	10	0	4	5	0	0	5	9a–2p
Business	President	6	0	4	0	5	0	0	1	8a–4p
Criminal	Counterfeiter	0	6	7	7	0	0	0	4	9a–3p
Culinary	Executive Chef	6	0	5	0	0	5	0	4	9a–3p
Law Enforcement	SWAT Team Leader	6	5	0	0	0	0	6	6	11a–6p
Medical	Surgeon	7	0	0	9	0	0	8	5	10a–4p
Military	Commander	0	7	0	5	5	0	0	4	9a–3p
Natural Scientist	Unnatural Crossbreeder	8	5	0	7	0	0	7	8	9a–4p
Paranormal	UFO Investigator	0	0	7	0	5	4	7	9	10a–5p
Politics	Judge	7	0	3	0	8	0	0	6	10a–2p
Science	Top Secret Researcher	8	0	0	0	0	6	7	3	10a–3p
Show Business	Leading Man/Lady	4	10	5	0	7	0	0	9	1p–7p
Slacker	Freelance Photographer	0	0	3	4	3	0	0	7	2p–7p

Days Off	# Work Days	Daily Salary	Weekly Average	Energy	Bladder	Hygiene	Social	Hunger	Fun	Comfort	Game
Sun, Tue, Thu	4	§1,785	§7,140	-5	-8	-4	-2	6	-4	4	University
Tue, Wed, Thu	4	§1,190	§4,760	-35	-56	-28	0	-28	28	-7	The Sims™ 2
Sun & Sat	5	§924	§4,620	-40	-64	-16	48	-32	-8	-8	The Sims™ 2
Tue & Thu	5	§896	§4,480	-30	-6	-24	-42	-24	36	-48	The Sims™ 2
Tue & Thu	5	§812	§4,060	-42	-21	-49	21	3	28	-21	The Sims™ 2
Sun & Sat	5	§826	§4,130	-30	-30	-24	36	-24	24	-24	The Sims™ 2
Sun & Sat	5	§875	§4,375	-30	-48	-12	36	-24	-6	-6	The Sims™ 2
Sun & Sat	5	§812	§4,060	-30	-18	-24	0	-24	24	18	The Sims™ 2
Sun & Sat	4	§1,344	§5,376	-5	-8	-4	-2	6	-4	4	University
Sun & Sat	5	§1,386	§6,930	-5	-8	-4	-2	-6	-4	-4	University
Sun & Sat	5	§840	§4,200	-30	-48	-12	36	-24	-6	-6	The Sims™ 2
Sun & Sat	5	§896	§4,480	-25	-20	-10	30	-20	20	20	The Sims™ 2
Mon, Wed, Fri	4	§1,312	§5,248	-5	-8	-4	-2	6	-4	4	University
Tue, Wed, Thu	4	§613	§2,452	-30	-48	-12	36	-24	-6	-6	The Sims™ 2

Days Off	# Work Days	Daily Salary	Weekly Average	Energy	Bladder	Hygiene	Social	Hunger	Fun	Comfort	Game
Sun, Wed, Fri, Sat	3	§2,232	§6,696	-5	-8	-7	-2	-6	-7	-1	University
Tue, Wed, Thu	4	§1,488	§5,952	-25	-40	-35	0	-35	5	-15	The Sims™ 2
Tue, Sat, Sun	4	§1,400	§5,600	-40	-64	-16	48	-32	8	0	The Sims™ 2
Sun & Sat	5	§1,064	§5,320	-30	-36	-42	-36	-42	18	48	The Sims™ 2
Tue, Wed, Thu	4	§1,208	§4,832	-30	-36	-24	36	3	42	-12	The Sims™ 2
Sun & Sat	5	§875	§4,375	-35	-28	-49	42	-49	42	-49	The Sims™ 2
Sun & Sat	5	§980	§4,900	-30	-48	-12	36	-24	6	-6	The Sims™ 2
Sun & Sat	5	§840	§4,200	-30	0	-18	0	-42	6	42	The Sims™ 2
Tue & Thu	4	§1,554	§6,216	-5	-8	-7	-2	6	-7	1	University
Sun, Tue, Sat	4	§2,100	§8,400	-5	-8	-7	-2	6	-7	1	University
Sat, Sun, Wed	4	§1,138	§4,552	-20	-32	-8	0	-16	4	20	The Sims™ 2
Tue & Thu	5	§1,036	§5,180	-25	-20	-10	-15	-35	40	35	The Sims™ 2
Sun, Wed, Fri, Sat	3	§2,205	§6,615	-5	-8	-7	-2	6	-7	5	University
Tue, Wed, Thu	4	§788	§3,152	-25	-40	-10	30	-20	5	0	The Sims™ 2

Level 9 Careers

Career	Job Name	Logic	Body	Creativity	Mechanical	Charisma	Cooking	Cleaning	Friends	Hours
Artist	Conceptual Artist	0	0	9	8	7	5	0	10	10a–5p
Athletic	Coach	0	10	0	7	7	0	0	6	9a–3p
Business	CEO	7	0	6	0	6	0	0	1	9a–4p
Criminal	Smuggler	0	7	9	7	0	0	0	5	2a–8a
Culinary	Restaurateur	7	0	7	0	0	8	0	6	2p–10p
Law Enforcement	Police Chief	9	7	0	0	0	0	7	8	8a–4p
Medical	Medical Researcher	8	0	0	0	0	0	9	7	11a–6p
Military	Astronaut	0	10	0	6	5	0	0	5	9a–3p
Natural Scientist	Dinosaur Cloner	10	6	0	9	0	0	8	10	11a–6p
Paranormal	Exorcist	0	0	8	0	6	5	8	10	9p–3a
Politics	Senator	8	0	5	0	9	0	0	8	9a–6p
Science	Theorist	9	0	0	0	0	7	9	5	10a–2p
Show Business	Blockbuster Director	5	10	7	0	9	0	0	11	10a–5p
Slacker	Freelance Web Designer	0	0	4	4	4	0	0	10	10a–3p

Level 10 Careers

Career	Job Name	Logic	Body	Creativity	Mechanical	Charisma	Cooking	Cleaning	Friends	Hours
Artist	Visionary	0	0	10	0	7	6	0	13	1p–6p
Athletic	Hall of Famer	0	10	0	7	10	0	0	8	11a–5p
Business	Business Tycoon	9	0	7	0	8	0	0	1	10a–4p
Criminal	Criminal Mastermind	0	8	10	10	0	0	0	7	5p–11p
Culinary	Celebrity Chef	8	0	10	0	0	10	0	7	3p–8p
Law Enforcement	Captain Hero	9	10	0	0	0	0	8	10	10a–4p
Medical	Chief of Staff	10	0	0	0	0	0	10	9	9a–4p
Military	General	0	10	0	8	7	0	0	6	10a–4p
Natural Scientist	Ecological Guru	10	8	0	10	0	0	8	12	12p–9a
Paranormal	Cult Leader	0	0	10	0	10	7	9	13	6p–3a
Politics	Mayor	10	0	7	0	10	0	0	10	10a–4p
Science	Mad Scientist	10	0	0	0	0	9	10	8	10p–2a
Show Business	Icon	6	10	9	0	10	0	0	14	4p–9p
Slacker	Professional Party Guest	0	0	5	4	5	0	0	13	10p–2a

Days Off	# Work Days	Daily Salary	Weekly Average	Energy	Bladder	Hygiene	Social	Hunger	Fun	Comfort	Game
Sun, Thu, Fri, Sat	3	§2,625	§7,875	-4	-8	-2	-2	-6	-4	-3	University
Tue, Wed, Thu	4	§1,750	§7,000	-24	-48	-12	0	-24	18	12	The Sims™ 2
Wed, Sat, Sun	4	§1,663	§6,652	-28	-56	-14	42	-28	7	7	The Sims™ 2
Mon, Tue, Wed	4	§1,575	§6,300	-60	-48	-12	36	-24	18	42	The Sims™ 2
Mon, Tue, Wed	4	§1,330	§5,320	-40	-32	-16	64	3	40	-8	The Sims™ 2
Sun & Mon	5	§910	§4,550	-32	-56	-16	56	-32	56	-16	The Sims™ 2
Fri, Sat, Sun	4	§1,356	§5,424	-28	-56	-14	-7	-28	7	21	The Sims™ 2
Sat, Sun, Mon	4	§1,094	§4,376	-24	-6	-12	0	-24	60	-30	The Sims™ 2
Sun, Mon, Sat	4	§2,283	§9,132	-4	-8	-2	-2	-6	-4	3	University
Mon, Tue, Thu, Sat	3	§2,494	§7,482	-4	-8	-2	-2	6	-4	-3	University
Sat, Sun, Mon	4	§1,225	§4,900	-36	-72	-18	54	-36	27	27	The Sims™ 2
Sun, Mon, Sat	4	§1,522	§6,088	-16	-24	-8	24	-16	12	24	The Sims™ 2
Sun, Wed, Fri, Sat	3	§3,051	§9,153	-4	-8	-2	-2	6	-4	3	University
Fri, Sat, Sun, Mon	3	§933	§2,799	-20	-40	-10	30	-20	5	5	The Sims™ 2

Days Off	# Work Days	Daily Salary	Weekly Average	Energy	Bladder	Hygiene	Social	Hunger	Fun	Comfort	Game
Sun, Mon, Wed, Fri	3	§4,549	§13,647	-4	-8	-2	-2	8	-4	2	University
Fri, Sat, Sun, Mon	3	§3,033	§9,099	-24	-48	-12	0	-24	12	12	The Sims™ 2
Fri, Sat, Sun	4	§2,100	§8,400	-24	-48	-12	48	-24	12	12	The Sims™ 2
Sun, Mon, Wed	4	§1,925	§7,700	-24	-30	-12	-30	-24	36	48	The Sims™ 2
Fri, Sat, Sun, Mon	3	§2,170	§6,510	-20	-20	-10	50	2	45	15	The Sims™ 2
Tue, Wed, Thu	4	§1,225	§4,900	-24	0	-12	48	-3	54	-12	The Sims™ 2
Sat, Sun, Mon	4	§1,488	§5,952	-28	-56	-14	56	-28	14	14	The Sims™ 2
Fri, Sat, Sun	4	§1,138	§4,552	-24	-42	-12	0	-24	12	30	The Sims™ 2
Mon, Tue, Thu, Fri, Sat, Sun	1	§10,497	§10,497	10	10	-10	10	10	10	10	University
Sun, Mon, Wed, Thu, Fri	2	§4,725	§9,450	5	-8	3	4	10	5	10	University
Fri, Sat, Sun	4	§1,313	§5,252	-24	-48	-12	48	-24	30	30	The Sims™ 2
Sun, Mon, Fri, Sat	3	§2,333	§6,999	-16	-12	-28	8	-16	28	12	The Sims™ 2
Sun, Mon, Fri, Sat	3	§5,022	§15,066	-4	-8	-2	-2	10	-4	10	University
Mon, Tue, Wed, Thu	3	§1,400	§4,200	-16	-32	-8	32	-16	8	8	The Sims™ 2

Teen/Elder Careers

Level 1 Careers

Career	Job Name	Logic	Body	Creativity	Mechanical	Charisma	Cooking	Cleaning	Friends	Hours
Athletic	Waterperson	0	0	0	0	0	0	0	0	3p–6p
Business	Gofer	0	0	0	0	0	0	0	0	3p–6p
Criminal	Street Hawker	0	0	0	0	0	0	0	0	3p–6p
Culinary	Dishwasher	0	0	0	0	0	0	0	0	3p–6p
Law Enforcement	School Crossing Guard	0	0	0	0	0	0	0	0	3p–6p
Medical	Nursing Home Attendant	0	0	0	0	0	0	0	0	3p–6p
Military	Paintball Attendant	0	0	0	0	0	0	0	0	3p–6p
Politics	Door to Door Poller	0	0	0	0	0	0	0	0	5p–9p
Science	Lab Glass Scrubber	0	0	0	0	0	0	0	0	3p–6p
Slacker	Golf Caddy	0	0	0	0	0	0	0	0	3p–6p

Level 2 Careers

Career	Job Name	Logic	Body	Creativity	Mechanical	Charisma	Cooking	Cleaning	Friends	Hours
Athletic	Locker Room Attendant	0	1	0	1	0	0	0	1	3p–6p
Business	Mailroom Technician	1	0	0	0	0	0	0	2	3p–6p
Criminal	Numbers Runner	0	0	1	0	0	0	0	1	3p–6p
Culinary	Drive Through Clerk	0	0	0	0	0	1	0	1	5p–9p
Law Enforcement	Parking Lot Attendant	1	1	0	0	0	0	0	1	6p–9p
Medical	Orderly	0	0	0	0	0	0	1	1	3p–6p
Military	Recruit Training Corps	0	0	0	0	1	0	0	1	6p–10p
Politics	Campaign Worker	0	0	0	0	1	0	0	2	3p–6p
Science	Test Subject	1	0	0	0	0	0	0	1	3p–6p
Slacker	Gas Station Attendant	0	0	0	1	0	0	0	2	3p–6p

Level 3 Careers

Career	Job Name	Logic	Body	Creativity	Mechanical	Charisma	Cooking	Cleaning	Friends	Hours
Athletic	Team Mascot	0	2	0	2	1	0	0	0	3p–6p
Business	Executive Assistant	1	0	1	0	1	0	0	6	3p–7p
Criminal	Pickpocket	0	1	2	1	0	0	0	1	3p–6p
Culinary	Fast Food Shift Manager	1	0	1	0	0	1	0	4	5p–10p
Law Enforcement	Security Guard	1	2	0	0	0	0	0	3	9p–1a
Medical	Emergency Medical Technician	0	0	0	2	0	0	2	3	7p–10p
Military	Recruit	0	1	0	0	1	0	0	2	3p–6p
Politics	Intern	1	0	1	0	1	0	0	4	3p–6p
Science	Lab Assistant	1	0	0	0	0	1	1	2	3p–6p
Slacker	Convenience Store Clerk	0	0	1	1	1	0	0	4	5p–9p

Days Off	# Work Days	Daily Salary	Weekly Average	Energy	Bladder	Hygiene	Social	Hunger	Fun	Comfort	Game
Sun & Fri	5	§97	§485	-31	-25	-9	13	-16	-13	-31	The Sims™ 2
Sun & Fri	5	§52	§260	-31	-25	-9	13	-16	-13	-31	The Sims™ 2
Mon & Thu	5	§50	§250	-31	-25	-9	13	-16	-13	-31	The Sims™ 2
Mon & Fri	5	§63	§315	-31	-25	-9	13	-16	-13	-31	The Sims™ 2
Sun & Sat	5	§45	§225	-31	-25	-9	13	-16	-13	-31	The Sims™ 2
Mon & Wed	5	§65	§325	-31	-25	-9	13	-16	-13	-31	The Sims™ 2
Mon & Sat	5	§57	§285	-31	-25	-9	13	-16	-13	-31	The Sims™ 2
Mon & Thu	5	§53	§265	-42	-33	-13	17	-21	-17	-42	The Sims™ 2
Sun & Fri	5	§64	§320	-31	-25	-9	13	-16	-13	-31	The Sims™ 2
Mon & Sat	5	§45	§225	-31	-25	-9	13	-16	-13	-31	The Sims™ 2

Days Off	# Work Days	Daily Salary	Weekly Average	Energy	Bladder	Hygiene	Social	Hunger	Fun	Comfort	Game
Mon & Sat	5	§110	§550	-24	-24	-9	12	-12	-9	-24	The Sims™ 2
Mon & Sat	5	§76	§380	-24	-24	-9	12	-12	-9	-24	The Sims™ 2
Mon & Wed	5	§62	§310	-15	-18	-12	12	-18	9	-6	The Sims™ 2
Mon & Wed	5	§84	§420	-32	-20	-40	-16	-40	-12	-12	The Sims™ 2
Tue & Thu	5	§75	§375	-15	-15	-15	-15	-15	-15	-15	The Sims™ 2
Sun & Wed	5	§87	§435	-24	-24	-21	12	-12	-9	-24	The Sims™ 2
Mon & Wed	5	§77	§385	-24	-24	-60	12	-20	-20	-28	The Sims™ 2
Wed & Sun	5	§72	§360	-27	-18	-18	15	-18	-12	-24	The Sims™ 2
Mon & Sat	5	§105	§525	-21	-21	-6	-9	-21	-21	-18	The Sims™ 2
Mon & Thu	5	§71	§355	-24	-24	-9	12	-12	-9	-24	The Sims™ 2

Days Off	# Work Days	Daily Salary	Weekly Average	Energy	Bladder	Hygiene	Social	Hunger	Fun	Comfort	Game
Sun & Mon	5	§125	§625	-24	-24	-9	12	-12	-9	-24	The Sims™ 2
Sun & Sat	5	§98	§490	-32	-32	-12	16	-16	-12	-32	The Sims™ 2
Wed & Thu	5	§105	§525	-36	-15	-24	-24	-27	-18	-21	The Sims™ 2
Wed & Thu	5	§91	§455	-40	-20	-50	5	-29	-5	-25	The Sims™ 2
Mon & Tue	5	§125	§625	-24	-28	-16	-16	-20	-12	-24	The Sims™ 2
Tue & Thu	5	§125	§625	-24	-24	-24	12	-12	-27	-24	The Sims™ 2
Sun & Wed	5	§100	§500	-30	-15	-30	3	-30	-15	-15	The Sims™ 2
Sun & Sat	5	§112	§560	-24	-24	-9	12	-12	-9	-24	The Sims™ 2
Sun & Sat	5	§115	§575	-24	-15	-30	-12	-30	-6	-21	The Sims™ 2
Mon & Tue	5	§96	§480	-32	-32	-12	16	-16	-12	-32	The Sims™ 2

Object	Price				Category	Game
Antique Metal Sconce	$155	$23	$15	$62	Lighting	The Sims 2
Antonio's Prize-Winning Wedding Cake	$400	$60	$40	$160	Miscellaneous	The Sims 2
Anytime Candles	$100	$15	$10	$40	Decorative	University
AOD Disco Dining Chair	$320	$48	$32	$128	Comfort	The Sims 2
AOD Disco Dining Table	$755	$113	$75	$302	Surfaces	The Sims 2
A Portrait of My First Holiday Memory	$900	$135	$90	$360	Decorative	Holiday
Apple of the Eye	$400	$0	$0	$0	Decorative	Glamour Stuff
AquaBox Five-Gallon Aquarium	$300	$45	$30	$120	Decorative	The Sims 2
AquaGreen Hydroponic Garden	$0	$0	$0	$0	Career	The Sims 2
AquaPlus Shower Stall	$1,100	$165	$110	$440	Plumbing	The Sims 2
Aryhist Soldier	$2,000	$0	$0	$0	Decorative	Glamour Stuff
A Touch of Autumn Cornucopia	$73	$10	$7	$29	Decorative	Holiday
Astrowonder Telescope	$550	$82	$55	$220	Hobbies	The Sims 2
"A Stroke" by Alfred D'Sinvo	$1,700	$0	$0	$0	Decorative	The Sims 2
A Sim Noir Print	$3,000	$450	$300	$1,200	Decorative	Nightlife
Armchair by Club Design	$629	$94	$62	$251	Comfort	The Sims 2
Aunt Julianna's Old Moneymaker	$225	$34	$23	$90	Electronics	Open for Business
Bachman Bushar	$600	$90	$60	$240	Miscellaneous	The Sims 2
Bangee Yenn from Simporters, Ltd.	$700	$0	$0	$0	Decorative	The Sims 2
Banquet Chair by Well Bred and Co.	$1,200	$180	$120	$480	Comfort	The Sims 2
Banquet of Six by Well Bred and Co.	$1,050	$158	$105	$420	Surfaces	The Sims 2
Barococo Loveseat by MiRE	$1,250	$187	$125	$500	Comfort	Nightlife
Barococo Sofa by MiRE	$1,500	$225	$150	$600	Comfort	Nightlife
Basically Bare Bulb from Electric Lighting	$25	$3	$2	$10	Lighting	Nightlife
BeamDlite Compacto Wall Lamp by Ray Diant	$210	$32	$21	$84	Lighting	Nightlife
BeamDlite Extendo Wall Lamp by Ray Diant	$225	$34	$23	$90	Lighting	Nightlife
Beary Cute Pedestal	$600	$0	$0	$0	Decorative	Open for Business
Bed by St. Ajoque Reproductions	$1,200	$180	$120	$480	Comfort	The Sims 2

Chapter 12

OBJECTS

Object Directory

Object	Price	Initial Depreciation	Daily Depreciation	Depreciation Limit	Hunger	Comfort	Hygiene	Bladder	Energy	Fun	Environment	Cleaning	Study	Charisma	Creativity	Body	Logic	Mechanical	Cooking	Function	Kids	Study	Dining Room	Outside	Living Room	Bathroom	Bedroom	Kitchen	Miscellaneous	Street	Outdoor	Shopping	Food	Game
? = (C²)!?	$70	$0	$0	$0	0	0	0	0	0	0	4									Decorative		X	X		X		X		X			X		The Sims 2
12th Century Song Dynasty Sculpted Vase	$470	$0	$0	$0	0	0	0	0	0	0	2									Decorative		X	X		X		X	X	X			X		The Sims 2
#4234 by C. Lee Funkensnooz	$4,000	$0	$0	$0	0	0	0	0	0	0	3									Decorative		X	X		X		X		X			X		Glamour Stuff
4 by 4 Designer Chandelier	$2,200	$330	$220	$880	0	0	0	0	0	0	10									Lighting		X	X		X				X			X		The Sims 2
"52 Pickup" Card Table	$630	$95	$63	$252	0	0	0	0	0	6	0									Hobbies	X	X					X		X			X		Nightlife
Absolutely Nothing Special	$20	$3	$2	$8	0	0	0	0	0	0	2									Decorative		X			X		X		X			X		The Sims 2
Abstrusionism by Gordon Flatcher	$85	$0	$0	$0	0	0	0	0	0	0	3									Decorative		X	X		X		X		X			X		The Sims 2
Ad-a-Quaint Barstool	$5,000	$750	$500	$2,000	0	3	0	0	0	0	0									Comfort			X					X	X			X	X	Glamour Stuff
Ad-a-Quaint Coffee Table	$285	$42	$28	$114	0	0	0	0	0	0	2									Surfaces					X				X			X		The Sims 2
Adorable Ocean Liner	$140	$21	$14	$56	0	0	0	0	0	0	2									Decorative	X	X			X		X		X					Family Fun Stuff
A Fantastic End Table!	$275	$41	$28	$110	0	0	0	0	0	0	2									Surfaces					X		X		X					Family Fun Stuff
Affluent Armoire by Well Bred and Co.	$925	$139	$93	$370	0	0	0	0	0	0	2									Decorative							X		X			X		Glamour Stuff
Alas, a Lamp	$140	$21	$14	$56	0	0	0	0	0	0	2									Lighting		X			X		X		X			X		The Sims 2
Almost Deco Wall Sconce	$340	$51	$34	$136	0	0	0	0	0	0	1									Lighting					X	X	X		X			X		The Sims 2
Aluminium Privacy Blinds by P. King Tom Trading Co.	$80	$12	$8	$32	0	0	0	0	0	0	2									Lighting		X	X		X		X		X			X		Glamour Stuff
A Luxurious Night's Sleep	$184	$27	$18	$73	0	8	0	0	7	0	0									Comfort							X		X			X		Open for Business
An Anonymous Masterpiece	$3,200	$0	$0	$0	0	0	0	0	0	0	4									Decorative		X	X		X		X		X			X		Nightlife
American Tableau Table	$1,050	$157	$105	$420	0	0	0	0	0	0	2									Surfaces			X		X				X					University
A-maz-ing Matey!	$425	$64	$43	$170	0	0	0	0	0	9	0									Decorative	X								X		X	X		Glamour Stuff
Ankle-Height Light by GamGleam Industries	$105	$15	$10	$42	0	0	0	0	0	0	1									Lighting				X		X	X							Nightlife
Ancient Transport Urn Sculpture	$500	$0	$0	$0	0	0	0	0	0	0	2									Decorative				X	X				X			X		Open for Business
Antebellum Wall Lamp	$360	$54	$36	$144	0	0	0	0	0	0	2									Lighting					X	X	X		X			X		The Sims 2
Anti-Quaint-Ed Ltd. Ed. Armoire	$250	$37	$25	$100	0	0	0	0	0	0	2									Miscellaneous							X		X			X		The Sims 2
Anti-Quaint-Ed-Medium Ltd. Ed. Armoire	$235	$35	$23	$94	0	0	0	0	0	0	0									Miscellaneous							X		X			X		Open for Business
Antique Lace Curtains	$165	$24	$16	$66	0	0	0	0	0	0	2									Decorative	X		X		X		X	X	X			X		The Sims 2

Object	Price	Initial Depreciation	Daily Depreciation	Depreciation Limit	Category	Collection
Cantankerous Splatters	$2,750	$0	$0	$0	Decorative	NIGHTLIFE
Caress of Teak Bed	$450	$67	$45	$180	Comfort	THE SIMS 2
"Castanoga" Counter by Wood You Believe Furnishings	$680	$102	$68	$272	Surfaces	NIGHTLIFE
Catamaran Kitchen Island	$210	$31	$21	$84	Surfaces	NIGHTLIFE
Cat-A-Strophic Luminous Lawn Ornament	$99	$14	$10	$21	Decorative	THE SIMS 2
Centerpieces Coffee Table	$370	$55	$37	$148	Surfaces	THE SIMS 2
Chabadii Chabudinky	$265	$39	$26	$106	Surfaces	THE SIMS 2
Chabadii "Yet Another" Coffee Table	$290	$43	$29	$116	Surfaces	HOLIDAY
Chair de la Mer	$170	$26	$17	$68	Comfort	THE SIMS 2
Chanukah Menorah	$91	$13	$9	$36	Decorative	HOLIDAY
Charming Reflections Mirror	$690	$104	$69	$276	Decorative	NIGHTLIFE
Chazz Bassed Incandescent Floor Tile	$30	$5	$3	$12	Decorative	THE SIMS 2
Cheap Eazzzze Morrissey Double Bed	$450	$67	$45	$180	Comfort	THE SIMS 2
Cheap Eazzzze Puffy Recliner	$515	$77	$51	$206	Comfort	THE SIMS 2
Chesterstick Cherry Dresser	$2,125	$318	$212	$850	Miscellaneous	THE SIMS 2
Chez Moi French Country Counters	$900	$135	$90	$360	Surfaces	THE SIMS 2
Chez Chaise	$800	$120	$80	$320	Comfort	THE SIMS 2
Chiclettina Executrone Desk	$790	$118	$79	$316	Surfaces	THE SIMS 2
Chiclettina "Archipelago" Kitchen Island	$500	$75	$50	$200	Surfaces	THE SIMS 2
Chiclettina "Fjord" All purpose Counter	$1,000	$150	$100	$400	Surfaces	THE SIMS 2
Chiclettina "Fjord" Kitchen Counter	$490	$73	$49	$196	Surfaces	GLAMOUR STUFF
Chiclettina "Sardinia" Kitchen Counter	$750	$113	$75	$300	Surfaces	NIGHTLIFE
Chiclettina "Sardinia" Kitchen Island	$780	$117	$78	$312	Surfaces	FAMILY FUN STUFF
Children Safety Sign	$70	$0	$0	$0	Decorative	NIGHTLIFE
Chimeway & Daughters Saloon Piano	$3,500	$525	$350	$1,400	Hobbies	THE SIMS 2
Chinese Opera Mask by Old Face	$150	$0	$0	$0	Decorative	THE SIMS 2

Object Directory

Object	Price	Initial Depreciation	Daily Depreciation	Depreciation Limit	Hunger	Comfort	Hygiene	Bladder	Energy	Fun	Environment	Cleaning	Study (Skill)	Charisma	Creativity	Body	Logic	Mechanical	Cooking	Function	Kids	Study (Room)	Dining Room	Outside	Living Room	Bathroom	Bedroom	Kitchen	Miscellaneous	Street	Outdoor	Shopping	Food	Game
Bella Squared	$1,000	$0	$0	$0							7									Decorative		X	X		X		X					X		The Sims 2
"Belle Epoque" Tiffany Wall Lamp by Frufru Lighting Design	$300	$45	$30	$120							2									Decorative Lighting		X	X	X			X		X			X		Nightlife
Berge the Proliferating Reindeer	$300	$45	$30	$120							2									Decorative				X							X			Holiday
Be There Designs "Bazaar Sofa"	$800	$120	$80	$320		8			2		3									Comfort					X							X	X	The Sims 2
Bibliofile Bookcase	$400	$60	$40	$160							1									Hobbies		X					X					X		Nightlife
"Bigger is Better" Wall Mirror by ExPand	$580	$87	$58	$232							2			X						Decorative						X	X					X		The Sims 2
Bit O'This and That	$150	$22	$15	$60							1	X						X		Surfaces		X			X								X	University
Black Lacquer Bar Counter	$1,000	$150	$100	$400														X	X	Miscellaneous								X	X				X	University
Blazin' Buckaroos Lantern	$50	$7	$5	$20							1									Lighting	X			X							X			The Sims 2
Blinding Soldier Wall Lamp	$230	$34	$23	$92																Lighting		X	X		X	X	X	X				X		The Sims 2
Blooms & Boomers End Table	$120	$18	$12	$48																Surfaces					X		X					X		The Sims 2
Blossoming Heart	$485	$0	$0	$0							4									Decorative			X		X		X		X	X				Nightlife
Blue Sky Bonsai Tree	$99	$14	$9	$39							2									Decorative		X			X							X		The Sims 2
Blue Suede Chair	$611	$91	$61	$244		7			3		2									Comfort			X		X								X	The Sims 2
Bon Appetit Dining Chair	$150	$22	$15	$60		3														Comfort			X					X					X	The Sims 2
Bowl of Plastic Fruit	$1,100	$165	$110	$440							1									Decorative			X		X			X					X	Nightlife
Brand Name "EconoCool" Refrigerator	$600	$90	$60	$240	1															Appliances								X	X					University
Brand Name Zip Zap	$250	$37	$25	$100																Appliances				X						X	X			University
Brand Name MetalKettle Microwave	$299	$44	$29	$120	2															Appliances								X					X	Nightlife
"3 Stroke" by Alfred D'Sirvo	$1,700	$0	$0	$0							10									Decorative		X	X		X		X		X			X		The Sims 2
Bubble-Up "Soaking Zone" Hot Tub	$6,500	$975	$650	$2,600		6				7	9									Plumbing				X							X			The Sims 2
Bureaucratic Bureau by Well Bred and Co.	$1,300	$195	$130	$520							2									Surfaces	X	X							X					The Sims 2
Burled Wood Dartboard	$180	$27	$18	$72						7	1									Hobbies	X										X			The Sims 2
Burnished Blaze Torchiere	$199	$29	$19	$79							1									Lighting		X	X	X			X				X			Glamour Stuff
Bust of Tylopoda	$3,130	$0	$0	$0							10									Decorative	X	X	X	X								X		Nightlife
Cafeteria-Style Steelate Counter Island	$810	$121	$81	$324							2									Surfaces								X					X	University
Candy Coated Sofa	$1,570	$235	$157	$628		10			2		2									Comfort	X				X							X		The Sims 2

Object	Price	Init. Depr.	Daily Depr.	Depr. Limit	(need / motive grid)								Category	Game
Colonial Ironwood Bed	$3,000	$450	$300	$1,200	0	7	0	0	6	0	0	5	Comfort	The Sims 2
Coloratura by Chrome Concepts	$1,500	$225	$150	$600	0	0	0	10	0	0	0	3	Plumbing	The Sims 2
Coming Up Roses Loveseat by OakTowne	$220	$33	$22	$96	0	6	0	0	0	0	0	2	Comfort	The Sims 2
Compact Stereo by Lo-Fi Audio	$99	$14	$9	$39	0	0	0	0	0	2	0	0	Electronics	The Sims 2
"Compulsion" Fragrance Display	$3,500	$525	$350	$1,400	0	0	0	0	0	0	0	0	Miscellaneous	Nightlife
Contempto Adirondack Chair	$400	$60	$40	$160	0	7	0	0	0	0	0	2	Comfort	The Sims 2
Contempto Adirondack End Table	$450	$67	$45	$180	0	0	0	0	0	0	0	0	Surfaces	The Sims 2
Contempto Adirondack Loveseat	$90	$13	$9	$36	0	6	0	0	0	0	0	0	Comfort	The Sims 2
Contempto Good Livin' Chair	$80	$12	$8	$32	0	4	0	0	0	0	0	0	Comfort	The Sims 2
Contempto Outdoor Living Lounge	$420	$63	$42	$168	0	6	0	0	0	0	0	0	Comfort	The Sims 2
Contempto Penn Station	$310	$46	$31	$124	0	7	0	0	0	0	0	0	Comfort	Nightlife
"Contorta" Dining Chair by Ernesto Doloroso	$850	$128	$85	$340	0	4	0	0	0	0	0	2	Comfort	Glamour Stuff
"Contorta" Side Chair	$46	$31	$42	$168	0	6	0	0	0	0	0	0	Comfort	University
Convex Stoneware by Simporters Inc.	$375	$0	$0	$0	0	0	0	0	0	0	0	3	Decorative	Holiday
Cool Shades	$0	$0	$0	$0	0	0	0	0	0	0	0	0	Decorative	University
CDPG Garland	$8	$1	$0	$3	0	0	0	0	0	0	0	5	Aspiration	Holiday
Corner Pocket Pool Table	$1,800	$270	$180	$720	0	0	0	0	0	10	0	1	Hobbies	The Sims 2
Cornerstone "Sentinel" End Table	$1,200	$180	$120	$480	0	0	0	0	0	0	0	3	Surfaces	The Sims 2
Cornerstone Veritable Vanity	$250	$37	$25	$100	0	0	0	0	0	0	0	2	Decorative	The Sims 2
Cornerstone Victoriana Velvet Drapes	$250	$37	$25	$100	0	0	0	0	0	0	0	0	Decorative	The Sims 2
Corporal Filbert	$450	$67	$45	$180	0	0	0	0	0	0	0	2	Decorative	The Sims 2
Counter Cooking Conundrum	$810	$121	$81	$324	0	0	0	0	0	0	4	0	Surfaces	Holiday
Counter Culture "Surface"	$200	$30	$20	$80	0	0	0	0	0	0	0	2	Surfaces	The Sims 2
Counter Productive Work Surface	$750	$112	$75	$300	0	0	0	0	0	0	0	0	Surfaces	The Sims 2
CounterRevolution Commercial Counter	$750	$112	$75	$300	0	0	0	0	0	0	0	2	Surfaces	The Sims 2
Countertop Game Display from Group Interaction LTD.	$3,500	$525	$350	$1,400	0	0	0	0	0	0	4	9	Miscellaneous	The Sims 2
Country Comfort Corner Table	$110	$16	$11	$44	0	0	0	0	0	0	0	0	Surfaces	The Sims 2

Object Directory

The following table spans these grouped columns: **Price and Depreciation** (Price, Initial Depreciation, Daily Depreciation, Depreciation Limit); **Needs** (Hunger, Comfort, Hygiene, Bladder, Energy, Fun, Environment); **Skills** (Cleaning, Study, Charisma, Creativity, Body, Logic, Mechanical, Cooking); **Function**; **Room Sort** (Kids, Study, Dining Room, Outside, Living Room, Bathroom, Bedroom, Kitchen); **Community Sort** (Miscellaneous, Street, Outdoor, Shopping, Food); and the source game/expansion.

Object	Price	Initial Depreciation	Daily Depreciation	Depreciation Limit	Hunger	Comfort	Hygiene	Bladder	Energy	Fun	Environment	Cleaning	Study	Charisma	Creativity	Body	Logic	Mechanical	Cooking	Function	Kids	Study	Dining Room	Outside	Living Room	Bathroom	Bedroom	Kitchen	Miscellaneous	Street	Outdoor	Shopping	Food	Game
Chinese Riddle Lantern	$175	$26	$17	$70	0	0	0	0	0	0	1									Lighting			X	X	X		X	X		X	X			The Sims 2
Christmas Tree	$295	$44	$30	$118	0	0	0	0	0	0	2									Decorative				X	X						X			Holiday
Ciao Time Bovinia Refrigerator Model BRRR	$1,500	$225	$150	$600	0	0	0	0	0	0	1									Appliances								X	X				X	The Sims 2
Ciao Time Espresso Machine	$450	$67	$45	$180	0	0	0	-1	3	2	2									Appliances			X					X	X				X	The Sims 2
Ciao Time "Mondo Fuego" Gas Stove	$650	$97	$65	$260	0	0	0	0	0	0	1							X	X	Appliances								X	X				X	The Sims 2
CinderBooks by Retratech	$200	$30	$20	$80	4	0	0	0	0	0	0	X								Hobbies	X	X	X		X		X		X					University
Circle of Light Friendship Lamp	$215	$32	$21	$86	0	0	0	0	0	1	1									Lighting			X		X	X	X		X					Nightlife
City Dweller "Dims"	$70	$10	$7	$28	0	0	0	0	3	0	1									Lighting				X	X		X		X		X			Nightlife
Civic Idol by Adora Wall Arts	$50	$0	$0	$0	0	0	0	0	0	0	1									Decorative		X			X							X		The Sims 2
Clean Water Shower System	$625	$93	$62	$250	0	0	8	0	0	0	5									Plumbing						X			X					The Sims 2
Clotheshorse Display Rack	$3,000	$450	$300	$1,200	0	0	0	0	0	0	0									Miscellaneous							X		X			X		The Sims 2
Club Distress Butcher's Block	$240	$36	$24	$96	0	0	0	0	0	0	0									Surfaces								X	X				X	Nightlife
Club Distress Square Coffee Table	$155	$23	$15	$62	0	0	0	0	0	0	0									Surfaces					X				X					Nightlife
Club Distress Wall Mirror	$580	$87	$58	$232	0	0	0	0	0	0	0			X						Decorative					X	X	X		X					Nightlife
Club Room Countertop	$600	$90	$60	$240	0	0	0	0	0	0	0									Surfaces								X	X			X		Open for Business
Club Room Countertop	$600	$90	$60	$240	0	0	0	0	0	0	0									Surfaces								X	X			X		Open for Business
Club Room Countertop	$600	$90	$60	$240	0	0	0	0	0	0	0									Surfaces								X	X			X		Open for Business
Club Distress Avignon Rectangular Coffee Table	$610	$91	$61	$244	0	0	0	0	0	0	0									Surfaces					X				X					Nightlife
ClubCube by Luminescent Projections	$65	$10	$7	$26	0	0	0	0	0	0	0									Lighting			X		X				X					Nightlife
Coffee for Four by Well Bred and Co.	$350	$53	$35	$140	0	0	0	0	0	0	0									Surfaces					X				X					University
Cold Warrior Light	$190	$28	$19	$76	0	0	0	0	0	0	1									Lighting			X		X		X		X					The Sims 2
Collectible Franky Bear	$250	$0	$0	$0	0	0	0	0	0	0	2									Decorative	X						X					X		Glamour Stuff
College in Black and White	$300	$0	$0	$0	0	0	0	0	0	0	4									Decorative		X	X	X	X		X					X		University
College Public Phone	$550	$82	$55	$220	0	0	0	0	0	0	0									Electronics		X	X		X	X	X	X	X					University
Colonial Bathtub by Imperial Plumbing Works	$1,800	$270	$180	$720	0	8	10	0	0	0	3									Plumbing						X			X					The Sims 2
Colonial ComboClean by Imperial Plumbing Works	$2,200	$330	$220	$880	0	8	8	0	0	0	4									Plumbing						X			X					The Sims 2

Item	Price 1	Price 2	Price 3	Price 4	Category	Game/Expansion
DinCo's Fountain of Fiery Jubilations	$75	$11	$8	$0	Miscellaneous	HOLIDAY
DinCo "Sparks N' Stuff"	$169	$30	$8	$0	Miscellaneous	The Sims 2
Discourse Dining Table	$1,200	$80	$20	$80	Surfaces	The Sims 2
Don Meswithis Bunny Pennant	$65	$0	$0	$480	Decorative	University
Double-Helix Designer Bookshelf	$650	$87	$65	$260	Hobbies	The Sims 2
Doublewide Tieback Curtains	$400	$60	$40	$160	Decorative	University
Downbeat Kit	$3,100	$585	$390	$1,560	Hobbies	The Sims 2
Downhill Snowmanning	$130	$19	$13	$52	Decorative	HOLIDAY
Dreams Alight by Guildsmen Industries	$125	$19	$13	$50	Lighting	The Sims 2
Dreams of a Gifted Mind	$35	$0	$0	$0	Decorative	The Sims 2
Dr. Vu's Automated Cosmetic Surgeon	$0	$0	$0	$0	Career	University
Dry Land Flotation Device	$250	$38	$25	$100	Decorative	The Sims 2
Durable Value Sofa	$250	$37	$25	$100	Comfort	The Sims 2
Durably Plush Teddy Bear	$49	$7	$4	$19	Miscellaneous	FAMILY FUN STUFF
Dynasty Armoire	$560	$84	$56	$224	Miscellaneous	The Sims 2
Dynasty Dining Chair	$45	$62	$41	$166	Comfort	The Sims 2
Dynasty Dresser 2	$900	$135	$90	$360	Miscellaneous	The Sims 2
Dynasty "Enlightenment" Lamp	$95	$14	$9	$38	Lighting	The Sims 2
El Sol Sofa by Gunter	$1,390	$208	$139	$556	Comfort	OPEN FOR BUSINESS
ElectroDance Sphere by Liminterse Unlimited	$3,500	$525	$350	$1,400	Electronics	The Sims 2
Election Day Retro Space-Age Action Pinball	$1,750	$262	$175	$700	Hobbies	NIGHTLIFE
Electrono-Ticket Machine	$499	$74	$49	$199	Electronics	OPEN FOR BUSINESS
Elegant Chef FlameBay Gas Range	$800	$135	$80	$360	Appliances	The Sims 2
Elixir of Life	$0	$0	$0	$0	Aspiration	The Sims 2
Empress's New Clothes Rack	$5,000	$750	$500	$2,000	Miscellaneous	The Sims 2
End-to-End Table	$135	$20	$13	$54	Surfaces	The Sims 2
Engineered Angst Full-Color Poster	$40	$0	$0	$0	Decorative	The Sims 2
Engineered Angst Poster in Red	$40	$0	$0	$0	Decorative	The Sims 2

Object Directory

Object	Price	Initial Depreciation	Daily Depreciation	Depreciation Limit	Hunger	Comfort	Hygiene	Bladder	Energy	Fun	Environment	Cleaning	Study	Charisma	Creativity	Body	Logic	Mechanical	Cooking	Function	Kids	Study (Room)	Dining Room	Outside	Living Room	Bathroom	Bedroom	Kitchen	Misc.	Street	Outdoor	Shopping	Food	Game
Courtly Sleeper Day Dreamer	$700	$105	$70	$280	0	3	0	0	3	0	2									Comfort							X					X		The Sims 2
Cowboy's Caboose Chair	$385	$57	$38	$154	0	5	0	0	0	7	0									Comfort					X		X		X			X		The Sims 2
Cozmo MP3 Player	$195	$0	$0	$0	0	0	0	0	0	0	0									Personal	X			X					X			X		Nightlife
Cozy Colonial End Table	$400	$60	$40	$160	0	0	0	0	0	0	0									Surfaces		X	X		X		X	X				X		The Sims 2
Craftmeister Booknook	$250	$37	$25	$100	0	0	0	0	2	0	0									Hobbies		X			X		X					X		The Sims 2
Craftmeister's Pine Bed	$300	$45	$30	$120	0	2	0	0	2	0	0									Comfort							X					X		The Sims 2
Crazy 8 Table	$65	$9	$6	$26	0	0	0	0	0	0	0									Surfaces			X	X				X				X	X	University
"C Stroke" by Alfred D'Simvo	$1,700	$0	$0	$0	0	0	0	0	0	0	10									Decorative		X	X		X		X					X		The Sims 2
Curvaceous Colonial End Table	$430	$64	$43	$136	0	0	0	0	0	0	0									Surfaces		X	X		X		X		X			X		Nightlife
CyberChronometer Alarm Clock	$60	$9	$6	$24	0	0	0	0	0	0	0									Electronics							X					X		The Sims 2
Dahlen Library Bookcases	$700	$105	$70	$280	0	0	0	0	0	1	1					X				Hobbies		X			X		X					X		University
Daisy Bouquet	$40	$6	$4	$16	0	0	0	0	0	0	2									Decorative			X	X	X		X					X	X	Open for Business
Dancing Fiend Jukebox	$1,100	$165	$110	$440	0	0	0	0	0	9	1					X				Electronics			X	X	X			X				X	X	Nightlife
Dangling Daylight Ceiling Lamp	$145	$21	$14	$58	0	0	0	0	0	0	2									Lighting		X	X	X	X		X	X				X	X	University
Deceptico Piano Glass	$580	$87	$58	$232	0	0	0	0	0	3	3				X					Decorative				X	X		X					X	X	Open for Business
Decorative House Armoire	$550	$82	$55	$220	0	0	0	0	0	2	2									Miscellaneous		X	X		X		X					X	X	The Sims 2
Decra-Chill Display by Refrigifreeze	$800	$149	$99	$399	0	0	0	0	0	0	0	X						X	X	Surfaces			X					X				X	X	Open for Business
Deep Blue Sleep System	$470	$71	$47	$188	—	1	0	0	1	0	0									Comfort							X					X		Family Fun Stuff
Deep Sleeper by Igor and Sons	$1,500	$225	$150	$600	0	7	0	0	7	0	2									Comfort							X		X			X		Nightlife
Deluxe Magazine Rack	$2,500	$375	$250	$1,000	0	0	0	0	0	4	7									Miscellaneous	X	X	X		X		X	X	X			X	X	The Sims 2
Deluxe Veil of Dreams	$150	$72	$15	$60	0	0	0	0	0	0	2									Decorative		X	X		X		X		X			X	X	The Sims 2
Dialectric ReadyPrep Range	$400	$60	$40	$60	0	0	0	0	0	0	0									Appliances	X		X				X	X				X	X	The Sims 2
Diamondback by Desert Designs	$900	$135	$90	$360	0	7	0	0	7	0	2									Comfort			X	X	X		X	X				X	X	The Sims 2
"Diamonds Forever" Wall Light	$500	$75	$50	$200	0	0	0	0	0	0	2									Lighting		X	X	X	X		X	X	X			X	X	Nightlife
DinCo "Box A' Noise"	$99	$15	$10	$40	0	0	0	0	0	5	0									Miscellaneous				X					X					Holiday
DinCo "Box O' Blasts"	$150	$23	$15	$60	0	0	0	0	0	2	0									Miscellaneous									X					Holiday
DinCo's Crackers	$50	$8	$5	$20	0	0	0	0	0	0	0									Miscellaneous									X					Holiday

Object	Price	Initial Deprec.	Daily Deprec.	Deprec. Limit	Category	Expansion Pack
Fancifully Fuzzy Fern	$170	$25	$17	$68	Decorative	The Sims™ 2
Fancy Fairy by OgreCorp	$190	$29	$19	$76	Decorative	Family Fun Stuff
Fancy Sycophancy Mirror	$1,400	$210	$140	$560	Decorative	Glamour Stuff
Farstar e3 Telescope	$2,100	$315	$210	$840	Hobbies	The Sims™ 2
Fat City Counters	$630	$95	$63	$252	Surfaces	University
Fearless Flyin' 4000 Treadmill	$2,250	$337	$225	$900	Hobbies	Nightlife
Feckless Accessories for the Kitchen	$70	$0	$0	$0	Decorative	Nightlife
FestiValue "HoliTime" Table Small	$405	$60	$40	$162	Surfaces	Holiday
FestiValue "HoliTime" Table Large	$855	$128	$85	$342	Surfaces	Holiday
FestiValue "HoliTime" Table	$815	$122	$81	$326	Surfaces	Holiday
Fighting Llamas Pennant	$65	$0	$0	$0	Decorative	The Sims™ 2
Fighting Llamas Tri-Pennant Combo	$65	$0	$0	$0	Decorative	University
Fighting Piranhas Tri-Pennant Combo	$65	$0	$0	$0	Decorative	University
Filigree Facebowl by Imperial Plumbing Works	$610	$91	$61	$244	Plumbing	University
First Class Shelves by Well Bred and Co.	$900	$135	$90	$360	Hobbies	The Sims™ 2
First Mate's Desk	$140	$21	$14	$56	Surfaces	Nightlife
Fists of Bunny Poster	$45	$0	$0	$0	Decorative	University
"Five Diamonds" Wall Light	$130	$20	$13	$52	Lighting	Nightlife
FLATWOOD Dining Table by Iseeya	$450	$67	$45	$180	Surfaces	University
Flickering Mercenary Table Lamp	$195	$29	$19	$78	Lighting	The Sims™ 2
Flight-Away Model Plane	$250	$0	$0	$0	Decorative	The Sims™ 2
Floor-Length Tieback Curtains	$335	$50	$33	$134	Decorative	The Sims™ 2
Floral Fancy Hanging Lamp	$445	$66	$44	$178	Lighting	The Sims™ 2
Floral Fantasy Sofa by OakTowne	$360	$54	$36	$144	Comfort	The Sims™ 2
Floral Sink	$330	$49	$33	$132	Plumbing	The Sims™ 2
Florid Font	$5,800	$0	$0	$0	Decorative	Nightlife
Flowin' Protozoan Double Bed	$520	$78	$52	$208	Comfort	University

Object Directory

Object	Price	Initial Depreciation	Daily Depreciation	Depreciation Limit	Hunger	Comfort	Hygiene	Bladder	Energy	Fun	Environment	Cleaning	Study	Charisma	Creativity	Body	Logic	Mechanical	Cooking	Function	Kids	Study	Dining Room	Outside	Living Room	Bathroom	Bedroom	Kitchen	Miscellaneous	Street	Outdoor	Shopping	Food	Expansion
Entablature Brightener Wall Sconce	$285	$42	$28	$114	0	0	0	0	0	0	—									Lighting		X	X		X	X	X	X	X			X	X	Open for Business
Enterprise Office Concepts Bushmaster Tele-Prompter	$0	$0	$0	$0	0	0	0	0	0	5	10									Career		X							X					The Sims 2
Enterprise Office Freestanding Game Rack	$4,000	$600	$400	$1,600	0	0	0	0	0	4	4									Miscellaneous	X	X			X				X			X		The Sims 2
Epikouros "Sleek Cuisine" Counter	$325	$48	$32	$130	0	0	0	0	0	0	2									Surfaces						X		X				X	X	The Sims 2
Epikouros "Sleek Cuisine" Island	$335	$50	$33	$134	0	0	0	0	0	0	2									Surfaces								X					X	The Sims 2
ErgoSupreme Dining Chair	$1,000	$150	$100	$472	0	7	0	0	0	0	10									Comfort			X		X		X					X	X	The Sims 2
Erratic Glass by Van Mel	$2,100	$315	$210	$840	0	0	0	0	0	0	2			X						Decorative			X		X		X		X			X	X	Glamour Stuff
Euro-Torchiere Floor Lamp	$400	$60	$40	$160	0	0	0	0	0	0	—									Lighting		X	X		X		X	X	X			X	X	The Sims 2
EverFlow Plutonium Rod	$75	$26	$17	$70	0	0	0	0	0	0	—									Lighting		X	X		X		X	X	X			X	X	Nightlife
EverFlow Uranium Rod	$70	$26	$18	$68	0	0	0	0	0	0	1									Lighting		X	X		X		X	X	X			X	X	Nightlife
Exceptionally Expensive Clothing Collator	$5,000	$750	$500	$2,000	0	0	0	0	0	0	—			X						Miscellaneous						X		X	X					Nightlife
Exclaim! Sign	$71	$0	$0	$0	0	0	0	0	0	0	1									Decorative									X					Open for Business
Execuputter	$0	$0	$0	$0	0	0	0	0	0	4	—									Career		X	X		X		X		X				X	The Sims 2
Exerto 5000 Multipress Exercise Machine	$1,400	$210	$140	$560	0	0	0	0	0	3	2					X				Hobbies		X	X		X		X		X			X		The Sims 2
Exerto Butterfly Exercise Machine	$900	$135	$90	$360	0	0	0	0	0	0	2					X				Hobbies		X			X				X					University
Exerto Free Press Exercise Machine	$900	$135	$90	$360	0	0	0	0	0	0	2					X				Hobbies		X	X		X				X					University
Exerto Leg Extension Exercise Machine	$900	$135	$90	$360	0	0	0	0	0	0	2					X				Hobbies		X			X				X					University
Exerto Punching Bag	$0	$0	$0	$0	0	0	0	-1	0	1	—					X				Career					X				X					University
Exerto Selfflog Obstacle Course	$0	$0	$0	$0	0	0	0	0	0	6	—					X				Career				X					X		X			University
Exotic (Non)Screen from Simports, Ltd.	$900	$135	$90	$360	0	0	0	0	0	0	6									Decorative			X		X		X		X			X		The Sims 2
Exotic Reflections Mirror	$340	$51	$34	$136	0	0	0	0	0	0	2			X						Decorative			X			X	X		X			X		The Sims 2
Exploding Dragon Dining Table	$755	$113	$75	$302	0	0	0	0	0	0	2									Surfaces			X					X				X	X	The Sims 2
Extra Pep Coffeemaker	$85	$12	$8	$34	0	0	0	-1	3	0	0									Appliances								X				X	X	The Sims 2
Falling Fern	$111	$16	$11	$44	0	0	0	0	0	0	1									Decorative			X	X	X	X	X	X	X	X	X	X	X	The Sims 2
Fallorayne Fountain	$625	$0	$0	$0	0	0	0	0	0	0	10									Decorative				X					X		X			University

Item	Price				Category	Game
Gingerbread House	$60	$9	$6	$24	Decorative	Holiday
Gleeful Welcome Mat by GleeCo	$375	$56	$37	$150	Decorative	Open For Business
Gliteri & Co. Trieste End Table	$310	$46	$31	$124	Surfaces	The Sims 2
Globe L'Empereur	$350	$53	$35	$140	Decorative	Open For Business
Good Taste Dining Table	$400	$60	$40	$160	Surfaces	Nightlife
Good Witch Counters	$790	$118	$79	$316	Surfaces	Nightlife
Great Taste Dining Table	$810	$122	$81	$324	Surfaces	Open For Business
Grand Parlour Chess Table	$500	$75	$50	$200	Hobbies	University
GreetMe Mat by GleeCo	$425	$63	$42	$170	Decorative	Nightlife
Hanging Flower by Capur Ceramics	$100	$15	$10	$40	Decorative	Nightlife
Handle and Spout	$2,500	$0	$0	$0	Decorative	Glamour Stuff
Ha-hye-tal Mask	$3,000	$0	$0	$0	Decorative	Glamour Stuff
Groovy Dresser by Keen Co.	$425	$63	$42	$170	Miscellaneous	Nightlife
"Grilled Cheese" by Renu Tumush	$850	$0	$0	$0	Decorative	Nightlife
Head on Marble	$4,200	$630	$420	$1,680	Decorative	Nightlife
Here and There Thing	$280	$42	$28	$112	Surfaces	Nightlife
High-Class Dresser by Well Bred and Co.	$520	$78	$52	$208	Miscellaneous	Open For Business
Hipster Barstool by Big Daddy	$340	$51	$34	$136	Comfort	The Sims 2
Hipster Metal Chair by Big Daddy	$350	$53	$35	$140	Comfort	The Sims 2
Hipster Mosaic in Pink	$150	$22	$15	$60	Decorative	Holiday
Hold Me Closer by Tiny Dresser Co.	$2,000	$300	$200	$800	Miscellaneous	Holiday
Holiday Bow	$15	$2	$1	$6	Decorative	Holiday
Holiday Candle	$23	$3	$2	$9	Decorative	Holiday
Holiday in Leukerbad	$2,600	$390	$260	$1,040	Decorative	Holiday
Holiday Wreath	$15	$2	$1	$6	Decorative	The Sims 2
Home Office Desk by Quaint Design	$220	$33	$22	$88	Surfaces	Holiday
Hosta La Vista	$60	$9	$9	$36	Decorative	The Sims 2
Hunka 711 by Hwang Motors	$11,950	$1,793	$1,195	$4,780	Miscellaneous	Nightlife
Hydronomic CleenSheen Basin	$410	$61	$41	$164	Plumbing	The Sims 2

Object Directory

Object	Price	Initial Depreciation	Daily Depreciation	Depreciation Limit	Hunger	Comfort	Hygiene	Bladder	Energy	Fun	Environment	Cleaning	Study	Charisma	Creativity	Body	Logic	Mechanical	Cooking	Function	Kids	Study	Dining Room	Outside	Living Room	Bathroom	Bedroom	Kitchen	Miscellaneous	Street	Outdoor	Shopping	Food	Game
Flowin' Protozoan Single Bed	$620	$63	$62	$248		3			3		1									Comfort							X					X		THE SIMS 2
Food Shrine Commercial Display Freezer	$5,000	$750	$500	$2,000						4	5									Appliances		X	X		X			X				X	X	OPEN FOR BUSINESS
Food Temple Commercial Display Freezer	$5,000	$750	$500	$2,000						4	5									Appliances		X	X		X			X				X	X	UNIVERSITY
Foulbreath's Mat	$225	$34	$23	$90							1									Decorative	X	X	X	X	X	X	X		X		X	X		THE SIMS 2
Founding Fathers Electric Lamp	$235	$35	$23	$94																Lighting	X	X			X		X		X			X		OPEN FOR BUSINESS
Fountain of Opulence	$1,000	$150	$100	$400							7									Decorative				X							X			THE SIMS 2
Four Dead Guys Luminous Lawn Ornament	$99	$14	$10	$21							1									Decorative				X							X			THE SIMS 2
Four Vegetables in Repose	$325	$0	$0	$0							3									Decorative		X	X		X		X		X			X		THE SIMS 2
Frost de Fleur Bud Vase	$30	$4	$3	$12							1									Decorative		X	X		X		X		X			X		FAMILY FUN STUFF
Fruitless Fig Tree	$333	$49	$33	$133							2									Decorative		X	X	X	X		X		X		X	X		GLAMOUR STUFF
Functional Eloquence Mirror	$600	$90	$60	$240										X						Decorative						X	X		X			X		THE SIMS 2
Fun-Kadelic Frequency Stereo System from Kauker Inc.	$375	$56	$37	$150						9				X						Electronics	X	X			X		X		X			X		THE SIMS 2
Funky the Snowman	$99	$14	$9	$39							4									Decorative				X					X					THE SIMS 2
Fusty Hors D'oeuvres	$700	$105	$70	$280					5	4										Miscellaneous			X		X		X	X	X				X	HOLIDAY
Futonesque Fantasy Sofa	$180	$27	$18	$72		5			2		3									Comfort		X	X		X									UNIVERSITY
Gagmia Simore "RefuseNik" Trash Compactor	$375	$56	$37	$150							3									Appliances								X					X	THE SIMS 2
Garden Fresh Pedestal Sink	$355	$53	$35	$142																Plumbing						X						X		THE SIMS 2
Garden Glow Spotlight	$35	$5	$3	$14							1									Lighting				X							X			THE SIMS 2
"Gastronomique" Restaurant Podium	$200	$30	$20	$80																Miscellaneous													X	NIGHTLIFE
GazeEase "Stow 'N' Show" Produce Bin	$3,000	$450	$300	$1,200																Appliances								X				X	X	THE SIMS 2
GentleGlow Table Lamp	$120	$18	$12	$48							1									Lighting		X			X		X		X		X	X		THE SIMS 2
Genuine Buck's Famous Counterfeiting Machine	$0	$0	$0	$0																Aspiration	X	X												UNIVERSITY
Geometry 101 by Mrs. Wieprecht	$2,200	$0	$0	$0							10									Decorative	X	X	X		X		X		X			X		OPEN FOR BUSINESS
Get Up! Alarm Clock	$30	$4	$3	$12																Electronics							X		X			X		THE SIMS 2

Object	Price	Depreciation (Start)	Depreciation (Daily)	Depreciation (Limit)	Category	Expansion Pack
Just Shelves	$400	$60	$40	$160	Surfaces	The Sims 2
Keister Kumpanion Barstool	$185	$27	$18	$74	Comfort	Open for Business
Kepler's Celestial Wall Mirror	$475	$72	$48	$190	Decorative	The Sims 2
Kepler's Planetary Floor Mirror	$550	$83	$55	$220	Decorative	The Sims 2
Kick BackYard Loungechair by Survivall	$130	$19	$13	$52	Comfort	Family Fun Stuff
King for a Day Outdoor Chess Table	$399	$59	$39	$159	Decorative	Family Fun Stuff
Korean Keumungo	$80	$12	$8	$32	Hobbies	The Sims 2
Kozy Kitsch Gnome	$68	$10	$6	$27	Decorative	The Sims 2
Krampft Industries "Hubba-Tubba" Economy Bathtub	$700	$105	$70	$280	Plumbing	The Sims 2
Krampft Industries Value Counter	$140	$21	$14	$56	Surfaces	The Sims 2
Kwanzaa Kinara	$91	$13	$9	$36	Decorative	Holiday
Labyrinth Rug	$900	$150	$100	$400	Decorative	University
Laganaphyllis Simnovorii	$0	$0	$0	$0	Career	University
Lamp on the Half Shell	$90	$13	$9	$36	Lighting	The Sims 2
Lap of Luxury Sofa	$1,700	$255	$170	$680	Comfort	The Sims 2
Large Flower Arrangement	$155	$24	$16	$62	Decorative	Nightlife
"La Table" Long Dining Table	$876	$131	$88	$350	Surfaces	The Sims 2
"La Table" Square Dining Table	$710	$107	$71	$284	Surfaces	The Sims 2
Legno's Modern Chandelier	$190	$28	$19	$76	Lighting	Nightlife
LeTournament Decahedron XS	$245	$37	$25	$98	Personal	Nightlife
Lifestyle of the Pharaoh Picture	$750	$113	$75	$300	Decorative	Glamour Stuff
Light Effects Ceiling Lamp	$65	$9	$6	$26	Lighting	The Sims 2
Light Orbiter Floor Lamp	$250	$37	$25	$100	Lighting	The Sims 2
Li'l Chimera's Plush Bunny-Bear	$49	$7	$4	$19	Miscellaneous	Holiday
"Lily Pads" by Mya Pia	$225	$34	$23	$90	Decorative	Nightlife
Little House Lantern	$90	$13	$9	$36	Lighting	The Sims 2
Little Sister, WD15	$2,800	$420	$280	$1,120	Electronics	The Sims 2
Llamark Electronic Cash Register	$205	$30	$20	$82	Electronics	The Sims 2
Llama Xing Sign	$70	$10	$7	$28	Decorative	Nightlife

Object Directory

Object	Price and Depreciation				Needs							Skills								Function	Room Sort								Community Sort					Game
	Price	Initial Depreciation	Daily Depreciation	Depreciation Limit	Hunger	Comfort	Hygiene	Bladder	Energy	Fun	Environment	Cleaning	Study	Charisma	Creativity	Body	Logic	Mechanical	Cooking	Function	Kids	Study	Dining Room	Outside	Living Room	Bathroom	Bedroom	Kitchen	Miscellaneous	Street	Outdoor	Shopping	Food	
Ilistara Lamp	$80	$12	$8	$32	0	0	0	0	0	0	–									Lighting	X	X	X		X	X	X	X				X		The Sims 2
Illuminating Angles by Newt Va	$250	$37	$25	$100	0	0	0	0	0	0	–									Lighting	X	X	X		X	X	X	X				X		The Sims 2
Immobile Chimes Mobile in Steel	$1,500	$0	$0	$0	0	0	0	0	0	0	10									Decorative		X	X		X		X		X			X		Nightlife
Impeccable Taste Dining Table	$850	$128	$85	$340	0	0	0	0	0	0	2									Surfaces			X					X				X	X	The Sims 2
Imperial Lyon Basin	$640	$96	$64	$256	0	0	0	0	0	0	–									Plumbing						X		X				X	X	The Sims 2
Imperial Plumbing Pole-Air Freezer Bin	$3,000	$450	$300	$1,200	0	0	0	0	0	0	3									Appliances				X				X			X	X	X	The Sims 2
Imperial Plumbing Works Tivoli Basin	$560	$84	$56	$224	0	0	0	0	0	0	–									Plumbing						X		X				X	X	The Sims 2
Impresso Espress-o-Matic	$1,495	$224	$149	$598	0	0	0	0	0	4	3									Appliances			X					X				X	X	The Sims 2
Independent Expressions Inc. Easel	$350	$52	$35	$140	0	0	0	0	0	0	6				X					Decorative		X							X			X		University
Industrial Steelate Counter	$560	$84	$56	$224	0	0	0	0	0	0	–									Surfaces			X					X				X	X	University
Infinite Repetition Infinite Repetition Mirror	$750	$112	$75	$300	0	0	0	0	0	0	4			X						Decorative						X	X		X			X		Open for Business
In the Beginning	$600	$0	$0	$0	0	0	0	0	0	0	–									Decorative		X			X				X			X		Open for Business
In The Park by Awalck	$675	$0	$0	$0	0	0	0	0	0	0	1									Decorative		X			X		X				X	X		University
Inverted Vertigo, Cover Art	$60	$0	$0	$0	0	0	0	0	0	0	–									Decorative		X	X		X		X		X			X		University
It's Reggae, Mon Poster	$870	$130	$87	$348	0	0	0	0	0	0	1									Decorative		X			X		X		X			X		Family Fun Stuff
It's MYSHUNO! (the Fabulously Zany Party Game)	$45	$0	$0	$0	0	0	0	0	0	10	0									Hobbies					X							X		Holiday
Itty Bitty Clay Vases	$175	$26	$18	$70	0	0	0	0	0	0	–									Decorative					X				X			X		Nightlife
Jack-O-Hattern Luminous Lawn Ornament	$99	$14	$10	$40	0	0	0	0	2	0	1									Decorative				X					X		X	X		Nightlife
Jacuster's "Last Stand" Sectional Booth	$300	$45	$30	$120	0	8	0	0	2	0	0									Comfort		X	X									X	X	Nightlife
Juice On the Wall Sculpture	$240	$0	$0	$0	0	0	0	0	0	0	2									Decorative		X	X						X			X	X	The Sims 2
Juniper Bonsai Tree	$120	$18	$12	$48	0	0	0	0	0	0	1									Decorative		X		X					X		X	X	X	Open for Business
Just Corner Shelves	$200	$30	$20	$80	0	0	0	0	0	0	3									Surfaces		X	X	X				X	X			X	X	The Sims 2
Just in Case Oars	$450	$68	$45	$180	0	0	0	0	0	0	4									Decorative		X	X	X	X		X	X	X		X	X	X	Family Fun Stuff
Just More Corner Shelves	$200	$30	$20	$80	0	0	0	0	0	0	3									Surfaces		X	X		X			X				X	X	Open for Business

Object	Price											Category	Game
Magic Mistletoe	$80	$12	$8	$32	0	0	0	0	0	1		Decorative	Holiday
Magisplay Tray	$50	$7	$5	$20	0	0	0	0	0	1	X	Surfaces	Open for Business
Magnificently Medieval Armchair	$1,000	$150	$100	$400	0	9	0	8	0	2		Comfort	University
Majestically Medieval Double Bed	$3,400	$510	$340	$1,360	0	0	0	0	8	6		Comfort	University
Manor House Multi-Mirror	$160	$16	$16	$64	0	0	0	0	0	0		Decorative	The Sims 2
Manor House Paree Dining Table	$1,080	$162	$108	$432	0	8	0	0	0	0		Surfaces	The Sims 2
Marketing Print by Seph Epia	$330	$0	$0	$0	0	0	0	0	0	3	X	Decorative	University
Masterfully Medieval Sofa	$840	$84	$84	$336	0	8	0	0	0	2		Comfort	University
Maturely Medieval Single Bed	$1,100	$165	$110	$440	0	0	0	0	5	0		Comfort	University
Maxis' Game Simulator	$560	$126	$56	$224	0	0	0	0	9	0		Electronics	The Sims 2
Mediocre Medieval Loveseat	$1,350	$202	$135	$540	0	8	0	2	0	2		Comfort	Nightlife
Medium Decorative House Armoire	$525	$78	$52	$210	0	0	0	0	0	2	X	Miscellaneous	Open for Business
Mentionable Porcelain Toilet	$950	$142	$95	$380	0	0	10	0	0	0		Plumbing	The Sims 2
Merokkan End Table	$210	$31	$21	$90	0	0	0	0	0	0		Surfaces	The Sims 2
Merokkan Loveseat	$500	$75	$50	$200	0	7	0	2	0	2		Comfort	The Sims 2
Merry-making Dining Table	$1,025	$153	$102	$410	0	0	0	2	0	2		Surfaces	Open for Business
Milano Royale Dining Table	$900	$135	$90	$360	0	0	0	0	0	2		Surfaces	Open for Business
Mini-Disco Dinette Table	$255	$38	$25	$102	0	0	0	0	0	0		Surfaces	University
Missionaire Dining Table	$950	$142	$95	$380	0	0	0	0	0	2		Surfaces	Nightlife
Mission Coffee Table by Lulu Designs	$230	$34	$23	$92	10	0	0	0	0	3		Surfaces	Open for Business
Mixed Flower Bouquet	$85	$12	$8	$34	0	0	0	0	0	1		Decorative	Nightlife
MMM Mini Fridge	$350	$52	$35	$140	0	0	0	0	0	2		Appliances	Nightlife
Modart Naudeco Mirror (1-panel)	$660	$87	$58	$232	0	0	0	0	0	3		Decorative	Nightlife
Modart Naudeco Mirror (3-panel)	$660	$87	$58	$232	0	0	0	0	0	3		Decorative	Nightlife
Moderniste Dining Chair	$720	$108	$72	$400	0	6	0	0	0	2		Comfort	University
Modest Medieval End Table	$255	$53	$35	$142	0	0	0	0	0	0		Surfaces	The Sims 2
Modular Image Full-length Mirror	$150	$22	$15	$60	0	0	0	0	0	0	X	Decorative	University
Molded Sectional by WorldMold	$150	$23	$15	$60	0	6	0	1	0	0		Comfort	Nightlife
Money Tree	$0	$0	$0	$0	0	0	0	0	0	0		Aspiration	The Sims 2
Moneywell Computer	$1,000	$150	$100	$400	0	0	0	0	7	0	X	Electronics	The Sims 2

Object Directory

Object	Price	Initial Depreciation	Daily Depreciation	Depreciation Limit	Hunger	Comfort	Hygiene	Bladder	Energy	Fun	Environment	Cleaning	Study	Charisma	Creativity	Body	Logic	Mechanical	Cooking	Function	Kids	Study	Dining Room	Outside	Living Room	Bathroom	Bedroom	Kitchen	Miscellaneous	Street	Outdoor	Shopping	Food	Game
Locker Room Counterfeet	$80	$13	$9	$36	0	0	0	0	0	0	0									Surfaces	X		X				X	X	X					UNIVERSITY
Loft Curtains by Sparse and Fine	$195	$29	$19	$78	0	0	0	0	0	0	2									Decorative		X	X		X		X		X					THE SIMS 2
London's Famous Birthday Cake	$30	$4	$3	$12	0	0	0	0	0	0	0									Miscellaneous	X							X	X				X	THE SIMS 2
Look Upon the Orient Mirror	$370	$55	$37	$148	0	0	0	0	0	0	2			X						Decorative		X	X		X	X	X		X			X		THE SIMS 2
Los Pescados of the Wall Two	$78	$12	$8	$31	0	0	0	0	0	0	2									Decorative	X	X	X		X	X	X		X			X		FAMILY FUN STUFF
Los Pescados of the Wall	$78	$12	$8	$31	0	0	0	0	0	0	0									Decorative		X	X		X	X	X		X			X		FAMILY FUN STUFF
Loveseat by Club Distress	$750	$112	$75	$300	0	6	0	0	0	0	0									Comfort			X		X				X					THE SIMS 2
Love Tub	$0	$0	$0	$0	0	8	6	0	2	7	10									Aspiration				X							X			OPEN FOR BUSINESS
Luscious Hanging Pendant	$400	$60	$40	$160	0	0	0	0	0	0	2									Lighting	X	X	X		X	X	X		X			X		THE SIMS 2
Luminous Pro Antique Camera	$0	$0	$0	$0	0	0	0	0	0	0	0				X					Career		X	X		X	X	X		X			X		UNIVERSITY
Lunatech Amber Ceiling Lamp	$220	$33	$22	$88	0	0	0	0	0	0	1									Lighting		X	X		X	X	X		X			X		THE SIMS 2
Lunatech BC7/6	$135	$20	$13	$54	0	0	0	0	0	0	1									Lighting	X	X	X		X	X	X	X	X			X	X	THE SIMS 2
Lunatech "GaulleVanizer" Wall Sconce	$85	$12	$8	$34	0	0	0	0	0	0	0									Lighting	X	X	X		X	X	X	X	X			X	X	THE SIMS 2
Lunatech Light Disc	$95	$14	$10	$38	0	0	0	0	0	0	0									Lighting		X	X			X			X			X		THE SIMS 2
Lunatech "Lighten Up" Lighting Fixture	$75	$11	$7	$30	0	0	0	0	0	0	0									Lighting	X	X	X		X	X	X	X	X			X	X	NIGHTLIFE
Lunatech Spare Fixture in "Crimson Light"	$45	$6	$4	$18	0	0	0	0	0	0	0									Lighting	X	X	X		X	X	X		X			X		THE SIMS 2
Lunatech Spare Fixture in "Grass"	$45	$6	$4	$18	0	0	0	0	0	0	0									Lighting	X	X	X		X	X	X		X			X		THE SIMS 2
Lunatech Spare Fixture in "Ocean"	$45	$6	$4	$18	0	0	0	0	0	0	0									Lighting	X	X	X		X	X	X		X			X		THE SIMS 2
Lushcroft Antique Loveseat	$1,140	$171	$114	$456	0	8	0	0	0	0	2									Comfort					X				X					OPEN FOR BUSINESS
Luxiary "Ample King" Dining Table	$850	$127	$85	$340	0	0	0	0	0	0	8									Surfaces			X					X	X				X	THE SIMS 2
Luxiary King Armchair	$1,200	$180	$120	$480	0	9	0	0	2	0	2									Comfort		X	X		X		X		X			X		THE SIMS 2
Luxuriare Loveseat	$900	$135	$90	$360	0	9	0	0	2	0	2									Comfort		X	X		X		X		X			X		THE SIMS 2
Lying in Wait Screen	$945	$135	$90	$360	0	0	0	0	0	6	0					X				Decorative					X		X		X			X		OPEN FOR BUSINESS
Magical Mystery's "Shape, Rattle & Roll"	$30	$4	$3	$12	0	0	0	0	0	0	0									Miscellaneous	X								X					THE SIMS 2

Object	Price	§b	§c	§d	Hunger	Comfort	Hygiene	Bladder	Energy	Fun	Environment	col13	col14	col15	col16	col17	col18	Category	c20	c21	c22	c23	c24	c25	c26	c27	c28	c29	c30	Set
Neukum Systems "Bubblegum Sugar" Pop Wall Speaker	§400	§60	§40	§160	0	0	0	0	0	2	0							Electronics						X		X	X	X		The Sims™ 2
Neukum Systems "En Fuego" Salsa Wall Speaker	§400	§60	§40	§160	0	0	0	0	0	2	0							Electronics						X		X	X	X		The Sims™ 2
Neukum Systems "Glo Stik" Techno Wall Speaker	§400	§60	§40	§160	0	0	0	0	0	2	0							Electronics						X		X	X	X		The Sims™ 2
Neukum Systems "Happy Shopping" Store Soundscape Wall Speaker	§400	§60	§40	§160	0	0	0	0	0	2	0							Electronics						X		X	X	X		Open for Business
Neukum Systems "Hep Cat" 50s Rock Wall Speaker	§400	§60	§40	§160	0	0	0	0	0	2	0							Electronics						X		X	X	X		Nightlife
Neukum Systems "Isorhythm" Classical Wall Speaker	§400	§60	§40	§160	0	0	0	0	0	2	0							Electronics						X		X	X	X		The Sims™ 2
Neukum Systems "The Badunkadunk" Hip Hop Wall Speaker	§400	§60	§40	§160	0	0	0	0	0	3	0				X			Electronics	X		X	X		X						The Sims™ 2
Neukum Systems "The Cold Train" R&B Wall Speaker	§400	§60	§40	§160	0	0	0	0	0	2	0							Electronics						X		X	X	X		The Sims™ 2
Neukum Systems "Totally Rad" New Wave Wall Speaker	§400	§60	§40	§160	0	0	0	0	0	2	0							Electronics						X		X	X	X		Open for Business
Neukum Systems Wall Speaker	§400	§60	§40	§160	0	0	0	0	0	2	0							Electronics						X		X	X	X		Nightlife
No-Fuss Ficus	§300	§45	§30	§120	0	0	0	0	0	0	2							Decorative		X	X	X			X	X		X	X	X	The Sims™ 2
Noodlesoother	§0	§0	§0	§0	0	0	0	0	0	0	7							Aspiration												The Sims™ 2
Novellas Nouveau Bookcase	§800	§120	§80	§320	0	0	0	0	0	1	2	X				X	X	Hobbies	X			X		X						The Sims™ 2
NOYIN 2680 Cellular Phone	§149	§0	§0	§0	0	0	0	0	0	0	0							Personal												University
Nuh-Uh Nutcracker	§650	§0	§0	§0	0	0	0	0	0	0	6							Decorative	X		X				X	X				Open for Business
NuMica Allinall Card Table	§95	§14	§9	§38	0	0	0	0	0	0	0							Surfaces		X				X				X		The Sims™ 2
Oaktowne Dining Chair	§615	§92	§61	§246	0	6	0	0	0	0	0							Comfort		X								X	X	The Sims™ 2
Oaktowne East Side Dining Chair	§250	§37	§25	§100	0	3	0	0	0	0	0							Comfort	X	X				X			X			The Sims™ 2
Obviously Modern Wall Mirror	§399	§59	§39	§159	0	0	0	0	0	0	2			X				Decorative			X	X	X			X				The Sims™ 2
Odd Reflection of Grace	§525	§79	§53	§210	0	0	0	0	0	0	4							Decorative	X		X			X						Glamour Stuff
Oil "Fantasy Scape"	§500	§0	§0	§0	0	0	0	0	0	0	4							Decorative	X	X	X		X			X	X			The Sims™ 2
Old Boys Club Commercial Counter	§710	§106	§71	§284	0	0	0	0	0	0	2							Surfaces						X						The Sims™ 2
Old Fashioned Change Room	§690	§103	§69	§276	0	0	0	0	0	4	0							Miscellaneous						X						The Sims™ 2
Ol' Grandfather Clock	§3,500	§525	§350	§1,400	0	0	0	0	0	0	3							Decorative	X	X	X			X						The Sims™ 2
Olive Peynter's City SkyScape	§4,000	§0	§0	§0	0	0	0	0	0	0	10							Decorative	X	X	X		X	X		X				The Sims™ 2

Object Directory

Note: the Skills block (Cleaning, Study, Charisma, Creativity, Body, Logic, Mechanical, Cooking) has no entries for any object on this page; all skill cells are blank. Needs values not listed are 0 (□).

Object	Price	Initial Depreciation	Daily Depreciation	Depreciation Limit	Comfort	Energy	Fun	Environment	Function	Room Sort	Community Sort	Expansion
Moor is More Coffee Table	$225	$33	$22	$84					Surfaces	Study, Living Room	Miscellaneous	THE SIMS 2
"More Sleeka" Dining Chair by Simplanics	$650	$98	$65	$260	6			1	Comfort	Study, Dining Room, Living Room, Kitchen	Miscellaneous, Food	GLAMOUR STUFF
Morphic to the Maxx	$3,000	$450	$300	$1,200			3		Decorative	Living Room	Miscellaneous, Outdoor	THE SIMS 2
Mr. Bearlybutts	$385	$54	$36	$146	5				Comfort	Kids	Miscellaneous, Shopping	OPEN FOR BUSINESS
Mr. Generic's Sign — The Ceiling Model	$150	$0	$0	$0					Decorative		Miscellaneous, Outdoor	OPEN FOR BUSINESS
Mr. Generic's Sign — The Floor Model	$175	$0	$0	$0					Decorative	Living Room	Miscellaneous	NIGHTLIFE
Mr. Lampy McFourlegs	$150	$23	$15	$60					Lighting	Study, Living Room	Miscellaneous	HOLIDAY
Mr. Sanblovian	$50	$7	$5	$20				2	Comfort	Study, Dining Room, Living Room	Miscellaneous, Outdoor	NIGHTLIFE
"Mr. Section" by Comfortitude	$255	$38	$26	$102	8	2			Comfort	Living Room	Miscellaneous, Shopping	NIGHTLIFE
"Mr. Section with Arms" by Comfortitude	$260	$39	$26	$104	8	2		2	Comfort	Living Room	Miscellaneous, Shopping	NIGHTLIFE
Mr. Shuffles	$95	$14	$10	$38				2	Decorative		Miscellaneous	THE SIMS 2
Musee Public "Collection Sculpture"	$200	$0	$0	$0				10	Decorative	Study, Living Room	Miscellaneous, Shopping	FAMILY FUN STUFF
My Impregnable Fortress Bed by Mystical Furnishings	$570	$86	$57	$228	3	3			Comfort	Bedroom	Miscellaneous	FAMILY FUN STUFF
Myne Cafeteria Table	$380	$57	$38	$152					Surfaces	Study, Dining Room, Kitchen	Miscellaneous, Food	UNIVERSITY
Mysteriously Medieval Dining Chair	$950	$142	$95	$380	7				Comfort	Study, Dining Room, Living Room, Kitchen	Miscellaneous, Food	UNIVERSITY
Mystery Presents	$775	$41	$27	$110				3	Decorative		Miscellaneous	HOLIDAY
Mystic Life "Flower Vase"	$150	$22	$15	$60				1	Decorative	Bedroom	Miscellaneous, Shopping	FAMILY FUN STUFF
My Valiant Steed Dining Chair by Mystical Furnishings	$240	$36	$14	$96	3			1	Comfort	Study, Dining Room, Kitchen	Miscellaneous, Food	FAMILY FUN STUFF
My Very First Castle Desk by Mystical Furnishings	$180	$27	$18	$72			3		Surfaces	Study	Miscellaneous	THE SIMS 2
Narcisco Rubbish Bin	$45	$6	$4	$18					Miscellaneous	Outside	Miscellaneous, Outdoor	NIGHTLIFE
"Nature's Perfection" by E.Z. Phun	$299	$0	$0	$0					Decorative		Miscellaneous, Shopping, Food	NIGHTLIFE
"NeonBar" by Neontrix	$2,100	$277	$185	$740					Miscellaneous		Miscellaneous, Outdoor, Food	NIGHTLIFE
Neon Flamingo	$225	$34	$23	$90					Lighting	Outside	Miscellaneous, Outdoor, Shopping	NIGHTLIFE
"NeonServe" by Neontrix	$590	$89	$59	$236					Surfaces		Miscellaneous, Food	NIGHTLIFE
Neukum Systems "Art of Darkness" Heavy Metal Wall Speaker	$400	$60	$40	$160			2		Electronics	Study, Living Room, Kitchen	Miscellaneous, Outdoor, Food	THE SIMS 2

Object	Price	Initial Dep.	Daily Dep.	Dep. Limit	Category	Game
Plasticity NodePad by Yoko Onasis	$500	$75	$50	$200	Comfort	The Sims 2
Podium of Bonnappitizon	$200	$30	$20	$80	Miscellaneous	Open for Business
Poetic Justice Wall Sconce	$270	$40	$27	$108	Lighting	Open for Business
Poinsettia Gift Pack from the All Seasons Nursery and Logging Camp	$95	$14	$9	$38	Decorative	Holiday
Poisonous Forest (In Love with a Curse)	$5,500	$0	$0	$0	Decorative	The Sims 2
Polychromed Seating Surface With Cushion	$375	$56	$37	$150	Comfort	The Sims 2
Poppin' Party Balloon Centerpiece	$7	$5	$3	$14	Decorative	The Sims 2
Porcelain Oval Mirror	$200	$30	$20	$80	Miscellaneous	Nightlife
Potted Ficus by Nature's Garden	$320	$48	$32	$128	Decorative	Nightlife
Potted Palm	$510	$77	$51	$204	Decorative	Nightlife
"Potted Plant in Spiral Elegance," an existential piece by Natural Pretzel	$600	$90	$60	$240	Decorative	Family Fun Stuff
Potted Potential	$300	$0	$0	$0	Decorative	Open for Business
Power Mirror	$525	$94	$63	$250	Decorative	The Sims 2
Pretty Pot O' Pansies	$180	$27	$18	$72	Decorative	The Sims 2
PrevenTek Luminlight Streetlamp	$439	$65	$43	$175	Lighting	The Sims 2
PrevenTek Tri-Luminlight Streetlamp	$600	$90	$60	$240	Lighting	The Sims 2
Prints Charming Fingerprinting Scanner	$0	$0	$0	$0	Career	The Sims 2
Prisoner of Azkalamp	$35	$5	$3	$14	Lighting	The Sims 2
Produce Market Shingle	$99	$14	$9	$39	Decorative	Open for Business
Prosperous Perch Sofa by Well Bred and Co.	$490	$74	$50	$198	Comfort	University
Psychedelic SimAtri Coffee Table	$145	$0	$0	$0	Surfaces	Glamour Stuff
Qadim Bauble Lamp	$150	$22	$15	$60	Lighting	The Sims 2
Queen Anne Coffee Table	$470	$70	$47	$180	Surfaces	The Sims 2
Quick Display by Sims Club Merchandise	$200	$30	$20	$80	Surfaces	Open for Business
Rackmaster 850 Bowling Ball Rack by Hurling Matters	$2,000	$0	$0	$0	Decorative	Nightlife

Object Directory

Object	Price	Initial Depreciation	Daily Depreciation	Depreciation Limit	Hunger	Comfort	Hygiene	Bladder	Energy	Fun	Environment	Cleaning	Study	Charisma	Creativity	Body	Logic	Mechanical	Cooking	Function	Kids	Study	Dining Room	Outside	Living Room	Bathroom	Bedroom	Kitchen	Miscellaneous	Street	Outdoor	Shopping	Food	Pack
On A Pedestal by Yucan Byall	$5,000	$0	$0	$0	0	0	0	0	0	0	10									Decorative		X		X	X	X	X	X	X		X	X	X	The Sims 2
Once Upon a Glowy Glow Glowlamp	$350	$52	$35	$140	0	0	0	0	0	0	2									Lighting		X	X	X	X	X	X		X		X			Open for Business
One Pin, Two Pin	$25	$19	$13	$50	0	0	0	0	0	0	0									Lighting		X	X		X	X	X		X					Open for Business
Open/Closed Sign of War and Commerce	$20	$3	$0	$0	0	0	0	0	0	0	0									Decorative												X	X	Nightlife
Open-Wall Wall Fan	$0	$0	$0	$0	0	0	0	0	0	0	1									Decorative		X		X	X	X	X		X		X			Open for Business
Opus by Rose Grace Wise	$3,500	$0	$0	$0	0	0	0	0	0	0	10									Decorative	X	X	X	X	X	X	X	X	X		X	X		The Sims 2
Orbs of Connectedness Ceiling Lamp	$180	$27	$18	$72	0	0	0	0	0	0	1									Lighting		X	X	X	X	X	X		X		X			University
Organic Material's Barstool	$700	$105	$70	$280	0	7	0	0	0	0	2					X				Comfort		X	X		X			X	X	X	X		X	The Sims 2
Outdoor Ergo Ergonomic Chair by Guldner-Ebadi	$320	$48	$32	$128	0	5	0	0	0	0	0									Comfort				X					X		X			The Sims 2
Outdoor Protector	$245	$36	$24	$98	0	0	0	0	0	0	0									Decorative														Glamour Stuff
Pampered Sounds Stereo	$3,000	$382	$255	$1,020	0	0	0	0	0	10	2									Electronics		X			X		X		X		X			The Sims 2
Paper Moon Ceiling Light	$300	$45	$30	$120	0	0	0	0	0	0	0									Lighting		X	X	X	X	X	X		X	X	X			The Sims 2
Park Plates Mini Outdoor Dining Table	$115	$17	$11	$46	0	0	0	0	0	0	1									Surfaces			X	X						X	X		X	The Sims 2
Party Juice Barrel	$45	$21	$14	$58	0	0	0	0	0	0	2									Miscellaneous		X	X	X	X	X	X		X		X		X	Nightlife
Passable Mission Chair	$790	$118	$79	$316	0	8	0	0	0	0	0									Comfort		X	X		X		X		X		X			The Sims 2
Pasteur's HomoGenius Smart Milk	$0	$0	$0	$0	1	0	0	0	0	6	6									Miscellaneous														University
PatioPlastics Dining Chair	$80	$12	$8	$32	0	8	0	0	0	0	0									Comfort			X	X						X	X		X	The Sims 2
Peace of Garbage Can	$30	$4	$3	$12	0	0	0	0	0	0	1									Miscellaneous				X					X		X		X	The Sims 2
Perfect Parquet	$150	$22	$15	$60	0	0	0	0	0	0	0									Aspiration														The Sims 2
Piece of Quiet Park Bench	$500	$75	$50	$200	0	2	0	0	2	0	6									Comfort				X					X		X			The Sims 2
Pimp Viking 3D Arcade Game	$1,050	$157	$105	$420	0	0	0	0	0	10	6					X				Electronics					X				X	X	X			Nightlife
"Pineapple" by Lynn D'Saye	$850	$0	$0	$0	0	0	0	0	0	0	0									Decorative				X					X	X	X	X	X	Nightlife
PINEGULTCHER Outdoor Mintable	$220	$33	$22	$88	0	0	0	0	0	0	6									Surfaces				X				X	X	X	X			Nightlife
"Pinmaster 300" Bowling Alley by Hurling Fun Products, Inc.	$5,500	$825	$550	$2,200	0	0	0	0	0	10	0					X				Hobbies									X			X	X	Nightlife
Fix-Arm Drafting Lamp	$30	$4	$3	$12	0	0	0	0	0	0	1									Lighting		X		X	X				X		X			The Sims 2

Object	Price	2	3	4	5	6	7	8	9	10	11	12	13	14	Category	A	B	C	D	E	F	G	H	I	J	K	L	Set
Ring a'Ding Earthquake Detection System Holiday Special!	§40	§6	§4	§16	0	0	0	0	0	0	1				Decorative		X	X					X				HOLIDAY
Rip Co. Little Baker Oven	§100	§15	§10	§40	0	0	0	0	0	1	0			X	Miscellaneous	X											THE SIMS™ 2
Rip Co. Toy Bin	§55	§8	§5	§22	0	0	0	0	0	7	0				Miscellaneous	X											THE SIMS™ 2
Rip Co. Wobbly Wabbit Head	§35	§5	§3	§14	0	0	0	0	0	10	0		X		Miscellaneous	X											THE SIMS™ 2
Rip Co. Xylophone	§40	§6	§4	§16	0	0	0	0	0	4	0			X	Miscellaneous	X											THE SIMS™ 2
Rob R. Barron "Nouveau" Medium Wardrobe	§950	§142	§95	§380	0	0	0	0	0	0	3				Miscellaneous						X		X			X	OPEN FOR BUSINESS
Rob R. Barron "Nouveau" Wardrobe	§1,000	§150	§100	§400	0	0	0	0	0	0	3				Miscellaneous						X						THE SIMS™ 2
Roedisplay by Grant Industries	§500	§75	§50	§200	0	0	0	0	0	0	4				Surfaces				X							X	OPEN FOR BUSINESS
Roedisplay Concave Corner by Grant Industries	§250	§37	§25	§100	0	0	0	0	0	0	3				Surfaces				X							X	OPEN FOR BUSINESS
Roedisplay Convex Corner by Grant Industries	§250	§37	§25	§100	0	0	0	0	0	0	3				Surfaces				X							X	OPEN FOR BUSINESS
R.O.I. Lighting	§500	§75	§50	§200	0	0	0	0	0	0	3				Lighting			X		X	X	X		X		X	X	GLAMOUR STUFF
Rolling Hills by H. Sean	§400	§0	§0	§0	0	0	0	0	0	0	3				Decorative		X	X		X		X		X			X	THE SIMS™ 2
Romantic Romance by Elle and Eey	§100	§15	§10	§40	0	0	0	0	0	0	1				Lighting		X	X		X		X		X		X	X	NIGHTLIFE
Rose Bouquet	§120	§18	§12	§48	0	0	0	0	0	0	2							X	X	X			X				OPEN FOR BUSINESS
Route 66	§200	§0	§0	§0	0	0	0	0	0	0	2				Decorative	X	X				X		X			X	NIGHTLIFE
Rubber Tree Plant	§165	§24	§16	§66	0	0	0	0	0	0	1				Decorative		X	X	X			X	X		X	X	X	THE SIMS™ 2
Rug de Exuberance	§1,100	§150	§100	§400	0	0	0	0	0	0	0				Decorative		X	X		X		X		X				GLAMOUR STUFF
Rugged Llamas of the North Souvenir Rugby Jersey	§115	§0	§0	§0	0	0	0	0	0	0	1				Decorative		X				X					X	UNIVERSITY
Sacred Star	§18	§2	§1	§7	0	0	0	0	0	0	1				Decorative			X		X	X	X	X				X	HOLIDAY
Sanitation Station Baby Changing Table	§400	§60	§40	§160	0	0	10	0	0	0	0				Miscellaneous	X						X					THE SIMS™ 2
Santa Skating	§415	§62	§41	§166	0	0	0	0	0	0	3				Decorative		X	X		X		X				X	X	HOLIDAY
Satinistics Loveseat	§150	§22	§15	§60	0	5	0	0	2	0	0				Comfort				X			X					THE SIMS™ 2
Save the Sheep Faux Sheepskin Diploma	§0	§0	§0	§0	0	0	0	0	0	0	0				Career												UNIVERSITY
Schokolade 890 Chocolate Manufacturing Facility	§0	§0	§0	§0	0	0	0	0	0	1	0			X	Career												THE SIMS™ 2
ScienStone "Dramatic" Coffee Table	§340	§51	§34	§122	0	0	0	0	0	0	0				Surfaces		X			X			X				THE SIMS™ 2
Scraps Ranch "CafeMate" Coffee Table	§90	§13	§9	§36	0	0	0	0	0	0	0				Surfaces		X			X			X				THE SIMS™ 2
SCTC Universal Public Phone	§550	§82	§55	§220	0	0	0	0	0	0	0				Electronics									X	X		THE SIMS™ 2

Object Directory

Object	Price	Initial Depreciation	Daily Depreciation	Depreciation Limit	Hunger	Comfort	Hygiene	Bladder	Energy	Fun	Environment	Cleaning	Study (skill)	Charisma	Creativity	Body	Logic	Mechanical	Cooking	Function	Kids	Study (room)	Dining Room	Outside	Living Room	Bathroom	Bedroom	Kitchen	Miscellaneous	Street	Outdoor	Shopping	Food	Game
Rainy Day Main Street	$350	$0	$0	$0	0	0	0	0	0	0	3									Decorative		X	X		X		X		X			X	X	The Sims 2
Rave Against the Machine Nightclub Lamp	$350	$52	$35	$140	0	0	0	0	0	0	2									Lighting		X	X		X		X		X			X		The Sims 2
Really Distressed Loveseat by Club Distress	$165	$24	$16	$66	0	5	0	0	2	0	0									Comfort					X				X			X		University
Recalling Rug	$500	$75	$50	$200	0	0	0	0	0	0	0									Decorative		X	X		X		X		X			X		University
Recalling Rug 3x3	$1,000	$150	$100	$400	0	0	0	0	0	0	1									Decorative		X	X		X		X		X			X		The Sims 2
Recherché Counter Island	$680	$102	$68	$272	0	0	0	0	0	0	0									Surfaces								X	X			X	X	Nightlife
Recherché Floor Runner	$325	$49	$33	$130	0	0	0	0	0	0	0									Decorative		X	X		X		X		X			X		The Sims 2
Recycled Relaxer	$250	$37	$25	$100	0	5	0	0	2	0	1									Comfort					X				X			X		Nightlife
Red vs. Blue Oil Portrait	$20	$0	$0	$0	0	0	0	0	0	0	1									Decorative		X	X		X		X		X			X		The Sims 2
Reflection V	$500	$75	$50	$200	0	0	0	0	0	0	4									Decorative		X	X		X		X		X			X		The Sims 2
Reflective Glass Mirror	$100	$15	$10	$40	0	0	0	0	0	0	1			X						Decorative			X		X	X	X		X			X		Nightlife
Regulars Only Barstool	$650	$97	$65	$260	0	6	0	0	0	0	0									Comfort								X	X			X	X	Nightlife
Renaissance Bookcase by Literary Designs	$950	$142	$95	$380	0	0	0	0	0	0	10	X						X	X	Hobbies		X			X		X		X			X		The Sims 2
ReNuYuSenso Orb	$100	$0	$0	$0	0	0	0	0	0	0	0									Aspiration		X			X				X			X		Open for Business
Reprint Serial #3-CDPU4	$130	$105	$70	$280	0	0	0	0	0	0	1									Decorative	X	X			X		X		X			X		The Sims 2
ResiStall Astro Divider 7	$700	$0	$0	$0	0	0	0	0	0	0	0									Plumbing						X			X			X	X	Nightlife
Restaurant Sign by Upturned Nose	$100	$0	$0	$0	0	0	0	0	0	0	1									Decorative				X						X	X		P	Nightlife
Resurrect-O-Nomitron	$0	$0	$0	$0	0	0	0	0	0	0	0									Career		X							X			X		The Sims 2
Retratech "Office Pal" Economy Desk	$80	$12	$8	$32	0	0	0	0	0	0	0									Surfaces		X			X		X		X			X		The Sims 2
Retratech Padded Egg Chair	$150	$22	$15	$60	0	3	0	0	0	0	0									Comfort	X	X	X		X		X		X			X	X	University
Retro Bodacious Loveseat	$615	$92	$61	$246	0	7	0	0	2	0	0									Comfort					X				X			X		The Sims 2
Retro Lounge "High Liquidity" Juice Bar	$800	$120	$80	$320	0	0	0	0	0	0	0									Miscellaneous		X	X		X			X	X			X	X	University
Retro Overeasy Eggseater	$620	$93	$62	$248	0	7	0	0	0	0	0									Comfort			X		X				X			X		The Sims 2
Retro Overeasy Eggseater Recliner	$640	$96	$64	$256	0	7	0	0	2	0	0									Comfort					X		X		X			X		The Sims 2
Revolutionary Rebellion Poster	$45	$0	$0	$0	0	0	0	0	0	0	1									Decorative		X			X		X		X			X		University
Ribbons Aplenty Lamp by Safestyle Inc	$475	$71	$48	$190	0	0	0	0	0	0	0									Lighting	X	X	X		X	X	X		X			X	X	University
Right Away Community Trash-Can	$75	$11	$7	$30	0	0	0	0	0	0	0									Miscellaneous				X		X	X	X	X	X	X	X	X	Glamour Stuff
Ring a'Ding Earthquake Detection System	$30	$4	$3	$12	0	0	0	0	0	0	3									Decorative			X		X		X	X	X				X	Holiday

Object	Price	Initial Depreciation	Daily Depreciation	Depreciation Limit	Category	Game
SimCity Championship Roster 1984–85 Season Poster	$55	$0	$0	$0	Decorative	University
SimCity SynapseSnapper Industrial Sign	$99	$14	$9	$39	Decorative	The Sims 2
Simgreek Letter Sign-Annya	$100	$14	$9	$39	Decorative	University
Simgreek Letter Sign-Cham	$100	$14	$9	$39	Decorative	University
Simgreek Letter Sign-Fruhm	$100	$14	$9	$39	Decorative	University
Simgreek Letter Sign-Hoh	$100	$14	$9	$39	Decorative	University
Simgreek Letter Sign-Nagard	$100	$14	$9	$39	Decorative	University
Simgreek Letter Sign-Var	$100	$14	$9	$39	Decorative	University
Simgreek Letter Sign-Uhele	$100	$14	$9	$39	Decorative	University
Simgreek Letter Sign-Dresha	$100	$14	$9	$39	Decorative	University
Simline Wall Phone	$75	$11	$7	$30	Electronics	University
Simline Table Phone	$50	$7	$5	$20	Electronics	University
Simple Sink from Krampft Industries	$275	$41	$27	$110	Plumbing	The Sims 2
Simple Sit Chair	$200	$30	$20	$80	Comfort	The Sims 2
Simple Structure End Table	$60	$9	$6	$24	Surfaces	The Sims 2
Simple Tub from Krampft Industries	$1,500	$225	$150	$600	Plumbing	The Sims 2
Simply Spindle Coffee Table	$40	$6	$4	$16	Surfaces	The Sims 2
SimSafety V Burglar Alarm	$250	$37	$25	$100	Electronics	The Sims 2
Simsanto Inc. Biotech	$0	$0	$0	$0	Career	The Sims 2
SimSentry Clothing Booth	$370	$55	$37	$148	Miscellaneous	The Sims 2
"Sims Must Wash Hands" Sign	$70	$0	$0	$0	Decorative	The Sims 2
SimVac	$0	$0	$0	$0	Aspiration	Nightlife
Single-Track Light Set	$200	$30	$20	$80	Lighting	Open for Business
"Sit n'Grin" Photo Booth from iBurn Commercial Imagery	$1,300	$195	$130	$520	Miscellaneous	Nightlife
Sit-Up-Straight Dining Chair	$700	$105	$70	$280	Comfort	Open for Business
Skimmer Securities Ceiling Sprinkler	$245	$36	$24	$98	Miscellaneous	University
Sled Track Holiday Wall Lights by Xtremeholiday Sporting	$10	$1	$1	$4	Decorative	Holiday
Sled Track Wall Lights by Xtremeholiday Sporting	$10	$1	$1	$4	Decorative	Holiday

Object Directory

Object	Price	Initial Depreciation	Daily Depreciation	Depreciation Limit	Hunger	Comfort	Hygiene	Bladder	Energy	Fun	Environment	Cleaning	Study	Charisma	Creativity	Body	Logic	Mechanical	Cooking	Function	Kids	Study	Dining Room	Outside	Living Room	Bathroom	Bedroom	Kitchen	Miscellaneous	Street	Outdoor	Shopping	Food	Game
Searing Indifference Wall Poster	$50	$0	$0	$0	0	0	0	0	0	0	1									Decorative		X	X		X		X		X			X		THE SIMS 2
Seatris by Ima Hack	$1,720	$183	$122	$488	0	8	0	0	0	0	6									Comfort		X	X		X		X					X		THE SIMS 2
Secure Sentinel Post Lamp	$185	$27	$18	$74	0	0	0	0	0	0	2									Lighting		X	X	X	X		X				X			THE SIMS 2
Sellafone Gadget Kiosk	$2,500	$375	$250	$1,000	0	0	0	0	0	0	0									Electronics										X	X	X		UNIVERSITY
SensoTwitch Lie Finder	$0	$0	$0	$0	0	0	0	0	0	0	0				X					Career					X				X					NIGHTLIFE
"Sent to My Room Without Dinner" by Picts Ellie	$500	$0	$0	$300	0	0	0	0	0	0	2									Decorative		X	X		X		X		X			X		THE SIMS 2
Serenity Sitter	$800	$120	$80	$300	0	8	0	0	0	0	2									Comfort					X	X	X		X			X		THE SIMS 2
Sewage Brothers Resteze Toilet	$300	$45	$30	$120	0	0	0	10	0	0	1									Plumbing						X							X	THE SIMS 2
Sewage Brothers Resteze Urinal	$400	$60	$40	$160	0	0	0	10	0	0	1									Plumbing						X						X	X	THE SIMS 2
Share the Bounty Nutcracker	$45	$6	$4	$18	0	0	0	0	0	0	1									Decorative					X		X		X					GLAMOUR STUFF
Sheer Radiance Vanity Light	$90	$13	$9	$36	0	0	0	0	0	0	2									Lighting						X	X							OPEN FOR BUSINESS
Shimmering Light of Elegance	$320	$48	$32	$128	0	0	0	0	0	0	2									Lighting		X	X		X		X		X			X		HOLIDAY
Shining Knight Standing Lamp	$315	$47	$31	$126	0	0	0	0	0	0	2									Lighting	X	X	X		X		X		X					THE SIMS 2
Shiny Things, Inc. Grandiose Grill	$1,100	$165	$110	$440	0	0	0	0	0	0	0									Appliances				X				X	X		X			THE SIMS 2
Shiny Things Inc. Whisp-Aire Dishwasher	$950	$142	$95	$380	0	0	0	0	0	0	0									Appliances								X	X					THE SIMS 2
ShinyTyme Cooktop	$900	$135	$80	$360	0	0	0	0	0	0	0									Appliances								X	X					NIGHTLIFE
Shinytyme Kitchen Sink by Gurglomics	$300	$45	$30	$120	0	0	5	0	0	0	0									Plumbing						X		X	X					FAMILY FUN STUFF
Ship Rotation Device	$250	$38	$25	$100	0	0	0	0	0	0	2									Decorative		X	X		X		X		X			X		THE SIMS 2
Shocking Pink Flamingo	$12	$1	$1	$4	0	0	0	0	0	0	0									Decorative				X					X		X			THE SIMS 2
Shoji Table Lantern	$75	$26	$7	$70	0	0	0	0	0	0	3									Lighting	X	X	X		X		X		X			X		THE SIMS 2
Show My Ride display by Extremo Cars	$500	$75	$50	$200	0	0	0	0	0	1	1									Surfaces		X	X	X	X		X	X			X			OPEN FOR BUSINESS
Signs of Elliptical Joy by Alexandra Workman	$100	$15	$10	$40	0	0	0	0	0	0	3									Decorative		X	X		X		X		X		X			NIGHTLIFE
Sill-Length Tieback Curtains	$300	$45	$30	$120	0	0	0	0	0	0	3									Decorative	X	X	X		X		X		X					THE SIMS 2
Simbic Bisecteur Bass	$1,800	$525	$350	$1,400	0	0	0	0	0	10	2				X					Hobbies	X	X	X	X	X		X	X	X		X	X	X	UNIVERSITY
SimCity at Night	$425	$0	$0	$0	0	0	0	0	0	0	3									Decorative		X	X		X		X		X			X	X	THE SIMS 2

Item	Price	Category	Game
St. Ajoque Reproductions "See Plus" Mirror	$750	Decorative	The Sims™ 2
Stark Inspiration Chair	$800	Comfort	Family Fun Stuff
Stewart Mourning Café Curtains	$97	Decorative	The Sims™ 2
Stick 'Em Up Bulletin Board	$75	Decorative	University
Stiff by Superfluous Seating	$750	Comfort	The Sims™ 2
Stinging Jelly Light	$90	Lighting	The Sims™ 2
Strut Your Stuff Communal Shower	$425	Plumbing	University
Studio Bakonni Deluxe Loveseat	$1,100	Comfort	The Sims™ 2
Studio Bakonni Deluxe Lounge	$830	Comfort	The Sims™ 2
Studio Bakonni Deluxe Chair	$880	Comfort	The Sims™ 2
Sunflowers	$45	Decorative	Nightlife
Sung-6vu Sunburst Oriental Rug	$800	Decorative	The Sims™ 2
Sun King Drawers by Royale Furniture Co.	$850	Miscellaneous	Open for Business
Superflux Über UV Guitar	$2,500	Hobbies	University
Superlative Sink by "The Greatest Designer Alive"	$250	Plumbing	Open for Business
Super Signguy Retail Sign	$175	Decorative	Open for Business
Super Signguy Retail Sign	$150	Decorative	Open for Business
Super Stuffer Mantle Warmers	$35	Decorative	Holiday
Supreme Cabinet of the Lesser Items	$535	Miscellaneous	Open for Business
Surfing the Universe Poster	$59	Decorative	The Sims™ 2
Suspense	$475	Decorative	University
Su-Tove Armoire	$1,200	Miscellaneous	The Sims™ 2
Sweet Tooth Survivor Pinball	$1,750	Electronics	The Sims™ 2
SwinganmGo 27" Multivid V Television	$750	Electronics	Nightlife
Swing Kidz Deluxe Swing Set	$450	Miscellaneous	The Sims™ 2
Tablablanca from Simporters, Ltd.	$690	Surfaces	The Sims™ 2
Tea Party in Teak	$100	Comfort	The Sims™ 2
TechTonic Touch Toaster Oven	$100	Appliances	The Sims™ 2

Object Directory

Object	Price	Initial Depreciation	Daily Depreciation	Depreciation Limit	Hunger	Comfort	Hygiene	Bladder	Energy	Fun	Environment	Cleaning	Study	Charisma	Creativity	Body	Logic	Mechanical	Cooking	Function	Kids	Study	Dining Room	Outside	Living Room	Bathroom	Bedroom	Kitchen	Miscellaneous	Street	Outdoor	Shopping	Food	Game
Sled Track White Lights by XtremeHoliday Sporting Simplonics	$10	$1	$1	$4	0	0	0	0	0	0	—									Decorative									X		X			HOLIDAY
"Sleeka" Barstool by Simplonics	$600	$90	$60	$240	0	5	0	0	0	0	1									Comfort			X		X			X	X					NIGHTLIFE
SmokeSentry SmokeSniffer 3000	$50	$7	$5	$20	0	0	0	0	0	0	—									Electronics	X	X	X		X	X	X	X	X					THE SIMS 2
Snapdragon Bouquet	$300	$45	$30	$120	0	0	0	0	0	0	3									Decorative		X	X		X		X	X	X					OPEN FOR BUSINESS
Snowman Construction Set - Base	$10	$1	$1	$5	0	0	0	0	0	0	0									Decorative				X					X		X			THE SIMS 2
Snowman Construction Set - Head	$15	$1	$1	$5	0	0	0	0	0	0	2									Decorative				X					X		X			HOLIDAY
Snowman Construction Set - Hat	$10	$1	$1	$5	0	0	0	0	0	0	2									Decorative				X					X		X			HOLIDAY
Snowman Construction Set - Middle	$15	$1	$1	$5	0	0	0	0	0	0	2									Decorative				X					X		X			HOLIDAY
Social Climbing Ivy Floor Lamp	$105	$15	$10	$42	0	0	0	0	0	0	2									Lighting	X	X	X		X		X		X					THE SIMS 2
Social Climbing Ivy Table Lamp	$79	$11	$7	$31	0	0	0	0	0	0	1									Lighting		X	X		X		X		X					THE SIMS 2
Sofa by Club Distress	$1,450	$217	$145	$580	0	8	0	0	2	0	2									Comfort					X				X					OPEN FOR BUSINESS
Sofa of Substance	$1,625	$243	$162	$650	0	10	0	0	2	0	2									Comfort					X				X					THE SIMS 2
Soldier's Quarter Recliner	$810	$121	$81	$324	0	7	0	0	2	0	2									Comfort					X				X					THE SIMS 2
Soma 44" PancakeTek Television	$3,500	$525	$350	$1,400	0	0	0	0	0	8	1					X				Electronics	X	X			X		X		X					THE SIMS 2
Soma AudioGeek TK421 Tower System	$2,550	$382	$255	$1,020	0	0	0	0	0	7	1					X				Electronics		X			X		X		X					UNIVERSITY
Soma "Wall-Eye" Large Screen Flat-Panel Television	$8,000	$1,200	$800	$3,200	0	0	0	0	0	10	2					X				Electronics		X			X		X		X					THE SIMS 2
Space Oddity	$50	$0	$0	$0	0	0	0	0	0	0	2									Decorative					X				X					NIGHTLIFE
Spaceship Spacious	$6,250	$0	$0	$0	0	0	0	0	0	0	2									Decorative	X				X				X					OPEN FOR BUSINESS
Spherical Splendor Fountain	$225	$0	$0	$0	0	0	0	0	0	0	2									Decorative				X					X		X			OPEN FOR BUSINESS
Spring Majesty	$291	$0	$0	$0	0	0	0	0	0	0	2									Decorative				X					X		X			NIGHTLIFE
Squat Pedestal by Selfless Salesman	$220	$33	$22	$88	0	0	0	0	0	0	2									Surfaces			X		X				X			X	X	UNIVERSITY
Squeezin' It Lemonade Stand	$120	$18	$12	$48	0	0	0	0	0	0	3								X	Miscellaneous				X					X		X		X	OPEN FOR BUSINESS
"Squintimacy" Votive Table Lamp by Dimview & Co.	$10	$17	$11	$44	0	0	0	0	0	0	1									Lighting		X	X		X		X		X		X	X	X	NIGHTLIFE
Stack-O-Flames Bonfire	$745	$0	$0	$0	0	0	0	0	0	10	10									Miscellaneous				X					X		X			UNIVERSITY

Object	Price										Category	Expansion Pack
The Gobo-a-Go-Go Spotlighter by LumiD	$425	$64	$43	$70	0	0	0	0	0	2	Lighting	Nightlife
The "Bold-end" Ratio Table	$190	$28	$19	$76	0	0	0	0	0	0	Surfaces	The Sims 2
The Good Butler End Table	$375	$56	$38	$150	0	0	0	0	0	10	Surfaces	The Sims 2
The Gray Woman of SimCity	$6,000	$0	$0	$0	0	0	0	0	0	0	Decorative	Nightlife
"The Grease Stands Alone" Island Bar	$1,780	$0	$0	$0	0	0	0	0	0	0	Miscellaneous	Glamour Stuff
The GrooveLayer 9000 Professional DJ Booth by HotBeets	$2,750	$413	$275	$1,100	0	0	0	0	10	3	Electronics	Nightlife
The Grillinator "BigBG"	$210	$31	$21	$84	1	0	0	0	4	8	Appliances	Open for Business
The Great Dress Rack	$3,000	$450	$300	$1,200	0	0	0	0	0	0	Miscellaneous	Open for Business
The HottCorp Burning 8-R Series Fire Jet	$325	$49	$33	$130	0	0	0	0	2	10	Surfaces	Nightlife
The Ideal Sim by Van Mel	$2,300	$345	$230	$920	0	0	0	0	0	2	Decorative	Glamour Stuff
The Impossible Mission Counter	$740	$111	$74	$296	0	0	0	3	10	3	Surfaces	Open for Business
The Impossible Mission Island Bar	$1,900	$277	$185	$740	0	0	0	0	0	1	Miscellaneous	Open for Business
The Impossible Mission Island Counter	$750	$112	$75	$300	0	0	0	0	12	10	Surfaces	Nightlife
The Inlaid Medallion	$875	$131	$88	$350	0	0	0	0	0	1	Decorative	Open for Business
The Inner Light	$200	$30	$20	$80	0	0	5	0	1	1	Lighting	The Sims 2
The Java de Pwi Barstool	$630	$94	$63	$252	0	0	0	0	2	2	Comfort	The Sims 2
The Kinder Koddler	$50	$7	$5	$20	0	0	0	0	0	0	Miscellaneous	Family Fun Stuff
The Kinder Kontainer	$275	$41	$27	$110	0	0	0	0	0	2	Miscellaneous	The Sims 2
The King's Jester	$3,200	$480	$320	$1,280	0	0	0	0	0	10	Decorative	Nightlife
The Lady On Red	$180	$0	$0	$0	0	0	0	0	0	1	Decorative	Open for Business
The Landwhale by Heavenla	$4,250	$638	$425	$1,700	0	4	0	0	1	2	Miscellaneous	Open for Business
The Larger Mission Coffee Table by Lulu Designs	$280	$42	$28	$112	0	0	0	0	6	4	Surfaces	Open for Business
The Legendary Bedscalibur Sleep System by Dulac Industries	$2,300	$345	$230	$920	0	6	0	0	6	4	Comfort	Open for Business
The Little Frock Tree	$80	$12	$8	$32	0	0	0	0	0	1	Decorative	Nightlife
The Lone Daisy	$285	$0	$0	$0	0	0	0	0	0	2	Decorative	Holiday
The Lying Fisherman Fountain	$1,200	$2	$0	$0	0	4	0	0	0	8	Decorative	Open for Business
The Meaning of Fruit	$1,500	$0	$0	$0	0	0	0	0	0	0	Decorative	The Sims 2
The Measure of a Sim Wooden Model	$100	$15	$10	$40	0	0	0	0	1	1	Decorative	The Sims 2
The Mighty Mighty by Gustav Stickler	$295	$44	$29	$118	0	0	0	0	0	10	Surfaces	Open for Business

Object Directory

Object	Price	Initial Depreciation	Daily Depreciation	Depreciation Limit	Hunger	Comfort	Hygiene	Bladder	Energy	Fun	Environment	Cleaning	Study	Charisma	Creativity	Body	Logic	Mechanical	Cooking	Function	Kids	Study	Dining Room	Outside	Living Room	Bathroom	Bedroom	Kitchen	Miscellaneous	Street	Outdoor	Shopping	Food	Game
Tell-Me-Tall by GrowCo	$90	$14	$9	$36	0	0	0	0	0	0	1									Decorative		X	X		X		X		X			X		FAMILY FUN STUFF
Tempered Tea Table	$221	$33	$22	$88	0	0	0	0	0	0	2									Surfaces		X	X		X		X		X			X		THE SIMS 2
Tempest Cooktop from Cuas	$2,500	$375	$250	$1,000	10	0	0	0	0	0	10									Appliances								X	X				X	OPEN FOR BUSINESS
Terribly Modern Counter	$650	$97	$65	$260	0	0	0	0	0	0	10									Surfaces		X	X					X	X				X	NIGHTLIFE
"That Place Over There" by Retina Bluri	$550	$0	$0	$0	0	0	0	0	0	0	10									Decorative		X			X		X		X			X		THE SIMS 2
The Aquadresser	$245	$37	$26	$98	0	0	0	0	0	0	4									Decorative						X			X			X		OPEN FOR BUSINESS
The Aquamoire	$300	$45	$30	$120	0	0	0	0	0	0	10									Miscellaneous		X	X		X		X		X			X		OPEN FOR BUSINESS
The Big Diver, by Big Yard Dudes Inc.	$4,750	$2	$0	$0	0	0	0	0	0	0	10									Miscellaneous				X					X		X			FAMILY FUN STUFF
The Big Gorilla, by Big Yard Dudes Inc.	$5,000	$2	$0	$0	0	0	0	0	0	0	10									Decorative				X					X		X			FAMILY FUN STUFF
The Big Knight, by Big Yard Dudes Inc.	$4,500	$2	$0	$0	0	0	0	0	0	0	10									Decorative				X					X		X			OPEN FOR BUSINESS
The Big Ninja, by Big Yard Dudes Inc.	$5,500	$2	$0	$0	0	0	0	0	0	0	10									Decorative				X					X		X			HOLIDAY STUFF
The Black and White "Bare" Bath	$900	$125	$90	$360	0	0	6	0	0	0	2									Plumbing						X			X					THE SIMS 2
The Castle Keep Toybox	$55	$8	$6	$22	0	0	0	0	0	7	6									Miscellaneous	X						X		X					FAMILY FUN STUFF
The "Classic" Wreath	$20	$3	$2	$8	0	0	0	0	0	0	6									Decorative			X				X		X			X		NIGHTLIFE
The Crazy Fun Toybench from "Craftin' It!" Industries	$1,500	$225	$150	$600	0	0	0	0	0	0	8									Hobbies	X	X					X		X					OPEN FOR BUSINESS
The Dragn's Horde by Mystical Furnishings	$345	$52	$36	$138	0	0	0	0	0	0	1									Miscellaneous	X	X	X		X		X	X	X			X		OPEN FOR BUSINESS
The Disguise of Mr. Romance	$140	$21	$14	$56	1	1	1	1	1	1	1									Miscellaneous				X					X					GLAMOUR STUFF
The Eclectic and Enigmatic Energizer	$0	$0	$0	$0	0	0	0	0	0	0	0									Aspiration									X				X	FAMILY FUN STUFF
The Etched Life by Anonymous	$1,200	$180	$120	$480	0	0	0	0	0	0	9									Decorative		X	X		X		X		X			X		THE SIMS 2
The Fishy Rug	$150	$23	$15	$60	0	0	0	0	0	0	0									Decorative		X	X		X	X	X	X	X			X		NIGHTLIFE
The Forbidden Fruit Counter by Neontrix	$590	$89	$59	$236	0	0	0	0	0	0	10									Surfaces		X	X		X	X	X	X	X			X		NIGHTLIFE
The Fourth Element Wall Hanging	$5,000	$0	$0	$0	0	0	0	0	0	0	0									Decorative	X	X	X		X	X	X	X	X			X		NIGHTLIFE
The Fun Spot Kids Rug	$135	$20	$14	$54	0	0	0	0	0	0	10									Decorative		X	X		X	X	X	X	X			X		NIGHTLIFE
The Classic Chair	$920	$138	$92	$368	0	9	0	0	0	0	2									Comfort		X	X		X		X		X			X		THE SIMS 2

The four numeric columns to the right of each item name (price/depreciation values) followed by the item's Category and originating Game/Expansion Pack.

Object	Price				Category	Game/Pack
The Talking Table	$775	$41	$77	$10	Surfaces	The Sims 2
The "That Smells Great" Floral Workstation from 'Craftin' it' Industries	$1,000	$150	$100	$400	Hobbies	Open for Business
The "Towel on a Metal Ring" by DecorCorp	$150	$0	$0	$0	Decorative	Open for Business
The "Towel on a Metal Rod" by DecorCorp	$200	$0	$0	$0	Decorative	Open for Business
The "Towel on a Wooden Ring" by DecorCorp	$125	$0	$0	$0	Decorative	Open for Business
The "Towel on a Wooden Rod" by DecorCorp	$200	$0	$0	$0	Decorative	Open for Business
The Tragic Stack-n-Stack Cube from UpbDuggery n Stuff	$150	$22	$15	$60	Surfaces	Open for Business
The Tray o' Orbs from Orby Designs	$850	$0	$0	$0	Decorative	Open for Business
The Truth is Somewhere	$55	$5	$3	$4	Decorative	Open for Business
The "Watt is it" Table Lamp	$35	$5	$3	$14	Lighting	The Sims 2
The Yomoshoto Evasion	$6,250	$338	$225	$2,500	Miscellaneous	University
Thinking Cap	$0	$0	$0	$0	Aspiration	The Sims 2
"Thirsty" the bath mat by Lumpen Lumeniat	$50	$8	$5	$20	Decorative	Nightlife
Thrice As Nice Floor Lamp	$100	$10	$7	$28	Lighting	Nightlife
Tibetan Desk	$670	$100	$67	$268	Surfaces	The Sims 2
Tinkle Trainer 6000 Potty Chair	$70	$10	$7	$28	Miscellaneous	The Sims 2
Titania Vineyards 1914 Toasting Set	$350	$52	$35	$140	Miscellaneous	The Sims 2
Torcher Clamshell Wall Sconce	$75	$11	$7	$30	Lighting	The Sims 2
Torcher "Luminescence" Sconce	$202	$30	$20	$80	Lighting	The Sims 2
Tornado Torch Floor Lamp	$330	$49	$33	$132	Lighting	The Sims 2
Total Mirror	$303	$45	$30	$121	Decorative	The Sims 2
Touch of Teak Bed	$1,800	$270	$180	$720	Comfort	The Sims 2
Touch of Teak Plymouth Armoire	$812	$121	$81	$324	Miscellaneous	The Sims 2
Touch of Teak Tansu Medium Dresser	$1,450	$217	$145	$580	Miscellaneous	Open for Business
Toyboxtopus	$55	$8	$5	$22	Miscellaneous	Family Fun Stuff
Transcendence by Joan Schnitzel	$800	$0	$0	$0	Decorative	The Sims 2
Trash Trapper 910i	$40	$6	$4	$16	Miscellaneous	Open for Business

Object Directory

Object	Price and Depreciation				Needs							Skills									Room Sort								Community Sort					
	Price	Initial Depreciation	Daily Depreciation	Depreciation Limit	Hunger	Comfort	Hygiene	Bladder	Energy	Fun	Environment	Cleaning	Study	Charisma	Creativity	Body	Logic	Mechanical	Cooking	Function	Kids	Study	Dining Room	Outside	Living Room	Bathroom	Bedroom	Kitchen	Miscellaneous	Street	Outdoor	Shopping	Food	
The Monster Under My Bed by Little Timmy	$35	$0	$0	$0	0	0	0	0	0	0	1									Decorative	X							X	X					The Sims™ 2
The More Impossible Mission Counter	$740	$111	$74	$296	0	0	0	0	0	0	1									Surfaces						X		X	X					Open for Business
The Muse by Stella Livorno	$3,200	$480	$320	$1,280	0	0	0	0	0	0	10									Decorative		X	X		X		X		X			X		Glamour Stuff
The My-Chi Sculpture Form	$2,500	$0	$0	$0	0	0	0	0	0	0	10									Decorative				X					X		X			The Sims™ 2
The Nofowle Armchair	$155	$23	$15	$62	0	5	0	0	0	0	0									Comfort					X				X			X		The Sims™ 2
The "Non-Deadly" Robot Crafting Station from 'Craftin' It!' Industries	$2,000	$300	$200	$800	0	0	0	0	0	0	0									Hobbies		X										X		Open for Business
The Oasis	$1,850	$277	$185	$740	0	0	0	0	0	3	0									Miscellaneous			X		X			X	X				X	Nightlife
The Old-Timer Recliner	$650	$97	$65	$316	0	7	0	0	0	0	0									Comfort					X				X					The Sims™ 2
The Parallelosign by Signalellocorp	$100	$15	$10	$40	0	0	0	0	0	0	1									Decorative									X		X			Nightlife
The Photon-Master 3000, Tabletop Edition	$220	$33	$22	$88	0	0	0	0	0	0	1									Lighting	X	X	X		X		X		X					Open for Business
The Pounding Waves Rug	$175	$26	$18	$70	0	0	0	0	0	0	0									Decorative	X	X	X		X		X		X			X		Family Fun Stuff
The Prismo RotoBall by LumiO	$550	$83	$55	$220	0	0	0	0	0	0	3									Lighting			X		X	X	X	X	X				X	Nightlife
The Qube	$340	$51	$34	$136	0	0	0	0	0	0	0									Surfaces		X			X				X					Nightlife
The Reef End Table	$100	$15	$10	$40	0	0	0	0	0	0	0									Surfaces					X		X					X		Family Fun Stuff
The Shadow Streamer	$375	$56	$38	$150	0	0	0	0	0	0	2									Lighting			X		X	X	X	X	X				X	Nightlife
The Simulated Succulent	$160	$24	$16	$64	0	0	0	0	0	0	1									Decorative			X	X	X			X	X		X	X	X	The Sims™ 2
The Slim System, by Jim Slimboy	$1,050	$157	$105	$420	0	4	0	0	4	0	2									Comfort							X							The Sims™ 2
The Slumber Saddle of Sleepnir by Dulac Industries	$1,080	$162	$108	$432	0	5	0	0	5	0	2									Comfort							X		X					Open for Business
The Smoogo Minima	$950	$143	$95	$380	0	1	0	0	0	2	0									Miscellaneous				X										Nightlife
The Smord P328	$2,250	$338	$225	$900	0	1	0	0	0	4	0									Miscellaneous				X										Nightlife
The Soma "Sleep Well"	$2,600	$390	$260	$1,040	0	6	0	0	6	0	5									Comfort							X							The Sims™ 2
The "Sometimes A Man Is An Island" Counter Island, by Fat City Counters	$630	$95	$63	$252	0	0	0	0	0	0	0									Surfaces								X	X				X	Nightlife
The Sorrowful Scions	$450	$0	$0	$0	0	0	0	0	0	0	4									Decorative		X		X					X		X			Nightlife
The "Spike Light"	$150	$22	$15	$60	0	0	0	0	0	0	1									Lighting				X					X		X			The Sims™ 2
The Stones of Stepping	$100	$15	$10	$40	0	0	0	0	0	0	0									Decorative		X	X	X	X		X		X		X	X		Family Fun Stuff
The Sumptuous Brasserie Barstool	$680	$102	$68	$272	0	6	0	0	0	0	1									Comfort					X			X	X				X	Nightlife

The Sims 2 Pets

Object	Price				Category	Game
Wall Flowers Sconce	$110	$16	$11	$44	Lighting	Open for Business
Wangauf Wall Planter	$200	$30	$20	$80	Decorative	The Sims™ 2
Way-Back Recliner	$149	$22	$14	$59	Comfort	University
Way Coolinary Countertop	$410	$61	$41	$164	Surfaces	University
Way Coolinary Island	$1,850	$277	$185	$740	Surfaces	University
Way Fluid Island Bar	$810	$121	$81	$324	Miscellaneous	University
Wear's the Sale? Shop Sign	$99	$14	$9	$39	Decorative	The Sims™ 2
We Call It Football Limited Edition Prints	$75	$0	$0	$0	Decorative	Open for Business
Weirdness is the Art Rug	$700	$150	$100	$400	Decorative	Family Fun Stuff
Well Rounded by Circulator	$3,100	$465	$310	$1,240	Comfort	The Sims™ 2
Werkbunnst Medium Stonewood Dresser	$490	$73	$49	$196	Miscellaneous	Open for Business
Werkbunnst Stonewood Dresser	$510	$76	$51	$204	Miscellaneous	Open for Business
Werkbunnst/Shuttlecraft Recliner	$790	$118	$79	$340	Comfort	The Sims™ 2
Whatay Buffet	$300	$45	$30	$120	Miscellaneous	University
White Rabbit Nirvana Blower	$1,720	$258	$172	$688	Lighting	The Sims™ 2
Whodunnit? Table Lamp	$300	$45	$30	$120	Lighting	Glamour Stuff
Wildflower Bouquet	$55	$8	$5	$22	Miscellaneous	The Sims™ 2
Will Lloyd Wright Dollhouse	$180	$27	$18	$72	Miscellaneous	The Sims™ 2
Winter Blossoms	$650	$0	$0	$0	Decorative	The Sims™ 2
Wishy-Washer from Brandname LX	$550	$82	$55	$220	Appliances	University
Wooden Post n' Lamp	$200	$30	$20	$26	Lighting	The Sims™ 2
Worldly Hue Streetlamp	$485	$72	$48	$194	Lighting	Open for Business
Wornable Easy Chair	$180	$27	$18	$72	Comfort	The Sims™ 2
Wornable Fridge	$375	$56	$37	$150	Appliances	The Sims™ 2
Wornable Sofa	$195	$27	$18	$72	Comfort	The Sims™ 2
Wrath of Sack Man Pinball	$1,750	$262	$175	$700	Electronics	University
XLR8R2 Food Processor	$220	$33	$22	$88	Appliances	University
Zecutime Cityside Loveseat	$400	$60	$40	$160	Comfort	The Sims™ 2
Zecutime Cityside Sofa	$550	$82	$55	$220	Comfort	The Sims™ 2
Zecutime Social Chair	$335	$50	$33	$134	Comfort	The Sims™ 2
Zenu Meditation Sleeper	$950	$142	$95	$380	Comfort	The Sims™ 2

Object Directory

Object	Price	Initial Depreciation	Daily Depreciation	Depreciation Limit	Hunger	Comfort	Hygiene	Bladder	Energy	Fun	Environment	Cleaning	Study	Charisma	Creativity	Body	Logic	Mechanical	Cooking	Function	Kids	Study	Dining Room	Outside	Living Room	Bathroom	Bedroom	Kitchen	Miscellaneous	Street	Outdoor	Shopping	Food	Game
TraumaTime "Incision Precision" Surgical Training Station	$0	$0	$0	$0	0	0	0	0	0	4	0									Career									X					The Sims 2
Trellisor Wedding Arch	$900	$135	$90	$360	0	0	0	0	0	0	2									Miscellaneous				X										The Sims 2
Tri-Tip Table	$155	$23	$15	$62	0	0	0	0	0	0	0									Surfaces			X					X						The Sims 2
Trattoa 27" MultiVid IV Television	$500	$75	$50	$200	0	0	0	0	0	6	0					X			X	Electronics					X		X		X					The Sims 2
Tulip Bouquet	$70	$10	$7	$28	0	0	0	0	0	0	2									Decorative			X		X		X	X						Nightlife
Tulip Light from Luxiary	$300	$45	$30	$120	0	0	0	0	0	0	0									Lighting					X		X							University
Tushugger Cushy Chair	$380	$57	$38	$152	0	7	0	0	0	0	0									Comfort					X		X							Nightlife
"Two Dogs and an Olive" by Mixt Hupp	$2,900	$435	$290	$1,160	0	0	0	0	0	0	10									Decorative		X	X		X		X	X						The Sims 2
Uber-Duper Deluxe Curves Ahead Sign	$72	$0	$0	$0	0	0	0	0	0	0	0									Decorative										X				Open for Business
Ug-No-More Makeover Station	$1,200	$180	$120	$480	0	0	0	0	0	0	2									Decorative					X	X	X		X					The Sims 2
Ultra Funky Curtain Clothes	$300	$45	$30	$120	0	0	0	0	0	0	0									Decorative					X		X							Nightlife
"Unbridled Braids" Oval Rug	$170	$25	$17	$68	0	0	0	0	0	0	2									Decorative					X		X	X						The Sims 2
Untitled by Len Bledgemann	$2,700	$405	$270	$1,080	0	0	0	0	0	0	10									Decorative		X	X		X		X	X				X		Open for Business
Used Propellers	$450	$68	$45	$180	0	0	0	0	0	0	1									Decorative					X		X							The Sims 2
ValueSpite Funny Bunny	$40	$6	$4	$16	0	0	0	0	0	7	0									Decorative	X													Holiday
VaporWare Submergence Spa	$8,500	$1,275	$850	$3,400	0	6	0	0	0	4	3									Plumbing						X					X			Family Fun Stuff
Vault of Mysteries Armoire by Mystical Furnishings	$400	$60	$40	$160	0	0	0	0	0	0	3									Miscellaneous							X					X		Glamour Stuff
VeggiStuf Produce Bin	$3,000	$450	$300	$1,200	0	0	0	0	0	0	0									Appliances				X				X			X	X		The Sims 2
Veil of Dreams	$120	$18	$12	$48	0	0	0	0	0	0	4									Decorative					X		X							Nightlife
Victor Victorian Pedestal Sink	$700	$105	$70	$280	0	0	0	0	0	0	0									Plumbing						X								The Sims 2
Vintage Retro Classic Dining Table	$235	$35	$24	$94	0	0	0	0	0	0	0									Surfaces			X					X						Nightlife
Vision Mirrors "Past Reflections"	$1,100	$165	$110	$440	0	0	0	0	0	0	6			X						Decorative					X	X	X					X		Nightlife
"Visivue" Dining Table	$500	$75	$50	$200	0	0	0	0	0	0	0									Surfaces			X					X						The Sims 2
VocoPhonicSim Karaoke Machine	$1,800	$270	$180	$720	0	0	0	0	0	8	0				X					Electronics					X								X	Nightlife
VroomMaster 4000	$149	$22	$14	$59	0	0	0	0	0	0	0									Electronics					X			X						The Sims 2
Waderfall	$35	$0	$0	$0	0	0	0	0	0	5	1									Decorative	X							X						The Sims 2

Chapter 13 — Socials

Interaction	Menu	Availability Daily A to B Above	Availability Daily A to B Below	And/Or	Availability Lifetime A to B Above	Availability Lifetime A to B Below	Crush	Love or Go Steady	Autonomous Personality	User Directed
About Grilled Cheese	Talk	-100	100	And	-100	100	-	-	-	Yes
About Interests	Ask	-10	100	And	0	100	Not allowed	Not allowed	-	Yes
Admire	Appreciate	0	100	And	0	100	-	-	Outgoing	Yes
Annoy	Irritate	-45	-1	Or	-30	-1	-	-	Mean	Yes
Apologize	Appreciate	-100	-20	And	-100	100	-	-	Nice	Yes
Apologize	Appreciate	-100	100	And	-100	100	-	-	-	Yes
Argue	Irritate	-100	100	Or	-100 (15)	100	-	-	Mean	Yes
Ask For Help	Sales	-	-	-	-	-	-	-	Outgoing	No
Ask to Go Out	Teen	-100	100	Or	-100	100	-	-	Not Autonomous	Yes
Ask to Leave	Ask to Leave	-100	100	Or	-100	100	-	-	Not Autonomous	Yes
Ask to Teach/ be Taught	Ask to Teach	-100	-100	Or	-100	100	-	-	Not Autonomous	Yes
Assign	Management	-	-	-	-	-	-	-	Not Autonomous	Yes
Attack	Fight	-100	-65	Or	-100	-65	-	-	Active	Yes
Attention	Ask For	-100 (0)	100	And	-100 (0)	100	-	-	Active	Yes
Back to My Place?	Ask	55	100	And	30	100	Not allowed	Not allowed	-	Yes
Backrub	Appreciate	40	100	And	15	100	-	-	Playful	Yes
Bad Mouth	Talk	0	100	And	0	100	-	-	-	Yes
Basic Sell	Sales	-	-	-	-	-	-	-	-	Yes
Bite Neck	Vampire	40	100	And	30	100	-	-	-	Yes
Blow Bubbles	Self	-	-	-	-	-	-	-	Nice	Yes
Blow Kiss	Dining	25	100	And	15	100	Sets	Sets	-	Yes
Bonfire Dance	Bonfire	-30	100	Or	-20	100	-	-	-	Yes
Brag	Talk	0	50	Or	10	50	-	-	Outgoing	Yes
Break Up	Break Up	-100	45	And	-100	45	-	-	Not Autonomous	Yes
Bust-a-Move!	Entertain	15	100	And	5	100	-	-	Active	Yes
Buy Lemonade	Lemonade Stand	-	-	-	-	-	-	-	-	Yes

Autonomous	If Accept, A's Social	If Accept, A's Daily	If Accept, A's Lifetime	If Accept, B's Social	If Accept, B's Daily	If Accept, B's Lifetime	If Reject, A's Social	If Reject, A's Daily	If Reject, A's Lifetime	If Reject, B's Social	If Reject, B's Daily	If Reject, B's Lifetime	Game
Yes	10	5	1	22	4	2	0	-10	-1	0	-7	-2	Nightlife
Yes	6	1	0	6	1	0	-3	-2	0	-3	-2	0	Nightlife
Yes	10	5	1	22	4	2	0	-10	-1	0	-7	-2	The Sims 2
Yes	0	0	0	0	0	0	4	-4	-1	-3	-10	-1	The Sims 2
Yes	16	10	0	16	10	0	0	0	0	0	0	0	The Sims 2
Yes	10	5	1	22	4	2	0	-10	-1	0	-7	-2	Nightlife
Yes	16	-7	-2	0	-9	-2	4	-6	-1	-2	-4	-1	The Sims 2
Yes	16	6	0	16	6	0	-5	-3	0	-5	-3	0	Open for Business
No	10	8	0	16	10	0	0	-8	-1	0	-2	0	The Sims 2
No	0	0	0	0	0	0	0	0	0	0	0	0	The Sims 2
No	14	6	0	20	13	0	-4	-4	0	-4	-4	0	The Sims 2
No	0	3	0	0	1	0	-	-	-	-	-	-	Open for Business
Yes	24	-7	-10	-8	-11	-10	-8	-11	-10	24	-7	-10	The Sims 2
Yes	14	5	0	20	13	0	-4	-4	0	-4	-4	0	The Sims 2
Yes	30	14	2	24	10	1	-10	-8	-1	-15	-10	-2	Nightlife
Yes	14	4	2	20	6	3	0	-7	-2	0	-10	-3	The Sims 2
No	24	5	0	24	5	0	10	-3	0	10	-6	0	Nightlife
Yes	8	3	0	8	3	0	-4	-2	0	-4	-3	0	Open for Business
Yes	14	6	2	20	13	2	-4	-4	-2	-4	-4	-2	Nightlife
Yes	-	-	-	-	-	-	-	-	-	-	-	-	Open for Business
Yes	14	8	1	14	8	1	8	-6	-1	0	-6	-1	Nightlife
Yes	20	5	1	20	5	1	-10	-4	-1	-10	-4	-1	University
Yes	14	6	0	20	4	0	0	-5	0	0	-5	0	The Sims 2
No	0	-20	-20	0	-50	-30	0	0	0	0	0	0	The Sims 2
Yes	18	9	2	18	9	2	-5	-5	-2	-5	-5	-2	University
Yes	-	-	-	-	-	-	-	-	-	-	-	-	Open for Business

Interaction	Menu	Availability Daily A to B Above	Availability Daily A to B Below	And/Or	Availability Lifetime A to B Above	Availability Lifetime A to B Below	Crush	Love or Go Steady	Autonomous Personality	User Directed
Call Over	Call Over	-100	100	Or	-100	100	-	-	Not Autonomous	Yes
Can't Afford	Sales	-	-	-	-	-	-	-	-	No
Caress	Flirt	65	100	And	40	100	Sets	Sets	Playful	Yes
Caress Hands	Dining	55	100	And	30	100	Sets	Sets	Nice	Yes
Change Diaper	Ask For	-100 (0)	100	Or	-100 (0)	100	-	-	Nice	Yes
Change Diaper	Social baby	-100 (20)	100	And	-100 (10)	100	-	-	Active	Yes
Change Diaper	Social toddler	-100 (20)	100	And	-100 (10)	100	-	-	Neat	Yes
Change Wage (Angry)	Management	-	-	-	-	-	-	-	Not Autonomous	Yes
Change Wage (Appreciative)	Management	-	-	-	-	-	-	-	Not Autonomous	Yes
Change Wage (Disappointed Neg)	Management	-	-	-	-	-	-	-	Not Autonomous	Yes
Change Wage (Disappointed Pos)	Management	-	-	-	-	-	-	-	Not Autonomous	Yes
Change Wage (Elated)	Management	-	-	-	-	-	-	-	Not Autonomous	Yes
Charm	Flirt	15	70	And	5	70	Sets	Sets	Nice	Yes
Chat	Talk	-100	100	Or	-100	100	-	-	None	Yes
Cheer Up	Appreciate	20	100	And	20	100	-	-	Nice	Yes
Complain About	Sales	-	-	-	-	-	-	-	Grouchy	No
Congratulate About	Memory	25	100	Or	25	100	-	-	Serious	No
Console	Memory	50	100	And	35	100	-	-	Nice	No
Cops and Robbers	Play	0	100	Or	10	100	-	-	Playful	Yes
Cuddle	Bed	35	100	And	25	100	Sets	Sets	Not Autonomous	Yes
Cuddle	Hot Tub	35	100	And	25	100	Sets	Sets	Not Autonomous	Yes
Cuddle	Love Tub	-5	100	And	-15	100	Sets	Sets	Not Autonomous	Yes
Cuddle	Sofa	35	100	And	25	100	Sets	Sets	Not Autonomous	Yes
Cuddle	Booth	35	100	And	25	100	Sets	Sets	-	Yes
Cuddle Baby	Social baby	-100 (0)	100	And	-100 (0)	100	-	-	Nice	Yes
Dance Close	Slow Dance	20	100	And	20	100	-	-	-	Yes
Dance Together	Dance	-10	100	Or	-10	100	-	-	Outgoing	Yes
Dance Together (on Shoes)	Dance	30	100	and	15	100	-	-	Nice	Yes
Dare to Peek	Coffin	-100	100	And	-100	100	-	-	Outgoing	Yes
Dazzle	Sales	-	-	-	-	-	-	-	Not Autonomous	Yes

Autonomous	If Accept, A's Social	If Accept, A's Daily	If Accept, A's Lifetime	If Accept, B's Social	If Accept, B's Daily	If Accept, B's Lifetime	If Reject, A's Social	If Reject, A's Daily	If Reject, A's Lifetime	If Reject, B's Social	If Reject, B's Daily	If Reject, B's Lifetime	Game
No	0	0	0	0	0	0	0	0	0	0	0	0	The Sims 2
Yes	22	5	0	24	3	0	-5	9	-3	-3	-4	-2	Open for Business
Yes	22	10	2	24	11	2	-5	-10	-3	-3	-10	-2	The Sims 2
Yes	20	9	1	20	10	1	-4	-9	-2	-3	-8	-2	Nightlife
Yes	14	6	0	20	13	0	-4	-4	0	-4	-4	0	The Sims 2
Yes	14	6	0	20	13	0	0	0	0	0	0	0	The Sims 2
Yes	14	6	0	20	13	0	-4	-4	0	-4	-4	0	The Sims 2
No	-15	-10	-4	-15	-12	-6	-	-	-	-	-	-	Open for Business
No	20	10	1	20	13	2	-	-	-	-	-	-	Open for Business
No	-10	-3	-2	-10	-4	-1	-	-	-	-	-	-	Open for Business
No	-10	-5	-2	-10	-7	-3	-	-	-	-	-	-	Open for Business
No	30	13	2	40	15	3	-	-	-	-	-	-	Open for Business
Yes	14	4	1	16	5	1	0	-4	-1	0	-6	0	The Sims 2
Yes	Variable	Variable	Variable	Variable	Variable	Variable	Variable	Variable	Variable	Variable	Variable	Variable	The Sims 2
Yes	16	6	1	30	8	2	0	-10	-1	0	-5	-1	The Sims 2
Yes	4	5	0	4	5	0	-2	-4	0	-2	-4	0	Open for Business
Yes	8	5	1	8	5	1	0	0	0	0	0	0	The Sims 2
Yes	8	5	1	8	5	1	0	0	0	0	0	0	The Sims 2
Yes	24	6	0	24	6	0	0	-5	0	0	-5	0	The Sims 2
No	20	6	2	20	10	2	0	-10	-3	0	-10	-2	The Sims 2
No	20	6	2	20	10	2	0	-10	-3	0	-10	-2	The Sims 2
No	20	6	2	20	10	2	0	-10	-3	0	-10	-2	The Sims 2
No	20	6	2	20	10	2	0	-10	-3	0	-10	-2	The Sims 2
Yes	20	6	2	20	10	2	0	-10	-3	0	-10	-2	Nightlife
Yes	20	4	1	40	4	1	0	0	0	0	0	0	The Sims 2
Yes	18	8	0	18	8	0	-5	-4	0	-2	-1	0	Nightlife
Yes	10	6	0	10	8	0	-2	-3	0	-2	-2	0	The Sims 2
Yes	16	5	2	16	6	2	0	-6	-2	0	-6	-2	Open for Business
Yes	22	9	1	6	4	0	-10	-10	-3	0	-7	-2	Nightlife
No	20	6	2	20	6	2	-10	-5	-3	-10	-6	-4	Open for Business

Interaction	Menu	Availability Daily A to B Above	Availability Daily A to B Below	And/Or	Availability Lifetime A to B Above	Availability Lifetime A to B Below	Crush	Love or Go Steady	Autonomous Personality	User Directed
Demote Manager	Management	-	-	-	-	-	-	-	Not Autonomous	Yes
Desire	Assess	-	-	-	-	-	-	-	Not Autonomous	Yes
Dirty Joke	Entertain	55	100	And	35	100	-	-	Playful	Yes
Do You Like What You See?	Ask	-100	100	And	-100	100	Not allowed	Not allowed	-	Yes
Encourage	Encourage	-100	100	Or	-100	100	-	-	Not Autonomous	Yes
Engagement	Propose	75	100	And	70	100	-	Required	Not Autonomous	Yes
Family Kiss	Kiss	-100	100	And	0	100	Not allowed	Not allowed	Nice	Yes
Family Kiss	Social toddler	-50 (-)	100	And	0 (-)	100	Not allowed	Not allowed	Nice	Yes
Feed a Bite	Dining	35	100	Or	25	100	Sets	Sets	-	Yes
First Kiss	Kiss	50	100	And	25	100	Sets	Sets	Not Autonomous	Yes
Food	Ask For	-100 (0)	100	Or	-100 (0)	100	-	-	Active	Yes
Freestyle Join	Entertain	25	100	Or	15	100	-	-	Outgoing	Yes
Friendly Hug	Hug	10	100	Or	10	100	-	-	Serious	Yes
Get Back to Work as...	Management	-	-	-	-	-	-	-	-	Yes
Go Steady	Propose	70	100	And	25	100	Required	-	Not Autonomous	Yes
Goose	Flirt	75	100	And	55	100	Required	Sets	Playful	Yes
Gossip	Talk	30	100	Or	35	100	-	-	Mean	Yes
Groom	Appreciate	50	100	And	25	100	-	-	Neat	Yes
Gross Out	Irritate	-100	-5	Or	-100	-5	-	-	Sloppy	Yes
Hand	Kiss	30	100	And	15	100	Sets	Sets	Playful	Yes
Handheld	Play	20	100	Or	10	100	-	-	-	Yes
Hang Out	Talk	10	100	Or	5	100	-	-	Outgoing	Yes
Hard-Sell	Sales	-	-	-	-	-	-	-	-	Yes
Head On Shoulders	Slow Dance	30	100	And	20	100	Sets	Sets	-	Yes
Hire	Management	-	-	-	-	-	-	-	Not Autonomous	Yes
Hit On	Flirt	45	80	And	25	80	Sets	Sets	Mean	Yes
Hold Hands	Flirt	55	100	And	30	100	Sets	Sets	Nice	Yes
Hot Smooch	Booth	60	100	And	45	100	Required	Sets	-	Yes
How Much Money Do You Have?	Ask	25	100	And	15	100	Not allowed	Not allowed	-	Yes
I Quit	Management	-	-	-	-	-	-	-	-	No

Autonomous	If Accept, A's Social	If Accept, A's Daily	If Accept, A's Lifetime	If Accept, B's Social	If Accept, B's Daily	If Accept, B's Lifetime	If Reject, A's Social	If Reject, A's Daily	If Reject, A's Lifetime	If Reject, B's Social	If Reject, B's Daily	If Reject, B's Lifetime	Game
No	20	-8	-2	-5	-9	-2	-	-	-	-	-	-	Open for Business
No	-	-	-	-	-	-	-	-	-	-	-	-	Open for Business
Yes	18	6	1	20	6	1	4	-8	-2	0	-12	-1	The Sims 2
Yes	0	0	0	0	0	0	0	0	0	0	0	0	Nightlife
No	14	6	0	20	13	0	-4	-4	0	-4	-4	0	The Sims 2
No	100	6	3	100	9	3	-30	-15	-5	-4	-8	-4	The Sims 2
Yes	18	5	1	20	6	1	0	-4	0	0	-5	0	The Sims 2
Yes	18	5	1	20	6	1	0	-4	0	0	-5	0	The Sims 2
Yes	20	10	1	16	9	1	-6	-8	-1	0	-6	-1	Nightlife
No	70	15	3	70	13	2	0	-15	-5	0	-10	-3	The Sims 2
Yes	14	6	0	20	13	0	-4	-4	0	-4	-4	0	The Sims 2
Yes	Variable	Variable	Variable	Variable	Variable	Variable	Variable	Variable	Variable	Variable	Variable	Variable	University
Yes	16	5	1	16	6	1	0	-5	-1	0	-5	-1	The Sims 2
Yes	4	-2	-1	4	-2	-1	-4	-4	-1	-4	-4	-1	Open for Business
No	30	6	3	30	9	3	-4	-10	-5	-4	-4	-4	The Sims 2
Yes	20	11	1	14	10	1	-2	-9	-2	-6	-11	-3	The Sims 2
Yes	24	9	0	24	9	0	0	-7	0	0	-6	0	The Sims 2
Yes	4	3	0	4	0	3	0	0	0	0	0	0	The Sims 2
Yes	24	6	0	24	6	0	6	-5	0	-4	-5	0	The Sims 2
Yes	16	9	1	16	9	1	8	-6	-1	0	-6	-1	Nightlife
No	0	4	0	0	4	0	-5	-2	0	-5	-2	0	University
Yes	Variable	Variable	Variable	Variable	Variable	Variable	Variable	Variable	Variable	Variable	Variable	Variable	University
Yes	12	4	0	12	4	0	-6	-3	0	-6	-4	0	Open for Business
Yes	16	5	1	16	6	1	0	-5	-1	0	-7	-1	Nightlife
No	20	6	0	20	10	0	-4	-8	0	-4	-5	0	Open for Business
Yes	18	8	1	14	9	1	4	-8	-1	0	-10	-2	The Sims 2
Yes	20	9	1	20	10	1	-4	-9	-2	-3	-8	-2	The Sims 2
Yes	22	13	2	20	11	2	0	-11	-2	0	-12	-3	Nightlife
Yes	30	13	1	30	6	1	-10	-7	-1	-15	-10	-1	Nightlife
Yes	24	-7	-5	-8	-13	-10	16	-10	-10	-10	-18	-10	Open for Business

Interaction	Menu	Availability Daily A to B Above	Availability Daily A to B Below	And/Or	Availability Lifetime A to B Above	Availability Lifetime A to B Below	Crush	Love or Go Steady	Autonomous Personality	User Directed
Insult	Irritate	-60	-5	Or	-45	-5	-	-	Mean	Yes
Introduce	Talk	35	100	And	20	100	-	-	Not Autonomous	Yes
Joke	Entertain	-10	100	Or	-5	100	-	-	Playful	Yes
Joy Buzzer	Prank	-100	100	And	-100	100	-	-	Mean	Yes
Kicky Bag	Play	15	100	Or	5	100	-	-	-	Yes
Kiss	Car	45	100	And	15	100	Required	Sets	Outgoing	Yes
Lay Off	Management	-	-	-	-	-	-	-	Not Autonomous	Yes
Leap into Arms	Hug	55	100	And	35	100	Required	Sets	Active	Yes
Look-for Mark	Self	-	-	-	-	-	-	-	-	Yes
Love Talk	Booth	40	100	And	25	100	Sets	Sets	-	Yes
Lower Hands	Slow Dance	45	100	And	35	100	Sets	Sets	-	Yes
Make Out	Bed	80	100	And	50	100	Required	Sets	Not Autonomous	Yes
Make Out	Hot Tub	80	100	And	50	100	Required	Sets	Not Autonomous	Yes
Make Out	Love Tub	40	100	And	20	100	Required	Sets	Not Autonomous	Yes
Make Out	Sofa	80	100	And	50	100	Required	Sets	Not Autonomous	Yes
Make Out	Kiss	80	100	And	50	100	Required	Sets	Outgoing	Yes
Make Out	Car	80	100	And	50	100	Required	Sets	Outgoing	Yes
Manipulation	Sales	-	-	-	-	-	-	-	Not Autonomous	Yes
Marriage (Join)	Propose	75	100	And	70	100	-	Required	Not Autonomous	Yes
Mary Mack	Play	15	100	Or	15	100	-	-	Lazy	Yes
Massage	Hot Tub	55	100	And	30	100	-	-	Not Autonomous	Yes
Massage	Love Tub	15	100	And	0	100	-	-	Not Autonomous	Yes
May I Help You?	Sales	-	-	-	-	-	-	-	-	Yes
Mood	Assess	-	-	-	-	-	-	-	Not Autonomous	Yes
Motivational Speech	Talk	-	-	-	-	-	-	-	Not Autonomous	Yes
Move In	Propose	60	100	And	45	100	-	-	Not Autonomous	Yes
Nag	Irritate	-100	100	And	25	100	-	-	Outgoing	Yes
Network	Talk	-	-	-	-	-	-	-	Not Autonomous	Yes
Noogie	Irritate	-25	50	And	-10	50	-	-	Playful	Yes
Offer At...	Sales	-	-	-	-	-	-	-	-	No

Autonomous	If Accept, A's Social	If Accept, A's Daily	If Accept, A's Lifetime	If Accept, B's Social	If Accept, B's Daily	If Accept, B's Lifetime	If Reject, A's Social	If Reject, A's Daily	If Reject, A's Lifetime	If Reject, B's Social	If Reject, B's Daily	If Reject, B's Lifetime	Game
Yes	16	-8	-1	-7	-14	-2	10	-10	-1	-7	-14	-2	The Sims 2
No	16	13	5	16	13	5	-5	-3	-1	-5	-3	-1	University
Yes	14	4	0	14	4	0	0	-4	0	0	-4	0	The Sims 2
Yes	18	4	0	16	4	0	-	-	-	-	-	-	University
Yes	10	1	0	10	1	0	0	-4	0	0	-4	0	University
No	18	10	2	16	10	2	8	-8	-2	0	-10	-2	Nightlife
No	24	6	0	20	6	0	20	-7	-5	-8	-13	-10	Open for Business
Yes	20	11	2	16	13	2	0	-15	-4	0	-10	-2	The Sims 2
No	-	-	-	-	-	-	-	-	-	-	-	-	Open for Business
Yes	18	6	1	18	8	1	0	-7	-1	0	-8	-1	Nightlife
Yes	18	10	2	16	10	2	8	-8	-2	0	-8	-3	Nightlife
No	30	19	4	30	19	4	8	-15	-4	0	-15	-4	The Sims 2
No	30	19	4	30	19	4	8	-15	-4	0	-15	-4	The Sims 2
No	30	19	4	30	19	4	8	-15	-4	0	-15	-4	The Sims 2
No	30	19	4	30	19	4	8	-15	-4	0	-15	-4	The Sims 2
Yes	30	19	4	30	19	4	8	-15	-4	0	-15	-4	The Sims 2
Yes	30	19	5	30	19	5	8	-15	-4	0	-15	-4	Nightlife
No	16	6	1	30	8	2	0	-10	-1	0	-5	-1	Open for Business
No	100	6	3	100	6	3	-100	-100	-85	-50	-50	-20	The Sims 2
Yes	30	8	0	30	8	0	0	-6	0	0	-7	0	The Sims 2
No	14	4	2	20	6	3	0	-7	-2	0	-10	-3	The Sims 2
No	14	4	2	20	6	3	0	-7	-2	0	-10	-3	The Sims 2
Yes	16	6	0	16	6	0	-5	-3	0	-5	-3	0	Open for Business
No	-	-	-	-	-	-	-	-	-	-	-	-	Open for Business
No	0	3	0	5	0	1	0	-5	0	-3	-1	0	Open for Business
No	40	6	3	40	6	3	-4	-10	-5	-4	-4	-4	The Sims 2
Yes	0	0	0	0	0	0	6	-4	0	-8	-8	-1	The Sims 2
No	40	6	1	40	6	1	-10	-7	-1	-10	-7	-1	Open for Business
Yes	14	6	1	6	-5	0	0	0	0	0	0	0	The Sims 2
Yes	16	5	0	16	5	0	-8	-4	-8	-8	-5	0	Open for Business

Interaction	Menu	Availability Daily A to B Above	Availability Daily A to B Below	And/Or	Availability Lifetime A to B Above	Availability Lifetime A to B Below	Crush	Love or Go Steady	Autonomous Personality	User Directed
On Date	Ask	0	100	And	0	100	Not allowed	Not allowed	-	Yes
On Outing	Ask	0	100	And	0	100	Not allowed	Not allowed	-	Yes
Pass On	Management	-	-	-	-	-	-	-	Not Autonomous	Yes
Peck	Hot Tub	40	100	And	20	100	Sets	Sets	Not Autonomous	Yes
Peck	Love Tub	0	100	And	-15	100	Sets	Sets	Not Autonomous	Yes
Peck	Sofa	40	100	And	20	100	Sets	Sets	Not Autonomous	Yes
Peck	Kiss	40	100	And	20	100	Sets	Sets	Nice	Yes
Perk Up	Talk	-	-	-	-	-	-	-	Not Autonomous	Yes
Pillow Fight	Play	40	100	Or	25	100	-	-	Playful	Yes
Play With	Social baby	-100 (0)	100	And	-100 (0)	100	-	-	Playful	Yes
Poke	Fight	-100	-15	Or	-100	-20	-	-	Mean	Yes
Power Network	Talk	-	-	-	-	-	-	-	Not Autonomous	Yes
Promote to Manager	Management	-	-	-	-	-	-	-	Not Autonomous	Yes
Punch U Punch Me	Play	45	100	Or	35	100	-	-	Mean	Yes
Rally Forth!	Self	-	-	-	-	-	-	-	Not Autonomous	Yes
Read To	Ask For	-50 (25)	100	And	-50 (15)	100	-	-	Serious	No
Read To	Social toddler	-50 (25)	100	And	-50 (15)	100	-	-	Outgoing	Yes
Red Hands	Play	35	100	Or	25	100	-	-	Active	Yes
Ride Home	Ask	-100	100	Or	-100	100	-	-	-	-
Rock Paper Scissors	Play	-10	100	and	5	100	-	-	Playful	Yes
Romantic Hug	Hug	35	100	And	25	100	Sets	Sets	Outgoing	Yes
Romantic Kiss	Sofa	60	100	And	35	100	Sets	Sets	Not Autonomous	Yes
Romantic Kiss	Kiss	60	100	And	35	100	Sets	Sets	Outgoing	Yes
Rub Belly	Baby	60	100	Or	50	100	-	-	Serious	Yes
School Cheer	Entertain	5	100	Or	5	100	-	-	Outgoing	Yes
Secret Handshake	Entertain	-100	100	Or	-100	100	-	-	Outgoing	Yes
Send Home for the Day	Management	-	-	-	-	-	-	-	Not Autonomous	Yes
Serenade	Flirt	70	100	And	60	100	Required	Required	Outgoing	Yes
Set Uniform	Management	-	-	-	-	-	-	-	Not Autonomous	Yes
Share Interests	Talk	35	100	Or	20	100	-	-	Not Autonomous	Yes

Autonomous	If Accept, A's Social	If Accept, A's Daily	If Accept, A's Lifetime	If Accept, B's Social	If Accept, B's Daily	If Accept, B's Lifetime	If Reject, A's Social	If Reject, A's Daily	If Reject, A's Lifetime	If Reject, B's Social	If Reject, B's Daily	If Reject, B's Lifetime	Game
No	14	6	0	20	4	0	0	-5	0	0	-5	0	Nightlife
No	10	1	1	22	4	2	0	-10	-1	0	-7	-2	Nightlife
No	30	6	1	30	9	2	0	-7	0	0	-5	-1	Open for Business
No	14	8	1	14	8	1	8	-6	-1	0	-6	-1	The Sims 2
No	14	8	1	14	8	1	8	-6	-1	0	-6	-1	The Sims 2
No	14	8	1	14	8	1	8	-6	-1	0	-6	-1	The Sims 2
Yes	14	8	1	14	8	1	8	-6	-1	0	-6	-1	The Sims 2
No	0	4	0	0	6	1	0	-5	-1	0	-3	0	Open for Business
Yes	Variable	Variable	Variable	Variable	Variable	Variable	-8	-5	-1	-2	-5	-2	University
Yes	20	4	3	2	25	1	0	0	0	0	0	0	The Sims 2
Yes	6	0	0	-6	-8	-2	10	-8	-2	10	-7	-2	The Sims 2
No	40	6	1	40	6	1	-10	-7	-10	-10	-7	-1	Open for Business
No	22	10	2	24	11	2	-	-	-	-	-	-	Open for Business
Yes	28	8	0	28	8	0	0	-5	0	0	-5	0	The Sims 2
No	0	0	0	0	0	0	0	0	0	0	0	0	Open for Business
No	14	6	0	20	13	0	-4	-4	0	-4	-4	0	The Sims 2
Yes	14	6	2	20	6	3	-4	-4	0	-4	-4	0	The Sims 2
Yes	24	6	0	24	6	0	0	-7	0	0	-5	0	The Sims 2
-	-	-	-	-	-	-	-	-	-	-	-	-	Nightlife
Yes	16	6	0	16	6	0	0	-5	0	0	-5	0	Open for Business
Yes	20	6	2	20	10	2	0	-10	-3	0	-10	-2	The Sims 2
No	24	16	3	26	16	3	8	-13	-3	0	-13	-4	The Sims 2
Yes	24	16	3	26	16	3	8	-13	-3	0	-13	-4	The Sims 2
Yes	20	11	3	32	13	3	-10	-12	-3	0	-10	-3	The Sims 2
Yes	12	4	0	12	4	0	-3	-2	0	-3	-2	0	University
Yes	20	5	1	20	5	1	-10	-4	-2	-10	-4	-2	University
No	-	-	-	-	-	-	-	-	-	-	-	-	Open for Business
Yes	28	13	2	30	15	2	-6	-12	-3	0	-10	-3	The Sims 2
No	-	-	-	-	-	-	-	-	-	-	-	-	Open for Business
No	6	0	0	6	0	0	-3	-3	0	-3	-3	0	The Sims 2

The Sims 2 Pets

Interaction	Menu	Availability Daily A to B Above	Availability Daily A to B Below	And/Or	Availability Lifetime A to B Above	Availability Lifetime A to B Below	Crush	Love or Go Steady	Autonomous Personality	User Directed
Shoo from Room	Shoo	-100	100	Or	-100	100	-	-	Not Autonomous	Yes
Shove	Fight	-100	-25	Or	-100	-30	-	-	Outgoing	Yes
Show Item	Sales	-	-	-	-	-	-	-	-	Yes
Show Off	Play	15	100	or	10	100	-	-	Active	Yes
Slap	Fight	-100	-40	Or	-100	-40	-	-	Serious	Yes
Slow Dance	Slow Dance	30	100	And	15	100	-	-	-	Yes
Smooch	Kiss	70	100	And	40	100	Required	Sets	Playful	Yes
Smooch	Slow Dance	65	100	And	45	100	Required	Sets	-	Yes
Snuggle	Social toddler	-50 (-)	100	And	0 (-)	100	-	-	Nice	Yes
Snuggle	Sofa	35	100	Or	30	100	Required	Required	Not Autonomous	Yes
Splash	Hot Tub	20	100	Or	15	100	-	-	Not Autonomous	Yes
Splash	Love Tub	-20	100	Or	-25	100	-	-	Not Autonomous	Yes
Squeeze	Hug	70	100	And	55	100	Required	Sets	Playful	Yes
Stay the Night	Propose	55	100	And	40	100	-	-	Not Autonomous	Yes
Steal a Bite	Dining	-100	100	Or	-100	100	-	-	-	Yes
Suggestion	Flirt	25	70	And	15	70	Sets	Sets	Playful	Yes
Surprise Engagement	Dining	75	100	And	70	100	Required	Required	-	Yes
Sweet Talk	Flirt	35	80	And	20	80	Sets	Sets	Outgoing	Yes
Tag	Play	-25	100	Or	5	100	-	-	Active	Yes
Take a Break	Management	-	-	-	-	-	-	-	Not Autonomous	Yes
Talk To	Social baby	-100 (-100)	100	And	-100 (-100)	100	-	-	Playful	Yes
Talk To	Social toddler	-50 (-50)	100	And	-50 (-50)	100	-	-	Outgoing	Yes
Talk to Belly	Baby	15	100	Or	25	100	-	-	Playful	Yes
Teach to Talk	Social toddler	25 (-)	100	And	15 (-)	100	-	-	Not Autonomous	Yes
Teach to Use Potty	Social toddler	-100 (-)	100	And	-100 (-)	100	-	-	Not Autonomous	Yes
Teach to Walk	Social toddler	25 (-)	100	And	15 (-)	100	-	-	Not Autonomous	Yes
Tease	Memory	-100	10	Or	-100	10	-	-	Mean	No
Tease	Play	-	-	-	-	-	-	-	Mean	Yes
Tell Secret	Talk	60	100	Or	60	100	-	-	Mean	Yes
Tender Kiss	Bed	50	100	And	25	100	Sets	Sets	Not Autonomous	Yes
Tender Kiss	Hot Tub	50	100	And	25	100	Sets	Sets	Not Autonomous	Yes
Tender Kiss	Love Tub	10	100	And	-10	100	Sets	Sets	Not Autonomous	Yes
Tender Kiss	Kiss	50	100	And	25	100	Sets	Sets	Nice	Yes

Autonomous	If Accept, A's Social	If Accept, A's Daily	If Accept, A's Lifetime	If Accept, B's Social	If Accept, B's Daily	If Accept, B's Lifetime	If Reject, A's Social	If Reject, A's Daily	If Reject, A's Lifetime	If Reject, B's Social	If Reject, B's Daily	If Reject, B's Lifetime	Game
No	14	6	0	20	13	0	-4	-4	0	-4	-4	0	The Sims 2
Yes	8	0	0	-8	-9	-3	10	-7	-1	14	-8	-3	The Sims 2
Yes	20	4	0	20	4	0	10	-5	0	10	-5	0	Open for Business
Yes	14	6	0	20	13	0	-4	-4	0	-4	-4	0	Open for Business
Yes	10	0	0	-15	-10	-5	14	-5	-3	30	-7	-3	The Sims 2
Yes	18	8	0	18	8	0	-5	-4	0	-5	-3	0	Nightlife
Yes	22	13	2	20	11	2	0	-11	-2	0	-12	-3	The Sims 2
Yes	22	13	2	20	11	2	0	-11	-2	0	-12	-3	Nightlife
Yes	20	6	2	20	10	2	0	-10	-3	0	-10	-2	The Sims 2
No	24	8	2	24	10	2	0	-10	-2	0	-10	-2	The Sims 2
No	12	5	0	14	8	0	0	-4	0	0	-8	-1	The Sims 2
No	12	5	0	14	5	0	0	-5	0	0	-5	0	The Sims 2
Yes	20	6	2	20	10	2	0	-10	-2	0	-10	-2	The Sims 2
No	14	6	0	20	13	0	-4	-4	0	-4	-4	0	The Sims 2
Yes	8	5	0	6	3	0	8	-3	0	0	-4	0	Nightlife
Yes	16	5	1	16	6	1	0	-5	-1	0	-7	-1	The Sims 2
No	100	6	3	100	9	3	-30	-15	-5	-4	-8	-4	Nightlife
Yes	18	6	1	18	8	1	0	-7	-1	0	-8	-1	The Sims 2
Yes	20	6	0	20	6	0	0	-5	0	0	-5	0	The Sims 2
No	10	1	0	10	3	0	-	-	-	-	-	-	Open for Business
Yes	16	5	2	16	10	2	-5	-2	-1	5	1	2	The Sims 2
Yes	14	6	2	20	6	3	-4	-4	0	-4	-4	0	The Sims 2
Yes	20	6	2	28	8	2	-10	-8	-2	0	-10	-3	The Sims 2
No	14	6	0	20	13	0	-4	-4	0	-4	-4	0	The Sims 2
No	0	6	0	0	13	0	0	-4	0	0	-4	0	The Sims 2
No	14	6	0	20	13	0	-4	-4	0	-4	-4	0	The Sims 2
Yes	14	6	1	10	6	1	-5	-4	-1	4	-10	-1	The Sims 2
Yes	-	-	-	-	-	-	-10	0	0	-10	-10	-3	Open for Business
Yes	24	9	0	24	9	0	0	-7	0	0	-6	0	The Sims 2
No	18	10	2	16	10	2	8	-8	-2	0	-8	-2	The Sims 2
No	18	10	2	16	10	2	8	-8	-2	0	-8	-2	The Sims 2
No	18	10	2	16	10	2	8	-8	-2	0	-8	-2	The Sims 2
Yes	18	10	2	16	10	2	8	-8	-2	0	-8	-2	The Sims 2

Interaction	Menu	Availability Daily A to B Above	Availability Daily A to B Below	And/Or	Availability Lifetime A to B Above	Availability Lifetime A to B Below	Crush	Love or Go Steady	Autonomous Personality	User Directed
Throw Drink	Irritate	15	15	And	10	10	-	-	-	Yes
Throw Drink	Dining	15	15	And	10	10	-	-	-	Yes
Throw Food	Dining	-100	100	And	-100	100	-	-	Playful?	Yes
Tickle	Play	20	100	Or	15	100	-	-	Playful	Yes
Tickle	Social toddler	20 (10)	100	And	15 (0)	100	-	-	Playful	Yes
Toast	Dining	20	100	And	10	100	-	-	-	Yes
Toss in Air	Social toddler	-50 (25)	100	And	-50 (10)	100	-	-	Active	Yes
Tune Up	Flirt	-	-	-	-	-	Sets	Sets	Not Autonomous	Yes
Unassign	Management	-	-	-	-	-	-	-	Not Autonomous	Yes
Up Arm Kiss	Kiss	55	100	And	30	100	Sets	Sets	Playful	Yes
Ventrilo-Fart	Prank	-100	100	And	-100	100	-	-	Sloppy	Yes
Water Balloon	Prank	-100	100	And	-100	100	-	-	Playful	Yes
What Are Your Skills?	Ask	-20	100	And	-10	100	Not allowed	Not allowed	-	Yes
What Do You Want/Fear?	Ask	15	100	And	5	100	Not allowed	Not allowed	-	Yes
What Is Your Job?	Ask	7	100	And	0	100	Not allowed	Not allowed	-	Yes
What Turns You On/Off?	Ask	5	100	And	0	100	Not allowed	Not allowed	-	Yes
What's Your Sign?	Ask	-100	100	And	-100	100	Not allowed	Not allowed	-	Yes
Wolf Whistle	Flirt	-15	50	And	-15	40	Sets	Sets	Sloppy	Yes
WooHoo	Car	85	100	And	65	100	Required	Required	Outgoing	Yes
WooHoo	Photo Booth	85	100	And	65	100	Required	Required	Outgoing	Yes
WooHoo/Try for Baby	Bed	85	100	And	65	100	Required	Required	Not Autonomous	Yes
WooHoo/Try for Baby	Hot Tub	85	100	And	65	100	Required	Required	Not Autonomous	Yes
WooHoo/Try for Baby	Love Tub	45	100	And	25	100	Required	Required	Not Autonomous	Yes
WooHoo/Try for Baby	Booth	-100	100	Or	-100	100	Required	Required	Not Autonomous	Yes
You're Fired	Management	-	-	-	-	-	-	-	Not Autonomous	Yes

Autonomous	If Accept, A's Social	If Accept, A's Daily	If Accept, A's Lifetime	If Accept, B's Social	If Accept, B's Daily	If Accept, B's Lifetime	If Reject, A's Social	If Reject, A's Daily	If Reject, A's Lifetime	If Reject, B's Social	If Reject, B's Daily	If Reject, B's Lifetime	Game
Yes	8	-7	-3	-10	-13	-4	-	-	-	-	-	-	Nightlife
Yes	8	-7	-3	-10	-13	-4	-	-	-	-	-	-	Nightlife
Yes	10	8	1	8	8	1	8	-6	-1	0	-6	-1	Nightlife
Yes	16	5	0	16	5	0	0	-5	-1	0	-6	-1	The Sims 2
Yes	16	5	0	16	5	0	0	-5	-1	0	-8	-2	The Sims 2
Yes	14	6	0	14	10	0	-	-	-	-	-	-	Nightlife
Yes	14	6	2	20	13	2	0	-10	-3	0	-10	-2	The Sims 2
Yes	14	5	1	14	8	1	-4	-6	-2	-4	-4	-1	Open for Business
No	0	1	0	0	1	0	-	-	-	-	-	-	Open for Business
Yes	20	11	1	24	11	2	8	-10	-1	0	-10	-1	The Sims 2
Yes	18	4	0	16	4	0	-	-	-	-	-	-	University
Yes	18	4	0	16	4	0	-	-	-	-	-	-	University
Yes	10	1	0	10	1	0	-4	-1	0	-4	-1	0	Nightlife
Yes	14	9	0	20	13	0	-4	-4	0	-4	-4	0	Nightlife
Yes	10	5	0	10	5	0	-4	-3	0	-4	-3	0	Nightlife
Yes	14	4	0	14	4	0	-4	-2	0	-4	-1	0	Nightlife
Yes	10	1	0	10	1	0	-4	-1	0	-4	-1	0	Nightlife
Yes	14	4	1	14	4	1	-8	-3	-1	0	-6	-2	University
No	50	13	8	50	13	8	0	-12	-5	0	-15	-5	Nightlife
No	50	13	8	50	13	8	0	-12	-5	0	-15	-5	Nightlife
No	50	9	1	30	9	1	-5	-6	-1	-45	-6	-1	The Sims 2
No	50	13	8	50	13	8	0	-12	-5	0	-15	-5	The Sims 2
No	50	13	8	50	13	8	0	-12	-5	0	-15	-5	The Sims 2
No	50	13	8	50	13	8	0	-12	-5	0	-15	-5	The Sims 2
No	24	-7	-5	-8	-13	-10	16	-10	-10	-10	-18	-10	Open for Business

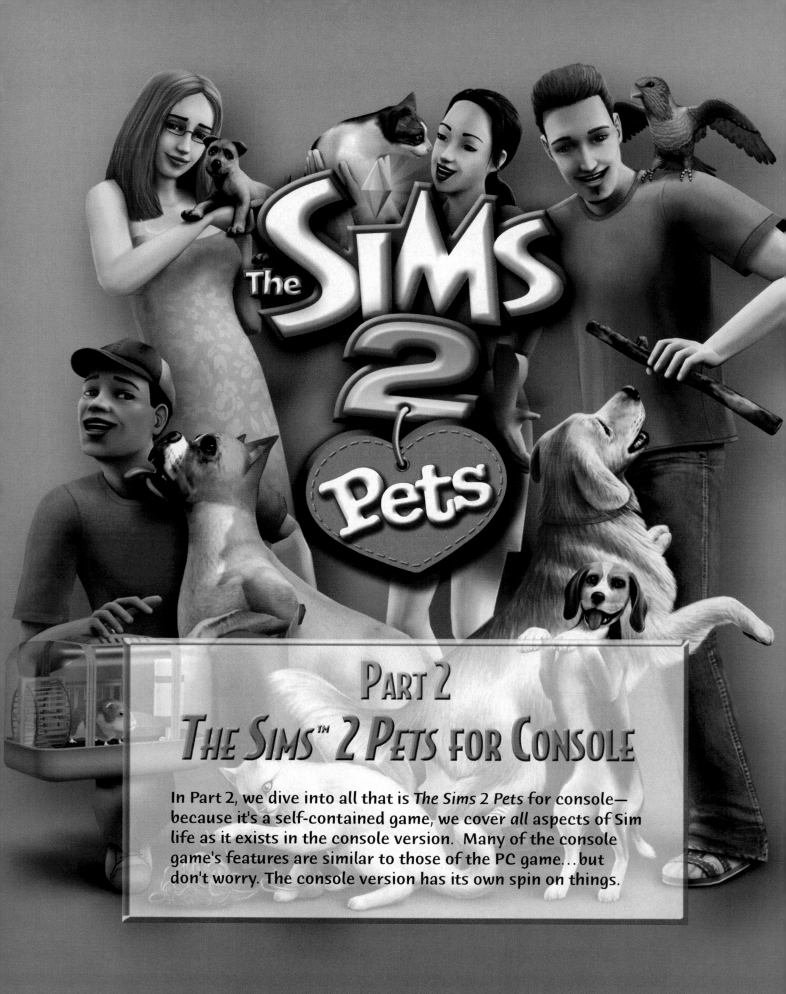

PART 2
THE SIMS™ 2 PETS FOR CONSOLE

In Part 2, we dive into all that is *The Sims 2 Pets* for console—because it's a self-contained game, we cover *all* aspects of Sim life as it exists in the console version. Many of the console game's features are similar to those of the PC game…but don't worry. The console version has its own spin on things.

Chapter 14

THE NEIGHBORHOOD VIEW AND CONTROL MODES

Pets change everything. Well, maybe not everything, but in the world of *The Sims 2 Pets*, they seem to have changed a whole lot. This chapter acquaints you with the structure of this latest console incarnation, whether you're an experienced PC player trying your hand at the console version, a console veteran who needs to know the differences between last year's version and this year's, or a newcomer who's never heard a word of Simlish or ever controlled a Sim (let alone a Sim's pet).

Game Overview

The Sims 2 Pets is an entirely freeform experience; there are no rigid goals and objectives you must attain to progress.

That's not to say there's nothing to strive for. In fact, there's *always* something, usually just out of reach, to propel your desires and attention. Within this seemingly shapeless sandbox are several organic goals you can strive toward:

◆ Make lots of money: Climbing the career ladder in as many careers as possible is a well-established and very challenging ambition.

◆ Train perfect pets. Teach your pets to behave perfectly and school them in all commands.

◆ Upgrade the Town Square: The more you utilize the services of the Town Square, the more useful it becomes, upgrading in both appearance and inventory, providing access to the most powerful objects and services.

◆ Unlock Create a Cat and Create a Dog colors, markings, collars, and apparel by satisfying pets' Wants.

◆ Unlock new neighbors for your Sims to meet and befriend by satisfying your Sims' Wants.

Or, you can just play any way you please, sailing by your own compass. No matter what you choose, this book will aid you in discovering how to best plot your course.

The journey begins at the Neighborhood map.

The Neighborhood Map

Your adventure begins with the naming of your Sims' town ("Whiskerton" by default, but the choice is yours).

The neighborhood consists of:

◆ Six occupied residential lots, including a tutorial lot.

◆ Four unoccupied residential lots

◆ The Real Estate Office (the doorway to Create A Family; see the "Creating Your Sims and Pets" chapter)

tip

Since pets are new to this version of the game, even experienced console players should begin with the tutorial lot.

You, therefore, have three choices:

1. Learn the ropes with the tutorial.
2. Kick off with a pre-made household.
3. Build a family of your own and move it into an empty lot.

Unoccupied Lots

To start a family of your own creation, take on one of the four unoccupied lots. These lots contain no families but also no structures or objects of any kind. They're clean slates for you to develop.

As the game goes on, you may have lots that are unoccupied but improved (saved with structures and/or objects). From the neighborhood view, these function the same as unoccupied lots.

Unoccupied (improved or not) lots offer three options: Move in Family, Bulldoze (deleting any structures and objects), or Build (entering Build mode to add or change structures).

note

For more on building a house, see the "Build Your Own Abode" chapter.

tip

If you want to start with a new family but don't want to build a whole new structure, move out one of the existing families to empty the lot and move your new family in. The former residents will inhabit the Family Bin in the Real Estate Office, awaiting a new home.

The four unoccupied lots are:

◆ Rock Ridge: §8,500
◆ Lemming Point: §14,000
◆ Redwood Glen: §8,500
◆ Fishbone Island: §14,000

note

The cost of unoccupied lots reflects the location. The two expensive lots have island and vista locations.

Occupied Lots

Occupied lots contain a structure, objects, and Sims (and pets). These lots can be played ("Enter House") or cleared of residents ("Move Out Family"). The latter option moves the family to the Real Estate Office's Family Bin and deletes all nonstructural objects on the lot (adding the current value of the objects to the Family Funds). After a family is moved out, a lot becomes unoccupied, with the option to Build or Bulldoze (see "Unoccupied Lots").

Dogwood Forest

◆ Family: Oakley
◆ Funds: §4,315
◆ Sims: Buck
◆ Pet(s): Rufus (male dog), Lucky (male dog), Hamhock (male dog)

Feline Farms

◆ Family: Simpson
◆ Funds: §1,111
◆ Sims: Dottie
◆ Pet(s): Shnookems (male cat), Daisy (female cat), Bella (female cat), Smokey (male cat), Oscar (male cat)

Firefly Lake

◆ Family: May
◆ Funds: §2,292
◆ Sims: Mira May, Penelope Arnold, Vivian Parker, Marsha Worthington
◆ Pet(s): Presto Parker (male dog), Falafel May (male cat)

Paw Valley Road

◆ Family: Townsend
◆ Funds: §8,986
◆ Sims: Linda, William
◆ Pet(s): Henrietta (female dog), Fauntleroy (male dog)

Serenity Falls

◆ Family: Hardiman
◆ Funds: §4,498
◆ Sims: Dan, Kate
◆ Pet(s): Buster (male dog)

Tutorial

- Family: Newbie
- Sims: Bob, Betty
- Funds: $3,562
- Pet(s): Buddy (male dog)

Control Modes

There are two ways to control your Sims; the second is exclusive to the console incarnation of this storied franchise:

1. Classic Control: Control your Sims indirectly by using the cursor to select an object or Sim you want your Sim to interact with, then choosing among the available interactions.
2. Direct Control: Control your Sims directly by moving them around the lot. Approach an object or Sim to interact with it.

 note To switch between control modes, press the Toggle Control Mode button. To cycle through all controllable Sims, press the Switch Sims button.

In Classic Control mode, you don't control your Sims as much as you control what you want them to interact with by choosing it with the cursor.

Each method has its advantages and its compromises.

In Direct Control mode, you control your Sim rather than a cursor. Want to interact with that trampoline? Walk right up to it and start bouncing.

 tip Though you could certainly play exclusively in either Classic or Direct Control mode, the most efficient and effective way to play is to switch between the modes for activities best done in each.

For instance, you could do most of your Need satisfaction (except Hunger) and skill work in Classic Control mode, switching to Direct Control to prepare food.

Classic Control Mode

Traditionally, Sims move at your command, but you have no direct control over the route they take or the way they opt to do things. As in Direct Control mode, the currently controllable Sim is highlighted with a green crystal (known as the "plumb bob") over his or her head. However, moving the control stick moves not your Sim but rather a green cursor that you use to select an object or Sim to interact with.

 note The shape of the Classic Control cursor changes according to the kind of object it's selected.

Icons along the bottom of the screen indicate the actions your Sim will do in order.

The benefits of the Classic Control system, however, substantially make up for this slight relinquishment of control. You can, for instance, queue up several activities for your Sim to perform in order and leave him or her to them. Moreover, you can see queued icons for actions your Sim has chosen autonomously. By contrast, in Direct Control, you can effectively only queue up social interactions.

 tip When trying to keep multiple controllable Sims busy, use Classic Control to queue up several interactions, then switch to another Sim and repeat, and so on.

Direct Control Mode

With direct Sim control, you control your Sims, well, directly. Want them to use the TV? Direct them to the TV and push the Select Interaction button. Any available interactions for the TV appear for your selection.

note

When interacting with or holding an object in Direct Control mode, your Sims have easier access to several special subinteractions. They can, for instance, read a magazine while on the toilet or search the cushions of a sofa for loose change or other surprises.

In Classic Control mode, you'd have to position your indicator over the object to activate these additional interactions.

Direct Control mode provides substantially greater command than Classic Control over your Sims' preparation of food (see the "Food Creation" chapter).

tip

Another advantage of Direct Control over Classic Control is your Sim's tendency to run. A Sim under Classic Control runs only when late for the carpool. Direct Control mode's speed of foot is much more time efficient and makes moving around the lot in Direct Control mode a must.

Food preparation is much easier in Direct Control mode since you choose what steps to take, rather than trying to override your Sim's own choices.

Many of the food preparation interactions are either inaccessible or more difficult in Classic Control mode, depending more heavily on fast button pushing.

For example, in food preparation, when Sims remove ingredients from a refrigerator, the surface or object they prepare the food on or with dictates what dish results. In Classic Control mode, you've only a brief time to direct this choice, requiring fast adjustment of the interaction indicator before your Sim makes a decision. In Direct Control mode, however, when the Sim closes the fridge, a new interaction selector pops up awaiting your preference on what to do with the food.

Social Interactions in Direct Control

Though queuing interactions is mostly exclusive to Classic Control mode, you can also do it in Direct Control mode when your Sim interacts with another Sim or a pet.

note

Actually, you CAN queue nonsocial interactions in Direct Control—it's just seldom available. Since all queued interactions would have to be in the immediate vicinity to be queued, these situations are very rare.

Once a social interaction is selected, additional (up to eight) social interactions with the same Sim or pet can be queued before the first interaction is even complete.

Town Square

The Town Square is the happenin' destination for Sims and their pets. It has a great deal to offer and you can help it offer even more.

The Town Square features five stores:

Pet Bakery: Pick up a treat for your pet.

Pet Emporium: Buy pet supplies including pet food, dishes, beds, houses, scratching posts, and litter boxes.

Pet Purveyors: Adopt a new pet or sell a household pet.

Pet Salon: Dog bathing and pet clothing are available here.

Pet Toy Store: Shop for fun items for your pet.

Pets are well served when visiting the Town Square, with its climbable trees and catnip patch, pet-level water fountains, and lots of open areas for playing and training.

As an additional bonus, the buildings in the Town Square passively satisfy Fun and Comfort for any nearby Sim or pet. The more a building upgrades, the more Fun and Comfort satisfaction it supplies.

Town Square Upgrades

Some features of the Town Square upgrade as the businesses in it improve. The fountain, the statue, and the kennel upgrade based on the overall quality of Town Square businesses:

◆ When 80 percent of the buildings and carts have elevated to the Good stage, the fountain, statue, and kennel upgrade to Good.

◆ When 40 percent of the buildings and carts are Good and 60 percent are Awesome, the fountain, statue, and kennel upgrade to Awesome.

Cat Day and Dog Day

Every Saturday on the Town Square is either Cat Day or Dog Day. During these special events, stores feature discounts on all objects for the species of the day. Likewise, the park is full of Sims and their dogs, and the decor will be changed to match.

 note
Cat or Dog Day occurs only if your Sim ARRIVES at the Town Square on Saturday. If they arrive late Friday and the day turns over, it never becomes Cat or Dog Day. Conversely, if your Sim stays past midnight on Saturday, it continues to be Cat or Dog Day until your Sim leaves.

 note
You can't build on the Town Square, and if you move any object from your Sims' inventories, the Sims will be fined by the Cop.

Pet Points

Pet Points are the only currency accepted at the Town Square; the more you spend, the more the Town Square will have to offer.

All of the Town Square's stores sell their goods in exchange for Pet Points, not Simoleons.

If you're running short of Pet Points, you can always trade Simoleons at the ATM.

Where do you get Pet Points? From two places:

◆ Every time you satisfy a pet's Want, the household earns Pet Points. The number of Pet Points a Want yields depends on how difficult the Want is to satisfy and is shown when you view the pet's Wants.

◆ Simoleons can be converted into Pet Points at the Town Square's ATM. Though this method yields Pet Points on demand, the conversion rate ($5 for 1 Pet point) is pretty steep.

The more Pet Points you spend, the more goods and services the Town Square will offer. The total Pet Points all your playable Sims collectively spend at each Town Square business eventually unlock larger versions of the stores with greater inventories.

Business	Pet Points Required to Upgrade to Good Level	Pet Points Required to Upgrade to Awesome Level	Upgrade Effect
Pet Bakery	360	400	More Objects to Buy
Pet Emporium	600	667	More Objects to Buy
Pet Purveyors	450	500	Larger Selection of Pets
Pet Salon	200	222	More Pet Accessories and Create-A-Pet options
Pet Toy Store	300	333	More Objects to Buy

The larger and more impressive upgraded buildings boast larger selections and bigger Motive effects for nearby Sims and pets.

Upgraded vending carts are critical if you want your Sims to have long stays at the Town Square.

Pet Points also unlock and upgrade three kinds of vending carts in the Town Square. One (the coffee cart) appears in the Town Square initially, but the other two are revealed only after certain amounts of Pet Points are spent at *all* Town Square businesses. Once a cart appears, it upgrades to larger versions via Pet Points spent at it:

Cart	Revealed by Spending Collective Pet Points	Pet Points Required to Upgrade to Good Level	Pet Points Required to Upgrade to Awesome Level
Coffee	Initially Revealed	156	222
Ice Cream	200	345	345
Smoothie	400	385	385

Chapter 15

CREATING YOUR SIMS AND PETS

Birth is the first step in all new Sims' and pets' lives. Who they are, however, depends heavily on the choices you make at their inception. The decisions you make—and those your Sims make later—matter too, but most of what is to come is shaped in this initial phase.

This section looks at how Sims and pets are built in Create A Family, including the steps, the considerations, and the implications of every choice you're asked to make. Turn your mind, therefore, to your new creation and all the other attributes that define a Sim or pet.

Create A Family

In the cozy living-room environment that is Create A Family, you can do several things:

- Select what you want to make: Sim, Dog, or Cat.
- Edit a created family member: Position the green plumb bob over the family member to be edited and select.
- Remove a family member: Position the green plumb bob over the family member to be removed and select.
- Enter an unlock code: Enter codes obtained from PC or other console players to liberate locked content. (See the "Unlockables Summary" chapter.)

The most important of these choices is the species of your family member. The choices are very different depending on whether you want a Sim or a pet.

Sims

The first step in the process is generating a Sim. You can either use the Sim provided or generate a new Sim exactly to your specifications.

Unless the default gender is what you desire, select your prospective Sim's gender. Next, you can change your Sim's starting state by pressing Randomize Sim to spit out a new Sim of the chosen gender. Once you're satisfied, press Customize to continue.

Create-A-Sim

The next phase of the process is Create-A-Sim, where you change and tune your Sim's:

- Body
- Fashion
- Aspiration
- Personality
- Name

> **note**
> There are no locked items in Create-A-Sim. All unlockable Create-a-Family items are pet only.

Body

Your Sim's body is shaped here.

You can alter many of these attributes in the Body section of Create-A-Sim.

> **note**
> Eye color can't be directly altered but changes when you switch skin tones.

Skin Tone

Choose from among 11 skin tones, including green alien skin.

Body Type

Your Sim may take shape as thin, medium, or stout.

Morph Body

Choose different body features and move the sliders to adjust.

The thickness and shapeliness of your Sim's legs, arms, and torso can be adjusted by shifting the morphing slider.

Morph Head

Head morphing can change your Sim's whole look.

The narrowness of the skull, thickness of the jaw, and the shape of the eyes, nose, and mouth can also be adjusted with a slider.

Hair

The style and color of your Sim's hair can be adjusted by choosing from all hairstyles.

Pick from all hairstyles.

Once a hairstyle is chosen, you may specify its color and apply any accessory sets (like headbands, propped sunglasses, etc.) designated for that style.

Fashion

Fashions are available to adorn Sims top to bottom.

What your Sim wears is as important as the form from which the clothes hang. Fashion choices abound.

Fashions are organized by category:

- ◆ Head
- ◆ Bottoms & Shoes
- ◆ Tops
- ◆ Accessories

 note

Many items are unisex, so there's some overlap in the counts between men and women.

Head

On your Sim's head, you can add hats or glasses. Facial hair and makeup are available for male and female Sims, respectively.

Hats come in many shapes, sizes, and colors.

Each selected hat can be adjusted for material (to change pattern and/or color) and style (how it's worn). For example, a baseball cap can come in a variety of colors and shapes and can be worn forward, backward, sideways, etc.

Glasses can be changed in color only.

Men can select facial hair.

As with hair, facial hair can be chosen from all styles. The color of the facial hair automatically matches the hair color you selected.

Makeup is applied in preset colors and configurations.

Tops

Tops come in three kinds.

- ◆ Undershirts
- ◆ Overshirts
- ◆ Jackets

Choosing tops in each category creates the layered look.

Your Sim can wear one shirt of each type or any combination of the types. There's no requirement to wear all three. The different kinds simply allow for a more flexible "layered" look that is the key to great fashion.

Adjusting sleeve length is very important in achieving the right layering.

Depending on the type, each kind of top can be adjusted in its material (color and pattern), sleeve (length and style), torso (whether a jacket is worn open or closed), and collar (worn up or down).

Bottoms & Shoes

The lower half of your Sim's body is covered by pants or a skirt (depending on gender) as well as shoes.

You can judge a Sim by the shoes she wears. Well, not really.

Pants and skirts are adjustable for material (color and pattern) and style (length or style of wear).

Accessories

Accessories include adornments to the arm and waist and jewelry (including neckties, scarves, and piercings) or tattoos for various body parts. Many accessories can be modified for materials (color and design), and arm accessories can be adjusted for style (on which arm they're worn).

Tattoos apply to various parts of the body but can't be further customized.

Accessories go on the wrists, around the waist, and on the head.

Aspiration

Sims are so much more than just the sum of their physical and psychological needs. Any Sim sociologist would tell you (it isn't a career track yet, but you never know) that what really makes life worth living for Sims is getting what they want.

Your Sim's Aspiration is one of your most crucial choices.

And what Sims want is pretty rich and complex. Much of it is a matter of Personality, but most is in some way directed by one overarching factor—their life's goal or Aspiration.

Game Impact

Satisfying your Sims' Wants and fulfilling their Aspirations significantly impact many aspects of *The Sims™ 2 Pets*:

- Aspiration affects which Wants your Sim sees in the Wants panel.
- Aspiration points unlock new Sims for your Sims to meet and befriend.
- When Aspiration level is high enough (the bar turns platinum white), the Sim's Motives decay more slowly.

The crux of the Aspiration challenge is to combine meeting your Sim's Motives and climbing up the career and earning ladder while satisfying specific Wants. This, in turn, makes meeting the Sim's Motives and career advancement easier and provides more befriendable Sims, both of which facilitate satisfying Wants, and so on.

Wants

A Want is an experience the Sim sees as positive and desirable.

What Sims want tells you a lot about them.

At any given moment, every Sim may have dozens of Wants, but the Wants panel shows only the top four. The displayed Wants are the only ones that matter for Aspiration scoring.

Wants can be as simple as the desire to cook food or buy a TV or talk to another Sim, or be as complex as a quest to completely master a skill or train a pet.

The goal is to do everything in your power to help your Sim get many of the displayed Wants. The more difficult the Want, the longer or more work it'll take and the more points will be at stake.

Sample Wants Categories

Wants come in several general categories:

- Socials and Relationships: These pertain to the desire to do a specific social interaction on or achieve a certain relationship level with any Sim or a specific Sim. This includes pets.
- Career: These are Wants regarding job promotions, acquisition of skill points, earning money, or going to work.
- Build/Buy: Sims want to purchase a general class of object or a specific object or change the structure of a lot.
- Sightseeing: Sims may want to travel to another lot just for fun.
- Food Creation: Sims may want to cook general or specific meals or prepare meals with certain effects and serve these meals to others.

How Displayed Wants Are Chosen

At any given moment, your Sim probably has more than four Wants, but only the most important appear in the Wants panel. These are the only ones that are visible and can score Aspiration points.

Your Sims' Wants reflect much about them and their current situation.

Which ones are ranked the highest can be affected by three factors:

- Current Circumstances: Relationships, skill levels, etc., can trigger Wants in your Sims.
- Personality: Your Sim's specific Personality can change which potential Wants are most pressing. A very Neat Sim has an increased desire to clean up messes, while a very Sloppy Sim assigns such concerns a very low priority. Active Sims raise the appeal of physical fun activities while Lazy Sims give higher priority to sedentary activities.
- Aspiration: Which Aspiration your Sim strives toward also aids in selecting your Sim's strongest Wants. Knowledge Sims fill their Wants panel with various desires for more skills and cerebral experiences, while Popularity Sims will be driven to meet as many Sims and pets as possible.

Each of these factors contributes to how important a Want is to your specific Sim and affects how it's ranked. Whenever the Wants panel is refreshed, the currently top-ranked Wants are selected to fill all available slots.

Refreshing Wants

Wants are constantly and invisibly changing in their ranking, based on circumstances, but you don't see all these fluctuations in the Wants panel. It only changes when it's refreshed.

When your Sim awakens, his or her Wants are scrambled to reflect any life changes.

When the panel refreshes, it replaces not only the satisfied Wants but any others that no longer rank in the top available positions. Wants that have dropped out of the top spots are replaced with whichever Wants are, at that moment, the most important.

The Wants panel refreshes only when certain triggers occur. Fortunately, one of these triggers is completely within your control. The triggers are:

◆ Your Sim wakes from sleep.

◆ A Want (of any kind) is fulfilled.

◆ You direct your Sim to use the telephone Services menu to Call Therapist.

 note
Wants don't refresh when you load a saved game. You find everything exactly the way it was when you last left the game.

At any moment you desire, you can refresh your Sim's Wants panel by using the telephone to Call Therapist. Doing so forces new Wants to replace any that are outdated or have been outranked by other Wants.

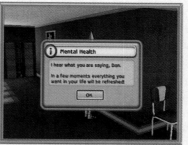

Calling the Sim Therapist instantly refreshes Wants.

If nothing has really changed since the last refresh, the call to the Therapist results in the same set of Wants.

Satisfying Wants

Wants are fulfilled in several ways. The satisfaction of a Want can arise from a random occurrence, a specific interaction, a sequence of actions that lead to a more complex result, or just about anything else that occurs in the game.

Full descriptions of Wants appear in the Wants/Aspiration panel in the Personal Info menu.

Be sure to read the description of a Want closely to understand precisely what conditions will fulfill it, and then do what's needed to make it occur.

 note
Sims never autonomously act to fulfill their Wants. They may do things that, by chance, end up doing so, but they never choose their actions based on what's in the Wants panel.

Aspiration Score and Meter

All playable Sims have constantly changing Aspiration scores that represent how many Wants they've recently fulfilled.

The Aspiration meter appears in the lower right corner of the screen when you press the Wants and Aspirations button.

This score is shown in the Aspiration meter. The meter's height and color indicate the Sim's current level of Aspiration success:

◆ Green: Normal (full Motive decay)
◆ Platinum: Excellent (50 percent Motive decay)

Each level of Aspiration score on the meter affects how quickly your Sim's Motives decay. Slow Motive decay means fewer trips to the bathroom or bed.

Changing Aspiration Score

Aspiration score can be raised and lowered by two things: realization of wants and Aspiration decay.

Every Want carries a point value that is added to Aspiration score if the Want comes to pass. This value is also added to your neighborhood-wide accumulated Aspiration points.

Aspiration score is high now, but if no more Wants are satisfied for a while, it decays back to zero.

Every hour, Aspiration score drops by 12.5 points (2.5 percent) until it reaches 0 (the line between red and green levels). Therefore, a Sim with a full Aspiration meter will, if no more Wants are realized, be reduced back to zero in 36 game hours. Decay *does not* affect accumulated Aspiration points, only the Aspiration meter.

Neighborhood-Wide Accumulated Aspiration Points

Separate but related to the Aspiration meter are your accumulated Aspiration points. This number controls the unlocking of new "residents" of your Sims' neighborhood. When you accumulate the required points a new set of Sims is added to the pool of "townie" Sims. Townies don't have homes you can see on the neighborhood map, but they are most often seen relaxing at the Town Square or, less often, walking by your Sims' homes. Once met, these townies can be called on the phone to visit, be invited to parties, be befriended, and even (if things go well) be added to a playable household.

Accumulated Aspiration points can be viewed in the Stats panel of the Personal Info menu.

This count, like Aspiration score, is raised points assigned to satisfied Wants, but the similarity ends there.

Unlike the Aspiration meter, the count in accumulated Aspiration points does not decay over time and can't be decreased.

Also, points in the Aspiration meter affect only the individual Sim to whom the meter belongs. Accumulated Aspiration points, on the other hand, are a common pool for all playable Sims in the entire neighborhood. Any time any controllable Sim (even one you're not currently playing) satisfies a Want or realizes a Fear, this count is changed to reflect it.

This commonality makes it deeply in your interest to make sure all controllable Sims are getting what they want.

The Five Aspirations

Sims can aspire to five goals.

◆ Creativity ◆ Popularity
◆ Family ◆ Wealth
◆ Knowledge

CREATIVITY

◆ Preferred Careers: Artist, Fashion
◆ Skill Bent: Creativity, Cooking
◆ Sample Wants: Make Food, Give Food, Create Group Meal, Change Clothes, Paint a Picture

A Creativity Aspiration Sim wants to live the inspired life—painting beautiful paintings, cooking powerful food, and building Creativity skill.

Buy this type of Sim easels, musical instruments, and harvesting objects.

Creativity Sims are happiest cooking and harvesting food.

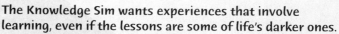

Personality for Creativity Sims should be very heavy on Playful since it impacts how quickly they develop Creativity skill.

FAMILY

- Preferred Careers: None
- Skill Bent: Cooking, Cleaning
- Sample Wants: Gain Skill in Cooking and Cleaning, Interact with Family

Family Sims are happiest at the center of a large family.

Sims with the Family Aspiration dedicate their lives to the enrichment of their families. Family Sims want to fall in love, get engaged, marry, and get pets. Once settled down, they want to interact with those in their household as much as possible.

A Family Sim has no particular career ambitions but wants to advance in a career if put in one. It won't, however, be a high-priority Want.

Family Sims should certainly have a high Neat/Sloppy score (10 if possible) so they can quickly become adept at cleaning and will tidy autonomously. Clearly, too, they should be good at cooking to provide the most satisfying meals; satisfying meals mean short meals, and that means more time for other household Sims to pursue their Wants. It might also be beneficial to make a Family Sim have very high Playful/Serious since high Creativity can be an income-producing aid for stay-at-home Sims (painting or writing a novel).

note

Though it will add to family income, time spent pursuing painting will detract from a Family Sim's ability to fulfill his or her Aspiration.

KNOWLEDGE

- Preferred Careers: Education, Medicine
- Skill Bent: All
- Sample Wants: Master a Skill, Find a Comet, Be Abducted by Aliens, Read a Book

The Knowledge Sim wants experiences that involve learning, even if the lessons are some of life's darker ones.

Skill building is a major preoccupation of Knowledge Sims, and they get their best Aspiration scoring from maxing out several, and eventually all, their skills.

Knowledge Sims also want to experience the truly bizarre. They hanker to be abducted by aliens (several times if possible).

Keep peering through the telescope, and maybe the Knowledge Sim will get her dearest wish. Hello, aliens.

When they have a low Mood, Knowledge Sims want to buy items that feed their thirst for knowledge—bookcases and telescopes.

Knowledge Sims are attracted to the Medicine and Education professions but want to quit or stay home from work to pursue their general love of learning. Their desire for all skills means they learn three skills mostly by doing: Cooking, Cleaning, and Mechanical. It helps (for Cleaning at least) if they're very Neat.

A good Personality profile for Knowledge Sims is 10 Neat/Sloppy, 10 or 0 in Playful/Serious, 5 in Nice/Grouchy, and (if Playful/Serious is 0) 10 in Outgoing/Shy or Active/Lazy. This gives them accelerated learning in three skills.

POPULARITY

- Preferred Careers: Government and Coaching
- Skill Bent: Charisma
- General Wants: Make a Friend, Make a Best Friend, Make Multiple Friends

Popularity Sims crave companionship and collect friends like trading cards.

Popularity Sims want notoriety and to be liked. Their Wants, therefore, revolve around making and keeping as many best friends as possible and throwing successful parties.

Their career ambitions fit their desire for fame.

Popularity Sims already spend much of their time making friends, so having enough for a career is no extra work.

Popularity Sims want to get the party started and keep it going.

Personality traits for Popularity Sims should center on those that help them make friends, develop Charisma, and succeed in one of the Aspiration's favored careers. They should certainly have 10 Outgoing/Shy and probably 10 Nice/Grouchy. Beyond that, it depends on career choice. If they stay at home, a high Neat/Sloppy score is helpful.

WEALTH

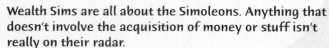

◆ Preferred Careers: Any

◆ Skill Bent: Only whatever is needed for career

◆ Sample Wants: Make Money, Have High Family Funds

Wealth Sims are all about the Simoleons. Anything that doesn't involve the acquisition of money or stuff isn't really on their radar.

Going to work and buying stuff are what Wealth Sims are all about.

Career is more important for this Aspiration than any other; Wealth Sims are the only Sims who won't sacrifice career success for other Wants.

Personality for Wealth Sims should be geared toward career. For the creation of valuable paintings and novels, Wealth Sims should always have high Playful/Serious to maximize their Creativity. Creativity can do double duty if you limit your Wealth Sims to careers that also require this skill. Wealth Sims can, but probably shouldn't, be Lazy. Lazy Sims want to quit their job when their Mood is bad, and this would be damaging to the family finances.

Personality

The very core of your Sims' being is their Personality. It drives countless things they do in their daily life. Here are but a few of the things Personality can affect.

Skill Acquisition Speed

Some skills are learned more quickly (up to twice as fast) by Sims with certain Personality traits. The more points a Sim has in a trait, the less time it takes to gain a point in that skill.

The time it takes to gain skill points can be cut significantly if your Sim has the right Personality.

Most skills have an aligned Personality trait that makes the skill easier to learn.

◆ Body: Active   ◆ Creativity: Playful
◆ Charisma: Outgoing   ◆ Logic: Serious
◆ Cleaning: Neat   ◆ Mechanical: None
◆ Cooking: None

Only a Sim of the specified Personality extreme sees any difference in skill speed. Sims with an Active/Lazy trait of 0–5, for example, increase Body skill at the normal rate, while Sims of Active/Lazy 6–10 do it faster (increasing how Active they are). Among Active Sims, the increase is gradual. A 6 gets a slight increase while a 10 works at double the normal rate.

Motive Decay Rate

Some Personality traits alter the rate at which Motives decay. In other words, they shorten or lengthen how long a Sim can go without satisfying a specific Motive.

- Hunger: Active decays faster; Lazy decays slower
- Bladder: None
- Energy: Lazy decays faster; Active decays slower
- Hygiene: Sloppy decays faster; Neat decays slower
- Fun: Playful decays faster; Serious decays slower
- Social: Outgoing decays faster; Shy decays slower
- Comfort: Lazy decays faster; Active decays slower

In each case, a neutral Sim (5 points) decays at the standard rate, while those above and below decay faster or slower. The farther from neutral, the greater the effect.

Career Affinities

Some Personality traits make a Sim more likely to succeed in certain careers. Each career focuses on three skills that must be developed for the Sim to advance. Sims whose Personality allows them to build those skills more easily advance more quickly in any career that requires the skill.

A Sim with extreme scores in one or more Personality traits has an easier time in these careers:

- Arts & Crafts: Outgoing, Playful
- Business: Serious or Playful, Outgoing
- Coaching: Active, Outgoing
- Construction: Active, Playful
- Education: Serious or Playful, Neat
- Government: Serious or Playful, Outgoing
- Law Enforcement: Serious, Active, Neat
- Medicine: Serious, Neat
- Parks & Recreation: Active, Serious, Neat
- Retail Clothing: Outgoing, Playful

note

Some careers benefit from conflicting traits (for example, Government has both Serious and Playful). Obviously, a Sim may only be one or the other, so any score other than neutral provides some advantage in the career.

Sloppy Sims are, well, sloppy.

Other Effects

Personality impacts many parts of Sims' lives:

- Whether they accept certain social interactions
- What they do when left to their own devices
- Whether they clean up after themselves or others
- Whether special object interactions are available
- Which Sims they get along with and which they clash with
- How successful they are at prank calls
- How much they enjoy music when dancing
- What they like to watch on TV
- Which Aspiration best suits them

Personality Traits

A Sim's Personality is the sum of five traits. These traits are expressed in terms of their extremes.

- Neat/Sloppy
- Playful/Serious
- Outgoing/Shy
- Nice/Grouchy
- Active/Lazy

Each trait has 10 settings—0 represents the "negative" extreme, and 10 represents the "positive." The more toward one extreme or the other Sims lean, the more often they autonomously behave in accordance with that extreme. For example, a Sim with Nice/Grouchy of 8 exhibits sweet and helpful behavior toward other Sims, Nice/Grouchy of 5 is neutral, and Nice/Grouchy of 2 is very surly indeed. The higher or lower the number, the more frequently these behaviors occur.

Personality is more than a Sim's autonomous mindset. It also affects which interactions a user-directed Sim will accept.

note

The term "negative" is a bit of a misnomer regarding Personality traits. Being Serious, for example, merely means your Sim tends toward reading, finds gregarious Sims insufferable, and learns Logic very quickly. A Serious Sim can make friends and find love, too, although perhaps not with extremely Playful Sims.

Assigning Personality points, however, requires choices. Every Sim has only 25 Personality points that can be distributed between these five traits. Unless you construct a perfectly balanced Sim with 5 points in each trait, you must put one trait in the negative to get another in the positive.

In the game, a playable Sim's Personality and Zodiac sign can be viewed in the Personality panel of the Personal Info menu.

Strategically, this means that you must make decisions about what you want your Sim to be. If you want a social butterfly with Outgoing 10, you may have to make your Sim a total slob or extremely slothful. Understanding the consequences of these choices is what this section is all about.

NEAT/SLOPPY

- Modify Motive Decay: Hygiene (Neat: Slower; Sloppy: Faster)
- Speeds Skill: Cleaning (Neat)
- Career Tilt (Neat): Parks & Recreation, Education, Law Enforcement, Medicine

Neat Sims (6–10) pick up after themselves and others. Sloppy Sims (0–4) rarely put anything away, make messes whenever possible, and never clean up things left by others.

Neat Sims LOVE to clean.

Neutral Sims (5) show weak tendencies toward both extremes.

- Hygiene decays much more quickly for Sloppy Sims than for Neat ones, meaning they require more showers/baths to keep their Mood high.
- Neat Sims develop Cleaning skill much more quickly than Sloppy ones. As such, much of the time Neat Sims "waste" cleaning things is offset by their impressive speed at doing it, the Fun they receive, and the further acquisition of skill (cleaning things bestows Cleaning skill).
- Because of their acumen at Cleaning skill, Neat Sims advance faster in careers that require it.

- The Sloppier Sims are, the faster they CREATE messes. For example, a very Sloppy Sim can foul a shower with a few visits, while a Neat Sim's shower doesn't need cleaning for several uses. They're also messier in the kitchen.
- Neat Sims get Fun from cleaning while Sloppy Sims lose Fun when forced to tidy.
- Sloppy Sims gobble their food, causing Neat Sims nearby to react.

OUTGOING/SHY

- Modify Motive Decay: Social (Outgoing: Faster; Shy: Slower)
- Speeds Skill: Charisma (Outgoing)
- Career Tilt (Outgoing): Coaching, Arts & Crafts, Business, Retail Clothing, Government

Outgoing Sims are the life of the party.

Outgoing Sims (6–10) thrive on social interaction; the more other Sims around the better. Shy Sims don't like to attract attention to themselves and are visibly uncomfortable with it, even if they actually like the interest. Because, on the other hand, Shy Sims (0–4) require less social interaction, they can spend more time in seclusion, working on skills or fulfilling their Aspirations. Neutral Outgoing/Shy Sims (5) have neither the benefits nor drawbacks of either extreme, which is not a desirable setting for any purpose.

 note
Outgoing Sims crave social interaction, so their Social motive decays at an accelerated rate. Shy Sims need less contact, and their Social need decays at a slower rate.

ACTIVE/LAZY

- Modify Motive Decay: Hunger (Active: Faster; Lazy: Slower), Energy (Lazy: Faster; Active: Slower), Comfort (Lazy: Faster; Active: Slower)
- Speeds Skill: Body (Active)
- Career Tilt (Active): Coaching, Law Enforcement, Construction, Parks & Recreation

Active Sims (6–10) have the undeniable benefit of needing less sleep and less time sitting, but they require a lot more visits to the feed bag. For the more physical professions, Active Sims build Body skill at a higher rate.

Neutral Sims (5) show weak tendencies toward both extremes.

Active Sims gravitate to physical pursuits.

Lazy Sims (0-4) require less food than others but must sit, nap, and sleep more frequently.

◆ There's a random chance that Lazy Sims will turn off their alarm clock, go back to sleep, and miss work.

◆ Active Sims tend toward Fun activities and objects that are more physical, while Lazy Sims tend toward the sedentary.

◆ Lazy Sims take longer to get out of bed, making their prework routine take even longer.

PLAYFUL/SERIOUS

◆ Modify Motive Decay: Fun (Playful: Faster; Serious: Slower)

◆ Speeds Skill: Creativity (Playful), Logic (Serious)

◆ Career Tilt (Serious): Medicine, Law Enforcement, Business, Education, Parks & Recreation, Government

◆ Career Tilt (Playful): Arts & Crafts, Business, Construction, Retail Clothing, Education, Government

Playful Sims (6-10) can find Fun in the oddest places where no other Sim can, but they need a heck of a lot more of it than their Serious counterparts. They are extremely well suited for creative endeavors.

Neutral Sims (5) show weak tendencies toward both extremes.

Serious Sims (0-4) can go longer between Fun activities and are naturally attracted to quieter, more cerebral endeavors (reading, playing chess, etc.). Serious is the only "negative" trait that speeds the learning of a skill; Serious Sims are very adept at Logic.

◆ Fun decays faster for Playful Sims. For Serious Sims it decays more slowly; they require only occasional Fun interactions.

NICE/GROUCHY

◆ Modify Motive Decay: None   ◆ Speeds Skill: None   ◆ Career Tilt: None

Nice Sims (6-10) are very considerate toward the feelings of others, autonomously engaging in social interactions that benefit both parties.

Grouchy Sims (0-4), on the other hand, bring down almost any relationship if left to their own devices. Sometimes Grouchy Sims even derive a positive benefit (Social, Relationship, or Fun) from being mean to others.

Generally, socializing is easier for Nice Sims because they can do stronger interactions earlier in relationships.

Nice/Grouchy is also a major factor in the acceptance of many social interactions. Which way a Sim tilts can change the difficulty of relationship building, but not fatally so.

Strategically, Nice/Grouchy is not a factor in either skills or career, so it's a theoretically expendable trait. That doesn't, however, mean that it should be set to zero; Grouchy Sims can do a lot of damage to hard-won relationships. Unless a surly Sim is what you want, never set Nice/Grouchy below 5.

note
Grouchy Sims watching other Sims compete are more likely to taunt the contestants while Nice Sims cheer.

Zodiac Signs

Every Sim sports one of the 12 astrological signs. Each star sign represents a set of Personality settings that approximates the real-world astrological character of the sign.

note
A Sim's Zodiac sign can be set in Create-A-Sim and viewed in the game in the Personality panel of the Personal Info menu.

As you change each Personality trait, the Sim's sign changes to fit an astrological profile. It also works the other way—change the sign, and all Personality traits change to the following settings.

Personality Presets by Zodiac Sign

Zodiac Sign	Neat	Outgoing	Active	Playful	Nice
Aries	5	8	6	3	3
Taurus	5	5	3	8	4
Gemini	4	7	8	3	3
Cancer	6	3	6	4	6
Leo	4	10	4	4	3
Virgo	9	2	6	3	5
Libra	2	8	2	6	7
Scorpio	6	5	8	3	3
Sagittarius	2	3	9	7	4
Capricorn	7	4	1	8	5
Aquarius	4	4	4	7	6
Pisces	5	3	7	3	7

These values are the default for each sign, but they aren't precise. You can tweak them a bit without changing the sign. Extreme changes eventually cause the sign to shift.

Sims may befriend and fall in love with anyone, but due to inherent differences in Personality types, some combinations are harder or easier than others. Keep the following affinities/aversions in mind to discover who's a more likely friend and who poses an interesting challenge.

Zodiac Sign Compatibility

Zodiac Sign	Attracted to	Repelled by
Aries	Gemini/Taurus	Cancer/Libra
Taurus	Aries/Libra	Virgo/Cancer
Gemini	Pisces/Virgo	Capricorn/Aries
Cancer	Taurus/Scorpio	Gemini/Aries
Leo	Sagittarius/Cancer	Capricorn/Gemini
Virgo	Aquarius/Sagittarius	Leo/Taurus
Libra	Virgo/Cancer	Pieces/Scorpio
Scorpio	Pieces/Leo	Libra/Aquarius
Sagittarius	Pisces/Capricorn	Libra/Scorpio
Capricorn	Aquarius/Taurus	Leo/Gemini
Aquarius	Capricorn/Sagittarius	Scorpio/Virgo
Pisces	Scorpio/Gemini	Leo/Aries

Interests

Upon a Sim's creation, Interest points are randomly distributed among the 18 Interests. An Interest can be assigned 0–10 points: 0 indicates no interest, 5 moderate interest, and 10 intense interest. The level in each Interest guides the Sim in Talk interactions.

Sims' Interests become apparent during Talk interactions. If they bring up or like a topic raised by another Sim, they flash that Interest's symbol. If not, they look bored or offended.

The 18 Interests are:

- Animals
- Crime
- Culture
- Entertainment
- Environment
- Fashion
- Food
- Health
- Money
- Paranormal
- Politics
- School
- Sci-Fi
- Sports
- Toys
- Travel
- Weather
- Work

Interest in Talk

The number of points in an Interest dictates how likely the topic is to arise in a Talk initiated by your Sim. The choice of topic in a given conversation is random, but the higher an Interest's level, the more likely it is to be picked.

note

Unlike Personality points, Interest points are distributed randomly and automatically at creation or birth.

note

In Direct Control mode, Talk interactions aren't extended by each Sim's interest in the topics. Each Sim takes one turn talking, then the other takes over. The level of interest dictates how many Relationship points result.

In Classic Control mode, Talk volleys back and forth between the Sims with level of interest dictating the chances of another round.

Name

Finally, give your Sim a name.

The final step is to give your Sim a name. It can be anything you like, but note that it can't be changed once the Sim is moved in.

tip

If you want your Sim to have a middle name or initial, make it part of the first name.

That's it. Your Sim is complete, and you have all the insight you need to be ready for how your choices will affect your Sim's ability to function in the world.

When your Sim's on the receiving end of a conversation, interest level in the other Sim's chosen topic determines how likely your Sim is to continue the conversation (if interest is high) or end it (if interest is low).

Using Interests Strategically

Neither your own Sims' Interests or those of the various resident Sims are directly visible in the game. The resident Sims' Interests are, however, specified in this guide in the "Social Interactions" chapter.

Since your Sims' Interests are chosen at random, it may seem as if there's no way to know what Interests your Sims have and, thus, no way to guide them to Sims they share Interests with. Well, that's not exactly true.

If you observe your Sims in Talk interactions and examine the Interest bubbles they use, you can determine which topics interest them and which don't. With that info in hand, you can compare these Interests to those of the NPCs to see who would make the most fruitful conversation partners.

Cats and Dogs

note

Create a Cat and Create a Dog are essentially identical. The only difference is in the Head panel. Dogs can have extra hair accessories on their heads, but cats can't.

The first step is to choose your species. On the same menu you used to start your new Sim, select whether you'd like to create a cat or a dog.

The Breed Bin

There are two ways to handle the issue of breed. The Breed Bin is chock-full of various real world breeds; choose whichever one appeals to you to begin.

Alternatively, you could make a randomized mixed breed by choosing Mixed Breed. Selecting this as your pet's breed and pressing the indicated button will yield a randomly generated combination of two Breed Bin breeds. The result may not be pretty, but it's surely unique.

Whether you pick a breed or fiddle with hybridization, you must next decide on your pet's gender. Gender only matters for two things: the pose in which the pet satisfies its Bladder Motive and with which gender the pet can breed

If it's your goal to make puppies or kittens, make sure the two dogs or cats in your family are opposite genders. If breeding is not in your plans, it doesn't matter which gender you choose.

Create a Pet

With these initial steps out of the way, it's time to get into the heart of the matter: sculpting an anonymous breed into a unique pet. The tools for this job are divided into five categories:

- Body
- Personality
- Head
- Name
- Fashion

Body

Body settings affect a pet's appearance from the tip of its tail to the top of its head.

Body Type

Body type is the pet's overall silhouette.

Body type cycles a pet through predefined classic body types. Though these settings don't change the pet's face, many will alter the neck and ears surrounding it.

Trimness

Athletic or a little lumpy?

This slider specifies if your pet will be skinny or stocky.

Customize Fur

Here you can set the pet's:

- Fur Style: This determines the texture of the coat (shaggy, smooth, etc.).
- Fur Color: The color of the pet's base coat. If you don't apply any markings on top of the base coat, this will be the pet's outer coat. If you do cover the base coat with markings, you may not see this base color on the finished pet.
- Extra Hair: Tufts and ruffs and other bushy bits can be added to a pet's coat.
- Fur Markings: Each pet can have up to three fur markings that sit on top of its base coat. For each layer, select a marking pattern and a color for that marking. Note that the higher layers can completely obscure lower ones, depending on the color of each. The outer fur style will affect the appearance of the marking.

Fur layers can create rich and detailed coats for your pets.

Tail

Chose wisely; a tail follows a pet for a lifetime.

Choose from available tails. Color is dictated by the pet's base coat color.

Head

The shape and adornment of a pet's head helps define it as a breed and as an individual.

Morph Face

This tool allows you change the shape of a pet's eyes, snout, and jowls.

Changing the slider and the pets it uses as its models will yield rich results.

Each of these mechanisms works identically. The slider shifts the pet's features between the two extremes shown in the thumbnails. Pulling the slider all the way to either end matches the features exactly to that extreme.

You can redefine the extremes by clicking on either portrait and selecting a new example to serve as the slider's end point. Now, pulling the slider to that extreme will match the newly selected features.

Extra Hair (Dogs Only)

Fur accessories provide a hint of wisdom…or something.

This selector applies one of four (the first of which is none) hair accessories (tufts, beards, etc.) to the dog's face.

Ears

Ears up? Ears down?

Use this selector to choose from varying ear shapes.

Fashion

Yes, pets can be fashionable.

note

If a fashion item has a closed-lock icon, you can't use it until you unlock it by either collecting enough neighborhood-wide Pet points or getting the unlock code from another PC or console player. For information on unlocking items, see the "Unlockables Summary" chapter.

note

If you want your pet dressed to the nines but don't want to tinker around with the fashion catalogs, just press Randomize Fashion to outfit it with a selection of apparel.

You can add fashions to a pet's:

- Head: Headwear such as hats, glasses, or neckwear (including collars)
- Body: Shirts and hoodies
- Paws: Shoes

Personality

Personality is the biggest choice you'll make for your pet.

Pets, like Sims, have individual Personalities that greatly impact their choices and behavior. A pet's Personality also affects its trainability. Pet traits are:

- Gifted/Normal/Doofus
- Hyper/Normal/Lazy
- Independent/Normal/Friendly
- Aggressive/Normal/Cowardly
- Pigpen/Normal/Snooty

Unlike Sims, however, pets' Personality traits are simpler in two important ways. First, pet traits aren't scaled like Sim traits. In other words, a Sim can be a little bit Outgoing (Outgoing/Shy 6) or very Outgoing (Outgoing/Shy 10), but a pet is Hyper, Normal, or Lazy; there's no "kind of Lazy." It's as if Sims could be given only 0, 5, or 10 for their traits.

Second, pets have no Personality points that must be distributed between their traits. You're free to set each trait wherever you wish to make the pet you want.

Personality Impact

A pet's Personality is very important in determining how the pet behaves and what interactions it will choose. Because you can't directly control pets, the autonomous effects of Personality are even more critical than for human Sims.

Specifically, Personality traits have six distinct effects:

Personality:

- Affects what pets will do to satisfy their Motives or occupy their time when their Motives are not pressing.
- Determines what objects a pet will or won't interact with. Snooty pets, for example, won't eat out of a dirty food dish no matter how hungry they are. Pigpen pets, on the other hand, will eat out of even the filthiest food dish.
- Dictates how quickly the pet can be trained. Gifted pets learn much more quickly than Normal or Doofus pets and will do trained behaviors more often without training.
- Shapes a pet's reactions to objects, events, and Sims. For example, when the doorbell rings, an Independent dog will growl and a Friendly dog will bark cheerily.
- Influences whom and how often pets will follow. For example, Pigpen pets will choose to follow Sims with low Hygiene.
- Impacts the outcome of social interactions.

tip

If you want to train your pets quickly, ALWAYS make them Gifted. You'll lose out on some of the amusing behavior that comes with the Doofus trait, but that may be a small price to pay for a well-mannered pet.

Name

Finally, name your pet whatever you like.

Sharing Pets

Once you've changed the basic attributes of a breed, the resulting pet is a unique creation of your making. Why keep such a masterwork to yourself? You can share pets with other console players by giving out your modified pet's genetic code.

Pet genetic code lets your console-playing friends use your pet as a template for their own.

A pet's genetic code can be found in its Pet Profile panel in the Personal Info menu. If other players (or you for that matter) enter this code in Create A Family or at the Pet Purveyor shop at the Town Square, they'll receive an exact copy of that pet as if it were a pre-made breed from the Breed Bin.

A genetic code will reproduce a pet's:

- Species
- Fur Color, Markings, Style, and Extra Hair
- Tail
- Ears
- Body Type
- Personality Traits
- Face and Body Shape Modifiers

The code will not include the pet's name, learned behaviors, or fashions.

note

If the shared pet was designed with an unlocked color or marking, this marking will carry over to another player's game for this pet but will not be unlocked for general use. You can, however, share the unlock code for that color or marking as well to give your friend the whole package.

Chapter 16

Pet Life

Pets in *The Sims* 2 are actual—though limited—Sims. Understanding what makes them tick is critical to making them powerful members of your human Sims' households.

This chapter examines the various aspects of pet "Simology" (or "Petology"), from their Motives and Moods to their Wants and everything in between.

Control

Unlike Sims, cats and dogs can't be directly controlled; you can't select a cat or dog and tell it where to go.

Pets can't be directly controlled, though you can select and view them. Their Action queue is grayed out because you can't cancel actions from it.

This doesn't, however, mean that pets are automatons that'll do what they want and can't be made to serve your will. While you can't direct pets, you can view their Action queue and their Motives, Moods, relationships, career info, and Petology.

Also, pets can be indirectly controlled through effective training in reinforced behaviors and commands (see the "Training and Reinforced Behavior" section). Because pets put interactions from your Sims ahead of all other actions, solid training can make them as responsive as other Sims so long as you keep them happy and well cared for.

Motives and Mood

Like human Sims, pets have Motives and an overall Mood that function separately and in concert to shape the pet's behavior, actions, and willingness to interact and behave as trained.

Pet Motives

Adult cats and dogs have eight Motives:

- Hunger
- Comfort
- Bladder
- Energy
- Fun
- Social
- Hygiene
- Chew or Scratch (depending on species)

All but the last of these Motives are identical to Sim Motives, though the ways pets satisfy them can be very different.

Hunger

Pets satisfy Hunger by eating. Since they're animals, however, they're dependent on human Sims to provide their food. A simple food bowl, kept filled and clean, will take care of Hunger.

Pets are fed in a variety of ways. You can always fill a food bowl with generic pet food for §10 a pop, or you can buy food at the Town Square Pet Emporium. The more expensive the store-bought food, the greater its Hunger satisfaction.

You can also buy a pet snacks from the Town Square carts, or make you pet food in a food processor. For prepared food, the finished product is related to the Hunger satisfaction of the ingredients.

Pets also get a bit of Hunger satisfaction from pet treats (purchased from the Town Square's Pet Bakery). Sims can feed pet treats with the Give Love…Feed Treat interaction if they have any in their family inventory.

Keep food sitting out, and have a bowl for each pet in the household to keep pets from fighting over food.

note

Sims abducted by aliens may come back with an extra special alien pet treat.

If pet food is not available, pets (depending on their Personality and training) will satisfy Hunger by eating Sim food left on the floor.

 note

Snooty pets won't eat from a bowl in its dirty state no matter how hungry they are. Regular pets won't refuse until the bowl gets VERY dirty (with flies and green stink cloud), and Pigpen pets don't care about their bowl's dirtiness.

Also, Snooty pets are less likely to eat from the Petology Food Dish.

Hyper pets deplete Hunger more quickly and Lazy pets more slowly.

When a pet's Hunger drops to critical levels, it begins to whine and you receive messages about the problem. If the Motive hits bottom, the pet collapses and eventually revives. Each time the pet passes out, the chance of it running away increases. If no food is provided within six hours, the pet runs away no matter how many times it has passed out.

 note

Passed out pets can be revived by the Paramedic.

Bladder

When a pet has to go, its natural and trained options depend on the species.

You can impact where a pet does its business with proper house-breaking.

Generally, pets satisfy their Bladder Motive either inside or outside, without much preference for either. Pets can be reinforced to pee outside by scolding for peeing where they shouldn't.

Having a dog means cleaning up puddles.

Pets trained to pee outside will do so on the ground or on a wide variety of objects: trees, flowers, bushes, flamingoes, gnomes, mailboxes, and so on. The result of Bladder satisfaction is a puddle that brings down the Room score. Puddles should be cleaned up regularly.

 tip

If your Sims' pets pee outdoors, it might be a good investment to hire some help to keep up with the mess. A Maid will take care of any puddles he or she finds, regardless of the source.

Cats don't need to be housebroken if there's a useable litter box.

The situation changes, however, if the pet is a cat and there's a litter box in the house. If your Sim's house has a litter box, any cats in the house will use it automatically without any reinforcement. Cats can also be trained to pee in the toilet. Once toilet-trained, a cat will use the toilet on command or by default if there's no litter box.

 note

The presence of a litter box doesn't guarantee a puddle-less floor in your cat-inhabited home. If a litter box gets too dirty, cats refuse to use it and revert to whichever way they've been trained.

When a pet's Bladder Motive drops too low, pets act distressed and show their Bladder Motive balloon. If it hits bottom, they pee where they stand.

Comfort

Pets satisfy Comfort by sitting or lying down. Generally, pets satisfy Comfort by using floors or terrain. All pets can relax in pet beds and pet houses if they're available, and they prefer them to the ground/terrain. Training lets you decide whether you want a pet to use furniture or the floor/ground/pet furniture to relax or sleep.

Lazy pets deplete Comfort faster than regular pets, and Hyper pets deplete Comfort more slowly. When Comfort drops too low, pets stretch a lot. When it hits bottom, they'll lie down anywhere.

Energy

Pets replenish their Energy by sleeping.

> ### note
> As with Sims, a pet's Energy level DOES NOT impact a pet's Mood.

Both cats and dogs can sleep on the floor or ground. Cats can also snooze on the Los Gatos Cat Condo.

Pet beds and houses provide faster Energy replenishment than the floor.

> ### note
> Sleeping pets have dreams and nightmares (depending on Mood), just like Sims.

Lazy pets deplete Energy more quickly. Hyper pets need less sleep, so they decay more slowly.

When pets get too low on Energy, they yawn more frequently. If it fails, they fall asleep where they stand.

Hygiene

Pet Hygiene is a very important Motive but possibly more so to your Sims than for their pets. How pets react to and fulfill this Motive depends on their species.

Dogs don't care if they're clean or not. In fact, the level of their Hygiene has no impact on their overall Mood. However, *others* might care how dogs smell. Dogs with depleted Hygiene bring down Room score in their immediate vicinity (lowering your Sims' Moods) and may cause Sims to react with a nose-crinkling "Ewwww!"

Odoriferous dogs can be cleaned only with a good bath.

Cats, being naturally clean animals, are affected by the level of their Hygiene. Low Hygiene significantly brings down a cat's Mood. A cat with low Hygiene—though this is unusual—has the same effect on Room and elicits the same response as a smelly dog.

The way each species replenishes its Hygiene is dramatically different. Dogs can't replenish Hygiene without your Sims' help.

> ### note
> Sims will never bathe even the stinkiest dog autonomously; you must direct them to do it.

Sims can bathe dogs in bathtubs, shower tubs (though not shower stalls), or at the Pet Salon.

Cats, by contrast, are self-cleaning, so your Sims need not—in fact, cannot—give a cat a bath. When a cat's Hygiene is sufficiently depleted, they clean themselves by licking until Hygiene is replenished. The level at which a cat considers itself dirty enough to self-clean depends on whether it's Personality is Pigpen, Normal, or Snooty. Snooty cats prioritize the activity more highly than other types, and Pigpens put it near the bottom of their to-do list.

Unless you keep a cat constantly busy, it will never allow its Hygiene to get too low.

Pigpen pets' Hygiene decays more quickly, while that of Snooty pets drops more slowly.

When Hygiene is too low, pets emit an Room score-reducing stink cloud. In the event of failure, dogs won't care and cats groom themselves until Hygiene is restored.

Fun

Pets desperately need to have lots of Fun, so replenish this Motive by interactions with objects, other pets, or (primarily) Sims.

> ### note
> Fun interactions with pets go both ways, but Sims get more Fun from playing with dogs than with cats.

What gives a pet Fun depends on its species. For example, dogs gain Fun from:

- Playing with other pets
- Playing with Sims
- Chewing toys
- Digging holes
- Rolling in dirt piles

There are lots of ways for pets to have Fun.

Cats get Fun from:

- Playing with other pets
- Playing with Sims
- Playing with the Feline Birdie Stick
- Scratching on the Scratch-O-Matic Scratching Post or Los Gatos Cat Condo
- Watching fish in aquariums or caged pets

Independent and Lazy pets have a slower Fun decay, while Hyper and Friendly pets' Fun Motive decays more quickly.

If Fun drops too low, pets will find a Sim and initiate Fun interactions. If the Motive hits bottom, they'll engage in destructive behavior (in spite of their training).

Social

note
Social interactions with pets go both ways, but Sims get more Social from playing with cats than with dogs.

Pets need to be around people and other pets to be happy. A good pet, however, gives back even more than it takes.

Pets need lots of social interaction to stay happy. Dogs in particular require lots of attention from Sims and other pets, as high Social plays a larger role in their Mood.

Social for pets is replenished by:

- Playing with other pets
- Playing with Sims
- Getting love from Sims

Friendly pets need more socializing, so their Social drops more quickly, while Independent pets can go longer without contact because of slower decay.

Critical levels and total failure of Social will drive pets to whine and engage in destructive behavior (in spite of their training).

Chew/Scratch

Sims care about their surroundings, so they have the Room Motive. Cats and dogs could care less about Room; instead, they have the Motive to Chew (dogs) or Scratch (cats).

There goes the living room set.

Chew/Scratch is depleted gradually over time and is replenished by chewing on or scratching something.

Pets continue to chew on or scratch an object until one of the following happens:

- You direct a Sim to scold the pet for chewing/scratching. This immediately stops the behavior as the pet awaits the Sim's arrival.
- The Chew/Scratch Motive is fully satisfied.
- The object is destroyed.

note
Chewable or scratchable objects can be destroyed if the assault goes on long enough, reducing the object to scraps that your Sims must clean up. To completely destroy an object, however, the pet must do all the damage in one uninterrupted session; damage does not carry over to the next scratch or chew session, nor does the object show any sign of wear and tear until it disintegrates. Therefore, as long as you interrupt a pet before the object is completely gone, it'll take another full session to lose it.

Pets can chew or scratch many household objects. Cats focus on furniture and rugs while dogs go after cat toys, newspapers, and bills.

There are a few objects that pets can never destroy:

- The ChompCo Chew Toy (dogs only)
- Scratch-O-Matic Scratching Post (cats only)
- Los Gatos Cat Condo (cats only)

Since there's no way to stop pets from fulfilling this Motive, your Sims must teach their pets to chew or scratch these indestructible objects instead of the furniture. Make sure every pet-inhabited house has a species-appropriate chewable/scratchable object, and scold any time a pet chews or scratches something it shouldn't.

Good training and easy access to acceptable chew and scratch objects will solve the problem.

Aggressive pets decay Chew/Scratch more quickly than regular pets, and for Cowardly pets the Motive drops more slowly.

If Chew/Scratch reaches critical or failure level, dogs and cats forget their training and chew or scratch on inappropriate objects. If there's nothing at all to chew or scratch, dogs will dig holes and cats will yowl.

Mood

A pet's Mood is extremely important in making and keeping it a positive asset to your Sims' household.

Mood Impacts

A pet's Mood impacts several things:

- Social Interaction Acceptance/Rejection: Along with relationship, most Sim-to-pet Social interactions are ruled by the pet's Mood. A happy pet with do anything a well-liked Sim wants it to do.
- Relationships: The pet's Mood affects the relationship decay rate.
- Commands: A pet in a bad Mood won't obey the commands it's been taught.
- Training: Pets in a bad Mood won't accept command training from Sims.
- Scolding: Pets in a bad Mood won't learn from a scolding.
- Faster Learning: Pets in a good Mood learn commands and reinforced behaviors faster.

- Deviance: Pets in a bad enough Mood forget their training (in proportion to their bad Mood) until good Mood is restored. Thus, a pet trained not to scratch or chew will be more likely to do so the worse its Mood is.
- Destruction: Pets in a VERY bad Mood will go on a chew/scratch frenzy, laying waste to your Sims' homes.
- Body Language: Happy dogs wag their tails while walking or sitting, and happy cats walk with their tails held high.

note

Most Motives have different impacts on Mood, depending on their level. For example, a fully satisfied Bladder has no amplified effect on Mood, but a very low Bladder has a huge impact. Though there are small variations between cats and dogs, the effect of each Motive is, approximately, the same as for Sims.

Unhappy pets are disobedient pets.

Pet Wants

Like their Sims, pets have Wants. Well, they probably have many, but they display only *one* Want—their most important—at a time.

If your Sims can help the pet satisfy this Want, the family earns Pet points that it can spend at the Town Square. Every pet Want has its own Pet point reward, depending how difficult it is to satisfy.

A Sim near a pet can sense what the pet most desires.

There are two ways to see a pet's Want. You could switch to control of the pet and press the Quick Text button; the Want and its reward appear atop the screen.

You can also check pets' Wants when controlling a Sim. If a Sim is close enough to a pet, pressing the Quick Text button shows the pet's current Want.

Satisfying pet Wants should be one of your major objectives. Though satisfying a pet's Want has no direct impact on the pet, there's usually an immediate relationship or Motive benefit to the pet. Plus, amassing Pet points is critical to upgrading the Town Square, making all objects available to you and your pets.

Ownership

Pets, somewhat like Sims and their beds, feel a sense of ownership over certain objects, preferring them over all others and using them exclusively unless unavailable. Unlike Sims, however, they tend to be very protective of things they've deemed to belong to them alone, even fighting to scare off an impinging rival.

To avoid fights, make sure every pet has its own bed.

Pets can claim ownership over:

◆ Pet Beds   ◆ Pet Toys
◆ Pet Bones   ◆ Pet Bowls
◆ Scratching Posts

 note
A pet can claim ownership over only one of each kind of item (the one with the highest Ownership score). In other words, each dog can own only one bowl.

 note
The first pet to use an object gets a big head start in ownership over the object.

Here's how it works. Every time a pet uses an object, it gains Ownership points over it. Once a pet has enough Ownership points toward an object, it will increasingly go to that object exclusively to satisfy its Motive.

 note
Any number of pets can amass Ownership points for an object at the same time. It's possible for every pet in a house to feel it "owns" a pet dish. Who owns a dish more is really the issue: when two pets have Ownership points over an object, challenges ensue.

Ownership battles may seem petty, but they're critical for pets.

When one pet witnesses another pet using an object for which it has gained significant Ownership points, it can Challenge the other pet. Challenge is an interaction in which each pet's Ownership points are compared—the pet with the most points further cements its dominance over the object. The pet with the higher Ownership points gains a bonus number of Ownership points, and the loser surrenders some of its points.

You can tell when a Challenge interaction is occurring when one pet hisses or growls at another that's using an object. The challenging pet's negative thought bubble also shows the object in dispute. The pet using the object stops interacting with it and engages in the challenge.

Whether or not a pet mounts an Ownership Challenge can depend on:

◆ Relationship: If the challenger has a Pack or Mine Relationship with the challengee, it may decide to forgo a challenge. Conversely, an Enemy Relationship increases the odds of a challenge.

◆ Relationship Level: The challenger's level of relationship can increase or decrease the likelihood of a challenge.

◆ Aggressive Trait: If the challenger has the Aggressive trait, it's more likely to mount a challenge.

How a pet reacts to or forces a challenge depends on its Personality. Given the combination of traits, the result is usually one of the following:

◆ The loser leaves.

◆ The loser leaves and the winner begins using the object.

◆ Both pets interact to dramatize the conflict—barking/hissing, chasing, fighting. Which of these occurs also depends on Personality. In the end, the loser leaves and the winner may or may not use the object.

Training and Learned Behavior

Pets can be trained to behave properly or perform special tasks. Training can only be imparted by household Sims with an established relationship to the pet and only when the pet is in a good Mood.

note
Commands and reinforced behaviors that a pet has learned, or is in the process of learning, are viewable in the Reinforced Behaviors panel of the Personal Info menu.

Once a pet accepts training, the time it takes to fully learn the training can be affected by the:

◆ Sim's Charisma: Every point of the trainer's Charisma speeds training by 2 percent.

◆ Gifted Trait: Gifted pets train 25 percent faster than Normal pets.

◆ Doofus Trait: Doofus pets train 25 percent slower than Normal pets.

◆ Relationship to Trainer: If the pet's relationship to the trainer is 50 or higher, it trains 10 percent faster. If relationship is less than 50, it trains 10 percent slower.

note
Training a pet builds a Sim's Charisma just like a mirror, so training a pet makes a Sim a better pet trainer.

Types of Training

Pets can be trained in two ways:

◆ Reinforced Behavior

◆ Commands

Reinforced Behavior

Reinforced behavior training stops pets from autonomously doing undesirable things. Pets can be trained in:

◆ No Peeing: Pets learn to not pee in the house.

◆ No Chewing: Dogs learn to not chew on anything except pet chew toys.

◆ No Scratching: Cats learn to not scratch anything but scratching posts.

◆ No Digging: Dogs learn to not dig in the yard.

Reinforced behavior training is done by using the Scold interaction whenever a pet does the undesirable activity.

While and shortly after peeing, digging, scratching, or chewing, pets can be scolded.

note
Scolding cats damages relationship, so follow up scolding with a bit of love or play.

Scolding is only available for a time after the pet does the activity and only for the last reinforceable activity. If, for example, a pet digs in the yard then pees in the house, your Sim can only scold for the peeing; the opportunity to scold for digging passed when the pet piddled on the rug.

During reinforced behavior training, a learning bar appears above the pet's head. When it's filled, the behavior is fully learned.

note
The training Sim also has a training bar overhead, representing Charisma skill development.

The more complete a pet's training, the less likely it'll be to do the undesirable behavior. So, even partial training can make life at home better.

Once a behavior is learned, it is learned for good and the pet will not do the undesirable activity again unless its Mood is seriously low.

When a pet's Mood drops below -50, it begins to forget its reinforced behavior. The farther Mood dips below -50, the more likely the pet will be to act against its training.

Once Mood is restored above -50, however, full training returns immediately.

Commands

Sure, pets can be taught *not* to do things, but they can also be taught some pretty nifty things *to* do. Teaching pets commands:

◆ Makes them indirectly controllable (through your Sims).

◆ Enables them to be even more helpful to your Sims.

◆ Satisfies Social and Fun Motives of both pet and trainer when learned commands are performed.

◆ Improves their value when sold at the Pet Purveyor.

All commands can be taught under the Teach…

Pets can be taught to:

◆ Come

◆ Dance (only after Sit Up is learned)

◆ Follow

◆ Guard

◆ Lie Down

◆ Play Dead

◆ Roll Over (only after Lie Down is learned)

◆ Shake

◆ Sing

◆ Sit Up

◆ Speak

◆ Stay Here

◆ Use Toilet (cat only)

A pet's process of learning commands is very similar to the way a Sim learns a skill. During training, a progress bar appears above the pet's head. If the training is interrupted (perhaps because the pet or the Sim had to sleep or eat), later training will pick up exactly where the pet left off.

Pets in training show a progress bar. Since the Sim is learning Charisma by teaching, the Sim has a bar overhead, too.

During training a pet quickly depletes its Fun Motive. To keep the pet in training, Sims can do two things to boost the pet's Fun. During training, the Sim can:

◆ Do the Instruct…Encourage interaction: This doesn't add as much Fun as the training is taking away, but it can buy some time if the pet is close to mastering the command.

◆ Do the Instruct…Feed Treat interaction: If your Sim has a treat in inventory, you can direct him or her to feed it to a pet during training. This significantly boosts the pet's Fun, allowing it to stay in training far longer. Treats, however, cost money and deplete the pet's Bladder Motive, so this can be a costly technique.

When a command is learned, it's never forgotten and the pet always obeys unless it's in an awful Mood.

Pet Breeding

Pets breed only on command—via the Try for Puppy/Kitten with… interaction—from your Sims and only if:

◆ There's a useable pet house on the lot.

◆ There's another pet of the same species, opposite gender, and not blood related in the household.

◆ Both pets have high Relationship scores with the commanding Sim.

◆ Both pets have high Relationship scores toward each other.

◆ The household isn't already holding the maximum number of Sims and pets.

First your Sim commands the pet to breed.

Then the pet sees if the other pet is willing.

Finally, they both retire to the nearest pet house for a little "alone time."

Immediately after the breeding, a single puppy or kitten arrives. During its one-day-long youth, the puppy or kitten exists in its basket, though it can be handled, nuzzled, played with, etc., by its parents and other pets and Sims.

After one day, the puppy or kitten grows into a full-grown pet and is added to the household. The adult version of the offspring resembles its parents in appearance, behavior, and even training. Bred pets inherit:

◆ Fur Texture: either mother or father

◆ Face: either mother or father or combination of both

◆ Fur: either mother or father

◆ Ear: either mother or father

◆ Tail: either mother or father

◆ Traits: either mother or father

◆ Training: 25 percent of parent's cumulative fully learned commands and reinforced behaviors. Thus, if Mom had two commands/behaviors and Dad had six, the offspring would get two. The actual commands or behaviors are randomly selected from its parents' commands and behaviors.

note
For every trait, there's a 20 percent chance the offspring will get a random trait from neither parent.

Runaways

Most pets are loyal to the core, but there may come a time when they feel it's necessary to run away into the cold cruel world of stray pets.

A happy, well-cared-for pet won't run away; only persistent and repeated neglect or abuse will compel a pet to depart its family.

Running away is driven by the following events:

◆ Pet passes out from Hunger.

◆ Pet's Master (dogs) or Mine (cats) Relationship is broken.

◆ Sim with whom the pet has a Master (dogs) or Mine (cats) Relationship passes out.

If five of these events happen to a pet, it immediately and permanently runs away. Don't say you didn't have it coming!

note
If, after a pet passes out from Hunger, food is not provided within six hours, the pet will run away regardless of how many runaway events have occurred.

Strays

The neighborhood is full of pets with no homes. These "strays" can show up on your Sims' lots and can forge relationships—even close ones—with your Sims. You may also get an opportunity to return a runaway pet to its owner.

There are two kinds of strays:

◆ Unowned Strays: These pets are generated randomly and may have behaviors or commands. Unowned strays initially have no Master or Mine Relationships with anyone. Using the Check Imbedded Microchip interaction reveals that the pet has no owner.

◆ Owned Runaway Pets: Pets with owners typically have a Master or Mine relationship with their previous owner. Using the Check Imbedded Microchip interaction reveals the owner of the pet and enables your Sim to use the phone to return the pet to its owner. Owned strays are more likely to visit Sims' lots than unowned strays.

Stray Visits

Unaccompanied pets are strays. But that doesn't mean they don't belong to someone.

Strays visit a lot in much the same way as townies, but several rules determine how often they visit and how long they'll stay.

note
You can exclude all strays from a lot by buying the Stray Away! sign from the pause menu Object Catalog.

All strays can stay on a lot for a specific time (unless something else forces them to leave earlier) based on their relationship with any Sim on the lot. The higher the pet's greatest relationship with any Sim on the lot, the longer it'll stay.

A stray will leave if:

- Its visit time expires.
- It loses too many collective relationship points with all Sims and pets in the household.
- Its Motives drop too low.
- It experiences the kind of events that would make an owned pet run away.

The higher a stray's relationship with a Sim in a household, the more often it will visit.

Dealing with Strays

Sims may do the Shoo interaction to force strays to leave the lot immediately. This will, however, reduce the relationship between Sim and stray.

If a stray is owned, your Sim can use the phone to report the lost pet. Shortly, the owner will (assuming the pet's former household has room for it) drop by to pick up the pet.

 note If a runaway pet and its former owner happen to visit your Sim's lot at the same time, they'll be reunited automatically.

Bonding

When a pet has gained a Master or Mine Relationship toward one Sim on a lot, the pet becomes part of the household.

If an adopted stray is a runaway, it can't thereafter be returned to its owner.

Caged Pets

In addition to cats, dogs, puppies, and kittens, your Sims can also own caged mammals and goldfish. These pets aren't as complex as cats and dogs, but they do require some responsibility from your Sims and offer a decent share of Fun for Sims, cats, and dogs.

Some of the joy and only a bit of the work make caged pet ownership an attractive option.

Caged pets come in two varieties:

- Piggle Puff: This small hamster-like mammal can be purchased from the home Object Catalog.
- Goldfish: A single fish in a fishbowl, the goldfish is immediately purchasable from the Town Square's Pet Emporium.

 note Sims gain Cleaning skill from cleaning pet cages and fishbowls.

Piggle Puff

The piggle puff is a Fun object that requires some care or interaction or it will become grumpy and bite and eventually run away.

To gain Fun from the piggle puff, Sims can take it out and play with it, and cats and dogs can watch it. It must, however, be regularly fed and its cage must be cleaned.

The piggle puff's Mood is based on whether its cage is clean and it's been recently fed. If a pet's Mood drops, it becomes foul-tempered, biting anyone who tries to interact with it. A bite reduces, rather than satisfies, the Sim's Fun.

If the piggle puff's Mood gets bad enough it runs away, leaving an empty and nonrefillable cage.

 note To dispose of a piggle puff cage, you must sell it in Buy mode.

You can sell a live piggle puff (with cage) in Buy mode. Its resale value is relative to its Mood when sold. For the most slam for the Simoleon, feed it and clean its cage before selling.

Goldfish

The goldfish is essentially a decorative object that can, if the fishbowl is not kept clean, lower your Sims' Moods.

Keep the bowl clean and the fish fed or they'll be floating for sure.

The goldfish must be fed regularly, and its bowl must be cleaned when it gets dirty. If the goldfish's bowl is filthy, it stops raising Room score and instead lowers it. If the bowl remains filthy for a long time or you don't direct your Sims to feed it, the goldfish eventually dies. A dead fish lowers Room score even more.

The fishbowl can be sold in Buy mode, but its value depends on how dirty it is and whether the fish is alive or dead.

Chapter 17

FACTS OF SIM LIFE

Higher callings and professional achievement are all for naught if Sims can't take care of their physical and emotional necessities. All Sims must spend time every day fulfilling their Motives, or they quickly find themselves unable to function. If they can satisfy these Motives with maximum efficiency, their rise in the world becomes a speedy one.

If, on the other hand, they fail to fulfill their Motives, or something untoward befalls them, a dramatic swoon awaits. Fortunately, the opportunities to see the Paramedic are relatively rare, and the road back to the full bloom of normality is an easy one.

This section discusses Sims' Motives and Mood, along with a few other miscellaneous issues that govern how Sims live their lives.

Motives and Mood

Every Sim is driven, at the most fundamental level, by his or her common physical and psychological Motives. This section examines how those Motives function, how to most efficiently satisfy them, and how to enable Sims to take care of them autonomously.

Taken together, the levels of a Sim's Motives dictate overall Mood.

Mood and Motives drive and impact several important elements of the game:

- Sims' performance at work is largely dictated by their Mood when they leave the lot.
- Mood affects the availability of social interactions.
- The acceptance of social interactions depends on Mood and Motives.
- Mood and Motives affect a Sim's willingness to build skills.
- Mood and Motives affect a Sim's willingness to use Fun objects.
- Certain special behaviors and interactions are triggered by the level of individual Motives or overall Mood.
- Many Wants arise based on Mood.
- Visitors stay only as long as they can fulfill certain Motives.
- Time management depends largely on your Sims' ability to quickly and efficiently tend to their Motives.

Motives Defined

Every Sim has eight basic Motives:

 Hunger   Energy   Hygiene

 Comfort   Fun   Room

 Bladder   Social

The Motives Panel

Motives are measured on a scale of -100 (fully depleted) to +100 (fully satisfied).

note

The numbers mentioned in this section, and others that describe the level of a Motive or Mood, are not seen in the actual game, but they should provide a guide to where on the meter the numbers would be. For example, if a Motive is at 0, the meter is dead center (50 percent full). If it's at -50, it's at 25 percent full. If it's at +50, it's at 75 percent full.

The Motives panel shows the current level of all your Sim's Motives. The size and color of the filled portion of the bars show the level of each Motive.

Motives are shown in the Motives panel. Next to each Motive is a horizontal bar. When a bar is filled with green, the Motive is fully satisfied (+100). When it's in the middle (yellow), the Motive is partially satisfied. When the bar is orange, the Motive is said to be "in distress" (around -60 to -80). When the bar is all red, the Motive is in "failure" (-100).

Arrows within the bars indicate that something is pushing a Motive's level either up or down. This can be an interaction, normal decay, or passive influence of some nearby object.

When a Motive is changing, arrows appear next to the bar. If they're pointing up, the Motive is being satisfied by whatever the Sim is doing. If they're pointing down, the Motive is decaying. The number of triangles indicates the speed of the change. Three triangles mean a fast change, and one indicates a gradual change.

> **note**
>
> If you see Fun rising for no apparent reason, look to see if your Sim is near a stereo or TV or even a pet. If so, the Sim is feeling the pull of those things' passive influence, gaining Fun just from being near them.

Mood

Sims' overall sense of well-being is reflected in their Mood. Mood, in turn, is the sum effect of all Motives (except Energy).

Mood (without regard for any of the individual Motives) dictates which social interactions are accepted, whether a Sim looks for a job or develops skills, how well a Sim is doing at work, and whether the Sim is eligible for a job promotion.

Not all the Motives impact Mood to the same extent. The level of each Motive dictates how much it affects overall Mood. If, for example, Hunger is just below fully satisfied, it affects Mood just a little. If it's in the middle, it affects Mood more, but at only a minimal level. Once Hunger gets very low, however, its effect is multiplied several times, growing stronger as the Motive creeps lower.

The Mood Meter

This is the Mood meter. If it's all green, your Sim is in a super Mood. The more red there is, the worse your Sim's Mood.

Mood is represented by the Mood meter (on the Motives panel), a curved bar running along the top of the onscreen control wheel in the lower left corner of the screen. The meter decays from right to left and fulfills from left to right. If the bar is mostly green, Mood is positive. If it's mostly red, Mood is negative.

Motive Decay

All Motives (except Room) decay over time. If left unsatisfied, they eventually drop to their lowest value (-100).

The speed of this decay dictates how often a Sim has to tend to a Motive and is influenced by several factors:

♦ Personality: Many Motives are tied to certain Personality traits that accelerate (if at one extreme) or slow (if at the other) decay. A Sim with 10 Active/Lazy decays Hunger the fastest, 5 is normal, and 0 is slowest.

♦ Sleep: Many Motives decay at a slower rate or not at all when a Sim is asleep. Energy and Comfort replenish during sleep.

♦ Objects and Interactions: Many objects or interactions speed the decay of certain Motives.

Distress and Failure

When Motives get very low, they enter two stages, distress and then failure.

Distress

Motive distress occurs in two stages, at -60 and -80. At -60, Sims gesture about their dwindling Motive and display blue thought bubbles indicating the Motive that's getting low.

Sims with dwindling Motives signal their distress.

If a Motive is below -80, Sims indicate their trouble in red thought bubbles and their general behavior. Tired Sims sag in posture, and Sims in Bladder distress pin their knees together. Either of these behaviors significantly slows Sims' speed.

Sleepy Sims walk very slowly like they're, well, extremely sleepy.

note

Sims with low Energy, Hunger, Fun (skill only), Comfort (if not seated for the activity), or Bladder (regardless of overall Mood) automatically exit out of or refuse to enter skill or Fun objects, wake from sleep, and refuse to look for a job.

Other Motives don't have this effect, though they bring down overall Mood as they decline. Low Mood causes some of the same kickouts as Energy, Hunger, Fun, Comfort, or Bladder distress.

Failure

Failure occurs when a Motive reaches -100. What happens then depends largely on the specific Motive.

Hunger

Hunger is the physical Motive for food and drink.

Sims satisfy Hunger by eating. The more nourishing the food, the more the satisfaction a meal contains.

Depletion

Hunger depletes at a steady rate all day, though it slows when the Sim is asleep. The speed of Hunger depletion depends also on Personality.

Hunger can also be depleted by social interactions.

Satisfaction

Hunger is satisfied by eating food or drinking liquid. The more satisfying a meal, the more Hunger it refills. The more Hunger is fulfilled, the fewer servings Sims need to become full, and the less time they must spend eating.

Desperate for food and low on cash? Have a seat on the couch and search the cushions. Your Sim may just find a treat. It won't help much, but every little bit counts.

note

For all the minute details on making the most satisfying food, see the "Food Creation" chapter.

Personality

Active Sims lose Hunger more quickly than other Sims. The more Active they are (the more Personality points they have in Active/Lazy), the more quickly Hunger depletes.

Mood Impact

Hunger has a low impact on Mood when it's high or even moderate. As the Motive descends into negative territory, Hunger's impact on Mood grows quickly. By the time it nears failure, Hunger has more impact on Mood than any other Motive.

Therefore, satisfied Sims don't give much thought at all to having a full stomach, but they care plenty when it starts to growl.

If Hunger declines too low, Sims either exit or refuse to use skill-building or Fun objects, even if Mood is still positive.

Distress and Failure

When Hunger gets low, Hunger icons appear above Sims' heads.

If Sims are prevented from eating and Hunger reaches -100, they go into Motive failure. In the case of Hunger, this means passing out and a revival. It's OK; other Sims can be directed to revive them or the Paramedic will be glad to help.

Comfort

Comfort is the physical Motive to get off your feet and the emotional Motive to feel safe, well, and cared for.

A nice, expensive chair is just the thing for flagging Comfort.

Depletion

Comfort is steadily depleted every minute a Sim is not sitting, reclining, or lying down. Like Energy, Comfort is satisfied when the Sim is sleeping anywhere but the floor.

Passing out on the floor? That's not so comfortable.

Comfort is also decreased by doing certain activities:

- Sleeping on the floor
- Standing
- Dancing
- Using exercise equipment

Satisfaction

Lounging in the hot tub brings back lost Comfort too.

Comfort is satisfied by sitting, reclining, using comfortable objects, and engaging in comforting activities:

- Sleeping or relaxing in bed
- Doing anything on a sofa
- Sitting or reclining in chairs
- Using a hot tub
- Taking a bath
- Using an expensive toilet
- Looking into a fireplace

 note
The main difference between a shower and a bath is that the bath provides Comfort in addition to Hygiene—hence the higher price of a bathtub with the identical Hygiene of a cheaper shower.

Any Comfort object or interaction has a speed of satisfaction and a cap. The more expensive an object, the more quickly it satisfies Comfort, and the higher it allows Comfort satisfaction to climb.

 note
Sims with desk jobs rather than more physical occupations come home with increased Comfort.

Sims can get Comfort just from being near any pet (even ones they don't own), even if they're not interacting with it. The higher the pet's Mood and the relationship of the pet to the Sim, the more Comfort the Sim will get.

Personality

Lazy Sims lose Comfort more quickly than other Sims. The lazier they are (the fewer Personality points they have in Active/Lazy), the faster Comfort depletes.

Mood Impact

Like Hunger, Comfort has no exaggerated effect on Mood until it gets very low. Unlike Hunger, however, this moment comes only after Comfort drops just shy of halfway into the red zone. As it drops farther and eventually empties, however, its effects are increasingly multiplied.

At its lowest point, Comfort has its greatest influence on Mood, though it's still considerably less than extremely low Hunger.

Low Comfort can knock a Sim out of skill building if the Sim is standing for the activity.

Distress and Failure

Sims in Comfort distress signal with a comfy chair thought bubble and look generally uncomfortable (stretching, fighting back pain).

There is no failure state for Comfort; Sims just waste a lot of time telling you how uncomfortable they are. Plus, their Mood is thoroughly tanked until you allow them to sit.

Bladder

Bladder is the physical Motive to use a toilet.

Depletion

Bladder decreases steadily all the time, albeit more slowly when a Sim is sleeping.

Depletion can be accelerated if a Sim eats food or drinks liquid (especially coffee and espresso).

Satisfaction

There's nothing complicated about how to satisfy the Bladder Motive.

Bladder can be satisfied anywhere (though most places aren't by choice), but there's only one place that doesn't simultaneously cause a total depletion of Hygiene—a toilet. All toilets fulfill the Bladder Motive at the same rate, but more expensive ones also give Comfort.

Personality

All Personalities have identical Bladder motives.

Mood Impact

Bladder has no heightened effect on Mood until it gets very low. At that point, its effect becomes quickly and profoundly serious.

If Bladder declines too low, Sims either exit or refuse to use skill-building or Fun objects, even if Mood is still positive.

Distress and Failure

Sims with low Bladder walk like they're "holding it."

Around the time Bladder begins to seriously affect Mood, Sims start to show their distress by displaying toilet thought balloons.

note

Sims "holding it" trudge to the bathroom with knees together; if they waited too long, they'll wet the floor before reaching the toilet.

At -100, failure occurs, and Sims wet themselves. This completely refills the Bladder Motive but also decimates the Hygiene Motive. Sims who've gone through Bladder failure don't need a toilet until Bladder decays again, but they need a bath or shower.

When Bladder failure occurs, nearby Sims react.

Energy

Energy is the basic physical Motive for sleep and rest.

Depletion

Every waking moment, Sims use Energy, though the rate varies by Personality.

Energy is depleted more quickly when Sims engage in physically demanding activities.

note

If using any objects or doing any interaction drops Sims' Energy too low, they automatically stop interacting.

Satisfaction

A bed is inarguably the best way to restore Energy.

When Sims sleep, the Energy Motive is refilled at a rate defined by what they're sleeping on:

- Couch: Power naps on couches refill Energy, but at a slower rate than on beds. They are also, unlike beds, capped with a maximum Energy restoration. The speed of and caps on Energy restoration generally rise with the cost of the couch.

- Bed: Beds are the primary engines for fulfilling Sims' Energy Motive. They tend to fill Energy more quickly than other furniture and fill the Motive to its top. The speed with which a bed restores Energy is generally tied to its cost, and the difference can be dramatic.

- The Floor or Standing: If Sims can't get to a bed or couch before their Energy Motive fails, they fall asleep on the ground. Not surprisingly, the ground provides very slow Energy satisfaction. Give them a few minutes to recharge, wake them up, and get them into a real bed.

tip

Spending Simoleons on a bed is a sound investment. A cheap bed provides full rest in about nine game hours, a medium bed in seven and a half hours, and an expensive bed in only six hours.

A frothy cup of espresso is just the thing for flagging Energy, but it means an earlier trip to the bathroom.

There is a less-obvious way to gain Energy—drinking espresso. This strong, brown brew adds a fixed amount of Energy but takes time to drink and causes Bladder to deplete.

Personality

Lazy Sims lose Energy more quickly than other Sims. The lazier they are (the fewer Personality points they have in Active/Lazy), the faster Energy depletes.

Mood Impact

Energy has no effect on Sims' overall Mood. Therefore, for job performance, it doesn't matter how high Energy is when they go to work. If it's too low, however, they collapse on the sidewalk when they return home.

If Energy declines too low, Sims either exit or refuse to use skill-buildling or Fun objects, even if Mood is still positive.

Distress and Failure

Sims in Energy distress show red thought balloons. This behavior wastes time. When Energy reaches rock bottom, Sims instantly fall asleep on the ground or where they're standing. Passed out Sims can't be revived until they gain sufficient Energy to get to a bed (about five game minutes).

If there isn't room to collapse, Sims fall asleep standing up. After a few moments, they can be awakened by clicking on them and selecting Wake Up. Take the opportunity to get them to bed.

Fun

Fun is the psychological Motive for amusement and relaxation.

Depletion

Fun decays steadily while a Sim is awake. No decay occurs during sleep.

Satisfaction

Anything amusing feeds the Fun Motive.

Fun is satisfied by engaging in any interaction with a Fun rating. The higher the rating, the more Fun it imparts. This rating is typically a measure both of the speed of satisfaction and the maximum to which Fun can rise.

tip

You know a Fun object has a maximum limit if the meter stops filling even if the Sim is still doing the activity. Sims also declare that an object is no longer or not sufficiently Fun once they exceed or reach that maximum.

This warning means Sims will do the directed interaction but they won't get any Fun satisfaction because the object is capped lower than the current Fun level.

A very expensive Fun object, for example, gives Fun quickly all the way up to 100. Less pricey diversions might get a Sim to max Fun but do it very slowly, or they might work quickly but only raise Fun to a fixed level. And still others might offer a fixed dose of Fun but allow Sims to go back for additional doses until Fun hits maximum.

note

Sims' Personality (whether they're more Playful or more Serious) has nothing to do with how much Fun they get out of an interaction. But it does affect which interactions Sims are attracted to when acting autonomously. If left to their own devices, Serious Sims pull a book off the shelf before they turn on the TV.

Directing Serious Sims to watch TV, however, gives them whatever Fun the TV offers, regardless of Personality.

Viewing a decorative object is an easy dose of Fun—small but easy.

Fun can be had from interactions with both objects and other Sims. In the latter case, many social interactions (in addition to Relationship and Social Motive benefits) also give Fun.

tip

Arcade machines are super Fun objects and money well spent.

Spectators can get Fun too.

Fun can also be had from watching other Sims engaged in a Fun activity.

One of the best sources of Fun, however, is pets. Not only do they get Fun satisfaction from playing with pets, they get it from just being near them (even pets they don't own). The higher the pet's Mood and the relationship of the pet to the Sim, the more Fun the Sim will get.

Personality

Playful Sims lose Fun more quickly than other Sims. The more Playful they are (the more Personality points in Playful/Serious), the faster Fun depletes.

note

Neat Sims receive Fun from cleaning while Sloppy Sims lose Fun.

note

Playful Sims (Playful/Serious less than 5) need about two hours of Fun per day while Serious Sims require only about an hour to be fully satisfied.

Mood Impact

Fun has its greatest impact on Mood when it's very high (about 50 to 100) or very low (about -50 to -100). Sims are never in a top-notch Mood unless their Fun is totally satisfied, but only truly bored Sims allow a lack of Fun to dampen their otherwise positive Mood.

Fun can, by itself, knock a Sim out of skill building if it gets too low. Less dire levels of Fun can indirectly have the same effect if they lower Mood below 0.

Distress and Failure

Sims without Fun slouch, look depressed, and show TV thought bubbles, all of which waste time. They're also likely to be in a pretty sour overall Mood.

There is no failure state for Fun; the effects of distress simply worsen.

Social

Social is the psychological Motive to interact with other Sims.

No Sim is an island, so Sims must interact in some way to feed their Social Motive.

tip

Whenever possible, get Sims to eat, watch TV, use the hot tub, etc., together so they can feed their Social Motive along with whatever else they're doing. Playing with their pets is one of the easiest ways to keep a Sim's Social Motive high.

Depletion

Any time Sims aren't directly interacting with another Sim or pet, Social is decaying at a steady rate.

Social is also reduced by negative social interactions. If the outcome of an interaction (mostly rejected ones but some positive) is negative, it probably reduces Social.

Satisfaction

Social is satisfied by having positive social interactions. In most such interactions, both sides receive some increase in the Social Motive.

tip

If the Social Motive is very low, focus social interactions on Sims with high-level relationships. The interactions that come with these relationships satisfy far more Social Motive than even the best low-level interactions.

A pet is an always-ready source of Social Motive satisfaction.

There are more ways to interact, however, than face-to-face. Sims can talk on the phone; chat over a computer; or talk in groups at meals, on the couch, or in hot tubs.

When Sims join an activity (like talking, watching TV, etc.), that activity usually gains a Social benefit for all involved.

Personality

Outgoing Sims lose Social more quickly than other Sims. The more Outgoing they are (the more Personality points they have in Outgoing/Shy), the more quickly Social depletes.

note

Shy Sims need about an hour of Social per day (on top of what they get at work), while Outgoing Sims need about two hours of interaction.

Mood Impact

Like Fun, Social has its strongest influence on Mood when it's very high and very low. Also as with Fun, Social's baseline impact on Mood is higher than for the physical Motives. Social's "normal" effect is twice that of the other Motives. This means when all Motives are high, Social and Fun are actually the strongest determinants of Mood.

Distress and Failure

Sims in Social distress show red socializing thought bubbles. These displays waste time and reduce efficiency. Really low Social is also a serious drag on Mood.

There is no failure state for Social.

Hygiene

Hygiene is the physical Motive to feel clean.

Depletion

If Sims are awake, they're gradually losing Hygiene. When they're sleeping, this rate is slowed but not stopped.

Just being near a smelly pet will bring down a Sim's Hygiene.

Many activities accelerate the loss of Hygiene, especially ones involving physical exertion.

When a Sim stands near any pet with low Hygiene, the stench affects the Sim's Hygiene. Even if Sim and pet aren't interacting, the Sim's Hygiene drops whenever the filthy pet is close. The higher the pet's Mood and the relationship of the pet to the Sim, the less Hygiene the Sim will lose.

Satisfaction

Showers are the quickest way to full Hygiene.

Hygiene is satisfied by several objects, primarily showers and bathtubs. Tubs provide slower Hygiene than showers but provide simultaneous Comfort. Hot tubs have even slower Hygiene satisfaction but also provide Comfort, Fun, and Social (if there's more than one soaking Sim).

Personality

Sloppy Sims lose Hygiene faster than other Sims. The sloppier they are (the fewer Personality points in Neat/Sloppy), the faster Hygiene depletes.

Mood Impact

Hygiene doesn't begin to seriously affect Mood until it reaches -40. At this point, its impact quickly multiplies (though not as much as the other physical Motives).

Hygiene does not, by itself, knock a Sim out of skill building except to the extent that it may lower Mood below 0.

Distress and Failure

When Sims' Hygiene is in distress, they're followed by a swarm of flies, and nearby Sims react to the odor.

Whew! This Sim needs a bath.

Low Hygiene doesn't directly affect Sims' ability to work on skills (unless it brings Mood down below medium), but it does make it difficult to interact socially. The clouds of flies are unpleasant, and the self-sniffing and scratching waste valuable time.

There is no failure state for Hygiene. Your Sim is just in a pretty bad Mood, stinks to high heaven, and is unable to interact (no Sim wants to get close enough to talk) or (if Mood is low enough) have Fun or work on skills.

Room

Room is the psychological Motive for order and cleanliness in one's surroundings. This Motive is unique in both the way it works and how it influences Mood.

An untidy home makes a full good Mood impossible.

The Room Motive doesn't decay like other motives. Rather, it exists as a score in a given location that pushes the Room Motive of any nearby Sim either up or down.

Generally, Room score is based on the quality and cleanliness of each room, though the amount of light and whether the Sim is indoors or out creates more localized effects.

note
Indoors, a "room" is defined as a place enclosed by walls with access only via doors. If two spaces are connected by a gap in the wall rather than a door or archway, the two spaces together form a single "room" for Room score purposes.

Calculating Room Score

Room score defines where Sims' Room Motive is set when they are in that room.

Two elements make up Room score:

◆ The "niceness" of the room (including presence of plants and decorative objects)

◆ The presence of any messes (including trash, dirty dishes, ashes, or dead plants)

The final score is determined by subtracting messiness from niceness. Which things influence these elements provide the strategy behind Room score.

note
Room score scales to the size of the room. Therefore, it takes more total Room score (and money) to top out a large room than a small one.

Niceness

Niceness reflects three elements:

◆ Purchase price of objects in the room (including lights)

◆ Purchase price of flooring

◆ Purchase price of wallpaper

Nice decorations from the Buy Catalog and floor and wall coverings from the Build Catalog contribute to Room.

Each of these elements has only a partial impact on Room. The bulk of the score comes from objects, but the rest comes from sizable allotments for each of the rest.

In other words, a room packed with expensive objects but no wall coverings or floor coverings offers only about 60 percent full Room score.

Objects

The combined purchase prices of all objects in a room dictates the first portion of the niceness calculation.

The more expensive a decorative object, the greater its positive effect on Room.

Every object is assigned a "niceness" factor that raises Room score in the room in which it's placed.

note
Every object has a niceness factor, but the factor is minimal for ordinary objects. Only the more expensive and decorative objects have really significant Room scores.

Each object in the room contributes its niceness to the overall Room score.

note

Given the strong but limited effect of objects on Room score, there always comes a point when spending money on decorative objects shows no further increase in Room score. The precise Simoleon amount of this point rises with the size of the room.

If, therefore, you're trying to improve Room score, and adding a new object doesn't show any effect, consider returning it and instead upgrading the lighting, flooring, or wall covering.

The cost of an object largely determines how much effect it has on Room, but decorative objects have a far greater effect per Simoleons spent.

Wall and Floor Covering

The plywood floors and sheetrock walls that you put up in Build mode contribute nothing to Room score. This leaves two massive chunks of niceness empty, making a full score impossible.

The quality (read: purchase price) of the coverings you place on walls and floors determines how much these two elements add to niceness. The more expensive they are, the more they contribute.

note

Each of these elements is scored as an average for the room. Therefore, if a room is mostly expensive wallpaper with some sections of the cheap stuff, top score isn't possible.

Messiness

Niceness is, however, only part of the Room equation. What separates overall Room score from niceness is the element of messiness.

A messy object in the room deducts a fixed amount from Room score everywhere in the room. Messy objects hold down Room score until they are cleaned or removed.

A filthy litter box and a dirty pet bowl mean low Room score for this room.

Messy objects include:

- Ash Piles
- Books Left Out
- Broken Objects
- Dirty Dishes
- Dirty Litter Boxes
- Dirty Pet Bowls
- Dirty Pet Beds and Pet Houses
- Flies (in addition to dirty object's messiness)
- Full Trash Cans
- Old Newspapers
- Puddles
- Spoiled Food
- Soiled Objects (dirty sinks, toilets, countertops)
- Trash Piles
- Uncovered Floor Sections
- Uncovered Wall Sections
- Unmade Beds

note

Messiness can be a result of noise, too. A ringing alarm clock pulls down Room score in its room until it's turned off.

Dirty objects detract from Room only if they're *visibly* dirty. Therefore, an object may show a Clean interaction before it begins to bring down Room.

Flies

Flies appear in Sims' homes in response to certain messes.

Flies appear above dirty dishes, spoiled food, or trash piles (including full trash cans) after a few hours. They create an additional Room reduction beyond the dirty object itself.

To get rid of flies, clean up the object that attracted them.

Room Outdoors

Outdoor environment works the same as indoor. Keep it clean and add nice decorations.

The game considers any outdoor space as one big "room" for Room score purposes. Just as in indoor spaces, nice objects raise Room score outdoors, and dirty things decrease it.

Personality

Room affects all Personality types equally.

Mood Impact

Room is the least Mood-influencing of all the Motives (other than Energy, of course). Like Fun and Social, it exerts greater effect when it's very high or very low.

Distress and Failure

Maybe maid service isn't such a waste of money after all.

When Sims suffer Room distress, they flash a door-shaped thought balloon. This wastes time, and the effect of low Room somewhat depresses overall Mood.

There is no failure state for Room.

Motives at Work

Every job has a distinctive effect on a Sim's Motives. When Sims are off the lot at a job, their Motives when they return are altered by this effect. So a Sim with a physical job returns home with a large deduction from Energy. Some of these effects are positive—Sims with desk jobs return home with higher Comfort. Most jobs, except really solitary ones (such as Security Guard), increase Social.

Passive Influence and Motives

Some objects satisfy Sims' Motives even when the Sims aren't directly interacting with them. This effect is called "passive influence."

Just being near a TV passively gives your Sim Fun.

Such objects raise or lower a Motive up to a limit for as long as the Sim is physically within the object's area of effect.

 tip

For efficient satisfaction of both Energy and Fun, power nap near a switched-on television. The nap doesn't provide complete Energy satisfaction, but it's fast, and you can get the passive Fun boost from the TV.

◆ All pets (even pets your Sim doesn't own) boost any nearby Sim's Fun and Comfort Motive in proportion to the pet's Mood and relationship to the Sim. Pets with low Hygiene deplete nearby Sims' Hygiene, again in proportion to the pet's Mood and relationship to each Sim.

◆ All switched-on televisions passively INCREASE Fun. Sim watches interestedly.

◆ All switched-on stereos passively INCREASE Fun. Sim dances slightly.

◆ Trash cans or piles of trash passively DECREASE Hygiene. Sim makes stinky gestures.

Awareness

Other Sims or pets can cause nearby Sims to react. This behavior is called "awareness."

When a Sim or pet autonomously reacts to another Sim or pet, the intensity of the awareness reaction depends on their relationship to that Sim or pet.

Reactions When Sim Passes near Another Sim or Pet

Relationship	Reaction
-100–-30	Scowl/Scoff
-29–40	Minor; turn head to look at Sim
41–100	Wave

Reactions When Dog Passes near Sim

Relationship	Reaction
-100–-60	Look and growl at Sim
-59–50	Look at Sim
51–100	Look at Sim, wag tail

 note

If the dog is Friendly, the values will be lower, reflecting the dog's easier-to-please nature:

Reactions When Friendly Dog Passes near Sim

Relationship	Reaction
-100–-80	Look and growl at Sim
-79–30	Look at Sim
31–100	Look at Sim, wag tail

Reactions When Cat Passes near Sim

Relationship	Reaction
-100–-1	Ignore Sim
0–100	Look at Sim

 note

If the cat is Independent, the values will be lower.

Reactions When Independent Cat Passes near Sim

Relationship	Reaction
-100–14	Ignore Sim
15–100	Look at Sim

Passing Out

Life has many surprises and not all of them are good. Sometimes, when your Sim receives one of these unpleasant experiences or just can't find the necessary food, he or she will pass out.

Oh, I feel that I shall swoon!

Fortunately, passing out isn't all that traumatic, but it's important to know how it works.

A Sim passing out drops to the floor and can't be controlled until someone revives him or her. Other playable Sims can be directed to revive the passed out Sim. Autonomous Sims won't do this on their own.

My hero!

Alternatively, controllable Sims can be directed to summon the Paramedic by telephone. Pets in the Sim's household will, depending on their Mood and relationship to the Sim, autonomously run off the lot to fetch the Paramedic. This is handy if there's no other controllable Sim on the lot.

note

For more information on the Paramedic, see the "Characters" chapter.

If there are no other controllable Sims or you choose not to revive the Sim, the Sim will eventually regain consciousness.

Why Sims Pass Out

Sims can pass out from three causes: starvation, object disaster, or fire.

Starvation

As described previously, if Sims' Hunger Motive goes into total failure and stays that way (they're unable to find any food source, or you actively prevent them from doing so), they eventually pass out from starvation.

Hunger is the only Motive that, if allowed to completely deplete, can cause a Sim to pass out.

Object Disaster

Using certain objects carries a chance for passing out. For most, however, this is usually a function of low skill. For others, the chance of passing out is either completely random or heightened by some condition (like a dirty fireplace), but the chances are usually very small.

Low Skill

Some objects require skill to use properly, and using them with too little of a certain skill can be bad news.

- Stove: Chance of fire depends on Cooking skill. Sim can pass out from smoke inhalation.
- Electrical Appliances: When repairing a broken TV, dishwasher, microwave, toaster, oven, or espresso maker, there's a chance of electrical shock if Mechanical skill is low.

The probability of passing out in every instance drops with each skill level, becoming nonexistent once your Sim reaches level 5.

Skill Level	Probability of Passing Out
0	20%
1	10%
2	5%
3	3%
4	1%
5 and higher	0%

Random Object-Induced Passing Out

Some objects just bear the mark of random misfortune. Still, it's not *completely* random. Such objects carry a risk factor that alters the probability. For example, all fireplaces can cause fires if there's a flammable object nearby, but the chances increase with the dirtiness of the fireplace. The dirtier it is, the greater the chance of an out-of-control fire and, if further misfortune ensues, passing out.

Fire

Sims can pass out from smoke inhalation if the space they're standing on catches fire. Most often, this occurs while Sims are standing around a fire, gawking and panicking. Suddenly, the fire is no longer in the next tile but rather right under the Sims' feet. If they don't move, they swoon.

Fires can be started by cooking or fireplaces.

Chapter 18

SKILLS AND CAREERS

What Sims do for a living is at least equally important to what they need and want. Skills enable Sims to have more of an impact on the things around them. Work defines Sims to themselves and the world, and more importantly, it pays the bills.

To become successful in both skills and career, it's crucial to understand how this finely balanced mechanism works and how you can use this knowledge to tilt it to your advantage.

Skills

Whether Sims are climbing the career ladder, staying home to pursue their Aspirations, or living a life of self-improvement, they need skills.

Skills can impact many things:

◆ To advance in any career, Sims must develop three defined skills. Career advancement increases Sims' income and provides fulfillment of career-related Wants.

◆ The Wants of many Sims are tied to the acquisition of a skill or all skills. Aspiration points increase with each skill level and pay off big time if the skill is maximized.

◆ Some skills provide the opportunity for extra income.

◆ Doing certain activities with high or low skill can elicit reactions from nearby Sims.

◆ Some skills make household chores faster and easier.

◆ Skills determine who wins a fight or many physical games.

High household skills lessen the need for hired help.

This section introduces you to the seven basic skills and details how they impact your Sims' everyday lives and entire lifetimes.

The Basic Skills

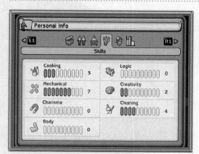

Your Sim's level in all skills can be viewed in the Skills panel of the Personal Info menu.

Seven basic skills appear in the Skills panel, under Personal Info. Basic skills affect many aspects of the game, including career and homemaking. The basic skills are:

◆ Cooking   ◆ Body   ◆ Creativity
◆ Mechanical ◆ Logic   ◆ Cleaning
◆ Charisma

Skill Building

Each basic skill is broken down into 10 increasingly difficult levels. Each level takes longer to master than the one before. For example, without any Personality-based acceleration, it should take a Sim one game hour to earn the first level of any skill. The 10th level of that skill should require 12 hours.

The Skill Meter

While your Sim is working on a skill, the Skill meter shows progress to date on the current level in development.

Progress in each skill level is displayed in the Skill meter that appears above the Sim's head while skill building. This meter fills, from bottom to top, as the Sim trains in the current skill level. When the

meter reaches the top, the number of the new skill level briefly appears, the Sim graduates to the next level, and he or she begins working on the following level. The meter resets to empty, and the process begins anew (more slowly with each more difficult level).

note

If you stop skill building in the middle of a level, the Sim's progress in that level is preserved for the next time he or she returns to build that skill.

Skills and Aspirations

Skills play a prominent role in the Aspirations game. Sims of all Aspirations want to gain skill levels, though some desire it more intensely and often than others. The higher the skill level, the more points the Aspiration bestows.

Eventually, some Sims want to get to the top of a skill or (in the case of Knowledge Sims) maximize *all* skills. The big payoffs for these Wants reflect how difficult a feat that is.

Intimately understanding the course of each Aspiration can guide you in how much to engage your Sims in skill building. For some Aspirations, it's central, and for others, it's a minor pursuit.

Skills and Careers

As detailed in the "Careers" section, Sims need skills for their careers. Each career requires development in three skills. With each level of the career, the skill requirements increase.

In the Career panel, the skill level required for the next promotion is shown as a green border around the target skill level.

tip

When choosing a career, consider how many of the career's required skills can be learned faster, thanks to your Sim's Personality. Having at least one skill match the Sim's Personality substantially aids career advancement.

Career Tracks, Featured Skills, and Helper Personalities

Career Track	Skill 1 (Personality)	Skill 2 (Personality)	Skill 3 (Personality)
Arts & Crafts	Creativity (Playful)	Mechanical (None)	Charisma (Outgoing)
Business	Logic (Serious)	Creativity (Playful)	Charisma (Outgoing)
Coaching	Body (Active)	Mechanical (None)	Charisma (Outgoing)
Construction	Body (Active)	Mechanical (None)	Creativity (Outgoing)
Education	Logic (Serious)	Creativity (Playful)	Cleaning (Neat)
Government	Logic (Serious)	Creativity (Playful)	Charisma (Outgoing)
Law Enforcement	Logic (Serious)	Body (Active)	Cleaning (Neat)
Medical	Logic (Serious)	Mechanical (None)	Cleaning (Neat)
Parks & Recreation	Body (Active)	Logic (Serious)	Cleaning (None)
Retail Clothing	Charisma (Outgoing)	Creativity (Playful)	Mechanical (None)

How Basic Skills Are Learned

Every basic skill can be learned in two ways: by interacting with objects and/or, for a few skills, by doing an activity that falls under a skill's domain ("practical skill building").

Object Interaction

Many objects impart skill building with certain interactions. Object skill building is the most common and effective method. The amount of skill building an interaction gives depends on the object. Normally, the more expensive a skill object is, the faster it provides skill.

Practical Skill Building

Cooks learn to cook by cooking. The Skill meter proves it.

Three skills offer skill building while performing the skill itself: Cooking, Mechanical, and Cleaning. Whenever Sims cook a meal, fix an object, or clean a mess, they're increasing their acumen in the skill. This increase is marked by the Skill meter over the Sim's head.

Practical skill training is equal in speed to object-based training, but the activities themselves don't last indefinitely. Sims can sit and study for as long as their Motives and Mood allow, but cleaning the toilet or cooking a meal lasts only a short time, after which skill building is over.

In two primary ways, however, practical skill building is preferable to object-based skill building:

- Efficiency: Sims have to either clean and repair things themselves or pay someone to do these things for them. Learning a skill by doing it means Sims get the job done and improve a skill at the same time, without having to spend money. On the flip side, they're spending something more valuable than money: time. This is, therefore, only an advantage if you intended the Sim to learn these skills anyway.

- Availability: Sims can't skill build with objects if Mood or certain Motives are too low. They can still get skill from cooking and cleaning (but not repairing) no matter what their Mood or Motives. On the other hand, there isn't always something to clean or someone to feed.

Another major difference between practical and object-based skill building arises when a Sloppy Sim gains practical Cleaning skill. The lower the Neat/Sloppy score, the more slowly the Sim learns Cleaning. This can be as low as one-third the rate that a Sim with a Neat/Sloppy of 10 would learn.

Speeding Skill Building

Many basic skills are learned (whether using an object or learning by doing) more easily by Sims of a certain Personality trait. The more extreme Sims are in the trait, the faster they learn the skill.

Put a Playful Sim in front of an easel, and the Creativity points just roll in.

The skill/Personality alliances are:

- Cooking: None
- Mechanical: None
- Charisma: Outgoing
- Body: Active
- Logic: Serious
- Creativity: Playful
- Cleaning: Neat

A Sim with an extreme Personality trait (such as 10 points in Active) trains at double the normal speed.

In each case, skill speed increases with every point toward the aligned skill. Therefore, a Sim with Outgoing/Shy of 0–5 would take a game hour to get the first level of Charisma skill, and one with Outgoing/Shy 10 would take only 30 game minutes. A Sim with 7 Outgoing/Shy would not gain full speed but would still do better than a neutral or Shy Sim: about 48 minutes.

There is one exception to this system—Sloppy Sims and practical Cleaning skill. In most cases, a Sim of the opposite Personality extreme trains at the same normal rate as a neutral Sim (5 points). However, in the case of practical Cleaning skill, the fewer points in Neat/Sloppy (0–4), the more slowly the Sim learns to clean. To gain the first level of Cleaning skill, for example, an extremely Sloppy Sim (Neat/Sloppy 0) would take about 90 minutes.

Skills, Mood, and Core Motives

Sims may build skills only when they're in a good Mood and their core Motives are reasonably satisfied.

Low Mood or low levels in the core Motives prevent Sims from skill building.

If Mood drops below 0, regardless of individual Motive levels, a Sim refuses to do object-based skill building and immediately ceases skill building if already engaged with a skill-building object.

Even if Mood is OK, five individual core Motives can, by themselves, forestall or end skill building:

- Energy
- Hunger
- Bladder
- Fun
- Comfort (if Sim isn't sitting to work on skill)

Other than these, no other Motive automatically bumps a Sim out of skill building. If the other Motives are low enough, however, they quickly reduce Mood to negative.

It's important to note that practical skill building in Cooking and Cleaning (but not Mechanical) is *not* affected by Motive level. A Sim gains skill building from practical avenues even if Mood is rock bottom and Motives are dwindling. It may not be the best choice of actions when Bladder is about to bottom out, but Sims do clean and learn the Cleaning skill if you tell them to.

 note
Skill levels, once acquired, can't be lost.

Skills in Detail

Cooking Skill

- Personality Acceleration: None
- Careers Used: None
- Objects: Bookshelves, Refrigerators/Counters/Cooking Appliances
- Practical: Cooking

Being skilled in Cooking is critical to making great meals.

Cooking influences how quickly Sims can cook, how nourishing (in terms of Hunger satisfaction) their efforts are, and the likelihood that that food has positive extra effects. Finally, Cooking skill determines the odds of Sims starting a cooking fire (the lower the skill, the greater the chance) and the chance that food they create is fatally poisonous.

tip

A Sim with no Cooking skill using any cooking appliance other than a microwave often starts a fire. Be sure to have a smoke alarm somewhere in the same room as the stove.

Mechanical

- Personality Acceleration: None
- Careers Used: Coaching, Law Enforcement, Construction, Parks & Recreation
- Objects: All Bookshelves (Study), Chess Tables (Play Paper Football)
- Practical: Repair Any Broken Object

Mechanical skill dramatically speeds the time required to repair broken objects. It also decreases the chance of electrocution when repairing electronic objects.

Mechanical skill can save your Sim oodles in repair costs.

note

When repairing an object, the Repair meter covers the Skill meter. The meter you see, therefore, is not reflecting progression to a new skill but rather the progress of the repair itself.

Mechanical can be learned using the Study interaction on any bookshelf, using objects that develop Mechanical skill, or by repairing any broken object. When the Sim is low in Mechanical skill, repairs take a very long time, and the Sim gives up frequently (requiring you to reactivate the interaction). On the upside, the Sim is learning Mechanical skill the entire time.

Charisma

- Personality Acceleration: Outgoing
- Careers Used: Government, Retail Clothing, Business, Arts & Crafts, Coaching
- Objects: All Mirrors (Practice Speech, Practice Kissing), Tombstones/Urns (Eulogize), Computers (Blog)
- Practical: N/A

Practicing kissing is one of the more flamboyant ways to build Charisma skill.

Charisma is primarily useful for careers that require it and is learned by practicing speeches or kissing in any mirror.

Working on a blog on the computer also develops Charisma.

Cerebral activities build Logic skill.

Body

- Personality Acceleration: Active
- Careers Used: Coaching, Law Enforcement, Construction, Parks & Recreation
- Objects: Exerto Self-Spot Exercise Machine
- Practical: N/A

Body is one of the most important skills because it impacts so many little things (too many to list). It's most prominently important as a career skill, but there's more.

Body skill affects which Sim wins in a fight, what tricks Sims can do on the surfing simulator, and who wins games.

Build body skill by using exercise equipment.

Logic

- Personality Acceleration: Serious
- Careers Used: Medical, Law Enforcement, Business, Education, Parks & Recreation, Government
- Objects: Computers (Design Video Game), Chess Sets (Play Chess), Astrowonder Telescope
- Practical: N/A

Logic is important primarily as a career skill.

tip

Time invested in building Logic skill eventually pays off. Designing video games can make your Sim a good living with top skill and a time commitment.

Logic is developed using several objects; sometimes it can be built up while tending to your Sim's Motives. Chess, for example, allows you to build Logic while taking care of Comfort (being seated while playing) and Social (if your Sim plays against another Sim).

Creativity

- Personality Acceleration: Playful
- Careers Used: Arts & Crafts, Business, Construction, Retail Clothing, Education, Government
- Objects: Pianos, Bookcases (Write in Journal), Independent Expressions, Inc. Easel, "Does it Rock!" Electric Guitar
- Practical: N/A

Creativity is important in several careers, but it has other applications as well, some of them financially beneficial. Painting on an easel teaches Creativity—and you can sell the paintings the Sim produces. The greater the Sim's Creativity, the higher the painting's sale price.

A Sim's performance of music is also affected by Creativity. Low Creativity Sims just bang away on the piano while high Creativity Sims play lovely music. Nearby Sims react to music's quality.

Cleaning

- Personality Acceleration: Neat
- Careers Used: Parks & Recreation, Education, Law Enforcement, Medical
- Objects: All Bookshelves (Study)
- Practical: Cleaning Any Object

Cleaning is a very important skill for Sims in careers that call for it and those who don't want to hire a Maid.

Sure, you can get Cleaning skill from a book, but multitasking is the way to glory.

The better Sims are at Cleaning, the faster they perform cleaning tasks. Faster cleaning means more free time for other things.

 note

High Cleaning skill doesn't make Sloppy Sims clean more often; it just makes them clean more quickly. If you want Sloppy Sims with high Cleaning skill to tidy up after themselves, you must direct them to the messes.

Careers

Learning to play the career game is absolutely essential if Sims are to have a reasonably efficient and successful life.

Without a regular and substantial income:

♦ Bills don't get paid.

♦ The refrigerator is empty.

♦ Environment score is hopelessly mediocre.

♦ Hired help is unaffordable.

As such, have a look at the mechanics of the working life.

Getting a Job

Sims find job listings in two sources: the newspaper and the computer. Each day at 7 am, the newspaper is delivered to the Sims' front walk. Select "Find Job" and you're presented with *three* job openings. The computer offers more variety, serving up *five* job openings a day.

More and better job listings are found on the computer than in the newspaper.

When a Sim with few skills or friends enters a new career track, he or she starts at level 1. Sims who leave or are fired from a track can get back into the career track at two levels below their previous job. For example, Sims fired at level 5 and still qualified for the job would reenter at level 3. If performance is good, they quickly regain their former position.

note

The job level boost for previously held careers only shows in computer job listings. All jobs in the newspaper are always level 1 positions, regardless of previous experience.

Career Structure

Every job has certain common attributes that tell you all you need to know about what is required of your Sim.

Skill Requirements

Every career features three skills that must be developed in order to climb the ladder. With every job level, the skill requirements may increase, requiring the Sim to meet all the skill thresholds before being eligible for promotion.

Friends Requirement

In the Career panel of the Personal Info menu, the number of friends needed for promotion is shown in the bar on the right.

Many jobs require, as a condition for promotion, that a Sim have a certain number of friends. What this means, though, isn't as clear as it seems.

note
The friend count on the Career panel shows the current number of the individual Sim's friends and, in the green brackets, the number needed for the next level.

For promotion purposes, a "friend" is any Sim with whom your individual Sim has a relationship of 40 points or higher. Friendships with housemates and pets also count for promotion purposes.

note
Job promotion only counts each individual Sim's friendships—not the friendships of housemates, roommates, or spouse ["family friends"].

note
Falling below the friend requirement for a Sim's current job doesn't result in demotion, but further promotion is impossible until the friend count is up to the next job's demands.

Hours

Jobs vary in their hours (both the start and quitting times and number of hours per shift).

note
Carpools arrive one hour before the job's start time and wait until the job's exact start time.

Sims return home 10 minutes after quitting time.

Unless your Sim is in a rockin' good Mood with all skills and friends needed for a promotion, spend the hour and a quarter the carpool waits getting more qualified.

Generally, higher-level jobs require fewer hours than lower-level jobs.

tip
Put a night table and an alarm clock next to your Sim's bed and set it [this only needs to be done once]. The clock automatically goes off one hour before the carpool arrives—two hours before the shift starts—awakening your Sim and, if needed, automatically taking the game out of triple speed.

To get to work on time, you may catch the carpool the instant it arrives (one hour before the shift begins) or use the hour it waits to feed Motives and work on skills. Don't cut it too close, however, or you'll miss work.

tip

If it looks like your Sim won't make the carpool, hold the pause button, switch to Classic Control mode, and use the indicator on the car to select Go to Work. The car won't pull away—even if it's after work start time—as long as Go to Work is the only item in your Sim's queue.

Daily Salary

With each higher job level, daily salary increases.

Motives Effects

Sims' Motives don't stand still while they're at work. When Sims return home, their Motive levels at their departure time are adjusted by fixed amounts.

note

If Sims' Energy or Bladder is near failure when they leave for work, it's possible that the at-work Motive adjustment will cause them to go into Motive failure upon their return. Send them to work too tired, and they'll come home and pass out on the sidewalk.

Every job decreases Energy, of course (none permit napping on the job, sadly). More physical jobs decrease Energy more. Not all Motives are, however, diminished at work. Some jobs increase Fun, and particularly cushy ones increase Comfort. All jobs, except the most solitary, increase Social.

Promotion

Come home with a promotion, and you get your Sim's new salary, work hours, and a nice fat promotion bonus.

Each day Sims go to work, there's a chance they'll be promoted to the next level. But whether a promotion's available and a Sim's odds of getting it depend on several factors.

Skills and Friends

To be eligible for promotion, a Sim must meet the next level's skill and friends requirements. If the Sim lacks these, there is no chance of promotion.

note

In the Career panel, needed skill levels are highlighted by green brackets on the indicator for the level.

Job Performance

The other variable in promotion is job performance. The higher it is, the greater the odds of promotion. High job performance isn't a guarantee of promotion, but it tilts the odds in the Sim's favor.

note

Going to work with all skill and friend qualifications and a Mood at least 75 percent positive guarantees a promotion.

Job performance is a product of Sims' Mood when they leave for work. The higher their Mood when they get in the car, the better their job performance for that day.

Promotion Bonus

On the happy day when a Sim rises to a new job level, he or she receives the daily salary for the old job, plus a promotion bonus of twice the daily salary of the new job level.

Getting Fired

Sims get fired from their job if they miss two consecutive days of work. To regain their prior position, they must use the computer (not the newspaper) to find a job listing in their previous career. This listing is two levels below the job they had when they were terminated.

tip

When going for the more difficult higher-level promotions, it pays to skip one day of work to develop skills and friends. If your Sim goes to work the day after a "mental health day" in a very good Mood, he or she will likely get the promotion.

Career Directory

Arts & Crafts

Level	Job Name	Friends	Cooking	Mechanical	Charisma	Body	Logic	Creativity	Cleaning	Daily Salary	Hours	Shift Length
1	Paste Wrangler	—	—	—	—	—	—	—	—	§145	2–6 pm	4
2	Brush Wrangler	—	—	—	—	—	—	1	—	§203	9 am–2 pm	5
3	Sign Painter	—	—	1	—	—	—	2	—	§269	9 am–3 pm	6
4	Mural Painter	—	—	2	1	—	—	2	—	§345	10 am–3 pm	5
5	Prom Director	2	—	2	2	—	—	2	—	§489	11 am–4 pm	5
6	Assistant Art Teacher	4	—	3	2	—	—	3	—	§697	6 pm–1 am	7
7	Art Teacher	5	—	3	3	—	—	4	—	§901	11 am–5 pm	6
8	Arts Council Member	7	—	4	3	—	—	5	—	§1,113	2–7 pm	5
9	Arts Council Chairperson	9	—	4	4	—	—	8	—	§1,521	10 am–3 pm	5
10	Art Gallery Owner	11	—	4	5	—	—	10	—	§1,924	11 am–3 pm	4

Coaching

Level	Job Name	Friends	Cooking	Mechanical	Charisma	Body	Logic	Creativity	Cleaning	Daily Salary	Hours	Shift Length
1	Waterboy/Girl	—	—	—	—	—	—	—	—	§154	3–9 pm	6
2	Towel Boy/Girl	—	—	—	—	1	—	—	—	§238	9 am–3 pm	6
3	Mascot Wrangler	—	—	—	—	2	—	—	—	§322	9 am–3 pm	6
4	Team Mascot	1	—	—	1	3	—	—	—	§420	9 am–3 pm	6
5	Little League Coach	2	—	—	2	6	—	—	—	§539	9 am–3 pm	6
6	Scout	3	—	1	3	8	—	—	—	§893	9 am–3 pm	6
7	Assistant Coach	4	—	2	4	10	—	—	—	§1,190	9 am–4 pm	7
8	Junior Varsity Coach	5	—	4	5	10	—	—	—	§1,500	9 am–2 pm	5
9	Varsity Coach	6	—	7	7	10	—	—	—	§1,750	9 am–3 pm	6
10	Athletic Director	8	—	7	10	10	—	—	—	§2,033	11 am–5 pm	6

Medical

Level	Job Name	Friends	Cooking	Mechanical	Charisma	Body	Logic	Creativity	Cleaning	Daily Salary	Hours	Shift Length
1	Emergency Medical Technician	—	—	—	—	—	—	—	—	§252	8 am–2 pm	6
2	Paramedic	—	—	—	—	—	—	—	1	§345	8 pm–2 am	6
3	Nurse	—	—	—	—	—	1	—	2	§416	7 am–2 pm	7
4	Intern	1	—	2	—	—	2	—	3	§524	9 am–6 pm	9
5	Resident	2	—	3	—	—	3	—	5	§642	6 pm–1 am	7
6	General Practitioner	3	—	4	—	—	4	—	6	§799	10 am–6 pm	8
7	Specialist	4	—	7	—	—	5	—	7	§975	10 am–4 pm	6
8	Surgeon	5	—	9	—	—	7	—	8	§1,380	10 am–4 pm	6
9	Medical Researcher	7	—	9	—	—	8	—	9	§1,756	11 am–6 pm	7
10	Chief of Staff	9	—	9	—	—	10	—	10	§2,299	9 am–4 pm	7

Law Enforcement

Level	Job Name	Friends	Cooking	Mechanical	Charisma	Body	Logic	Creativity	Cleaning	Daily Salary	Hours	Shift Length
1	Crossing Guard	—	—	—	—	—	—	—	—	§286	7 pm–2 am	7
2	Security Guard	—	—	—	—	1	—	—	—	§345	9 am–3 pm	6
3	Cadet	—	—	—	—	2	—	—	—	§395	3–11 pm	8
4	Dispatch Officer	1	—	—	—	2	1	—	—	§479	9 am–3 pm	6
5	Patrol Officer	2	—	—	—	3	3	—	—	§564	10 am–4 pm	6
6	Desk Sergeant	2	—	—	—	3	4	—	2	§670	9 am–3 pm	6
7	Detective	3	—	—	—	5	5	—	4	§816	9 am–3 pm	6
8	Lieutenant	4	—	—	—	6	6	—	6	§915	11 am–6 pm	7
9	Chief Detective	6	—	—	—	8	9	—	7	§1,210	8 am–4 pm	8
10	Police Chief	7	—	—	—	10	9	—	8	§1,640	10 am–4 pm	6

Business

Level	Job Name	Friends	Cooking	Mechanical	Charisma	Body	Logic	Creativity	Cleaning	Daily Salary	Hours	Shift Length
1	Mailroom Technician	—	—	—	—	—	—	—	—	§250	9 am–3 pm	6
2	Executive Assistant	—	—	—	—	—	—	—	—	§300	9 am–4 pm	7
3	Field Sales Rep	—	—	—	2	—	—	—	—	§374	9 am–4 pm	7
4	Junior Executive	1	—	—	2	—	—	1	—	§448	9 am–4 pm	7
5	Executive	3	—	—	4	—	2	1	—	§585	9 am–3 pm	6
6	Senior Manager	4	—	—	4	—	3	3	—	§748	8 am–5 pm	9
7	Vice President	5	—	—	5	—	4	3	—	§924	8 am–4 pm	8
8	President	6	—	—	5	—	6	4	—	§1,210	9 am–4 pm	7
9	CEO	7	—	—	6	—	7	6	—	§1,565	9 am–4 pm	7
10	Business Tycoon	8	—	—	9	—	9	7	—	§2,100	10 am–4 pm	6

Construction

Level	Job Name	Friends	Cooking	Mechanical	Charisma	Body	Logic	Creativity	Cleaning	Daily Salary	Hours	Shift Length
1	Ditch Technician	—	—	—	—	—	—	—	—	§168	9 am–3 pm	6
2	Cleanup Crew	—	—	1	—	—	—	—	—	§252	9 am–5 pm	8
3	Roofer	—	—	2	—	1	—	—	—	§350	8 am–4 pm	8
4	Mason	1	—	2	—	2	—	—	—	§448	9 am–4 pm	7
5	Electrician	3	—	3	—	3	—	1	—	§560	9 am–4 pm	7
6	Assistant Site Foreman	4	—	4	—	3	—	1	—	§728	3 pm–11 pm	6
7	Site Foreman	5	—	5	—	5	—	2	—	§924	9 am–3 pm	6
8	Contractor	6	—	7	—	6	—	2	—	§1,400	9 am–3 pm	6
9	Architect	7	—	8	—	7	—	3	—	§1,665	2–8 am	6
10	Developer	8	—	10	—	8	—	3	—	§2,100	5–11 pm	6

Retail Clothing

Level	Job Name	Friends	Cooking	Mechanical	Charisma	Body	Logic	Creativity	Cleaning	Daily Salary	Hours	Shift Length
1	Lint Manager	—	—	—	—	—	—	—	—	§180	7 am–12 pm	5
2	Mannequin Wrangler	—	—	—	—	—	—	—	—	§221	3–9 pm	6
3	Inventory Technician	—	—	—	—	—	—	2	—	§268	9 am–3 pm	6
4	Cashier	—	—	1	—	—	—	2	—	§344	10 am–3 pm	5
5	Alterations and Tailoring	2	—	2	—	—	—	3	—	§414	11 am–4 pm	5
6	Customer Service Clerk	4	—	3	1	—	—	5	—	§564	6 pm–1 am	7
7	Assistant Manager	5	—	3	2	—	—	6	—	§744	11 am–5 pm	6
8	Manager	7	—	3	3	—	—	7	—	§1,050	2–7 pm	5
9	Buyer	9	—	4	4	—	—	9	—	§1,356	10 am–3 pm	5
10	Owner	11	—	4	5	—	—	10	—	§1,800	10 pm–2 am	4

Education

Level	Job Name	Friends	Cooking	Mechanical	Charisma	Body	Logic	Creativity	Cleaning	Daily Salary	Hours	Shift Length
1	Private Tutor	—	—	—	—	—	—	—	—	§217	11 am–5 pm	6
2	Substitute Teacher	—	—	—	—	—	—	1	1	§322	4–10 pm	6
3	Intern	—	—	—	—	—	1	1	2	§448	9 am–3 pm	6
4	Test Administrator	1	—	—	—	—	1	2	4	§525	9 am–3 pm	6
5	Teacher's Aide	2	—	—	—	—	2	3	5	§630	10 am–5 pm	7
6	Teacher	3	—	—	—	—	4	4	5	§756	10 am–7 pm	9
7	Department Head	3	—	—	—	—	5	6	6	§896	8 am–1 pm	5
8	Assistant Principal	3	—	—	—	—	7	7	7	§1,016	8 am–1 pm	5
9	Principal	5	—	—	—	—	8	8	7	§1,562	10 am–2 pm	4
10	Superintendent	8	—	—	—	—	10	9	8	§2,200	10 pm–2 am	4

Parks & Recreation

Level	Job Name	Friends	Cooking	Mechanical	Charisma	Body	Logic	Creativity	Cleaning	Daily Salary	Hours	Shift Length
1	Garbage Collector	—	—	—	—	—	—	—	—	§215	7 am –1 pm	6
2	Groundskeeper	—	—	—	—	1	—	—	—	§285	9 am–3 pm	6
3	Facilities Manager	—	—	—	—	2	—	—	—	§392	3–11 pm	8
4	Volunteer Organizer	1	—	—	—	2	1	—	—	§556	9 am–3 pm	6
5	Community Sports Coordinator	2	—	—	—	3	2	—	—	§686	10 am–4 pm	6
6	Events Manager	2	—	—	—	3	4	—	2	§756	9 am–3 pm	6
7	Public Affairs Manager	3	—	—	—	4	5	—	4	§826	9 am–3 pm	6
8	Horticulturalist	4	—	—	—	6	6	—	6	§1,157	11 am–6 pm	7
9	Naturalist	6	—	—	—	8	8	—	7	§1,520	8 am–4 pm	8
10	Park Ranger	7	—	—	—	10	9	—	8	§2,000	10 am–4 pm	6

Government

Level	Job Name	Friends	Cooking	Mechanical	Charisma	Body	Logic	Creativity	Cleaning	Daily Salary	Hours	Shift Length
1	Campaign Worker	—	—	—	—	—	—	—	—	§245	9 am–6 pm	9
2	Intern	—	—	—	1	—	—	—	—	§310	9 am–4 pm	7
3	Volunteer Coordinator	—	—	—	2	—	—	—	—	§350	9 am–4 pm	7
4	Campaign Manager	2	—	—	4	—	—	—	—	§448	9 am–4 pm	7
5	City Council Member	4	—	—	5	—	2	—	—	§560	9 am–3 pm	6
6	Planning Commissioner	6	—	—	5	—	3	1	—	§728	8 am–5 pm	9
7	City Manager	7	—	—	5	—	4	2	—	§924	8 am–4 pm	8
8	Comptroller General	8	—	—	6	—	6	3	—	§1,400	9 am–4 pm	7
9	Judge	10	—	—	7	—	6	4	—	§1,665	9 am–4 pm	7
10	Mayor	12	—	—	10	—	7	5	—	§2,300	10 am–3 pm	5

Chapter 19

Social Interactions

Even the grumpiest Sim needs to interact with others to have a chance at happiness. Thus, social interactions have always been at the heart of Sim life. Now that Sims have pets to interact with, the horizons have opened even wider.

This chapter details how the social interaction system functions and how cats and dogs fit into the social fabric.

General Principles

note
Interactions are always between two Sims: the Sim who initiates the interaction and the Sim who is the target of it. For clarity, the initiator is referred to as "Sim A," and the target is referred to as "Sim B."

Relationship Score

Each Sim has some degree of relationship with every Sim he or she has met. Relationship scores are measured on a scale of 100 to -100. The higher the score, the stronger the relationship and the more powerfully positive or negative available interactions are.

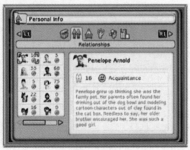

Relationship scores for every Sim your Sim knows are viewable in the Relationships panel of the Personal Info menu.

It's crucial to understand that the Relationship score between two Sims may not be the same for both Sims. It's possible, therefore, for Sim A to have a 35 Relationship score toward Sim B while Sim B has a 28 Relationship score toward Sim A. So don't rely on your Sim's relationship to another Sim to determine if the other Sim will accept an interaction.

Relationship Score Decay

Relationships decay toward zero with time (down if positive and up if negative). Every day that two Sims don't interact, the Relationship score shifts toward zero by 3 points. If the score drops below a relationship threshold (below 40 for a Friend, for example), the relationship shifts to the next level (from Friend to Acquaintance).

tip
Decay occurs every day at 4 pm and only if the Sim with whom your Sim has a relationship is not on the lot with your Sim. Therefore, if a Sim and a roommate or a Sim and a visitor are both on the lot at 4 pm (even if they're not interacting), their Relationship score doesn't decay for that day.

note
Losing a friend through neglect is particularly problematic since you need certain numbers of friends to get job promotions. If, just before going to work fully qualified for a promotion, your Sim loses a friend due to decay, your Sim won't get the promotion.

As a friendship nears the point of falling to a lower level, you receive an onscreen warning reminding you to touch base with the Sim involved. Heed it if you want to be ready when that next promotion is in sight.

tip
Because of relationship decay, you shouldn't stop socializing with a Sim when you reach Friend status. Finish the job by building the score to as close to 100 as possible.

Keeping in Touch

The way you keep relationships going is to interact with anyone your Sim knows on a regular basis. Whenever such Sims are around, direct your Sim to chat for a while and get the Relationship score as high as possible. As long as you stay ahead of the pace of decay, the relationship will grow.

Simply picking up the phone may be all you need to keep a relationship from drifting.

Finding time for friends is hard enough. Sometimes just finding them at all is a challenge. There are four ways to meet up with Sims to work on your relationship:

- Chats on the Phone or Computer: You don't have to be together to talk, thanks to the wonders of modern communication. A few Relationship points can be gleaned by calling a Sim on the phone or chatting on the computer for a few minutes. This doesn't make a friendship grow, but a daily call can easily overcome decay.

- Invitations to Come Over: The phone and computer are also your means to bringing your friends and acquaintances to you. They don't always accept an invitation to drop by, but they usually do if you invite them during civilized hours. Once they're at the house, your Sim can interact freely, building the relationship as much as possible.

- Drop By Visits: You hear the doorbell ringing all day; that's the sound of other Sims popping by to say hello. They wait for a while before giving up, so greet them at the first opportunity. Once in your home, they stay until you ask them to leave, or until a Motive or the hour forces them to, so make use of your time together.

- Town Square Encounters: The Town Square is always teeming with Sims and pets. Regular visits to the Town Square are great chances to build relationships with known Sims and forge new ones with strangers.

Social Motive

Even most failed social interactions feed the Social Motive.

The Social Motive is a Sim's need to be interacting with other Sims in any way. Interactions sway this Motive one way or the other.

tip

Higher relationships lead to better social interactions. Better social interactions give more Social Motive points.

Of course, Sims can fulfill their Social Motive by interacting with pets. In fact, their ability to fulfill a Sim's Social Motive is one of the best reasons to have pets.

Relationship Levels

Sims have some kind of relationship with every Sim they meet. What level of relationship it is, however, depends on Relationship score and (for romantic relationships) specific interactions.

tip

Make food with attraction effects and serve it to your Sim and, if possible, the other Sim. For a limited time, it becomes much easier to do romantic social interactions. This is valuable only when the Relationship score with the other Sim is high but you can't quite get the love relationship established.

There are four relationship levels:

Relationship Levels and Requirements

Relationship	Relationship Score Range	Icon
Best Friend	75–100	
Friend	40–74	
Acquaintance	-10–39	
Enemy	-30– -11	
Archenemy	-100– -31	

The kind of relationship two Sims have doesn't impact the kind of social interactions they can do; what matters there is the actual Relationship score.

Where one of these labels really matters is in career promotion; only your Sims' Friends and Best Friends—including relationships with other members of the household and pet friends—count toward job promotion requirements. Household Friends and even pet Friends count toward job promotions.

Icons in the Relationships panel highlight significant relationships.

The level of relationship is reflected in the Relationships panel of the Personal Info menu by the relationship icon next to the Sim's picture.

Availability

Whether interactions are available to you depends on *your Sim* and has nothing to do with the other Sim. Each interaction appears on your Social menu based on a combination of Mood and your relationship toward Sim B.

Availability, however, is no guarantee of acceptance. Normally, the qualifications for availability are likely to arise before the conditions for acceptance. So don't try an interaction as soon as it arises because it's unlikely to be accepted. Instead, precede newly available interactions with safe interactions to build Relationship score a bit more.

Acceptance

Interactions are accepted based on several possible attributes *of Sim B* and not on anything to do with your Sim. Sims accept or reject interactions based on several factors.

 note
The acceptance of some interactions depends on one attribute of Sim A: Hygiene. If Sim A is stinky, Sim B will probably reject a romantic advance.

How an interaction is received is out of your hands, but you can make educated guesses and take calculated risks.

 note
Most interactions carry a base probability of success to which Sim B's various factors are added or subtracted.

Acceptance can be based on:

- Sim B's Relationship score toward Sim A
- Sim B's Outgoing/Shy Personality
- Sim B's Neat/Sloppy Personality
- Sim B's Playful/Serious Personality
- Sim B's Active/Lazy Personality
- Sim B's Nice/Grouchy Personality
- Sim B's Mood
- Sim A's Hygiene

 tip
If it helps to think about these things in more aggressive terms, think of socializing as a battle to get to 100 over the Mood defense of the other Sim. The lower Mood is, the more resistant Sim B is to interactions. If possible, therefore, engage Sims when you suspect or can verify that their Mood is high. For playable Sims, you can simply switch to them and check their Mood. For NPC Sims, observe them for signs of Motive distress and approach them after they've satisfied a Motive and seem to be gravitating toward other interactions.

In the "Social Interaction Directory" table, the factors that go into acceptance feature a number in their column. The bigger the number, the more impact that factor has in whether the interaction is accepted.

Interaction Effects

Most interactions impact both Sims' Relationship score toward the other Sim, their Social Motive, and various memories.

The effect, however, depends on whether the interaction is accepted or rejected. In most cases, the result varies dramatically.

Positive interactions flash green plus signs to indicate an increase in Relationship points. Double plus signs mean a big change.

note

Only a few interactions (i.e. Nyah-Nyah) deplete the Social Motive. Pretty much any interaction, positive or negative, satisfies the Social Motive.

You can see some of these effects in action if you watch your Sim and his or her socializing partner carefully:

- Relationship: When an interaction finishes, icons indicate the level of change to the relationship. Single plus signs mean a small positive change, and double plus signs mean a large shift. Minus signs and double minus signs signify negative changes small and large.

- Social Motive: If the Motives' meters are visible during the interaction, arrows indicate the direction of the effect. Up is good, down is bad.

Boredom

If you do the same interaction five times in a row, the other Sim gets bored and automatically rejects it, even if he or she would otherwise accept. Sim B continues to reject it until you successfully attempt another interaction; you can then go back to the repeated interaction.

tip

If there's one interaction you know to be effective and powerful, do it four times, pick another interaction that's extremely likely to work, then do the preferred interaction four more times. Repeat.

Becoming a Couple or Moving In

Nearly any Sim can become a spouse or roommate if you develop the relationship correctly.

Weddings are lovely but quick affairs with little fanfare but cool outfits.

Either of these living arrangements converts the other Sim into a playable Sim on all lots. In fact, roomies and spouses differ in only two ways:

- Availability: Not surprisingly, the relationship and Mood requirements for the marriage interaction are quite a bit higher than for roommates.

- Kicking Out: Both kinds of living arrangements are undone by using the Kick Out interaction. What happens next, however, differs between the two.

Roomies just move out with no hard feelings. Kicked-out spouses, on the other hand, take rejection less gracefully. Relationship drops by -25 for both dumper and dumpee.

Acceptance

Whether your Sim can extend a roommate invitation or a marriage proposal depends on both Mood and relationship to the other Sim.

Roommates can be invited if your Sim's Relationship score to them is at least 60. Marriage is a bit more demanding. The Propose interaction is only available if your Sim's Relationship score to the other Sim is topped at 100.

 Married relationships are indicated by an interlocked ring icon in the Relationships panel.

Pet Socializing and Relationships

Pets have their own kinds of relationships, which have a strong effect on how they relate to Sims and other pets. The kinds of relationships available to a pet depend on its species.

Sims' Relationships to Pets

Once a Sim's relationship toward a pet, even nonhousehold pets, rises above 50, the Sim considers the pet a Friend. These friendships are just as valuable as Sim friendships because they too count toward a working Sim's promotion requirements.

Dogs

Dogs have two kinds of special relationships: Pack and Master.

Pack

 The Pack Relationship is roughly equivalent to Friend for Sims but is available to any Sim, dog, or cat.

Once a dog reaches a 50 Relationship score with a Sim or pet, it decides that the Sim, dog, or cat is part of its pack. Sims with the Pack Relationship with a dog get a larger increase in Fun when issuing commands or playing with the dog. When a dog looks to fulfill its Motives, it will favor any Pack Relationships over any others except its Master.

The Pack Relationship is destroyed if Relationship score of the dog toward the other pet/Sim drops below 0 or the dog becomes the other creature's Enemy.

Master

 Dogs need to know their place in the hierarchy of the household, so they'll eventually get to know a Sim so well that they'll declare him or her their "Master." Master is roughly equivalent to the "Best Friend" for Sims.

The first Sim to gain a Relationship score of 90 from the pet becomes the dog's one and only Master. A Sim can be Master to more than one dog, but each dog can have only one Master.

The primary benefit of the Master Relationship is an even greater increase in Fun satisfaction when a Master issues a command or plays with the dog. Additionally, many Sim-to-pet social interactions are more likely to be accepted when the Sim is the dog's Master. Dogs will seek out their Master first when trying to fulfill their Motives.

A Master Relationship is broken if:

◆ The dog moves out.

◆ The dog is sold.

◆ The Relationship score with the Master falls below -50.

◆ An Enemy Relationship arises between the Master and dog.

Cats

Instead of Friend and Best Friend, cats have one nonexclusive kind of signature relationship: Mine.

Mine

 Cats, feeling that they own others, rather than the other way around, wouldn't demean themselves by considering anyone their "Master."

Social Interaction Directory

Interaction	Who?	Base Probability	Minimum Relationship (A to B)	Maximum Relationship (A to B)	Minimum Mood (Sim B)	Maximum Mood (Sim B)	Minimum Hygiene (Sim B)	Maximum Hygiene (Sim A)	Mean/Nice Modifier	Shy/Outgoing Modifier
Admire	Sim-to-Sim	40	1	100	-100	100	0	0	10	10
Annoy	Sim-to-Sim	0	-33	0	-100	100	0	0	0	0
Apologize	Sim-to-Sim	100	-100	-1	-100	100	-150	100	0	0
Argue	Sim-to-Sim	0	-100	100	-100	100	0	0	0	0
Ask to Move In	Sim-to-Sim	100	60	100	-100	100	0	0	0	0
Ask to Move Out	Sim-to-Sim	100	-100	100	-100	100	0	0	0	0
Attack	Sim-to-Sim	0	-100	-50	-100	100	0	0	0	0
Backrub	Sim-to-Sim	20	33	100	-100	100	-50	50	5	2
Bark/Growl/Hiss	Pet-to-Pet	-100	100	-50	100	0	0	2	0	0
Bark/Growl/Hiss	Pet-to-Sim	50	-100	100	-50	0	0	0	2	0	0
Brag	Sim-to-Sim	50	-20	33	-100	100	0	0	5	0
Break Up	Sim-to-Sim	100	-100	-1	-100	100	0	0	0	0
Chase	Pet-to-Pet	50	-100	100	-50	100	0	0	2	2
Chase	Pet-to-Sim	20	-100	100	-50	100	0	0	0	6
Chat	Sim-to-Sim	100	-100	100	-100	100	0	0	0	1
Cheer up	Sim-to-Sim	40	1	100	-100	100	-150	50	10	5
Congratulate	Sim-to-Sim	100	-100	-1	-100	100	0	0	0	0
Console	Sim-to-Sim	100	-100	-1	-100	100	0	0	0	0
Dance Together	Sim-to-Sim	15	-50	100	-100	100	-150	100	0	0
Family Kiss	Sim-to-Sim	15	1	100	-100	100	-50	50	0	0
Fetch	Sim-to-Pet	20	-100	100	-100	100	0	0	0	0
Fight	Pet-to-Pet	—	—	—	—	—	—	—	—	—
Finger Wiggle	Sim-to-Pet	10	-100	100	-100	100	0	0	0	0
Finger Wiggle (Scratched)	Sim-to-Pet	10	-100	100	-100	100	0	0	0	0

Moreover, they don't have the collective mentality of dogs that could lead to a Pack Relationship (though dogs can consider cats to be part of their pack).

Instead, cats claim those they know well as their very own with the Mine Relationship. This special status is given to any household Sim or pet iwho develops a Relationship score of 50 with the cat.

Any Sim or pet that a cat considers Mine gets special treatment. The cat is more likely to accept social interactions from a Sim/pet it has a Mine Relationship with even when its Mood would normally cause it to reject. Cats are much more inclined to interact with those they consider Mine than with others, favoring the familiar to the less well known. They're even more likely to walk near "their" Sims and pets.

On the downside, cats will react jealously toward any Sim or pet that socializes with a Sim/pet it has a Mine Relationship with.

Finally, any creatures with a Mine Relationship get more Comfort from affectionate interactions.

A Mine Relationship is broken if:

- The cat moves out.
- The cat is sold.
- Relationship drops below -50.
- Enemy Relationship arises between the cat and the one it considers Mine.

All Pets

Pets can have Enemies too. If Relationship score to any Sim or pet drops below -50, the pet considers that creature to be its Enemy.

Lazy/Active Modifier	Sloppy/Neat Modifier	Serious/Playful Modifier	Master/Mine Modifier	Accept Sim/Pet A Relationship	Accept Pet/Sim A Social	Accept Pet/Sim B Relationship	Accept Pet/Sim B Social	Reject Pet/Sim A Relationship	Reject Pet/Sim A Social	Reject Pet/Sim B Relationship	Reject Pet/Sim B Social
0	10	0	0	4	6	3	6	-2	3	-4	3
0	0	0	0	—	—	—	—	-5	3	-3	3
0	0	0	0	8	6	8	6	-1	3	-2	3
0	0	0	0	—	—	—	—	-6	3	-4	3
0	0	0	0	10	5	10	5	—	—	—	—
0	0	0	0	-10	6	-15	6	—	—	—	—
0	0	0	0	—	—	—	—	-10	-3	-8	10
0	0	2	0	6	7	4	7	-2	3	-3	3
0	2	0	0	0	0	0	-3	-3	-3	5	
0	0	2	0	0	0	0	0	-3	-3	-3	5
0	0	0	0	3	6	2	6	-1	3	-2	2
0	0	0	0	-25	-20	-25	-20	—	—	—	—
0	0	2	0	1	2	-3	10	-2	2	-4	10
0	0	0	0	2	5	2	5	-1	3	-2	3
0	0	0	0	1	2	1	2	0	2	0	2
0	0	0	0	6	6	4	6	-2	2	-2	2
0	0	0	0	4	7	3	6	—	—	—	—
0	0	0	0	4	4	7	6	—	—	—	—
-3	0	0	0	5	5	5	6	-3	2	-3	2
0	0	0	0	3	6	3	6	-2	2	-2	2
0	0	0	10	5	10	5	10	-1	3	-2	3
—	—	—	—	1	5	-2	10	-2	2	-3	10
0	0	10	10	5	10	5	10	-1	3	-2	3
0	0	10	10	5	8	5	8	-1	3	-2	3

Social Interaction Directory continued

Interaction	Who?	Base Probability	Minimum Relationship (A to B)	Maximum Relationship (A to B)	Minimum Mood (Sim B)	Maximum Mood (Sim B)	Minimum Hygiene (Sim B)	Maximum Hygiene (Sim A)	Mean/Nice Modifier	Shy/Outgoing Modifier
First Kiss	Sim-to-Sim	0	60	100	-100	100	-150	100	0	0
Friendly Hug	Sim-to-Sim	25	20	100	-100	100	-150	100	0	5
Generic	Sim-to-Pet	20	-100	100	-100	100	0	0	0	0
Give	Pet-to-Sim	35	-50	100	-50	100	0	0	0	0
Give	Sim-to-Pet	20	-100	100	-100	100	0	0	0	0
Give	Sim-to-Sim	40	-100	100	-100	100	0	0	0	0
Gossip	Sim-to-Sim	80	20	66	-100	100	0	0	-10	0
Greet	Pet-to-Sim	100	30	100	-100	100	0	0	0	0
Greet	Sim-to-Pet	100	30	100	-100	100	0	0	0	0
Greet	Sim-to-Sim	100	-100	100	-100	100	0	0	0	0
Gross Out	Sim-to-Sim	50	-33	33	-100	100	0	0	0	0
Group Talk	Sim-to-Sim	100	-100	100	-100	100	0	0	0	0
Hug	Pet-to-Sim	20	-100	100	-100	100	0	0	0	0
Hug	Sim-to-Pet	20	-100	100	-100	100	0	0	0	0
Insult	Sim-to-Sim	30	-25	-1	-100	100	0	0	-20	0
Joke	Sim-to-Sim	100	1	100	-100	100	0	0	0	0
Nag	Sim-to-Sim	0	-33	0	-100	100	0	0	0	0
Nyah-Nyah	Sim-to-Sim	100	-33	0	-100	100	0	0	0	0
Peck	Sim-to-Sim	20	1	50	-100	100	-150	100	1	-1
Play	Pet-to-Pet	20	-100	100	-50	100	0	0	2	2
Play Razzle	Sim-to-Pet	30	-100	100	-100	100	0	0	10	0
Play Toy Dangle	Sim-to-Pet	20	-100	100	-100	100	0	0	0	0
Poke	Sim-to-Sim	0	-50	-20	-100	100	0	0	0	0
Propose	Sim-to-Sim	100	100	100	-100	100	0	0	0	0
Punch U	Sim-to-Sim	30	50	100	-100	100	0	0	0	10
Punch U (Sim A Grouchy)	Sim-to-Sim	30	50	100	-100	100	0	0	0	10
Red Hands	Sim-to-Sim	50	10	49	-100	100	0	0	0	-5
Revive	Sim-to-Pet	100	-100	100	-100	100	0	0	0	0
Revive	Sim-to-Sim	100	-100	100	-100	100	0	0	0	0
Romantic Hug	Sim-to-Sim	5	60	100	-100	100	-150	100	0	-4
Romantic Kiss	Sim-to-Sim	0	75	100	-100	100	-150	100	0	-5
Rub Belly	Sim-to-Pet	20	-100	100	-100	100	0	0	0	10
Serenade	Sim-to-Sim	10	50	100	-100	100	-150	100	0	-5
Shove	Sim-to-Sim	100	-100	-33	-100	100	0	0	0	0
Slap	Sim-to-Sim	100	-100	-33	-100	100	0	0	0	0
Sniff	Pet-to-Pet	25	-100	100	-50	100	0	0	2	2
Stroke	Sim-to-Pet	40	-100	100	-100	100	0	0	0	0
Tell Tall Tale	Sim-to-Sim	25	-75	50	-100	100	0	0	-5	3
Tender Kiss	Sim-to-Sim	0	65	100	-100	100	-150	100	0	0
Tickle	Sim-to-Sim	15	25	75	-100	100	-100	100	0	0
Try for Offspring	Pet-to-Pet	50	-100	100	-50	100	0	0	2	2
Try for Offspring	Sim-to-Pet	30	-100	100	-100	100	0	0	0	0
Tug of War	Sim-to-Pet	20	-100	100	-100	100	0	0	0	15

Lazy/Active Modifier	Sloppy/Neat Modifier	Serious/Playful Modifier	Master/Mine Modifier	Accept Sim/Pet A Relationship	Accept Pet/Sim A Social	Accept Pet/Sim B Relationship	Accept Pet/Sim B Social	Reject Pet/Sim A Relationship	Reject Pet/Sim A Social	Reject Pet/Sim B Relationship	Reject Pet/Sim B Social
0	0	0	0	10	10	10	10	-8	2	-10	2
0	0	0	0	5	6	5	6	-3	2	-4	2
0	0	0	10	2	5	2	5	-1	3	-2	3
0	0	0	0	2	5	2	10	-1	3	-2	3
0	0	0	20	5	10	5	10	-1	3	-2	3
-5	0	-5	0	5	6	5	6	-5	2	-5	2
0	0	0	0	3	6	3	6	-2	2	-4	2
0	0	0	0	5	5	5	10	-1	3	-2	3
0	0	0	0	2	5	2	5	-1	3	-2	3
0	0	0	0	3	6	3	6	-1	2	-2	2
0	-20	10	0	5	7	3	6	-4	2	-6	2
0	0	0	0	2	2	2	2	-1	2	-1	2
0	0	0	10	5	5	5	10	-1	3	-2	3
0	0	0	10	5	10	5	10	-1	3	-2	3
0	0	0	0	-2	6	-4	6	-6	2	-8	2
0	0	0	0	4	6	4	6	—	—	—	—
0	0	0	0	—	—	—	—	-5	2	-8	2
0	0	0	0	0	5	0	-1	-4	2	-5	2
0	0	0	0	4	6	4	6	-4	2	-5	2
1	0	5	0	4	8	4	8	-1	3	-2	3
0	0	0	5	5	10	5	10	-1	3	-2	3
0	0	0	10	5	10	5	10	-1	3	-2	3
0	0	0	0	2	6	1	6	—	—	—	—
0	0	0	0	0	0	0	0	—	—	—	—
4	0	5	0	2	6	2	6	-3	2	-3	2
4	0	5	0	-3	6	-8	6	-6	2	-8	2
-3	0	10	0	5	7	5	7	-2	2	-2	2
0	0	0	0	2	2	2	2	—	—	—	—
0	0	0	0	5	6	8	6	—	—	—	—
0	0	0	0	7	8	7	8	-4	2	-5	2
0	0	0	0	8	7	8	7	-4	2	-3	2
0	-10	10	0	5	10	5	10	-1	3	-2	3
0	0	5	0	3	6	5	6	-1	2	-2	2
0	0	0	0	-3	5	-3	4	—	—	—	—
0	0	0	0	-5	6	-8	6	-5	2	-12	2
0	0	0	0	2	5	2	5	-1	3	-2	3
0	10	0	0	5	10	5	10	-1	3	-2	3
0	0	10	0	5	8	5	9	-1	2	-1	2
0	0	0	0	6	6	6	6	-2	2	-3	3
0	0	10	0	4	6	4	6	-2	2	-3	2
0	0	2	0	5	15	5	15	-1	3	-2	3
0	0	0	0	5	10	5	10	-1	3	-2	3
0	0	0	5	5	20	5	20	-1	3	-2	3

Visitor Behavior

Hospitality means tending to your visitor's Motives. This is especially important since visitors always arrive with their Motives fairly low.

tip

Since visitors arrive with their Motives depressed, hold off on socializing until they've had a chance to have a bite to eat and a bit of Fun.

Keep good, nourishing food servings available to visitors by making group meals.

Well-cared-for visitors stay for a very long time (until 1 am), providing ample opportunity for socializing. Offer them no way to refuel their Motives, however, and they leave abruptly.

note

Since acceptance of most social interactions depends in large part on the recipient's Mood, you have another reason to make sure your visitor's Motives are being met.

Since only members of a household may use certain objects (cooking appliances, beds, etc.), it's up to you to provide objects and courtesies that allow your visitors to feed their Motives:

- Hunger: Serve a meal with multiple portions. It costs more, but this makes six plates of food, more than enough for a small gathering of hungry Sims.
- Energy: Equip your house with objects that supply Energy without sleep. The best bet is an espresso machine.
- Comfort: Provide lots of comfy places to sit.
- Hygiene: Your guests' Hygiene needs can be met with sinks for hand washing. Alternatively, your guests can follow your Sim into the hot tub if he or she gets in first to set the tone.
- Social: You provide this by letting your Sim interact freely with the guests. Guests can also satisfy their Social Motive by joining a group object interaction, such as the TV, air hockey table, or the hot tub.
- Bladder: Make sure the toilets are clean and easily accessible in roomy bathrooms. More than one bathroom can't hurt, and multiple doors make access easy.
- Fun: Furnish your Sim's house with Fun activities. Even better, make them group activities so he or she can socialize with guests while everyone fuels Fun. Note that visitors use many objects on their own initiative but must be invited by a household member to get into joinable activities.

- Room: Keep messes to a minimum and decorate your home with strong Room score–enhancing objects. Make sure you have plenty of art objects, and keep those trash cans plentiful and accessible.

tip

Visitors don't turn on the TV by themselves. Do it for them before they arrive so you don't need to break stride while greeting guests.

Parties

Parties are initiated via phone. Your Sim automatically invites five Sims with whom your Sim has a Relationship score of 90 or more. If your Sim knows fewer than five Sims at that level, the rest are chosen at random from all other Sims your Sim knows.

note

Pets can't be invited to parties.

Parties begin within moments of the phone invitation.

Within moments, the guests arrive, and the party begins. It ends six hours later, or earlier if two or more Sims depart prematurely. Sims only blow off your party if their Motives aren't being met. Lots must be equipped with toilets, available food (visitors can't use the fridge), a sink for hand washing (visitors can't take baths), and espresso (they can't sleep on beds or sofas) if you want your guests to stay the full six hours.

note

While a party is going on, guests' Motives decay more slowly than normal.

If the party goes beyond 2 am, the police come and fine your Sim §100. Once your Sim's been fined he or she won't be fined again on the same day, so why not keep the party going for its full duration?

tip

For fiscal reasons, therefore, it's always best to start parties no later than 8 pm.

The goal of a party is to have a large gathering of Sims in a place where your Sim can keep his or her Motives well tended. This is an optimal relationship-building environment, and a lot of socializing can be done in a very short period.

Chapter 20

OBJECTS

Sims, no matter how lofty their Aspirations, are still materialists at heart. They *love* stuff, but not just any stuff—stuff that satisfies their basic Motives and helps them learn new skills. Not that appearance isn't important—the cooler an object is, the better.

This section guides you through the objects that can make your Sim's world a humming, efficient utopia.

Objects, Motives, and Skills

Objects serve two primary functions: satisfying your Sims' Motives or improving their skills. When looking to spend your Simoleons, look carefully at which Motives could be filled more efficiently and which skills need work.

Every object's impact on a skill or Motive is listed in the catalogs later in this section.

Of course, objects have other functions. Some are just cool to have. And some serve a specific purpose beyond Motives or skills. A telephone, for example, serves no Motive or skill function, but it's absolutely essential to Sim life.

Object Quality and Price

Generally, the more expensive an item is, the more it satisfies its assigned Motives or skills.

The more-expensive skill objects pay off with faster skill development and maybe some Motive-feeding ability. Plus, they look really cool.

For Motive-satisfying objects, the object's power is indicated in the catalog—the higher the number, the faster or more completely the object satisfies the Motive. Often, however, an object's increased value is due to other factors like secondary Motive satisfactions (an expensive toilet, for example, feeds both Bladder and Comfort).

For skill-building objects, the price directly reflects the rate of skill acquisition (the cheapest item feeds at the slowest rate and the most expensive one at a higher rate) and the presence of secondary effects (such as multiple skill training, a Room score impact, etc.).

> ### note
> Occasionally, an object can drain a Motive. Coffee machines, for example, lower Bladder as they raise Energy.

The Basics

Every smoothly running Sim household needs certain basics for your Sims' eight essential Motives. Generally, you can start with the cheapest objects, but sometimes spending a little more money pays off in spades.

Reading while using the toilet is Sim multitasking at its finest.

- Hunger: Get a refrigerator. If you don't want to spend all your money on cheap but nutritionally empty snack foods, also look into a countertop and a stove or microwave. A little extra money gets you a food processor or a blender. The better the cooking objects in your Sims' homes, the more ingredients and preparations they can access and the more powerful the food they create.

- Comfort: Make sure you have chairs for dining tables (standing up while eating reduces Comfort) and a good couch for TV watching and the occasional power nap. A bed provides simultaneous Comfort and Energy, so consider both Motives when selecting one.

- Hygiene: Get a shower. To reduce time spent bathing, extend a little and buy a good one. Stay away from bathtubs early on. Though they offer Comfort, they tend to offer slower satisfaction than a comparably priced shower. Your Sim doesn't need a bathroom sink (instead, shower after every second or third toilet visit), but there must be one for guests to wash up and restore their Hygiene.

- Bladder: You must have a toilet unless you like wetting the floor. A more expensive toilet provides Comfort while you sit. Time on the toilet doesn't have to be wasted. Playing handheld games and reading magazines while on the can both satisfy Fun, and reading can lead to the discovery of recipes and game tips.

- Energy: The floor is no real alternative to even the most awful bed, so get one immediately. An expensive bed lets you refuel on dramatically fewer sleep hours than a cheap one, so this is a good place to splurge.
- Fun: Right off the bat, get a cheap TV to put in front of the couch. It's inexpensive, you can get Comfort at the same time, and it can be a social activity.
- Social: A telephone allows you to invite friends over and even maintain friendships over the landline. A phone is also your lifeline to services like the Maid and Repairman, as well as the Police and Fire Department.
- Room: The best thing you can do for Room score when money is tight is to let the sun (or the electric equivalent) shine in. Make sure your house has numerous windows and spend freely but wisely on interior lights. Decorations help Room, too, but they can be very expensive for a relatively small boost.

Depreciation

All objects depreciate immediately once placed on a lot. Every day thereafter, the object's resale value drops by a fixed amount per day ("daily depreciation") until it reaches a set floor ("depreciation limit") below which it can't go. No object is ever worth less than 40 percent of its original value.

 note
Depreciation isn't an entirely bad thing. It lowers your net worth, and that, in turn, lowers the amount of your bills.

Fire Code

The Fire Code governs how many objects can be placed on a lot.

The Fire Code Meter shows how close to capacity the lot is. When the meter reaches the top, you've violated the Fire Code.

When you place an object, the Fire Code Meter appears, representing how close the lot is to full capacity. When the red bar hits the top of the meter, the limit is reached. Additional objects can be placed, but with a stern warning and at a cost.

When a lot is over its object limit, placing another object generates, upon return to the game, an immediate fire somewhere on the lot.

To avoid this fiery penalty, don't place objects in violation of the Fire Code. If something needs to be placed, remove some objects or walls from the lot first, then place the new object.

 note
Placing multiple versions of the same object (for example, six of the same chair around a table) increases a lot's object count less than the same number of different objects (like six unmatched chairs). To avoid running afoul of the Fire Code in a large house, therefore, use many of the same objects whenever possible. It lets you put more stuff on the lot and provides a decorative continuity, too.

Flammability

Your beloved objects can be burned and destroyed if a fire breaks out, reducing them to useless (and Room score-depressing) ash if not extinguished in time.

Fire isn't totally preventable, but it helps to know what causes it.

- Objects: Objects with open flames (stoves, grills, fireplaces, etc.) carry a chance of igniting any adjacent object. Keep the area around these objects clear if possible.
- Exceeding the Fire Code: If you place objects in a lot that's already at its object capacity (Fire Code limit), there's a random chance of a fire until the total object count is reduced below the limit.

Fires are extinguished by summoning the Fire Department. This is done by phone or automatically if there's a smoke detector in the same room as the fire.

 tip
There should always be a smoke detector in any kitchen or room with a fireplace.

To extinguish flames yourself, use the Extinguish interaction on the fire.

Objects and Building on Lots

You may put your fingerprint on your Sims' own lots, but you can't make a profit off objects that preexist on the lot. Preexisting objects on the Town Square can be moved, rotated, or deleted, but never sold.

You also cannot place inventory objects from your Sim's home on the Town Square lot. This kind of behavior results in a fine from the Cop.

Selling Objects

When you need cash, you can of course sell off (via Buy mode) your items for their current depreciated value. Once an object is placed, you never get back the full purchase price.

Bills

Bills arrive every three days and represent three percent of the depreciated value of objects on the current lot. The more and nicer things you own, the higher your bills.

Watch your mailbox for bills and pay them promptly.

Bills are delivered to your mailbox and due 10 days from receipt. Take them from the mailbox and pay them as soon as possible. After 10 days, an unpaid bill becomes past due, and the Repo Man comes to take objects roughly equivalent to your debt. If there aren't enough objects to cover the bills, the Repo Man takes as many as possible and forgives the remaining liability.

tip
In Direct Control mode, you can take the bills from the mailbox and immediately pay them or set them down somewhere they can be more effectively ignored (if that's your thing).

Object Breakage

Objects eventually break after frequent use; every use brings the object steps closer to a breakdown. Broken objects display a Repair interaction and either work (but with detrimental side effects) or can't be used until fixed.

Getting your Sims' hands dirty repairing things themselves saves repair costs but takes time and (depending on the object) can delivery a painful shock.

Your Sims can do this themselves (though less than three Mechanical skill points means a good chance of electrocution and death), but this can be slow if they're not high in Mechanical skill. A better use of time might be to call the Repairman, who comes and fixes every broken object in your home in a single visit.

When Sims are self-repairing, the meter above their head indicates the progress of the repair, not the acquisition of Mechanical skill.

Theft

At night (midnight to be exact), if everyone in the house is asleep or at work, your Sim's home can be invaded by the Thief, who enters and selects the most-expensive accessible item and makes off with it.

To combat this, install a burglar alarm. Note that an alarm protects only single rooms, so full protection requires one in every room with an exterior entrance. The alarm automatically summons the Police, who may (or may not) catch the Thief.

note
Pets trained in the Guard command can serve as living burglar alarms, too. See the "Pet Life" and "Characters" chapters for more details.

If the Thief is apprehended, the cost of the object is refunded, but the object is not returned.

tip
Since outdoors counts as one big room, cheap protection can be had by building single wall segments at the sidewalk corners of your lot and putting alarms on each. Thus, the instant the Thief sets foot on your lot the alarm sounds, prompting the Thief to flee.

Object Directory

Object Directory

Object	Category	Price	Hunger	Comfort	Hygiene	Bladder	Energy	Fun	Social	Room	Chew/Scratch
!!!!Espresso.it.supremo!!!!	Appliances	§250	0	0	0	0	2	0	0	0	0
A.M.P. Wall Lamp	Indoor Lighting	§55	0	0	0	0	0	0	0	1	0
AE Arcade Unit	Electronics	§300	0	0	0	0	0	4	0	0	0
Animal Armoire	Miscellaneous	§750	0	0	0	0	0	0	0	0	0
Apex Park Bench	Seating	§650	0	5	0	0	0	0	0	0	0
Appalachian Torchiere	Indoor Lighting	§235	0	0	0	0	0	0	0	3	0
Astrowonder Telescope	Skill	§500	0	0	0	0	0	0	0	0	0
Atlantis Jr.	Miscellaneous	§500	3	0	0	0	0	0	0	3	0
Auditus Gladiolas	Indoor Plants	§180	0	0	0	0	0	0	0	2	0
Beetle Yak Rug	Indoor Decorations	§5,500	0	0	0	0	0	0	0	10	0
Bel-Air Blue Moon Edition	Seating	§310	0	6	0	0	0	0	0	0	0
Bel-Air Diner Seat	Seating	§115	0	3	0	0	0	0	0	0	0
Bel-Air Dining Table	Surfaces	§95	0	0	0	0	0	0	0	0	0
Belmont Double Bed	Beds	§3,000	0	8	0	0	10	0	0	1	0
Belmont Twin Bed	Beds	§1,200	0	6	0	0	8	0	0	1	0
BFF, Best Friends 4-ever	Indoor Decorations	§350	0	0	0	0	0	3	0	4	0
Birth of Venus Master Sink	Plumbing	§520	0	0	3	0	0	0	0	1	0
Blade Vision VERY High HD TV	Electronics	§3,500	0	0	0	0	0	5	0	2	0
Blast Off Rocket Bench	Skill	§2,000	0	0	0	0	0	0	0	0	0
Boronica by d'Lange	Indoor Decorations	§950	0	0	0	0	0	3	0	5	0
Bright Lights, Big Doggy	Indoor Decorations	§50	0	0	0	0	0	3	0	1	0
Callow Lily	Indoor Plants	§75	0	0	0	0	0	0	0	2	0
Cheapovision Television Set	Electronics	§500	0	0	0	0	0	3	0	2	0
Chez Moi French Country Counters	Surfaces	§590	6	0	0	0	0	0	0	1	0
Chimeway & Daughters Piano	Skill	§5,000	0	0	0	0	0	1	0	0	0
Chow Town Eco-Fridge	Appliances	§750	6	0	0	0	0	0	0	0	0
CiaoTime 360 Moderna Range	Appliances	§500	8	0	0	0	0	0	0	0	0
Claymore Ceramic Sink	Plumbing	§310	0	0	2	0	0	0	0	0	0
Comic Dehydrator	Miscellaneous	§550	0	0	0	0	0	3	0	2	0
Concreta Display Counter	Surfaces	§140	4	0	0	0	0	0	0	0	0
Curio Counters	Surfaces	§250	6	0	0	0	0	0	0	0	0
Curvaceous Colonial End Table	Surfaces	§410	0	0	0	0	0	0	0	1	0
CyberChronometer Alarm Clock	Electronics	§50	0	0	0	0	0	0	0	0	0
Destructo-Kat Scratching Post	Pet Supplies	§50	0	0	0	0	0	0	0	0	6
Dialectric Free Standing Range	Appliances	§350	4	0	0	0	0	0	0	0	0
Discourse Dining Table	Surfaces	§750	0	0	0	0	0	0	0	1	0
Does it Rock! Electric Guitar	Skill	§1,500	0	0	0	0	0	1	0	0	0
Doggy Dining	Surfaces	§475	0	0	0	0	0	0	0	0	0
Driver Pro 2006: "Chip Shots"	Miscellaneous	§975	0	0	0	0	0	6	0	0	0
EconoCool Refrigerator	Appliances	§500	4	0	0	0	0	0	0	0	0
El Sol Sofa by Günter	Seating	§390	0	3	0	0	0	0	0	0	0
Elementary Memories Dining Chair	Seating	§80	0	3	0	0	0	0	0	0	0
Entropix Blending Hutch	Appliances	§200	3	0	0	0	0	0	0	0	0

Object	Category	Price	Hunger	Comfort	Hygiene	Bladder	Energy	Fun	Social	Room	Chew/Scratch
Ergonom Biblio-Tech	Skill	§3,000	0	0	0	0	0	2	0	3	0
Estremita Chair	Seating	§215	0	3	0	0	0	0	0	0	0
Exerto Self-Spot Exercise Machine	Skill	§750	0	0	0	0	0	0	0	0	0
EZ Empire Light Sconce	Indoor Lighting	§210	0	0	0	0	0	0	0	2	0
EZ Green Camping Chair	Seating	§250	0	6	0	0	0	0	0	0	0
Fitzroy Dreamers' Rock Pool	Plumbing	§8,500	0	7	8	0	0	3	0	0	0
Floral Fantasy by Plastiqkue	Seating	§450	0	7	0	0	0	0	0	0	0
Frood Orchard	Miscellaneous	§650	4	0	0	0	0	0	0	4	0
Frood Tree	Miscellaneous	§150	0	0	0	0	0	0	0	2	0
Frood Tree 2.0	Miscellaneous	§400	2	0	0	0	0	0	0	2	0
Furniture Kamp Floor Lamp	Indoor Lighting	§255	0	0	0	0	0	0	0	3	0
Furniture Kamp Table Lamp	Indoor Lighting	§150	0	0	0	0	0	0	0	2	0
Garden Swing	Seating	§700	0	7	0	0	0	0	0	0	0
GenoLife Garden Hutch	Miscellaneous	§450	3	0	0	0	0	0	0	3	0
GenoLife Garden Hutch Grande	Miscellaneous	§550	2	0	0	0	0	0	0	2	0
GenoLife Garden Hutch Supreme	Miscellaneous	§700	4	0	0	0	0	0	0	5	0
Guppy Pond	Miscellaneous	§350	2	0	0	0	0	0	0	1	0
Hans und Hans Chair	Seating	§245	0	6	0	0	0	0	0	0	0
Hawaiian Fantasy Tiki Torch	Indoor Lighting	§110	0	0	0	0	0	0	0	1	0
Headhunter Battle Mask	Indoor Decorations	§360	0	0	0	0	0	3	0	4	0
Home Office Desk by Quaint Design	Surfaces	§250	0	0	0	0	0	0	0	1	0
Hounds Brothers Loveseat	Seating	§350	0	5	0	0	0	0	0	0	0
Hugs and Hisses	Indoor Decorations	§250	0	0	0	0	0	3	0	3	0
Hydronomic Kitchen Sink	Plumbing	§190	0	0	2	0	0	0	0	0	0
In Memory of Johnny Gnome	Indoor Decorations	§50	0	0	0	0	0	3	0	1	0
Independent Expressions, Inc. Easel	Skill	§750	0	0	0	0	0	1	0	0	0
Iterative Dishwasher	Appliances	§550	0	0	0	0	0	0	0	0	0
Jousterfield Loveseat	Seating	§950	0	7	0	0	0	0	0	1	0
Katty Kouch	Seating	§850	0	7	0	0	0	0	0	0	0
Krampft Industries Wonder Tubba	Plumbing	§950	0	5	5	0	0	0	0	0	0
Lazy-Day Eazy-Chair	Seating	§100	0	3	0	0	0	0	0	0	0
MacGrugor's Desk Lamp	Indoor Lighting	§140	0	0	0	0	0	0	0	2	0
MacGrugor's Wall Lamp	Indoor Lighting	§25	0	0	0	0	0	0	0	1	0
Mad Dog Growleth	Indoor Decorations	§400	0	0	0	0	0	3	0	4	0
Manila 1000 Marine Aquarium	Miscellaneous	§750	4	0	0	0	0	0	0	5	0
MaxArts 5pOr3 Gaming Kit	Electronics	§598	0	0	0	0	0	4	0	0	0
Mentionable Plastic Litter Box	Pet Supplies	§50	0	0	0	8	0	0	0	0	0
MeowTron X-11	Electronics	§400	0	0	0	0	0	5	0	0	0
Mission Coffee Table by Lulu Designs	Surfaces	§110	0	0	0	0	0	0	0	1	0
Missionaire Dining Table	Surfaces	§150	0	0	0	0	0	0	0	0	0
ModMan Office Chair	Seating	§200	0	3	0	0	0	0	0	0	0
Moneywell Computer	Electronics	§1,300	0	0	0	0	0	6	0	0	0
Moth Ball Incorporated Floor Lamp	Indoor Lighting	§480	0	0	0	0	0	0	0	3	0
Mr. Snugglepaws Double Bed	Beds	§850	0	6	0	0	8	0	0	0	0
Mr. Snugglepaws Twin Bed	Beds	§350	0	6	0	0	8	0	0	0	0
Nostalgix Gas Range	Appliances	§750	10	0	0	0	0	0	0	0	0
Nostalgix Refrigerator	Appliances	§1,200	8	0	0	0	0	0	0	0	0

Object	Category	Price	Hunger	Comfort	Hygiene	Bladder	Energy	Fun	Social	Room	Chew/Scratch
Office Chair	Seating	§80	0	3	0	0	0	0	0	0	0
Old Thyme Dining Table	Surfaces	§750	0	0	0	0	0	0	0	0	0
Old Thyme End Table	Surfaces	§440	0	0	0	0	0	0	0	1	0
Oriental "Master" Bathtub	Plumbing	§1,300	0	6	6	0	0	0	0	0	0
P.B. Jellies Loveseat	Seating	§250	0	3	0	0	0	0	0	0	0
P5 4400SX+ DS	Electronics	§3,900	0	0	0	0	0	8	0	0	0
Paw'ed Cushion Dining Chair	Seating	§265	0	6	0	0	0	0	0	0	0
Paw'ed Page Bookshelf	Skill	§1,200	0	0	0	0	0	2	0	3	0
Paw'ed Pillow Easy Chair	Seating	§410	0	6	0	0	0	0	0	0	0
Paw'ed Reading Lamp	Indoor Lighting	§165	0	0	0	0	0	0	0	2	0
Paw'ed Sconce	Indoor Lighting	§50	0	0	0	0	0	0	0	1	0
Pawttern Rug	Indoor Decorations	§2,300	0	0	0	0	0	0	0	5	0
People Invaders	Electronics	§450	0	0	0	0	0	6	0	0	0
Pet Project I—Patience	Indoor Decorations	§750	0	0	0	0	0	3	0	5	0
Pet Project II—Sorrow	Indoor Decorations	§1,100	0	0	0	0	0	3	0	6	0
Pet Project III—Cruelty	Indoor Decorations	§2,500	0	0	0	0	0	3	0	7	0
Petology Food Dish	Pet Supplies	§25	3	0	0	0	0	0	0	0	0
Plaank Bookcase	Skill	§3,000	0	0	0	0	0	2	0	3	0
Positive Potential Microwave	Appliances	§200	4	0	0	0	0	0	0	0	0
Post-Staunton "Strugatsky" Chess Set	Skill	§400	0	0	0	0	0	0	0	0	0
Procedural Music System	Electronics	§2,550	0	0	0	0	0	7	0	3	0
Puppy Palette	Indoor Decorations	§2,500	0	0	0	0	0	3	0	7	0
Radioproactive Heating Stove	Appliances	§1,100	10	0	0	0	0	0	0	0	0
Recycled Couch	Seating	§290	0	5	0	0	0	0	0	0	0
ResiStall Eco-Toilet	Plumbing	§750	0	0	0	10	0	0	0	0	0
Rhapsody in Paws	Indoor Decorations	§125	0	0	0	0	0	3	0	2	0
Rose Bush	Indoor Plants	§255	0	0	0	0	0	0	0	3	0
RPG "Paladin" Food Processor	Appliances	§200	4	0	0	0	0	0	0	0	0
Rubber Tree Plant	Indoor Plants	§115	0	0	0	0	0	0	0	2	0
Ruggo Boombox	Electronics	§99	0	0	0	0	0	2	0	0	0
See Me, Feel Me Pinball Machine	Electronics	§300	0	0	0	0	0	5	0	0	0
Sewage Brothers RestEze Toilet	Plumbing	§300	0	0	0	10	0	0	0	0	0
Shapes in Space	Indoor Decorations	§3,500	0	0	0	0	0	3	0	9	0
Shifty Sam the Garden Gnome	Indoor Decorations	§150	0	0	0	0	0	3	0	2	0
Shower of Power	Plumbing	§800	0	0	10	0	0	0	0	0	0
ShowHeuristic Hygiene System	Plumbing	§450	0	0	6	0	0	0	0	0	0
Simple Sink	Plumbing	§180	0	0	2	0	0	0	0	0	0
SimSafety V Burglar Alarm	Electronics	§150	0	0	0	0	0	0	0	0	0
Single High or Less Bed	Beds	§300	0	1	0	0	4	0	0	0	0
SirPlus! Metal Desk	Surfaces	§100	0	0	0	0	0	0	0	0	0
Sit Rover Sit!	Indoor Decorations	§100	0	0	0	0	0	3	0	2	0
SmokeSentry SmokeSniffer	Electronics	§100	0	0	0	0	0	0	0	0	0
Snuzi Double Bed	Beds	§1,800	0	8	0	0	10	0	0	0	0
Snuzi Twin Bed	Beds	§800	0	6	0	0	8	0	0	0	0
Spacious Spaces	Indoor Decorations	§200	0	0	0	0	0	3	0	3	0
Spielbunnst Lawn Seatery	Seating	§320	0	3	0	0	0	0	0	0	0

Object	Category	Price	Hunger	Comfort	Hygiene	Bladder	Energy	Fun	Social	Room	Chew/Scratch
Splash Fountain	Plumbing	§550	0	0	5	0	0	3	0	0	0
Stainless Steel Fridge	Appliances	§1,500	10	0	0	0	0	0	0	0	0
Stellar Loveseat	Seating	§750	0	7	0	0	0	0	0	0	0
Stray Away!	Pet Supplies	§50	0	0	0	0	0	0	0	0	0
Suds de Souffle Imperial Tub	Plumbing	§1,500	0	8	8	0	0	0	0	0	0
Super Settee by Sputnix Furnishings	Seating	§1,100	0	7	0	0	0	0	0	0	0
SynergyTrek Pro 9000	Skill	§600	0	0	0	0	0	0	0	0	0
Tasty Wonders Chow Bone	Pet Supplies	§20	0	0	0	0	0	0	0	0	2
Tenon Chair	Seating	§1,150	0	10	0	0	0	0	0	1	0
The Arcadian Bookshelf	Skill	§250	0	0	0	0	0	2	0	0	0
The Chesler Sofa	Seating	§510	0	5	0	0	0	0	0	0	0
The Christof Torchiere	Indoor Lighting	§280	0	0	0	0	0	0	0	3	0
The Earl of Ruester's Reading Lamp	Indoor Lighting	§315	0	0	0	0	0	0	0	3	0
The Grillinator "BigBQ"	Appliances	§500	5	0	0	0	0	0	0	0	0
The Honey Spooners	Indoor Decorations	§3,000	0	0	0	0	0	3	0	8	0
The Impossible Mission Counter	Surfaces	§180	4	0	0	0	0	0	0	0	0
The Kilmister Queen Bed.	Beds	§550	0	4	0	0	6	0	0	0	0
The Kilmister Twin Bed	Beds	§300	0	4	0	0	6	0	0	0	0
The Kitchen Sink	Plumbing	§500	0	0	3	0	0	0	0	0	0
The Lone Daisy	Indoor Decorations	§50	0	0	0	0	0	3	0	3	0
The Luxuriare	Seating	§1,350	0	7	0	0	0	0	0	1	0
The McMurdo Chair	Seating	§1,200	0	10	0	0	0	0	0	1	0
The Meowing	Indoor Decorations	§1,300	0	0	0	0	0	3	0	6	0
The Pet-estal	Surfaces	§220	0	0	0	0	0	0	0	1	0
The Piggle Puff	Pet Supplies	§150	0	0	0	0	0	6	0	0	0
The Plushocrat Lounge Chair	Seating	§690	0	10	0	0	0	0	0	1	0
The "Saved from the Curb" Couch	Seating	§200	0	5	0	0	0	0	0	0	0
The Scoot-a-Bout	Seating	§320	0	3	0	0	0	0	0	0	0
The "SculpToilette" Porcelain Lavatory	Plumbing	§950	0	0	0	10	0	0	0	2	0
The Slums Pet House	Pet Supplies	§100	0	0	0	0	0	0	0	0	0
The Stodgy Badger Family Portrait	Indoor Decorations	§75	0	0	0	0	0	3	0	2	0
The Super Nova	Indoor Lighting	§450	0	0	0	0	0	0	0	4	0
The "Tahdis" Wardrobe	Miscellaneous	§750	0	0	0	0	0	0	0	0	0
Thomas Plank Double Bed	Beds	§750	0	6	0	0	8	0	0	0	0
Thomas Plank Twin Bed	Beds	§450	0	4	0	0	6	0	0	0	0
Tiny Table	Surfaces	§350	0	0	0	0	0	0	0	0	0
Trampoline	Miscellaneous	§2,100	0	0	0	0	0	9	0	0	0
Trottco MultiVid Television	Electronics	§2,250	0	0	0	0	0	4	0	2	0
Up Dining Chair	Seating	§1,100	0	10	0	0	0	0	0	1	0
Wall Mirror	Skill	§100	0	0	0	0	0	0	0	0	0
Werkbunnst All Purpose Chair	Seating	§80	0	3	0	0	0	0	0	0	0
What a Steel Economy Trash Can	Miscellaneous	§30	0	0	0	0	0	0	0	0	0
Wireless Wall Phone	Electronics	§75	0	0	0	0	0	0	0	0	0
Wurl 'N' Hurl Retro Jukebox	Electronics	§580	0	0	0	0	0	5	0	3	0
X-Ray Wall Torch	Indoor Lighting	§120	0	0	0	0	0	0	0	1	0
Zaparoni Table Lamp	Indoor Lighting	§250	0	0	0	0	0	0	0	2	0

Object Catalog

Seating

Seating allows for replenishment of Comfort and/or Energy, provides a few Fun interactions, and opens up several Social interactions if two Sims share an object.

These objects come in several types:

◆ Moveable Chairs: These dining and desk chairs can be used for sitting at surfaces (tables, etc.).

◆ Stationary Chairs: These lounge chairs, etc., can't be used at tables but provide more comfort than dining chairs.

◆ Sofas: Group seating allows Sims to talk and perform romantic Social interactions. All sofas can be searched for loose change, food, or other surprises.

Elementary Memories Dining Chair
◆ Cost: §80
◆ Motive(s): Comfort 3

Werkbunnst All Purpose Chair
◆ Cost: §80
◆ Motive(s): Comfort 3

Office Chair
◆ Cost: §80
◆ Motive(s): Comfort 3

Lazy-Day Eazy-Chair
◆ Cost: §100
◆ Motive(s): Comfort 3

Bel-Air Diner Seat
◆ Cost: §115
◆ Motive(s): Comfort 3

The "Saved from the Curb" Couch
◆ Cost: §200
◆ Motive(s): Comfort 5

"ModMan" Office Chair
◆ Cost: §200
◆ Motive(s): Comfort 3

Estremita Chair
◆ Cost: §215
◆ Motive(s): Comfort 3

Hans und Hans Chair
◆ Cost: §245
◆ Motive(s): Comfort 6

EZ Green Camping Chair
◆ Cost: §250
◆ Motive(s): Comfort 6

P.B. Jellies Loveseat
◆ Cost: §250
◆ Motive(s): Comfort 3

Paw'ed Cushion Dining Chair
◆ Cost: §265
◆ Motive(s): Comfort 6

Recycled Couch
◆ Cost: §290
◆ Motive(s): Comfort 5

Bel-Air Blue Moon Edition
◆ Cost: §310
◆ Motive(s): Comfort 6

Spielbunnst Lawn Seatery
◆ Cost: §320
◆ Motive(s): Comfort 3

The Scoot-a-Bout
◆ Cost: §320
◆ Motive(s): Comfort 3

Hounds Brothers Loveseat
◆ Cost: §350
◆ Motive(s): Comfort 5

El Sol Sofa by Günter
◆ Cost: §390
◆ Motive(s): Comfort 3

Paw'ed Pillow Easy Chair
◆ Cost: §410
◆ Motive(s): Comfort 6

"Floral Fantasy" by Plastiqkue
◆ Cost: §450
◆ Motive(s): Comfort 7

"The Chesler" Sofa
- Cost: §510
- Motive(s): Comfort 5

Apex Park Bench
- Cost: §650
- Motive(s): Comfort 5

"The Plushocrat" Lounge Chair
- Cost: §690
- Motive(s): Comfort 10, Room 1

Garden Swing
- Cost: §700
- Motive(s): Comfort 7

Steller Loveseat
- Cost: §750
- Motive(s): Comfort 7

Katty Kouch
- Cost: §850
- Motive(s): Comfort 7

Jousterfield Loveseat
- Cost: §950
- Motive(s): Comfort 7, Room 1

Super Settee by Sputnix Furnishings
- Cost: §1,100
- Motive(s): Comfort 7

"Up" Dining Chair
- Cost: §1,100
- Motive(s): Comfort 10, Room 1

Tenon Chair
- Cost: §1,150
- Motive(s): Comfort 10, Room 1

The McMurdo Chair
- Cost: §1,200
- Motive(s): Comfort 10, Room 1

Luxuriare
- Cost: §1,350
- Motive(s): Comfort 10, Room 1

Beds

Beds allow for replenishment of Comfort (while relaxing) or Energy and Comfort (while sleeping).

The Kilmister Twin Bed
- Cost: §300
- Motive(s): Energy 6, Comfort 4

Single High or Less Bed
- Cost: §300
- Motive(s): Energy 4, Comfort 1

Mr. Snugglepaws Twin Bed
- Cost: §350
- Motive(s): Energy 8, Comfort 6

Thomas Plank Twin Bed
- Cost: §450
- Motive(s): Energy 6, Comfort 4

The Kilmister Queen Bed
- Cost: §550
- Motive(s): Energy 6, Comfort 4

Thomas Plank Double Bed
- Cost: §750
- Motive(s): Energy 8, Comfort 6

Snuzi Twin Bed
- Cost: §800
- Motive(s): Energy 8, Comfort 6

Mr. Snugglepaws Double Bed
- Cost: §850
- Motive(s): Energy 8, Comfort 6

Belmont Twin Bed
- Cost: §1,200
- Motive(s): Energy 8, Comfort 6, Room 1

Snuzi Double Bed
- Cost: §1,800
- Motive(s): Energy 10, Comfort 8

Belmont Double Bed
- Cost: §3,000
- Motive(s): Energy 10, Comfort 8, Room 1

Pet Supplies

The household Buy Catalog contains a smattering of basic but essential pet objects. More powerful pet objects can be found in the Town Square stores (see the "Town Square Catalogs" section.)

Tasty Wonders Chew Bone
- Cost: §20
- Motive(s): Chew 2

Petology Food Dish
- Cost: §25
- Motive(s): Hunger 3

Mentionable Plastic Litter Box
- Cost: §50
- Motive(s): Bladder 8

 Destructo-Kat Scratching Post
- Cost: §50
- Motive(s): Scratch 6

 Stray Away!
- Cost: §50
- Motive(s): N/A

This sign eliminates all strays from visiting lots on which it's posted.

 The Slums Pet House
- Cost: §100

 The Piggle Puff
- Cost: §150
- Motive(s): Fun 6

Lighting

Lighting makes spaces easier to see and can enhance Room score.

 MacGrugor's Wall Lamp
- Cost: §25
- Motive(s): Room 1

 Paw'ed Sconce
- Cost: §50
- Motive(s): Room 1

 A.M.P. Wall Lamp
- Cost: §55
- Motive(s): Room 1

 Hawaiian Fantasy Tiki Torch
- Cost: §110
- Motive(s): Room 1

 X-Ray Wall Torch
- Cost: §120
- Motive(s): Room 1

 MacGrugor's Desk Lamp
- Cost: §140
- Motive(s): Room 2

 Furniture Kamp Table Lamp
- Cost: §150
- Motive(s): Room 2

 Paw'ed Reading Lamp
- Cost: §165
- Motive(s): Room 2

 EZ Empire Light Sconce
- Cost: §210
- Motive(s): Room 2

 Appalachian Torchiere
- Cost: §235
- Motive(s): Room 3

 Zaparoni Table Lamp
- Cost: §250
- Motive(s): Room 2

 Furniture Kamp Floor Lamp
- Cost: §255
- Motive(s): Room 3

 The Christof Torchiere
- Cost: §280
- Motive(s): Room 3

 The Earl of Ruester's Reading Lamp
- Cost: §315
- Motive(s): Room 3

 The Super Nova
- Cost: §450
- Motive(s): Room 4

 Moth Ball Incorporated Floor Lamp
- Cost: §480
- Motive(s): Room 3

Appliances

Appliances generally go in a kitchen. When it comes to food prep objects, the higher the object's Hunger score the more Hunger satisfaction it contributes to the final food product. In the case of refrigerators, the score also represents the breadth of the ingredient selection within.

For more information on how each food-related appliance affects food preparation, see the "Food Creation" chapter.

 "Positive Potential" Microwave
- Cost: §200
- Motive(s): Hunger 4
- Skill(s): Cooking

 Entropix Blending Hutch
- Cost: §200
- Motive(s): Hunger 3
- Skill(s): Cooking

RPG "Paladin" Food Processor

- Cost: §200
- Motive(s): Hunger 4
- Skill(s): Cooking

Any prepped, cooked, or served dish of food can be put into the food processor to produce homemade pet food. The Hunger satisfaction of the food depends on the quality of the original ingredients.

!!!!Espresso.it. supremo!!!!

- Cost: §450
- Motive(s): Energy 2, Bladder -1

> **note**
> Drinking espresso replenishes Energy but at the cost of your Sim's Bladder.
>
> If the machine breaks, it can still make espresso, but the drink will cause nausea.

Dialectric Free Standing Range

- Cost: §350
- Motive(s): Hunger 4
- Skill(s): Cooking

CiaoTime 360 Moderna Range

- Cost: §500
- Motive(s): Hunger 8
- Skill(s): Cooking

The Grillinator "BigBQ"

- Cost: §500
- Motive(s): Hunger 5
- Skill(s): Cooking

Grills are part of the food creation system but can be used independently of it, too. For their role in the food system, see the "Food Creation" chapter. When used independently (Barbeque), grills cost money (§25), spontaneously producing ingredients that are cooked immediately.

Cleaning a grill is very important. Using a clean grill adds a bonus to the resulting food's Hunger satisfaction, while a dirty grill contributes to a food's nausea effect. Grills also have an elevated fire risk when cooking with low Cooking skill.

Outgoing and Active Sims autonomously prefer to use the grill over an indoor stove.

EconoCool Refrigerator

- Cost: §500
- Motive(s): Hunger 4

Iterative Dishwasher

- Cost: §550
- Skill(s): Cleaning

> **note**
> The dishwasher can serve as a countertop for food preparation.

Nostalgix Gas Range

- Cost: §750
- Motive(s): Hunger 10
- Skill(s): Cooking

Chow Town Eco-Fridge

- Cost: §750
- Motive(s): Hunger 6

Radioproactive Heating Stove

- Cost: §1,100
- Motive(s): Hunger 10
- Skill(s): Cooking

Nostalgix Refrigerator

- Cost: §1,200
- Motive(s): Hunger 8

Stainless Steel Fridge

- Cost: §1,500
- Motive(s): Hunger 10

Electronics

Electronic items are a major source of Fun.

CyberChronometer Alarm Clock

- Cost: §50

Once set, the alarm clock goes off every day one hour before your carpool arrives. Alarm clocks can be especially important when all playable Sims are asleep or at work because it's difficult to catch the carpool when the game's running at triple speed. The alarm clock instantly changes game speed back to normal as it awakens your Sim.

> **note**
> Prof. Feather's Chicken Checkers functions as an alarm clock, too. See the "Town Square Catalogs" section.

Wireless Wall Phone

- Cost: §75

Call for services, chat with friends, or invite other Sims over for a visit. A telephone is required to receive random, social, and work-related calls.

Additionally, the phone can be used to initiate parties and make prank calls. There are three possible prank calls, the success of which

depends on a different Personality trait or, in one case, a Motive:

◆ Fake Sweepstakes: Charisma

◆ Fake Names: Creativity

◆ Fart on Phone: Bladder (success of call is guaranteed if Bladder is less than 50 percent)

Succeeding in a prank call increases Fun while failure causes depletion of Fun.

Ruggo Boombox

◆ Cost: §99

◆ Motive(s): Fun 2

When activated, this item plays a random station or the last station played. Stations include:

◆ Alternative
◆ Ambient Dub
◆ Bluegrass
◆ Industrial
◆ Lounge Music
◆ Nu Metal
◆ Pop
◆ Punk Pop
◆ Trance Dance

Sims can dance to the music but do so uninterestedly if the music isn't to their liking. They at least moderately enjoy the music if they're Playful and Active and their Energy and Mood are relatively high. If not, enjoyment of music is purely random.

SmokeSentry SmokeSniffer

◆ Cost: §100

This sounds when a fire breaks out in the same room as the detector, automatically summoning the Fire Department. Since most fires begin in the kitchen, that should be the first place you put one.

SimSafety V Burglar Alarm

◆ Cost: §150

The alarm sounds if a Thief enters a room containing one, so place one in each room with an exterior doorway. Alarms wake all sleeping Sims and automatically summon Police.

AE Arcade Unit

◆ Cost: §675

◆ Motive(s): Fun 4

"See Me, Feel Me" Pinball Machine

◆ Cost: §300

◆ Motive(s): Fun 5

MeowTron X-11

◆ Cost: §400

◆ Motive(s): Fun 5

People Invaders

◆ Cost: §450

◆ Motive(s): Fun 6

Cheapovision Television Set

◆ Cost: §500

◆ Motive(s): Fun 3, Room 2

Sims watch TV for Fun and randomly select from the available channels:

◆ Food: Enjoyed by all

◆ Horror: Outgoing Sims enjoy while Shy Sims dislike

◆ Music: Enjoyed by all

◆ News: Serious Sims enjoy while Playful Sims dislike

Fixing a broken TV with low Mechanical skill (below 5) can be injurious.

Wurl 'N' Hurl Retro Jukebox

◆ Cost: §580

◆ Motive(s): Fun 5, Room 3

> **note**
> The jukebox works like the Ruggo Boombox; see that section.

MaxArts 5p0r3 Gaming Kit

◆ Cost: §598

◆ Motive(s): Fun 4

> **note**
> This holographic game system doesn't require a television. It can be played alone or you can invite another Sim with the Call Over interaction.

Moneywell Computer

◆ Cost: §1,300

◆ Motive(s): Fun 6

◆ Skill(s): Logic

Computers can be used for several things:

◆ Find a Job: It contains more daily listings than the newspaper.

◆ Chat: Talk to other Sims for Social Motive or invite them over just as on the telephone.

◆ Design Video Games: This increases Logic. When the game is complete, your Sim may sell it for money; price depends on your Sim's Logic skill.

◆ Play Video Game: This satisfies Fun.

◆ Blog: This increases Charisma. The more often a Sim blogs, the more popular the blog becomes, and the more Fun the Sim gains for blogging. Neglecting a blog decreases popularity, reducing Fun until it can be rebuilt.

Trottco MultiVid Television

◆ Cost: §2,250

◆ Motive(s): Fun 4, Room 2

note
This item works like the Cheapovision Television Set; see that section.

"Procedural" Music System

◆ Cost: §2,550

◆ Motive(s): Fun 7, Room 3

note
The jukebox works like the Rugged Boombox; see that section.

Blade Vision VERY High HD TV

◆ Cost: §3,500

◆ Motive(s): Fun 5, Room 2

note
This item works like the Cheapovision Television Set; see that section.

P5 4400SX+ DS

◆ Cost: §3,900

◆ Motive(s): Fun 8

◆ Skill(s): Logic

note
This works like the Moneywell Computer; see that section.

Skills

Skill objects can affect Sims' Motives but are primarily intended to build their various skills. Generally, the more expensive an object, the faster it develops skill, especially at higher levels.

Wall Mirror

◆ Cost: §100

◆ Skill(s): Charisma

note
Practice speaking or kissing to build Charisma.

The Arcadian Bookshelf

◆ Cost: §250

◆ Motive(s): Fun 2 (Read Book)

◆ Skill(s): Cooking (Study), Mechanical (Study), Cleaning (Study), Creativity (Write in Journal)

Bookcases are repositories of many important Sim skills but have several other uses as well. From books, your Sims can study to gain skill in Cooking, Cleaning, and Mechanical. Make sure a very comfy chair is the closest chair to the bookshelf. These cram sessions can last a while, and it helps to refresh Comfort simultaneously.

note
Reading books can lead to the discovery of new recipes.

Sims can also build their Creativity skill by writing in their journals.

Finally, a Sim can read a good book just for Fun.

Bookshelves work differently in Direct vs. Classic Control modes. In Classic Control mode, you make your selection at the bookshelf itself. In Direct Control mode, your Sim grabs a book from the shelf, then you select what to do with that book.

What your Sim does with a book when finished also depends on the control mode. In Direct Control, you can direct your Sim to put a finished book down or return it to the shelf. In Classic Control, Sims' Neat/Sloppy Personality trait dictates where they dispose of their used books.

note
Leaving books on the floor reduces Room score, driving down the Mood of any Sims in the room.

Post-Staunton "Strugatsky" Chess Set

◆ Cost: §400

◆ Skill(s): Logic (Play Chess), Mechanical (Play Paper Football)

Playing Chess or Paper Football results in both skill gain and Social interaction between the players (feeding Social Motive and building relationships).

Chess builds Logic skill while Paper Football develops Mechanical skill. Playing Chess solo still builds Logic but doesn't feed Social or Fun. Single-player Paper Football, however, *does not* develop Mechanical skill and results in less Fun than a real game because, really, it's kind of sad.

Astrowonder Telescope

◆ Cost: §500

◆ Skill(s): Logic

The telescope can be used at night (Stargaze) to view heavenly bodies and during the day (spy) to peek at more earthbound bodies. Both uses build Logic.

While stargazing, high Logic Sims have a small chance of discovering a new comet and receiving a large cash prize. For Sims of any Logic, stargazing carries a small chance of alien abduction (fear not, your visit to the saucer only lasts about four hours).

SynergyTrek Pro 9000

♦ Cost: §600
♦ Skill(s): Body

This Body skill-building device is extremely efficient and can be used by pets.

Sims may run on the treadmill to build Body skill but slowly deplete both Hygiene and Energy. If the machine is visibly dirty from use, the Hygiene loss is doubled.

Sims' current Body skill dictates how well they run. The lower the skill, the clumsier they are.

Independent Expressions, Inc. Easel

♦ Cost: §750
♦ Motive(s): Fun 1
♦ Skill(s): Creativity

Painting is an excellent way to build Creativity skill and, if your Sim has substantially developed that skill, to make a bit of extra cash.

Your Sim's Creativity skill determines both how quickly the painting is completed (the higher the skill, the faster the job) and for how much it sells.

Once a painting is complete, you must either sell or dispose of it before a new painting can be started. The sale price is directly related to your Sim's Creativity when he or she began the painting and how high it developed by the end.

Exerto Self-Spot Exercise Machine

♦ Cost: §750
♦ Skill(s): Body

Sims pump iron to build Body skill. At the outset, select what level of weight to attempt, keeping in mind your Sim's current Body skill—lifting above the Sim's abilities heightens the chance of failure. On the upside, the medium and heavy weight levels develop skill at a faster rate (120 percent for medium and 150 percent for heavy).

tip
Generally, Sims with 0–3 Body should lift only light weight. Sims with 4–7 Body should limit themselves to light or medium weight. Strong Sims (Body 8–10) can safely lift at all levels with only a slight chance of failure for heavy weight.

Failure occurs when the Sim fumbles the weights and results in a drop in Energy.

Paw'ed Page Bookshelf

♦ Cost: §1,200
♦ Motive(s): Fun 2 (Read), Room 3
♦ Skill(s): Cooking (Study), Mechanical (Study), Cleaning (Study), Creativity (Write in Journal)

note
This works like The Arcadian Bookshelf; see that section.

"Does it Rock!" Electric Guitar

♦ Cost: §1,500
♦ Motive(s): Fun 1
♦ Skill(s): Creativity

This instrument builds Creativity, and the quality of the music your Sim makes is dictated by the current level of that skill. While playing, use the Shoot Flame sub-interaction to put on a bit of pyrotechnics. There's only a small chance of setting something nearby ablaze.

Sims listening to a guitar player also react according to the player's Creativity skill.

Blast Off Rocket Bench

♦ Cost: §2,000
♦ Skill(s): Mechanical

This workbench is used to build model rockets, develop Mechanical skill, and make a bit of extra cash.

The higher your Sim's Mechanical skill, the faster the rocket gets built, the fancier it looks, and the more money your Sim earns per rocket.

If a rocket is launched indoors, it starts an immediate fire on the nearest flammable object. Just keep it outside, OK?

Ergonom Biblio-Tech

♦ Cost: §1,200
♦ Motive(s): Fun 2 (Read), Room 3
♦ Skill(s): Cooking (Study), Mechanical (Study), Cleaning (Study), Creativity (Write in Journal)

note
This works like The Arcadian Bookshelf; see that section.

Plaank Bookcase

- Cost: §3,000
- Motive(s): Fun 2 (Read), Room 3
- Skill(s): Cooking (Study), Mechanical (Study), Cleaning (Study), Creativity (Write in Journal)

note
This works like The Arcadian Bookshelf; see that section.

Chimeway & Daughters Piano

- Cost: §5,000
- Motive(s): Fun 1
- Skill(s): Creativity

Sims can play either traditional classical music or more discordant experimental music to build Creativity skill.

Regardless of the kind of music chosen, the quality of the Sims' music is dictated by their existing Creativity skill. Other Sims can listen and react according to the player's skill.

Indoor Plants

Callow Lily

- Cost: §75
- Motive(s): Room 2

Rubber Tree Plant

- Cost: §115
- Motive(s): Room 2

Auditus Gladiolas

- Cost: §180
- Motive(s): Room 2

Rose Bush

- Cost: §255
- Motive(s): Room 3

Surfaces

Surfaces include dining tables, counters, and any other table-like surfaces. Things may, unsurprisingly, be placed upon them.

Counters are an important element of the food preparation system. For more information, see the "Food Creation" chapter. To remain effective, counters must be cleaned regularly. Dirty counters contribute to the nausea effect of food prepared on them.

Bel-Air Dining Table

- Cost: §95

SirPlus! Metal Desk

- Cost: §100

Mission Coffee Table by Lulu Designs

- Cost: §110
- Motive(s): Room 1

"Concreta" Display Counter

- Cost: §140
- Motive(s): Hunger 4
- Skill(s): Cleaning

Missionaire Dining Table

- Cost: §150

The Impossible Mission Counter

- Cost: §180
- Motive(s): Hunger 4
- Skill(s): Cleaning

The Pet-estal

- Cost: §220
- Motive(s): Room 1

Curio Counters

- Cost: §250
- Motive(s): Hunger 6
- Skill(s): Cleaning

Home Office Desk by Quaint Design

- Cost: §250
- Motive(s): Room 1

Tiny Table

- Cost: §350

Curvaceous Colonial End Table

- Cost: §410
- Motive(s): Room 1

Old Thyme End Table

- Cost: §440
- Motive(s): Room 1

Doggy Dining

- Cost: §475

Chez Moi French Country Counters

- Cost: §590
- Motive(s): Hunger 6, Room 1
- Skill(s): Cleaning

Discourse Dining Table

- Cost: §750
- Motive(s): Room 1

 Old Thyme Dining Table
- Cost: §750

Plumbing

Plumbing objects provide necessary Bladder and Hygiene satisfaction. Generally, showers and baths are more effective than sinks at satisfying Hygiene.

 Simple Sink
- Cost: §180
- Motive(s): Hygiene 2

 Hydronomic Kitchen Sink
- Cost: §190
- Motive(s): Hygiene 2

note
While using a toilet, Sims can entertain themselves by reading or playing a handheld video game. Reading can lead to the discovery of new recipes.

 Sewage Brothers Resteze Toilet
- Cost: §300
- Motive(s): Bladder 10 (Use)

 Claymore Ceramic Sink
- Cost: §310
- Motive(s): Hygiene 2

 ShowHeuristic Hygiene System
- Cost: §450
- Motive(s): Hygiene 6

 The Kitchen Sink
- Cost: §500
- Motive(s): Hygiene 3

 "Birth of Venus" Master Sink
- Cost: §520
- Motive(s): Hygiene 3, Room 1

 Splash Fountain
- Cost: §550
- Motive(s): Hygiene 5, Fun 3

note
Sims can view this item as they would any decorative object or splash around in it for Fun and a bit of Hygiene.

 ResiStall Eco-Toilet
- Cost: §750
- Motive(s): Bladder 10

note
This works just like household toilets but without the option to read or play games while your Sims do their business.

 Shower of Power
- Cost: §800
- Motive(s): Hygiene 10

 The "SculpToilette" Porcelain Lavatory
- Cost: §950
- Motive(s): Bladder 10, Room 2

 Krampft Industries Wonder Tubba
- Cost: §950
- Motive(s): Hygiene 5, Comfort 5

 Oriental "Master" Bathtub
- Cost: §1,300
- Motive(s): Hygiene 6, Comfort 6

 "Suds de Souffle" Imperial Tub
- Cost: §1,500
- Motive(s): Hygiene 8, Comfort 8

 Fitzroy Dreamers' Rock Pool
- Cost: §8,500
- Motive(s): Hygiene 8, Comfort 7, Fun 3

note
Since this tub is actually a natural spring, it doesn't break or need repair.

Decorative

Decorative objects are used to adorn locations and raise Room score. Viewing some decorative objects satisfies Fun (sculptures and paintings give more Fun than plants).

 In Memory of Johnny Gnome
- Cost: §50
- Motive(s): Fun 3, Room 1

 Bright Lights, Big Doggy
- Cost: §50
- Motive(s): Fun 3, Room 1

The Lone Daisy
- Cost: §34
- Motive(s): Fun 3, Room 3

The Stodgy Badger Family Portrait
- Cost: §75
- Fun 3, Room 2

Sit Rover Sit!
- Cost: §100
- Motive(s): Fun 3, Room 2

Rhapsody in Paws
- Cost: §125
- Motive(s): Fun 3 (View), Room 2

Shifty Sam the Garden Gnome
- Cost: §150
- Motive(s): Fun 3, Room 2

Spacious Spaces
- Cost: §200
- Motive(s): Fun 3, Room 3

Hugs and Kisses
- Cost: §250
- Motive(s): Fun 3, Room 3

BFF, Best Friends 4-ever
- Cost: §350
- Motive(s): Fun 3, Room 4

Headhunter Battle Mask
- Cost: §360
- Motive(s): Fun 3, Room 4

Mad Dog Growleth
- Cost: §400
- Motive(s): Fun 3, Room 4

Pet Project I—Patience
- Cost: §750
- Motive(s): Fun 3, Room 5

Boronica by d'Lange
- Cost: §950
- Motive(s): Fun 3, Room 5

Pet Project II—Sorrow
- Cost: §1,100
- Motive(s): Fun 3, Room 6

The Meowing
- Cost: §1,300
- Motive(s): Fun 3, Room 6

Pawttern Rug
- Cost: §2,300
- Motive(s): Room 5

Pet Project III—Cruelty
- Cost: §2,500
- Motive(s): Fun 3, Room 7

Puppy Palette
- Cost: §2,500
- Motive(s): Fun 3, Room 7

The Honey Spooners
- Cost: §3,000
- Motive(s): Fun 3, Room 8

Shapes in Space
- Cost: §3,500
- Motive(s): Fun 3, Room 9

Beetle Yak Rug
- Cost: §5,500
- Motive(s): Room 10

Miscellaneous

These objects play a variety of roles but just don't fit in anywhere else.

"What a Steel" Economy Trash Can
- Cost: §30

note
This inexpensive trash can eventually fills up with garbage and must be emptied into the curbside can. When it's full, the can depresses Room score.

"Frood" Tree
- Cost: §150
- Motive(s): Room 2

note
From this tree, your Sims can extract fruits for use in cooking. For full info, see the "Food Creation" chapter.

Guppy Pond
- Cost: §350
- Motive(s): Hunger 2, Room 1

note
From this tank, your Sims can extract seafood for use in cooking. For full info, see the "Food Creation" chapter.

"Frood" Tree 2.0
- Cost: §400
- Motive(s): Hunger 2, Room 2

note

From this tree, your Sims can extract fruits for use in cooking. For full info, see the "Food Creation" chapter.

GenoLife Garden Hutch

◆ Cost: §450
◆ Motive(s): Hunger 3, Room 3

note

From this garden, your Sims can extract vegetables for use in cooking. For full info, see the "Food Creation" chapter.

Atlantis Jr.

◆ Cost: §500
◆ Motive(s): Hunger 3, Room 5

note

From this tank, your Sims can extract seafood for use in cooking. For full info, see the "Food Creation" chapter.

Comic Dehydrator

◆ Cost: §550
◆ Motive(s): Fun 3, Room 2

This humidor is for serious comic book connoisseurs who want their comic books nice and dry. Functionally, it works just like a bookshelf except it dispenses only comic books that can be read for Fun. No other bookshelf options (skill building, etc.) are available. Certain recipes are unlocked only from reading comics.

GenoLife Garden Hutch Grande

◆ Cost: §550
◆ Motive(s): Hunger 2, Room 2

note

From this garden, your Sims can extract vegetables for use in cooking. For full info, see the "Food Creation" chapter.

"Frood" Orchard

◆ Cost: §650
◆ Motive(s): Hunger 4, Room 4

note

From this tree, your Sims can extract fruits for use in cooking. For full info, see the "Food Creation" chapter.

GenoLife Garden Hutch Supreme

◆ Cost: §700
◆ Motive(s): Hunger 4, Room 5

note

From this garden, your Sims can extract vegetables for use in cooking. For full info, see the "Food Creation" chapter.

Animal Armoire

◆ Cost: §750

Using this dresser takes your Sims back to Create-A-Sim, where they can alter their look from all available and unlocked clothing.

The "Tahdis" Wardrobe

◆ Cost: §750

note

This works like the Animal Armoire.

"Manila 1000" Marine Aquarium

◆ Cost: §750
◆ Motive(s): Hunger 4, Room 5

note

From this tank, your Sims can extract seafood for use in cooking. For full info, see the "Food Creation" chapter.

Driver Pro 2006: "Chip Shots"

◆ Cost: §975
◆ Motive(s): Fun 6

note

After balls are hit from this Fun object, the sound that follows (chosen at random) indicates where (or on what) the ball landed.

Trampoline

◆ Cost: §2,100
◆ Motive(s): Fun 9

note

Only one Sim may jump at a time. The higher the Sim's Body skill, the more elaborate the tricks he or she can perform.

Town Square Catalogs

All the best pet supplies are available from stores in the Town Square, but the upper tiers of these objects will be carried by the stores only if they see there's a sufficiently free-spending clientele in town. Spend enough Pet Points at each of the three merchandise stores, and their structures and selections will expand to the most powerful items.

Object	Store	Store Level	Price (Pet Points)	Hunger	Comfort	Hygiene	Bladder	Energy	Fun	Social	Room	Chew/Scratch
Amusement Sphere	Pet Toy Store	Good	25	0	0	0	0	0	4	0	0	0
Anise	Ice Cream Cart	Good	38	60	0	0	-20	0	35	0	0	0
Aztec-spice Hot Chocolate	Coffee Cart	Good	24	40	0	0	-20	22	0	0	0	0
Baby Cat Bungalow	Pet Emporium	Basic	150	0	7	0	0	8	3	0	0	5
Bagel Tots by Biotic Chemical	Pet Bakery	Good	30	30	0	0	-15	0	0	0	0	0
Beef-a-hol Meat-brand Slurry	Pet Emporium	Basic	45	125	0	0	-40	0	0	0	0	0
Butter Pecan	Ice Cream Cart	Basic	34	60	0	0	-20	0	27	0	0	0
Café Latte	Coffee Cart	Basic	17	40	0	0	-20	8	0	0	0	0
Cappucino	Coffee Cart	Basic	20	40	0	0	-20	14	0	0	0	0
Captain Peghead's Original Fish Puffs	Pet Bakery	Basic	12	12	0	0	-6	0	0	0	0	0
Cashmere Chai Latte	Coffee Cart	Good	25	40	0	0	-20	24	0	0	0	0
Cat Mint Carrot Top	Pet Toy Store	Awesome	35	0	0	0	0	0	5	0	0	0
Cat Scratchies	Pet Emporium	Basic	75	0	0	0	0	0	0	0	0	7
Charming Pet House	Pet Emporium	Good	150	0	0	0	0	0	0	0	0	0
Cheese Biscotti by Biotic Chemical	Pet Bakery	Awesome	44	44	0	0	-22	0	0	0	0	0
Chewie Shewie by Droolz, Inc.	Pet Toy Store	Good	35	0	0	0	0	0	0	0	0	7
Chicken Croissants by Biotic Chemical	Pet Bakery	Awesome	40	40	0	0	-20	0	0	0	0	0
Chocolate	Ice Cream Cart	Basic	28	60	0	0	-20	0	15	0	0	0
ChompCo Chew Toy	Pet Toy Store	Basic	20	0	0	0	0	0	0	0	0	5
Classic Goldfish by Chabel!	Pet Emporium	Basic	150	0	0	0	0	0	4	0	0	0
Cobblestone Fudge	Ice Cream Cart	Awesome	41	60	0	0	-20	0	42	0	0	0
Coconut Carnage	Smoothie Cart	Basic	32	75	0	0	-30	6	12	0	0	0
Colonel Nash's Baked Swamp Dumpling	Pet Bakery	Basic	6	6	0	0	-3	0	0	0	0	0
Colonel Nash's Baked Swamp Squirrel	Pet Bakery	Good	30	30	0	0	-15	0	0	0	0	0
Coney Island Recyclo-Dog	Pet Toy Store	Good	35	0	0	0	0	0	0	0	0	7
Cozy Companion Pet Basket	Pet Emporium	Basic	50	0	3	0	0	4	0	0	0	0
Cup O'Joe	Coffee Cart	Basic	16	40	0	0	-20	5	0	0	0	0
Cute 'n Fluffy Pull Toy	Pet Toy Store	Good	30	0	0	0	0	0	5	0	0	0
Dangle Silk Spider by Droolz, Inc.	Pet Toy Store	Awesome	25	0	0	0	0	0	8	0	0	0
Delectable Dinners	Pet Emporium	Good	75	175	0	0	-65	0	0	0	0	0
Donkeyball Treat Ball	Pet Toy Store	Basic	20	0	0	0	0	0	0	0	0	0
Extreme Grape Attack	Smoothie Cart	Awesome	47	75	0	0	-30	22	22	0	0	0
Feline Birdie Stick	Pet Toy Store	Basic	20	0	0	0	0	0	2	0	0	0
Flavorful Cupcake by Biotic Chemical	Pet Bakery	Basic	14	14	0	0	-7	0	0	0	0	0
Flavorful Pretzel by Biotic Chemical	Pet Bakery	Good	20	20	0	0	-10	0	0	0	0	0
Floaty-O Flying Ring Toy	Pet Toy Store	Awesome	50	0	0	0	0	0	4	0	0	0
Foucault's Mailman	Pet Toy Store	Awesome	50	0	0	0	0	0	4	0	0	0
Fuzzy Wuzzy Bunny Fun	Pet Toy Store	Good	25	0	0	0	0	0	5	0	0	0
Gaia Theory Organic Cat Food	Pet Emporium	Awesome	100	250	0	0	-99	0	0	0	0	0
Gingermail Cookies by Droolz, Inc.	Pet Bakery	Awesome	50	50	0	0	-25	0	0	0	0	0
Gooseberry Surprise	Smoothie Cart	Good	38	75	0	0	-30	11	15	0	0	0
Happy Kat Catnip	Pet Toy Store	Basic	10	0	0	0	0	0	4	0	0	0

Object	Store	Store Level	Price (Pet Points)	Hunger	Comfort	Hygiene	Bladder	Energy	Fun	Social	Room	Chew/Scratch
Happy Times Catnip Toy	Pet Toy Store	Awesome	30	0	0	0	0	0	5	0	0	0
Herbal Tea	Coffee Cart	Basic	11	40	0	0	-20	11	0	0	0	0
Hibernosis Pet Basket	Pet Emporium	Awesome	150	0	8	0	0	8	0	0	0	0
Himalayan Heights	Pet Emporium	Awesome	200	0	8	0	0	8	3	0	0	5
Iced Raspberry Whipped Soy Chocolate Frostino	Coffee Cart	Awesome	26	40	0	0	-20	26	0	0	0	0
Indestructiball	Pet Toy Store	Awesome	35	0	0	0	0	0	5	0	0	0
King Pone Dog Bone	Pet Bakery	Basic	10	10	0	0	-5	0	0	0	0	0
Kitty Latrine	Pet Emporium	Basic	100	0	0	0	0	8	0	0	0	0
Lavender Jasmine Rose	Ice Cream Cart	Good	39	60	0	0	-20	0	38	0	0	0
Lavishware Dish	Pet Emporium	Good	150	7	0	0	0	0	0	0	0	0
Le Clown Tragique by Droolz, Inc.	Pet Toy Store	Awesome	150	0	0	0	0	0	0	0	0	10
Lemon Strawberry Sprinkle Rainbow Explosion	Ice Cream Cart	Awesome	43	60	0	0	-20	0	45	0	0	0
Los Gatos Cat Condo	Pet Emporium	Basic	100	0	5	0	0	5	3	0	0	5
Luscious Limon Lemon	Smoothie Cart	Good	39	75	0	0	-30	13	15	0	0	0
Mailman-o-War Pull Toy	Pet Toy Store	Awesome	40	0	0	0	0	0	6	0	0	0
Mango Tango Fandango	Smoothie Cart	Basic	37	75	0	0	-30	10	13	0	0	0
Mega-Hork Pull Toy	Pet Toy Store	Good	25	0	0	0	0	0	4	0	0	0
Mint Chocolate Chip	Ice Cream Cart	Basic	32	60	0	0	-20	0	24	0	0	0
Mood Enhancing Protein USA	Smoothie Cart	Basic	5	0	0	0	0	0	0	0	0	0
Nature's Husk Pet Nutrition	Pet Emporium	Good	60	150	0	0	-50	0	0	0	0	0
Newsie Wewsie by Droolz, Inc.	Pet Toy Store	Basic	25	0	0	0	0	0	0	0	0	6
Organico Shade-Harvested Neo-Coffee	Coffee Cart	Good	23	40	0	0	-20	20	0	0	0	0
Passionfruit Disaster	Smoothie Cart	Basic	32	75	0	0	-30	3	10	0	0	0
Pet Bone	Pet Toy Store	Good	30	0	0	0	0	0	0	0	0	5
Pet Plumbob	Pet Toy Store	Basic	25	0	0	0	0	0	0	0	0	6
Pet-a-cino	Coffee Cart	Basic	40	110	0	0	-20	0	0	0	0	0
Pet-astic Liver Cream	Ice Cream Cart	Basic	30	90	0	0	-20	0	0	0	0	0
Pett Tennis Ball	Pet Toy Store	Basic	15	0	0	0	0	0	4	0	0	0
Pistachio Current	Ice Cream Cart	Good	36	60	0	0	-20	0	31	0	0	0
Power Pet Blast	Smoothie Cart	Basic	35	100	0	0	-20	0	0	0	0	0
Prof. Feather's Chicken Checkers	Pet Emporium	Awesome	750	0	0	0	0	0	9	0	0	0
Quadruple Espresso	Coffee Cart	Basic	22	40	0	0	-20	18	0	0	0	0
Rasin the Roof	Smoothie Cart	Basic	35	75	0	0	-30	8	11	0	0	0
Raspberry Refreshado	Smoothie Cart	Basic	35	75	0	0	-30	7	12	0	0	0
Rope Pet Bone	Pet Toy Store	Awesome	50	0	0	0	0	0	0	0	0	9
Rope-o-War Pull Toy	Pet Toy Store	Basic	20	0	0	0	0	0	4	0	0	0
Sack o' Catnip	Pet Toy Store	Good	20	0	0	0	0	0	4	0	0	0
Scientifix Amino-Gratin	Pet Emporium	Awesome	150	200	0	0	-75	0	0	0	0	0
ScratchMaster	Pet Emporium	Good	100	0	0	0	0	0	0	0	0	8
Scratchpaw Manor Pet House	Pet Emporium	Awesome	200	0	0	0	0	0	0	0	0	0
Sisyphus' Feather	Pet Toy Store	Basic	10	0	0	0	0	0	6	0	0	0
Slim Licken's Pet Chow	Pet Emporium	Basic	30	100	0	0	-30	0	0	0	0	0
Snooty-Frooty-Smoothy	Smoothie Cart	Awesome	44	75	0	0	-30	18	20	0	0	0
Speckled Trout Tease Toy	Pet Toy Store	Good	20	0	0	0	0	0	8	0	0	0
Stick Au Natural	Pet Toy Store	Basic	5	0	0	0	0	0	2	0	0	0
Strawberry	Ice Cream Cart	Basic	29	60	0	0	-20	0	15	0	0	0
Swirly Lumps-n-Chunks	Smoothie Cart	Good	40	75	0	0	-30	15	15	0	0	0

Object	Store	Store Level	Price (Pet Points)	Hunger	Comfort	Hygiene	Bladder	Energy	Fun	Social	Room	Chew/Scratch
The Astro Pad	Pet Emporium	Awesome	300	0	0	0	0	0	0	0	0	0
The Gravel Palace	Pet Emporium	Awesome	150	0	0	0	8	0	0	0	0	0
The Mouse Fisher	Pet Toy Store	Basic	15	0	0	0	0	0	7	0	0	0
The Mouse of Destiny	Pet Toy Store	Good	30	0	0	0	0	0	3	0	0	0
The Supper Saucer	Pet Emporium	Basic	100	5	0	0	0	0	0	0	0	0
The Whizzle-Bee Flying Disc	Pet Toy Store	Basic	20	0	0	0	0	0	7	0	0	0
Triple Caramel Mocha Orange Cinnamon Coffee	Coffee Cart	Awesome	28	40	0	0	-20	30	0	0	0	0
Vanilla	Ice Cream Cart	Basic	30	60	0	0	-20	0	20	0	0	0
Wasket Pet Basket Deluxe!	Pet Emporium	Good	100	0	5	0	0	6	0	0	0	0

Pet Emporium

The Pet Emporium deals in pet food, scratching posts, beds, and baskets.

Baby Cat Bungalow

- Pet Points: 150
- Motive(s): Energy 8, Comfort 7, Fun 3, Scratch 5
- Store Level: Basic

Beef-a-hol Meat-brand Slurry

- Pet Points: 45
- Motive(s): Hunger 125, Bladder -40
- Store Level: Basic

Cat Scratchies

- Pet Points: 75
- Motive(s): Scratch 7
- Store Level: Basic

Charming Pet House

- Pet Points: 150
- Store Level: Good

Classic Goldfish by Chabell!

- Pet Points: 150
- Motive(s): Fun 4
- Store Level: Basic

Cozy Companion Pet Basket

- Pet Points: 50
- Motive(s): Energy 4, Comfort 3
- Store Level: Basic

Delectable Dinners

- Pet Points: 75
- Motive(s): Hunger 175, Bladder -65
- Store Level: Good

Gaia Theory Organic Cat Food

- Pet Points: 100
- Motive(s): Hunger 250, Bladder -99
- Store Level: Awesome

Hibernosis Pet Basket

- Pet Points: 150
- Motive(s): Comfort 8, Energy 8
- Store Level: Awesome

Himalayan Heights

- Pet Points: 200
- Motive(s): Comfort 8, Energy 8, Fun 3, Scratch 5
- Store Level: Awesome

Kitty Latrine

- Pet Points: 100
- Motive(s): Bladder 8
- Store Level: Basic

Lavishware Dish

- Pet Points: 150
- Motive(s): Hunger 7
- Store Level: Good

Los Gatos Cat Condo

- Pet Points: 100
- Motive(s): Comfort 5, Energy 5, Fun 3, Scratch 5
- Store Level: Basic

Nature's Husk Pet Nutrition

- Pet Points: 60
- Motive(s): Hunger 150, Bladder -50
- Store Level: Good

Prof. Feather's Chicken Checkers

- Pet Points: 750
- Motive(s): Fun 9 (Play)
- Skill(s): Logic (Practice)
- Store Level: Awesome

You may choose to play against the chicken just for Fun (Play) or for both Fun and Logic skill (Practice). The chance of beating the chicken increases with your Sim's Logic skill.

note

This builds Logic faster than any other object.

If your Sim wins, the chicken lays a Golden Egg that can be used in food preparation. Each Golden Egg goes directly into the Harvested Animals section of your fridge.

tip

The Chicken Checkers set can also be used as an alarm clock. Place it in the same room with your Sim's bed; when set, it functions just like a regular alarm clock.

If Chicken Checkers gets dirty, it depresses Room score for the room it's in. Clean it regularly to prevent or undo this effect.

Scientifix Amino-Gratin

- Pet Points: 150
- Motive(s): Hunger 200, Bladder -75
- Store Level: Awesome

ScratchMaster

- Pet Points: 100
- Motive(s): Scratch 8
- Store Level: Good

Scratchpaw Manor Pet House

- Pet Points: 200
- Store Level: Awesome

Slim Licken's Pet Chow

- Pet Points: 30
- Motive(s): Hunger 100, Bladder -30
- Store Level: Basic

The Supper Saucer

- Pet Points: 100
- Motive(s): Hunger 5
- Store Level: Basic

The Astro Pad

- Pet Points: 300
- Store Level: Awesome

The Gravel Palace

- Pet Points: 150
- Motive(s): Bladder 8
- Store Level: Awesome

Wasket Pet Basket Deluxe!

- Pet Points: 100
- Motive(s): Energy 6, Comfort 5
- Store Level: Good

Pet Bakery

Bagel Tots by Biotic Chemical

- Pet Points: 30
- Motive(s): Hunger 30, Bladder -15
- Store Level: Good

Captain Peghead's Original Fish Puffs

- Pet Points: 12
- Motive(s): Hunger 12, Bladder -6
- Store Level: Basic

Cheese Biscotti by Biotic Chemical

- Pet Points: 44
- Motive(s): Hunger 44, Bladder -22
- Store Level: Awesome

Chicken Croissants by Biotic Chemical

- Pet Points: 40
- Motive(s): Hunger 40, Bladder -20
- Store Level: Awesome

Colonel Nash's Baked Swamp Dumpling

- Pet Points: 6
- Motive(s): Hunger 6, Bladder -3
- Store Level: Basic

Colonel Nash's Baked Swamp Squirrel

- Pet Points: 30
- Motive(s): Hunger 30, Bladder -15
- Store Level: Good

Flavorful Cupcake by Biotic Chemical

- Pet Points: 14
- Motive(s): Hunger 14, Bladder -7
- Store Level: Basic

Flavorful Pretzel by Biotic Chemical

- Pet Points: 20
- Motive(s): Hunger 20, Bladder -10
- Store Level: Good

Gingermail Cookies by Droolz, Inc.
- ◆ Pet Points: 50
- ◆ Motive(s): Hunger 50, Bladder -25
- ◆ Store Level: Awesome

King Pone Dog Bone
- ◆ Pet Points: 10
- ◆ Motive(s): Hunger 10, Bladder -5
- ◆ Store Level: Basic

Pet Toy Store

The toy store carries the full line of quality pet toys. Many of these objects are required for some Play interactions (i.e., Fetch is only available if the Sim has a stick in inventory). Many toys wear out, so be mindful of when it's time to replace them.

Amusement Sphere
- ◆ Pet Points: 25
- ◆ Motive(s): Fun 4
- ◆ Store Level: Good

Cat Mint Carrot Top
- ◆ Pet Points: 35
- ◆ Motive(s): Fun 5
- ◆ Store Level: Awesome

Chewie Shewie by Droolz, Inc.
- ◆ Pet Points: 35
- ◆ Motive(s): Chew 7
- ◆ Store Level: Good

ChompCo Chew Toy
- ◆ Pet Points: 20
- ◆ Motive(s): Chew 5
- ◆ Store Level: Basic

Coney Island Recyclo-Dog
- ◆ Pet Points: 35
- ◆ Motive(s): Chew 7
- ◆ Store Level: Good

Cute 'n Fluffy Pull Toy
- ◆ Pet Points: 30
- ◆ Motive(s): Fun 5
- ◆ Store Level: Good

Dangle Silk Spider by Droolz, Inc.
- ◆ Pet Points: 25
- ◆ Motive(s): Fun 8
- ◆ Store Level: Awesome

Donkeyball Treat Ball
- ◆ Pet Points: 20
- ◆ Store Level: Basic

Feline Birdie Stick
- ◆ Pet Points: 20
- ◆ Motive(s): Fun 2
- ◆ Store Level: Basic

Floaty-O Flying Ring Toy
- ◆ Pet Points: 50
- ◆ Motive(s): Fun 4
- ◆ Store Level: Awesome

Foucault's Mailman
- ◆ Pet Points: 50
- ◆ Motive(s): Fun 4
- ◆ Store Level: Awesome

Fuzzy Wuzzy Bunny Fun
- ◆ Pet Points: 25
- ◆ Motive(s): Fun 5
- ◆ Store Level: Good

Happy Kat Catnip
- ◆ Pet Points: 10
- ◆ Motive(s): Fun 4
- ◆ Store Level: Basic

Happy Times Catnip Toy
- ◆ Pet Points: 30
- ◆ Motive(s): Fun 5
- ◆ Store Level: Awesome

Indestructiball
- ◆ Pet Points: 35
- ◆ Motive(s): Fun 5
- ◆ Store Level: Awesome

Le Clown Tragique by Droolz, Inc.
- ◆ Pet Points: 150
- ◆ Motive(s): Chew 10
- ◆ Store Level: Awesome

Mailman-o-War Pull Toy
- ◆ Pet Points: 40
- ◆ Motive(s): Fun 6
- ◆ Store Level: Awesome

Mega-Hork Pull Toy
- ◆ Pet Points: 25
- ◆ Motive(s): Fun 4
- ◆ Store Level: Good

Newsie Wewsie by Droolz, Inc.

- Pet Points: 25
- Motive(s): Chew 6
- Store Level: Basic

Pet Bone

- Pet Points: 30
- Motive(s): Chew 5
- Store Level: Good

Pet Plumbob

- Pet Points: 25
- Motive(s): Chew 6
- Store Level: Basic

Pett Tennis Ball

- Pet Points: 15
- Motive(s): Fun 4
- Store Level: Basic

Rope Pet Bone

- Pet Points: 50
- Motive(s): Chew 9
- Store Level: Awesome

Rope-o-War Pull Toy

- Pet Points: 20
- Motive(s): Fun 4
- Store Level: Basic

Sack o' Catnip

- Pet Points: 20
- Motive(s): Fun 4
- Store Level: Good

Sisyphus' Feather

- Pet Points: 10
- Motive(s): Fun 6
- Store Level: Basic

Speckled Trout Tease Toy

- Pet Points: 20
- Motive(s): Fun 8
- Store Level: Good

Stick Au Natural

- Pet Points: 5
- Motive(s): Fun 2
- Store Level: Basic

The Mouse Fisher

- Pet Points: 15
- Motive(s): Fun 7
- Store Level: Basic

The Mouse of Destiny

- Pet Points: 30
- Motive(s): Fun 3
- Store Level: Good

The Whizzle-Bee Flying Disc

- Pet Points: 20
- Motive(s): Fun 7
- Store Level: Basic

Chapter 21

CHARACTERS

Any neighborhood with Sims will be abuzz with activity; even the Lazy ones don't stay still for long. From the get-go, there are several Sims and pets in town for you to control and for your Sims to meet. As you help your Sims fulfill their Wants, more Sims will move to the happy burg, expanding your Sims' social circles whenever they visit the Town Square.

Not every Sim, however, is merely an unmet friend. Many have jobs that impact your Sim. Some are helpful and some can cause big trouble.

This chapter introduces you to the citizens (both four- and two-legged), civil servants, and other nefarious figures that live in your new neighborhood.

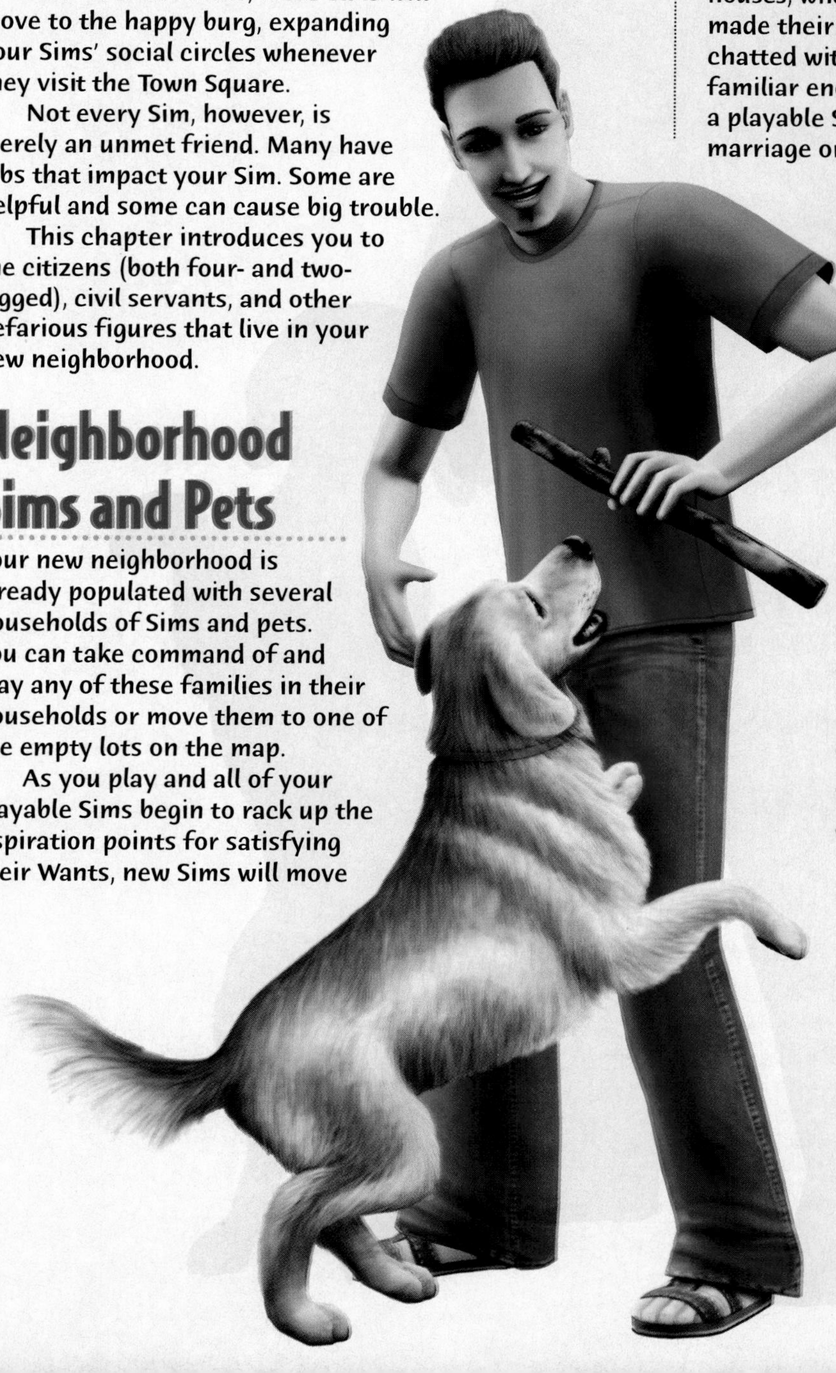

Neighborhood Sims and Pets

Your new neighborhood is already populated with several households of Sims and pets. You can take command of and play any of these families in their households or move them to one of the empty lots on the map.

As you play and all of your playable Sims begin to rack up the Aspiration points for satisfying their Wants, new Sims will move

to the neighborhood. These Sims don't move into any of the empty lots, but they do increase its population. These so-called "townies" are most often seen at the Town Square, but they occasionally walk by your Sims' houses, where they can be greeted. Once your Sims have made their acquaintance, the townie can be invited over, chatted with on the phone, etc. If one of your Sims gets familiar enough with a townie, the townie can become a playable Sim if brought into your Sims' houses via marriage or as a roommate.

> **note**
> Townies are unlocked when your entire neighborhood passes five cumulative Aspiration point scores. The "Neighborhood Sims" and "Neighborhood Pets" tables show the score at which various townies become available.

The tables display each neighborhood Sim's:

◆ Name
◆ Portrait
◆ Household (if any)
◆ Unlock Score (if a townie)
◆ Aspiration (if Sim) or Species (if pet)
◆ Gender
◆ Personality Traits
◆ Interests (Sims only)
◆ Cooking Skill Level (Sims only)

Neighborhood Sims

First Name	Last Name	Image	Household	Unlocked at Cumulative Aspiration Point Total	Aspiration	Gender	Neat	Outgoing	Active	Playful
Babette	Lambert		Unlockable townie	10,000	Knowledge	F	10	0	6	2
Betty	Newbie		Cozy Acres	—	Knowledge	F	5	10	2	3
Bob	Newbie		Cozy Acres	—	Family	M	10	1	5	3
Buck	Oakely		Dogwood Forest	—	Knowledge	M	0	2	10	7
Charlie	Prescott		Unlockable townie	100	Family	M	6	6	2	8
Cindy Lou	Boyle		Unlockable townie	100	Popularity	F	3	10	5	2
Claire	Seville		Unlockable townie	1,000	Wealth	F	8	5	8	1
Dan	Hardiman		Serenity Falls	—	Creativity	M	4	1	8	8
Dottie	Simpson		Feline Farms	—	Creativity	F	3	0	6	10
Eddie	Howard		Unlockable townie	1,000,000	Knowledge	M	2	10	5	2
Huckleberry	Wong		Unlockable townie	100,000	Creativity	M	3	5	1	10
Jim	Lester		Unlockable townie	10,000	Wealth	M	7	8	2	5
Joyce	Howard		Unlockable townie	1,000,000	Creativity	F	2	3	2	9
Kate	Hardiman		Serenity Falls	—	Family	F	4	7	0	5
Kiki	Pickens		Unlockable townie	100,000	Popularity	F	8	2	4	6
Linda	Townsend		Paw Valley Road	—	Family	F	4	4	7	7

Nice	Media	Clothes	Sports	Food	Crime	Politics	Space	Health	Travel	Money	Work	Weather	Animals	Paranormal	Cooking Skill
7	6	7	1	4	0	0	1	7	4	8	8	6	8	6	3
5	10	5	5	5	0	0	5	5	5	5	10	5	5	5	3
6	5	5	5	5	5	0	5	5	10	5	5	10	5	0	3
6	0	0	10	5	5	5	5	5	5	5	5	5	10	5	3
4	5	10	5	0	5	5	5	5	5	10	5	0	5	5	3
5	5	5	0	5	10	5	5	5	5	5	0	5	5	10	3
3	5	5	10	5	5	0	5	5	0	10	5	5	5	5	3
5	5	0	10	5	5	5	5	10	5	0	5	5	5	5	3
6	0	3	0	6	1	0	7	6	3	1	3	5	10	10	3
6	10	5	5	5	10	5	5	0	5	5	5	0	5	5	3
6	5	5	5	10	0	5	5	5	0	5	5	5	5	10	3
3	5	5	5	10	5	5	5	0	10	5	0	5	5	5	3
8	10	5	0	5	5	5	5	5	5	0	5	5	5	10	3
9	5	5	5	5	5	5	5	10	5	5	5	10	5	5	3
5	5	0	5	10	5	5	5	10	5	0	5	5	5	5	3
3	0	5	5	5	5	5	0	10	5	5	5	5	10	5	3

Neighborhood Sims continued

First Name	Last Name	Image	Household	Unlocked at Cumulative Aspiration Point Total	Aspiration	Gender	Neat	Outgoing	Active	Playful
Marsha	Worthington		Firefly Lake	—	Wealth	F	7	9	3	5
Mira	May		Firefly Lake	—	Knowledge	F	5	5	5	5
Patty	Prescott		Unlockable townie	100	Popularity	F	7	10	3	5
Penelope	Arnold		Firefly Lake	—	Family	F	2	8	2	8
Timothy	Pickens		Unlockable townie	100,000	Wealth	M	2	5	7	3
Varian	Parker		Firefly Lake	—	Wealth	F	4	8	2	8
Walter	Mellon		Unlockable townie	1,000	Knowledge	M	4	2	9	3
Wanda	Mellon		Unlockable townie	1,000	Popularity	F	4	9	1	6
William	Townsend		Paw Valley Road	—	Family	M	5	7	10	3

Neighborhood Pets

First Name	Last Name	Image	Household	Unlocked at Cumulative Aspiration Point Total	Species	Sex	Gifted/Normal/Doofus
Bella	Simpson		Feline Farms	—	Cat	F	Gifted
Boogie	Howard		Unlockable townie	1,000,000	Dog	M	Normal
Buddy	Newbie		Cozy Acres	—	Dog	M	Gifted
Buster	Hardiman		Serenity Falls	—	Dog	M	Normal
Daisy	Simpson		Feline Farms	—	Cat	F	Normal
Deltoid	Lambert		Unlockable townie	10,000	Dog	M	Normal

Nice	Media	Clothes	Sports	Food	Crime	Politics	Space	Health	Travel	Money	Work	Weather	Animals	Paranormal	Cooking Skill
1	5	10	5	5	5	5	5	5	10	5	5	5	5	5	3
5	5	5	5	5	5	5	5	0	5	5	5	5	5	0	3
0	5	5	5	5	5	10	10	5	0	5	0	5	5	5	3
5	5	0	5	5	5	5	5	5	5	5	0	5	10	10	3
8	5	5	5	10	5	5	5	5	5	5	5	5	5	5	3
3	10	5	0	5	0	5	5	5	5	5	10	5	5	5	3
7	0	5	5	5	10	5	5	5	0	5	5	10	5	0	3
5	5	5	10	10	5	5	5	0	5	5	0	5	5	5	3
0	5	5	5	5	5	5	5	5	5	5	5	5	5	5	3

Hyper/Lazy	Friendly/Independent	Aggressive/Cowardly	Snooty/Pigpen
Lazy	Independent	Normal	Snooty
Normal	Friendly	Aggressive	Normal
Lazy	Normal	Normal	Normal
Hyper	Normal	Normal	Pigpen
Normal	Friendly	Cowardly	Normal
Normal	Independent	Aggressive	Normal

Neighborhood Pets continued

First Name	Last Name	Image	Household	Unlocked at Cumulative Aspiration Point Total	Species	Sex	Gifted/Normal/Doofus
Falafel	May		Firefly Lake	—	Cat	M	Normal
Fauntleroy	Townsend		Feline Farms	—	Dog	M	Normal
Hamhock	Oakely		Dogwood Forest	—	Dog	M	Gifted
Henrietta	Townsend		Paw Valley Road	—	Dog	F	Normal
Honey Butter	Pickens		Unlockable townie	100,000	Dog	F	Normal
Lucky	Oakely		Dogwood Forest	—	Dog	M	Gifted
Mobius	Howard		Unlockable townie	1,000,000	Dog	M	Gifted
Morty	Howard		Unlockable townie	1,000,000	Cat	M	Gifted
Oscar	Simpson		Feline Farms	—	Cat	M	Normal
Paisley	Prescott		Unlockable townie	100	Cat	M	Normal
Presto	Parker		Firefly Lake	—	Dog	M	Gifted
Rufus	Oakley		Dogwood Forest	—	Dog	M	Normal
Shnookems	Simpson		Feline Farms	—	Cat	M	Doofus
Smokey	Simpson		Feline Farms	—	Cat	M	Normal
Whistle	Pickens		Unlockable townie	100,000	Cat	M	Normal
Yappy	Lester		Unlockable townie	10,000	Dog	M	Normal

Hyper/Lazy	Friendly/Independent	Aggressive/Cowardly	Snooty/Pigpen
Normal	Friendly	Aggressive	Normal
Normal	Independent	Normal	Snooty
Normal	Friendly	Normal	Normal
Normal	Friendly	Normal	Pigpen
Lazy	Friendly	Aggressive	Normal
Normal	Independent	Normal	Normal
Lazy	Normal	Normal	Normal
Normal	Normal	Cowardly	Normal
Lazy	Friendly	Normal	Normal
Hyper	Friendly	Normal	Normal
Lazy	Normal	Normal	Pigpen
Hyper	Normal	Aggressive	Pigpen
Lazy	Independent	Normal	Normal
Hyper	Friendly	Cowardly	Normal
Hyper	Normal	Aggressive	Normal
Hyper	Friendly	Normal	Normal

Service Sims

Thanks to your handy-dandy wall phone, the most loyal and efficient Sim services are only a phone call away. Dial up any of these services when you need them.

 note
All service NPCs and public servants with the power to fine your Sims for their misdeeds aren't very understanding if your Sims lack the funds to pay the bill/fine.

In all cases, they repossess an object of approximately the value of the outstanding bill or fine. If the NPC has an ongoing service with your Sim (like a Maid who comes every day), he or she cancels the contract.

 note
One further service can be requested over the phone, but no NPC arrives to provide the it: the Therapist is available over the phone only to provide a way for your Sims to refresh their list of Wants.

Maid

The Maid does the most valuable service in town. Keeping a house clean yourself, even when all Sims are high in Neat, consumes great gobs of time. Even Sims in the first level of their career should feel their time is too valuable for mopping and dishwashing. Better to just call the Maid and pay her reasonable fee of §10 per hour.

With Cleaning skill of 10 and a diligent work ethic, she stays until all messes (trash, full trash cans, dirty objects, dishes, food, ashes, unmade beds, and puddles) are cleaned. She also cleans dirty litter boxes, pet beds, and pet houses, and mops up pet's puddles. Therefore, the dirtier the house, the more she costs.

Gardener

The potted plants in your Sims' homes, as well as plants used to harvest vegetables and fruits, need watering every few days, or they'll die. Dead plants kill Room score, and that's trouble. To keep your plants nice and producing with no effort on your part, the Gardener may just be a sound investment. For §10 per hour every three days, he replants any dead plants and keeps everything watered and healthy.

The Gardener also fills in holes dug by untrained dogs.

Obedience Trainer

The Obedience Trainer can quickly train your pets for your Sims, leaving them free to pursue other matters. He isn't, however, reachable by telephone.

The Obedience Trainer appears in the Town Square in the vicinity of the smoothie cart after at least four Town Square buildings have upgraded to the second (Good) level. Your Sim may interact with him to hire him for training.

Once retained for the reasonable price of 20 Pet Points per hour, the Trainer will school the specified pet in any commands you choose until the pet is fully trained or its Motives force it to refuse training.

Repair Woman

When things are broken and you just don't have the time or the Mechanical skill to do it yourself, call the Repair Woman. She comes over quickly but charges a pretty penny (§50 per hour) to fix any broken items. She stays as long as there's something in need of fixing and charges you when she's done.

Fire Department

When a fire breaks out, get on the phone to the Fire Department. Only call them when there is a fire ablaze, though, or you'll be punished with a "tsk-tsk" and a §500 fine. If there's a smoke detector in the same room as the fire, the Fire Department comes running automatically.

Firefighters can also be called if a cat gets stuck in a climbable tree. Unlike a fire, a treed cat isn't a critical emergency, so Firefighters will only be summoned autonomously if there's a Gifted pet on the lot. When a cat gets stuck in a tree, Gifted pets leave the lot and bring back the Firefighters.

Police

During an invasion of your home, the Thief swipes one of your Sim's most valuable items. One way to catch the Thief is to call the Police as soon as you get the message that the burglar is in your home. Calling the Police frivolously, however, gets you in trouble to the tune of a §500 fine.

If the Cops catch the Thief, you get your item back and a §500 reward.

You also see the Police if your Sims' parties continue after 2 am. When the clock strikes 2 in the morning, the Police come calling and write your Sim a ticket for §100. That's what you get for having too much fun.

tip

Once you've gotten nabbed for a late party, the Cops don't come back, no matter how long the party goes, so there's no need to break it up once the fine's been assessed.

Cops also act as animal control officers and guardians of the Town Square. Returned runaway pets will be escorted home by the Cop. The Cop also keeps an eye on what objects are placed in the Town Square. You may not place from your inventory:

- Bathtubs
- Beds
- Blenders
- Food Processors
- Refrigerators
- Showers
- Sinks
- Stoves
- Toilets

Placing illegal objects results in an immediate fine (5 Pet Points). Your Sims will also be fined if you ever direct them to put a Guard-trained pet in Guard mode (10 Pet Points). That's just not allowed on community property.

Sims Who Call on You

A few other NPCs provide services (of sorts) for your Sims.

Mail Carrier

The Mail Carrier delivers new bills every three days at 10 am. Whenever you pay the bills by putting them in the mailbox (even if the Mail Carrier isn't scheduled to come), the mail is picked up automatically the next time the clock reaches 10 am.

Newsie

The Newsie brings the newspaper each morning at 7 am. If there are more than five newspapers on the lot, the Newsie refuses to deliver any more until you throw enough away to get below five.

Paramedic

The Paramedic is always on call to revive passed out Sims or pets. If a Sim or pet passes out, the Paramedic can be summoned by telephone. If there's a pet on the lot with a high relationship or a Master or Mine bit with the passed out Sim, it may run off the lot and bring back the Paramedic.

 note

Any Sim can be directed to revive a passed out pet or Sim, but the Paramedic can do it more quickly and may be the only choice if there are no other playable Sims on the lot when your Sim passes out.

The Paramedic will revive any passed out Sims or pets on the lot until everyone present is OK and upright.

Repo Man

Fail to pay your bills within 10 days of their arrival, and the Repo Man pays a visit. He takes an item or items with a total depreciated value at or above the amount you owe.

 note

Once the Repo Man is on the lot, you can't access Buy or Build Catalogs, so there's no way to sell off items or move them to inaccessible locations to keep them from being taken.

Thief

The Thief comes randomly at midnight if all residents are either asleep or at work and steals the most valuable item (purchased by your Sims) within reach. Unless you have a pet, a Thief can be stopped only by a burglar alarm or the Police.

If there are pets on the lot, they may scare the burglar away. When the Thief and pet are in the same room, the Thief will attempt to "buy off" the pet with a treat. Whether the pet accepts or not depends on its relationship to the household Sims and its Personality (Cowardly dogs can be counted upon to accept). If the pet accepts, it'll ignore the Thief. If the pet rejects, it'll bark or hiss, chasing the Thief from the lot.

To make a pet into a sure and unbribable toothy burglar alarm, direct your Sims to train it in the Guard command. A fully trained guard pet will sense the arrival of a Thief anywhere on the lot (not just in the same room) and cannot be bought off with a treat. It will always chase the Thief from the lot.

Chapter 22

FOOD CREATION

Hunger is the most important and constantly demanding of your Sim's Motives. It's just as essential as Energy, but, unlike Energy, it contributes mightily to a Sim's Mood. Want more evidence? It's the only Motive that gets its own extra section.

How you satisfy your Sim's Hunger is one of the key differences between playing *The Sims 2 Pets* and playing it well. The amount of efficiency that can be wrung out of preparing and eating food is absolutely unmatched if you take the time to learn how things function.

This section introduces you to the mechanics of how your Sims can satisfy their Hunger Motive and how you can harness the power of the food-creation system to rise to the heights of Sim existence.

note

Though the food-creation system can be used (albeit a bit awkwardly) in Classic Control mode, we highly recommend using it exclusively in Direct Control mode due to its greater efficiency and, above all, control.

Food in General

Your Sims satisfy their Hunger Motive by consuming food. Nothing else in the entire game can fully take its place. The question is not whether to eat, but how much time you're going to consume doing it.

note

Sims can eat at the Town Square at the three vending carts. The more upgraded these carts are, the better the food they sell.

Sims satisfy Hunger by eating. Satisfying it fully in the shortest amount of time is a function of the quality of the food.

Every food object your Sim eats, no matter how it's created, satisfies a fixed amount of Hunger and takes a fixed amount of time to prepare and consume. Efficiency, therefore, arises from creating food with the highest possible Hunger satisfaction and the shortest possible prep and eating time relative to Hunger satisfaction.

This requires balancing. Preparing great food requires two things—time for your Sim to learn to cook and money to purchase the best possible tools. It also requires balancing of satisfaction and time. A snack from the fridge is quicker than making a big meal, but your Sim has to come back for more food much more quickly.

To tame these various issues, it's necessary to understand how the food chain works.

The Food Chain

note

There are two ways to create food: generically and by using the food-creation system. The principles discussed here apply to both methods.

By interacting with the fridge, you see all the options of what kind of meal to cook.

Food gets its Hunger satisfaction from several sources:

- Inherent: Every generic meal and every ingredient carries in it a quantity of Hunger satisfaction. Generic meals have an assigned satisfaction amount, while prepared meals' satisfaction is based on the inherent attributes of the ingredients the meal comprises.

- Preparation: How a food is prepared (on a countertop, in a blender, in a food processor, or not at all) adds an additional amount of Hunger satisfaction. All combinations of ingredients have results that skip this step and go directly to the stove.

- Completion: All food combos have results that can be completed on a counter, in a food processor, in the blender, or in the stove. The better (more expensive) the stove, processor, or blender, the greater the added satisfaction.

- Cooking Skill: The Cooking skill (acquired by reading books from the bookshelf and by cooking) of the Sim preparing the food shortens food preparation time and adds additional Hunger satisfaction to the resulting food.

Finished foods tossed into the blender can be consumed very quickly, though they lose some of their Hunger satisfaction.

tip

Any finished food can be further processed by putting it in the blender. This makes the finished product drinkable and, thus, faster to consume. On the downside, it reduces the Hunger impact of the food by 20. Still, the time efficiency may be worth it.

note

Generic meals and ingredients have defined effects on Hunger satisfaction but also a negative effect on Bladder. Many ingredients also satisfy Energy and carry hidden effects that can dramatically impact your Sim for better or worse.

Meals, Ingredients, and the Refrigerator

With one exception (grilling) all food begins in the refrigerator.

All refrigerators feature the same slate of interactions:

- Get Ingredients (Direct Control)/Cook a Meal (Classic Control): This starts the food-creation system to make a single serving of a custom food.
- Get a Snack (§5): Your Sim extracts a preprocessed snack that's faster to eat than preparing a full meal but delivers only minimal Hunger satisfaction (especially relative to the time it takes to consume).
- Get Group Meal Ingredients: This starts the food-creation system to make six servings of a custom food. All ingredient costs are tripled.
- Get Generic Ingredients (§12): This bypasses ingredient selection and makes a generic meal.

note

Generic meals have fixed attributes:
- Cost: §12
- Hunger: 40/45/50/55 [depending on the fridge]
- Energy: 5
- Bladder: -20

Where you prepare a meal, even a generic one, decides what the final product is.

You can prepare generic meals on the counter (such as shabu-shabu to eat as is or roast and veggies to go in the stove), in the blender (dinner in a cup), in the food processor (casserole or soup) and then the stove, or directly in the stove (roast).

tip

Unless there's only one Sim in the household, always prepare group meals. It takes no extra time, and even though it costs more money, a group meal makes six times the amount of food for only three times the cost of a single meal. It's less expensive than letting the other Sims on the lot autonomously make their own single servings of generic meals (which are less nutritious than what you can make with a well-trained and controlled Sim).

Refrigerators differ in two factors: Hunger satisfaction of their contents and in the ingredients available.

Refrigerator Bonuses

The same ingredients and generic meals (except snacks) have different Hunger satisfaction power, depending on the fridge from which they were pulled. In fact, each fridge modifies everything taken from it by a fixed bonus amount:

- EconoCool Refrigerator: 0
- Chow Town Eco-Fridge: +5
- Nostalgix Refrigerator: +10
- Stainless Steel Fridge: +15

Refrigerators do not alter foods' other Motive effects or their special effects (if any).

Ingredient Selection

In the food-creation system, different refrigerators contain different ingredients. The more expensive the fridge, the wider the selection.

The most expensive fridge offers all ingredients.

note

Harvested fruits, vegetables, and animals have the same selection regardless of the fridge. The differences in selection apply only to ingredients "bought" from the fridge.

Food Selection by Fridge

Ingredient	Category	EconoCool Refrigerator	Chow Town Eco-Fridge	Nostalgix Refrigerator	Stainless Steel Fridge
Apple	Fruit		X	X	X
Banana	Fruit				X
Beef	Meat	X	X	X	X
Beet	Vegetable				X
Broccoli	Vegetable			X	X
Broth	Liquid		X	X	X
Butter	Oil		X	X	X
Canola Oil	Oil		X	X	X
Carrot	Vegetable	X	X	X	X
Celery	Vegetable	X	X	X	X

Ingredient	Category	EconoCool Refrigerator	Chow Town Eco-Fridge	Nostalgix Refrigerator	Stainless Steel Fridge
Cheese	Dairy				X
Cherry	Fruit		X	X	X
Chicken	Meat	X	X	X	X
Corn Oil	Oil	X	X	X	X
Egg	Dairy	X	X	X	X
Fauxlestra	Oil				X
Juice	Liquid				X
Lamb	Meat		X	X	X
Lemon	Fruit	X	X	X	X
Lettuce	Vegetable		X	X	X
Lime	Fruit	X	X	X	X
Llama	Meat				X
Milk	Dairy	X	X	X	X
Oat Flour	Grain				X
Olive Oil	Oil	X	X	X	X
Onion	Vegetable	X	X	X	X
Orange	Fruit	X	X	X	X
Ostrich	Meat				X
Peanut Oil	Oil	X	X	X	X
Pork	Meat	X	X	X	X
Potato	Vegetable	X	X	X	X
Rye	Grain		X	X	X
Sourdough	Grain	X	X	X	X
Soy Flour	Grain		X	X	X
Soy Milk	Dairy		X	X	X
Strawberry	Fruit				X
Tofu	Meat	X	X	X	X
Tomato	Vegetable				X
Turkey	Meat		X	X	X
Water	Liquid	X	X	X	X
White Flour	Grain	X	X	X	X
Whole Wheat Flour	Grain	X	X	X	X
Yogurt	Dairy		X	X	X

Food Preparation

Ingredients can be eaten directly out of the fridge or go straight to the stove, but more Hunger satisfaction is had with some preparation. Some preparation methods are the final step in the cooking process while others result in a pot of food ready to meet the heat of the stove.

Whether it's at a counter or in a food processor, more Hunger satisfaction is added with a prep stage.

tip
It's tempting to skip preparation to save time, but it's not a wise tradeoff, especially early in the game. First, you're losing considerable Hunger satisfaction by not going through more steps. Second, and more important, your Sims develop Cooking skill while cooking, so the more steps they use to make a meal, the more Cooking skill they acquire. Multitasking is way more efficient than making a quick meal, studying cooking at the bookshelf, and having to make another meal sooner because the first wasn't very satisfying. Sims go longer before the next meal and get more Cooking skill in the same time by fully preparing the meal and THEN sitting down to study (or do whatever).

Food can be prepped in or on two things:

◆ Countertops: Food can be prepped for the stove or for uncooked meals on any open countertop or on top of a dishwasher (which acts like a countertop). Hand-prepping food on the countertop is slower and adds fewer Hunger points to the process than if you use the food processor. If you can't afford the food processor, or if you desire the food that results from raw prepping, the countertop is all you need.

◆ Food Processor: The food processor is faster, adds more Hunger satisfaction than the countertop, and makes a different variety of foods from the same ingredients. It also acts as a food completion device for an uncooked result. Any prepped, cooked, or leftover food can be converted into pet food when it's taken for a spin in the food processor.

note
When deciding what to do with ingredients once you take them from the fridge, stand your Sim in front of a counter, appliance, or stove to see what interactions are available. In general, if the interaction stars with the word "Prep," it means that using it results in a pot of food to be cooked on the stove. If the interaction starts with "Make," it means selecting it creates a final product.

Completion

Foods can be completed in many different ways.

note
Blenders and counters get dirty. If you complete food in a dirty blender or on a dirty counter, it adds 2 to the meal's nausea effect.

To choose the next step, carry the food to the counter, processor, blender, or stove and choose what you want to make or prep.

Ingredients directly from the fridge can be finished without a preparation step (raw); on the counter; or in the food processor, blender, or stove. These results require no prep and contain only Hunger satisfaction from the ingredients, the fridge, and the device used to complete them.

 note

Microwave ovens act as stoves as far as the results they produce, but they have some advantages and disadvantages. Cooking foods in the microwave is faster than on the stove, but it adds 1 to the resulting food's nausea effect and deducts 5 from its Hunger satisfaction.

Prepped foods can receive an additional infusion of Hunger satisfaction if prepared on a stove. The amount of Hunger added to the food depends on the quality of the stove—the more expensive it is, the more Hunger satisfaction it imparts.

Grilling

The Grillinator "BigBQ" grill is not a completion device for any foods except those taken from its built-in cooler. It can't, therefore, act as a stove for anything extracted from a refrigerator.

Instead, for §25, your Sim pulls a generic barbeque meal from the grill and cooks it for a dish that supplies the following:

- Hunger: 31
- Energy: 5
- Bladder: -20

Cooking Skill

Cooking skill can be learned from books.

Cooking skill has several effects on food:

- Time: Reduces the time it takes to prep and cook food with all devices and countertops.
- Hunger Satisfaction: Imparts additional Hunger satisfaction with every step.
- Fire: Reduces the chance of fire when using stoves (level 5 or higher makes your Sim accident-proof).

Or you could just have your Sims cook A LOT and get all their Cooking skill from time served in the kitchen.

Cooking skill is learned passively from studying Cooking at any bookshelf or learned practically by cooking. The latter is the most efficient since it permits your Sims to produce a meal and develop skill simultaneously.

 tip

The payoff of having a high-level Cooking Sim early in the game is tremendous. The time and Motive efficiency of always having nutritious food to eat is unmatched by any other strategy. Spend more time than you think necessary in early lots studying Cooking.

Ingredients and Meals

Now that you know how the hardware works, let's talk software: the ingredients.

Food ingredients are the raw materials that your Sim uses to make meals. To master the kitchen in *The Sims 2 Pets*, you must understand how ingredients work and how they are combined.

Ingredient Attributes

The stats you see in the ingredient selection screen are only small parts of the equation.

Your Sims cook using 79 ingredients, each with unique attributes. These attributes come in two forms—basic and special.

Basic Attributes

Every food is identified by several factors:

- Type: This lets you know in what drawer of the fridge you can find it and controls how the ingredient is used in food combinations.
- Cost: Cost is per individual serving and is the same in every fridge. When making group meals (six servings), the ingredients' cost is tripled.
- Hunger: This is the number of points toward Hunger satisfaction. This number is altered by the fridge from which the ingredient comes, the objects used in its preparation, the Cooking skill of the chef, and other minor factors.

* Energy: This is the amount of Energy Motive satisfaction supplied by eating the food.
* Fun: Several ingredients are just a hoot to eat and satisfy the Fun Motive when consumed. This value isn't shown in the fridge or food descriptions you see onscreen. It also contributes to a food's potential for an Energy boost effect.
* Bladder: This is the amount of Bladder Motive DEPLETED by consuming the food. The greater the amount of Bladder reduction in the foods your Sims eat, the more often they have to visit the toilet. Choose your foods to balance the highest possible Hunger satisfaction with the least possible Bladder depletion, or much of the time you gain with good cooking will be lost in more-frequent potty breaks.

When food is prepared, these factors are simply added to determine the food's cost and final attributes.

The types of the ingredients determine what dish results, regardless of the specific ingredients. For example, any combination of a grain, a vegetable, and a fruit results in the same dish from each possible prep and completion. Make it in a food processor, and you always get a jam and veggie sandwich. The attributes of the particular sandwich you make, however, depend on the specific ingredients used.

Special Attributes

Every food has at least one special attribute that can combine to make the food even more powerful. Understand how these attributes function and how the resulting food is crafted, and you can create your own edible power-ups.

Love is in the air, or so that heart-spouting dish would suggest. That is evidence of a very special effect.

Most attributes work by accumulation. If the finished product contains 3 or more points in any attribute, the final food is imbued with the attribute's effect. If, therefore, three ingredients feature 1 point of nausea each, the resulting food causes anyone who eats it to immediately vomit. If all ingredients add up to less than 3 points of nausea, the food does not cause nausea.

note

Note that food attributes can be increased or reduced by other forces. For example, using a dirty blender or countertop adds 2 nausea points to any food made in it. If, therefore, there is already 1 nausea point in the ingredients, the 2 from the dirty blender convert the meal into a gastronomical boomerang.

There are five special attributes:

* Repulse: Food emits black hearts, and its description reads, "While there's nothing about this food that looks improper, there's something about it that makes you feel vaguely angry about it."
* Diuretic: Food drips water droplets and, when consumed, depletes the eater's Bladder Motive by nearly half (-40). If your Sims are even a bit below medium in that Motive, they immediately wet the floor. Description of the final product reads, "Just looking at this makes your stomach gurgle. Something about it just isn't right, but you feel like maybe if you were going to eat it, you should be somewhere near a restroom."
* Nausea: Food emits a green haze and, when consumed, causes the eater to immediately vomit. As a side effect, this dramatically depletes Hygiene Motive (-60). Description of the final product reads, "Something about it doesn't look quite right, and frankly, that makes you feel a bit sick to your stomach."
* Attract: Food emits red hearts. Description of the final product reads, "You can't take your eyes off it. It's the most beautiful thing you've ever seen."
* Skill Boost: Food emits stars, and anyone who eats it has all skills boosted by three levels for a short time. Description of the final product reads, "There's something about this food that just looks perfect. Each piece is perfectly placed, every aspect of it is expertly prepared. Merely being in its presence makes you feel better about yourself."

The description of the finished food provides clues as to its effects.

The visual effect around the food (hearts, stars, etc.) and the food's description confirm which effect, if any, the food contains. If a food contains no special effects, the description reads, "It looks tasty and well prepared."

Foods may have more than one effect if the ingredients combine for more than 3 points in several attributes. Only the strongest, however, is indicated by the visual effect and the description, so check your ingredients carefully in this book to make sure there isn't a lesser effect that will cause problems. Nothing is more unseemly than an aphrodisiac that induces vomiting.

One special effect works a bit differently: the Energy boost. Above and beyond the inherent Energy satisfaction effect of the food, the right combination can offer an even greater pick-me-up.

A food contains an Energy boost if the ingredients' collective Energy, Fun, and Skill boost attributes equal more than 80. If so, the resulting food has an additional 30-point boost to Energy Motive for a short time. Food

with an Energy boost effect emits sparks, and the resulting description reads, "One look at this dish and you know that if you ate it, you could take on the world. Or leap over tall buildings. Well, maybe not the tall buildings thing."

Ingredient Sources

Ingredients come from three sources:

◆ Refrigerators ◆ Harvesting Objects ◆ Other Sources

Refrigerator Ingredients

Most ingredients come from refrigerators. The supply of these ingredients is infinite, but each serving costs a fixed number of Simoleons. The cost triples if your Sim makes a six-serving group meal (what a bargain).

The ingredients available in each fridge depend on the appliance's quality and cost. The more expensive the fridge, the wider the selection of built-in ingredients. To get all possible refrigerator ingredients, you must purchase the Stainless Steel Fridge.

Harvesting Objects

Scooping fish out of this tank is one of the best ways to cook.

Nine objects can provide potentially infinite sources of free food:

Resource Type	Level 1 Object	Level 2 Object	Level 3 Object
Fruit	"Frood" Tree	"Frood" Tree 2.0	"Frood" Orchard
Seafood (Harvested Animals)	Guppy Pond	Atlantis Jr.	"Manila 1000" Marine Aquarium
Vegetables	GenoLife Garden Hutch	GenoLife Grande Garden Hutch	GenoLife Garden Hutch Supreme

Each object yields only some of the possible fruits, fish, or vegetables. To have the full selection, you must have all three objects of each type. If, however, you only want to have the tree, garden, or tank that provides the exact product you need, it pays to know what comes from where:

Ingredient	Category	Level 1	Level 2	Level 3
Asparagus	Vegetable			X
Avocado	Vegetable		X	
Bell Pepper	Vegetable			X

Ingredient	Category	Level 1	Level 2	Level 3
Bok Choy	Vegetable		X	
Carrot	Vegetable	X		
Chupa-Chupa	Fruit			X
Coconut	Fruit	X		
Cod	Meat		X	
Crayfish	Meat		X	
Dangleberry	Fruit			X
Edamame	Vegetable		X	
Eel	Meat		X	
Grapes	Fruit		X	
Halibut	Meat	X		
Jicama	Vegetable			X
Lobster	Meat			X
Mangosteen	Fruit			X
Mini-Swordfish	Meat			X
Passionfruit	Fruit	X		
Peas	Vegetable	X		
Persimmon	Fruit		X	
Pineapple	Fruit		X	
Plum	Fruit	X		
Portabella Mushroom	Vegetable			X
Prawns	Meat	X		
Purslane	Vegetable			X
Raspberry	Fruit	X		
Red Snapper	Meat			X
Salmon	Meat		X	
Shark	Meat			X
Soursop	Fruit		X	
Spinach	Vegetable	X		
Squid	Meat			X
Starfruit	Fruit			X
Tuna	Meat	X		
White Truffle	Vegetable			X

The vegetable gardens and the fruit trees function identically. Ripe fruit or vegetables are picked off them and added to refrigerator inventory ("Harvested Fruit" or "Harvested Vegetables") with the Harvest interaction. Both must be watered every day, or the tree/garden stops producing. If neglected long enough, the resource dies. Dead plants must be replaced with the Replant interaction, and the new plant must be watered for two days before it can produce again.

The aquariums function similarly. You must feed the fish every day or they'll die, requiring a tank restock. The tank must also be cleaned regularly. A dirty tank adds 1 Bladder attribute to every fish harvested from it while it's dirty.

All harvested ingredients in the refrigerator are finite and will run out if not restocked.

Other Sources

An extremely powerful food is obtained from an unexpected place. The Golden Egg is won by defeating the chicken in Prof. Feather's Chicken Checkers.

Regular games of Chicken Checkers with a high Logic Sim should supply a steady flow of Golden Eggs.

note

Prof. Feather's Chicken Checkers can be purchased from the Town Square's Pet Emporium, but only after the emporium has been upgraded to its highest "Awesome" level. Start spending those Pet Points at the emporium if you want to cook with Golden Eggs.

As with other harvested foods, these go automatically into the harvested drawers of the fridge ("Animals").

Ingredient Directory

note

Harvested fruits and veggies qualify as "Fruits" and "Vegetables," respectively, and harvested animals count as "Meat."

The following table lists every ingredient and its attributes:

Ingredient	Type	Cost	Hunger	Energy	Fun	Bladder	Repulse	Healthy	Diuretic	Nausea	Attract
Apple	Fruit	§3	9	0	0	-10	0	1	1	0	0
Asparagus	Vegetable	§0	9	0	0	-10	0	1	0	0	0
Avocado	Vegetable	§0	12	0	5	-2	0	1	0	0	1
Banana	Fruit	§3	6	10	10	-2	0	1	0	1	1
Beef	Meat	§6	15	0	0	-10	0	0	0	0	0
Beet	Vegetable	§5	9	0	10	-2	0	0	0	1	0
Bell Pepper	Vegetable	§2	8	5	0	-5	0	0	1	0	0
Bok Choy	Vegetable	§0	8	10	0	-2	0	1	1	0	0
Broccoli	Vegetable	§3	8	5	10	-5	0	1	0	0	0
Broth	Liquid	§5	8	0	0	-5	0	0	0	0	0
Butter	Oil	§5	5	0	5	-5	0	0	0	0	0
Canola Oil	Oil	§5	4	0	0	-5	0	1	1	0	0
Carrot	Vegetable	§3	6	0	10	-2	0	1	0	0	1
Celery	Vegetable	§2	8	10	0	-10	0	0	1	0	0
Cheese	Dairy	§4	8	0	0	-10	1	1	0	1	0
Cherry	Fruit	§6	6	10	0	-2	0	0	0	0	1
Chicken	Meat	§5	15	-2	0	-10	1	1	0	0	0
Chupa-Chupa	Fruit	§0	9	0	10	-2	0	0	0	0	0
Coconut	Fruit	§3	6	10	5	-2	0	0	0	0	0
Cod	Meat	§5	9	10	5	-10	0	0	1	0	1
Corn Oil	Oil	§2	6	0	0	-5	0	0	0	0	0
Crayfish	Meat	§8	12	15	10	-10	0	0	1	0	0
Dangleberry	Fruit	§0	30	25	25	-25	2	0	0	0	0
Edamame	Vegetable	§4	10	10	5	-2	1	2	0	0	0
Eel	Meat	§0	9	25	10	-15	0	0	1	1	0
Egg	Dairy	§2	10	5	0	-5	0	1	0	0	0
Fauxlestra	Oil	§2	5	0	0	-10	0	0	1	1	0
Golden Egg	Dairy	§0	10	5	10	-5	0	2	0	0	1
Grapes	Fruit	§2	6	10	5	-5	1	0	0	0	0
Halibut	Meat	§0	9	10	10	-10	0	1	0	1	1
Jicama	Vegetable	§0	10	0	0	-2	2	1	0	0	0
Juice	Liquid	§3	6	1	0	-10	0	0	0	1	0
Lamb	Meat	§7	18	0	0	-10	0	0	0	0	0
Lemon	Fruit	§2	6	10	0	-2	0	0	0	0	0
Lettuce	Vegetable	§2	6	10	0	-2	0	0	1	0	0
Lime	Fruit	§2	6	10	0	-2	0	0	0	0	0
Llama	Meat	§15	15	20	10	-15	0	0	0	0	1
Lobster	Meat	§0	18	20	15	-15	0	0	0	1	2
Mangosteen	Fruit	§0	6	25	10	-2	0	2	1	0	1
Milk	Dairy	§2	8	0	0	-10	1	1	0	0	0
Mini-Swordfish	Meat	§0	14	15	25	-5	0	1	1	1	2
Oats	Grain	§4	12	10	0	-5	0	1	0	0	0
Olive Oil	Oil	§5	3	0	10	-5	0	1	0	0	0
Onion	Vegetable	§2	8	0	-10	-2	0	0	0	0	0
Orange	Fruit	§2	6	10	0	-2	0	0	0	0	0
Ostrich	Meat	§12	9	30	0	-10	0	1	0	0	1
Passionfruit	Fruit	§0	9	10	0	-2	0	0	0	0	2
Peanut Oil	Oil	§2	2	0	10	-5	0	0	0	0	0
Peas	Vegetable	§2	6	5	10	-2	0	0	0	0	0
Persimmon	Fruit	§0	9	10	0	-2	0	0	0	0	0
Pineapple	Fruit	§0	9	15	15	-10	1	0	1	0	1
Plum	Fruit	§0	9	10	0	-2	0	2	2	0	0
Pork	Meat	§5	9	10	0	-10	0	0	0	0	0
Portabella Mushroom	Vegetable	§0	11	5	10	-2	0	2	0	0	1
Potato	Vegetable	§2	10	0	0	-2	0	0	0	0	0
Prawns	Meat	§0	9	10	10	-5	0	0	0	1	0
Purslane	Vegetable	§0	6	0	5	-2	0	2	0	0	0
Raspberry	Fruit	§2	6	10	0	-2	0	0	1	0	1
Red Snapper	Meat	§0	9	10	10	-10	0	1	1	1	1
Rye	Grain	§5	9	0	10	-5	0	1	0	0	0
Salmon	Meat	§5	9	10	10	-10	0	1	0	0	1
Shark	Meat	§0	18	20	15	-10	0	0	0	0	2
Sourdough	Grain	§5	12	5	5	-10	1	0	0	0	1
Soursop	Fruit	§0	9	0	0	-2	2	0	2	0	0
Soy Flour	Grain	§4	9	5	5	-5	0	1	0	1	0
Soy Milk	Dairy	§6	8	5	0	-5	0	0	1	0	0
Spinach	Vegetable	§0	6	10	0	-2	0	2	0	0	0
Squid	Meat	§0	14	15	25	-5	0	1	1	2	0
Starfruit	Fruit	§0	9	10	15	-2	0	0	0	0	1

Ingredient	Type	Cost	Hunger	Energy	Fun	Bladder	Repulse	Healthy	Diuretic	Nausea	Attract
Strawberry	Fruit	§5	9	20	0	-2	0	1	1	0	1
Tofu	Meat	§5	9	10	0	-5	0	2	0	1	0
Tomato	Vegetable	§5	9	0	0	-5	0	0	0	0	1
Tuna	Meat	§0	9	15	0	-5	0	1	1	1	0
Turkey	Meat	§4	15	-10	5	-10	1	1	0	0	0
Water	Liquid	§0	2	0	0	-10	0	0	0	0	0
White Flour	Grain	§3	9	0	0	-5	1	0	0	0	0
White Truffle	Vegetable	§0	15	0	30	-2	0	1	0	0	2
Whole Wheat Flour	Grain	§4	9	0	10	-5	0	1	0	1	0
Yogurt	Dairy	§5	8	0	10	-5	0	1	0	0	0

Food Combinations and Results

The secret to crafting food with exactly the effects you desire is knowing how they combine.

 note

You may use only one of each ingredient, but you may use multiple ingredients in the same type. Though the second ingredient of the same type adds its attribute points to the final result, it doesn't determine what the dish is. Two pieces of meat completed in the stove make a roast just as if you used one piece. The dish does, however, benefit from the extra attribute points of the additional ingredient.

Generally, food can be made from one to four ingredients, and its effects are the sum of the ingredients' individual attributes, both basic and special. The food's final Hunger satisfaction attribute is increased by the equipment used to prepare it.

The next question, therefore, is *what* to cook. Frankly, you can take any one or combine any four ingredients and get something edible, or you could consider only the ingredients and their effects and make whatever results.

Sometimes, however, it's better to know what you're going to get before you select ingredients. There are two sources for this: in-game recipes and this book.

Recipes

Thirty recipes are always available for you to use in your Sim's cooking. Found in both the Pause menu and via each fridge's Get Ingredients interaction, the recipe book is an excellent reference and a tool for quickly making complex meals.

Each recipe displays the required ingredients and what if any prep and cooking stages will be required. To quickly assemble a recipe's ingredients, access the recipe book through the fridge, highlight the recipe you want, and press the Select Recipe Ingredients button. This quickly puts all the required ingredients in your Sim's hands; doing the correct prep and cooking process is still up to you.

Recipe Book

Dish	Cost per Serving	Ingredient 1	Ingredient 2	Ingredient 3	Ingredient 4	Prep	Completion	Hunger	Bladder	Energy
Roast	§6	Beef	—	—	—	—	Stove	19	-10	0
Sandwich	§12	Beef	Onion	Whole Wheat Flour	—	—	Counter	47	-17	0
Sweet Vegetable Soup	§2	Carrot	Lime	Passionfruit	—	Counter	Stove	30	-6	20
Fruit Shake	§10	Strawberry	Yogurt	—	—	—	Blended	24	-7	20
Fruitspacho	§5	Apple	Peanut Oil	—	—	—	Processor	16	-20	0
Salad	§7	Lettuce	Olive Oil	—	—	—	Counter	10	-7	10
Chef's Salad	§5	Shark	Yogurt	Bok Choy	Plum	—	Counter	59	-19	40
Ceviche	§4	Halibut	Lime	Corn Oil	—	—	Counter	27	-12	20
Hors D'Oeuvres	§17	Llama	White Truffle	Fauxlestra	—	—	Counter	42	-7	15
Soup	§5	Squid	Juice	Milk	—	Processor	Stove	37	-25	16
Fruit in Pastry	§8	Juice	White Flour	Dangleberry	Corn Oil	Counter	Stove	68	-35	26
Samosas	§4	Mini-Swordfish	Oat Flour	Soursop	—	Processor	Stove	42	-12	35
Combo Pizza	§16	Turkey	Cheese	White Flour	Tomato	Counter	Stove	57	-25	-10
Roast & Fruit Sauce	§14	Beef	Whole Wheat Flour	Orange	Fauxlestra	—	Stove	50	-15	10
Salad-in-a-Cup	§6	Milk	Lettuce	Corn Oil	—	—	Blended	24	-12	10
Burrito	§14	Beef	Broth	White Flour	Avocado	Processor	Stove	60	-17	0
Kebabs	§17	Llama	Onion	Chupa-Chupa	—	—	Counter	42	-9	15
Parfait	§14	Cherry	Yogurt	Juice	—	—	Counter	Stove	30	-17	11

Recipe Book continued

Dish	Cost per Serving	Ingredient 1	Ingredient 2	Ingredient 3	Ingredient 4	Prep	Completion	Hunger	Bladder	Energy
Fruit Smoothie	§7	Yogurt	Soursop	Fauxlestra	—	—	Processor	28	-7	10
Gratin Shake	§7	Cheese	Broccoli	—	—	—	Blended	25	-15	5
Wellington Roast	§19	Beef	Broth	White Flour	Canola Oil	—	Stove	48	-20	0
Ceviche Puree	§7	Lobster	Lime	Olive Oil	—	—	Processor	33	-22	30
Cheeseless Pizza	§4	Golden Egg	Oat Flour	Carrot	Soursop	Processor	Stove	49	-14	20
Casserole	§5	Pork	Golden Egg	Spinach	Dangleberry	Processor	Stove	82	-42	45
Lasagna	§26	Ostrich	Cheese	Sourdough	Tomato	—	Stove	51	-35	35
Dumpling Stew	§7	Salmon	Crayfish	Egg	Rye	—	Stove	51	-30	30
Jam Sandwich	§10	Soy Flour	Whole Wheat Flour	Mangosteen	Corn Oil	Processor	—	42	-12	30
Pizza	§28	Tofu	Cheese	Whole Wheat Flour	Llama	Counter	Stove	54	-25	25
Vege Stir Fry	§2	Carrot	Celery	Bok Choy	Edamame	Counter	Stove	39	-16	30
Barbeque Sausage	§10	Pork	Orange	Passionfruit	Bananas	Processor	Stove	50	-14	40

Though the recipes simplify the Direct Control cooking process, you don't really need them to create food. It's much more important to know how the system works so you can independently make these recipes and scores of others. For that, you need to look under the game's hood a bit.

Food Type Combinations

Which food you get from combining ingredients is a result of up to three elements:

* Type of Each Ingredient: For determining the result rather than the food's statistics. The specific ingredient within the type isn't important.
* Prep Equipment (if any): Counter, food processor
* Completion Equipment (if any): Counter, food processor, blender, stove

This information can be used so you know how to make a specific dish. If, for example, you wanted to make a pizza, you know you need to combine any meat, any dairy, and any grain, prep it on the counter, and bake it in the stove. This doesn't tell you what the food's attributes are, but you can backward-engineer the result by considering the actual ingredients.

The more useful way to employ this information is to design a food that does what you want it to do. For this, use the attribute data in the "Ingredient Directory" to determine what ingredients you wish to use, then check the "Food Results by Type Combinations and Prep/Completion" table to see what (based on their types) they combine to form, using each prep/completion tool.

tip

IF maximum Hunger satisfaction is essential to any meal you cook, always utilize both the Food processor and the stove.

Food Results by Type Combinations and Prep/Completion

Ingredient 1	Ingredient 2	Ingredient 3	Ingredient 4	Raw	Counter Complete	Food Processor Complete	Stove Complete (No Prep)	Counter Prep and Stove Complete	Food Processor Prep and Stove Complete	Blender Complete
Dairy	—	—	—	Drink	Drink	Drink	Drink	Drink	Drink	Drink
Dairy	Grain	—	—	Ingredients	Dough	Dough	Bread	Bread	Bread	Dough Slurry
Dairy	Vegetable	—	—	Ingredients	Bowl of Soup	Bowl of Soup	Bowl of Soup	Gratin	Gratin	Gratin Shake
Dairy	Fruit	—	—	Ingredients	Fruit Salad	Shake	Fruit Sauce	Fruit Sauce	Fruit Shake	Smoothie
Dairy	Oil	—	—	Power Shake	Power Shake	Power Shake	Power Shake	Power Shake	Power Shake	Power Shake
Dairy	Grain	Vegetable	—	Ingredients	Vegetable Sandwich	Vegetable Sandwich	Veggie Bread	Veggie Bread	Veggie Bread	Veggie Power Shake
Dairy	Grain	Fruit	—	Ingredients	Jam Sandwich	Jam Sandwich	Fruity Bread	Fruity Bread	Fruity Bread	Fruity Power Shake
Dairy	Grain	Oil	—	Ingredients	Raw Dough	Raw Dough	Foccacia	Foccacia	Foccacia	Power Shake
Dairy	Vegetable	Fruit	—	Ingredients	Soup	Soup	Soup	Casserole	Casserole	Drink
Dairy	Vegetable	Oil	—	Ingredients	Salad	Salad	Salad	Salad	Salad	Salad-in-a-Cup
Dairy	Fruit	Oil	—	Ingredients	Fruit Salad	Smoothie	Fruit Soup	Fruit Soup	Fruit Soup	Smoothie
Dairy	Grain	Vegetable	Fruit	Ingredients	Veggies on Toast	Soup	Bread	Veggie Casserole	Veggie Casserole	Veggie Shake
Dairy	Grain	Vegetable	Oil	Ingredients	Sandwich	Sandwich	Quiche	Veggie Pizza	Veggie Burrito	Veggie Shake
Dairy	Grain	Fruit	Oil	Ingredients	Toast & Jam	Fruit Soup	Fruit Foccacia	Fruit Foccacia	Fruit Foccacia	Fruit Shake

Food Results by Type Combinations and Prep/Completion continued

Ingredient 1	Ingredient 2	Ingredient 3	Ingredient 4	Raw	Counter Complete	Food Processor Complete	Stove Complete (No Prep)	Counter Prep and Stove Complete	Food Processor Prep and Stove Complete	Blender Complete
Fruit	—	—	—	Ingredients	Bowl of Fruit	Fruit Smoothie	Fruit Soup	Fruit Compote	Fruit Compote	Fruit Smoothie
Fruit	Oil	—	—	Ingredients	Marinated Fruit	Fruitspacho	Fruit Stew	Bowl of Preserves	Bowl of Jam	Drink
Grain	—	—	—	Ingredients	Dough	Dough	Bread	Bread	Bread	Dough Smoothie
Grain	Vegetable	—	—	Ingredients	Veggie Sandwich	Veggie Sandwich	Veggie Casserole	Veggie Casserole	Veggie Casserole	Veggie Power Shake
Grain	Fruit	—	—	Ingredients	Jam & Toast	Fruit Slurry	Fruity Bread	Fruity Bread	Fruit Pancake	Drink
Grain	Oil	—	—	Ingredients	Bowl of Stuff	Bowl of Stuff	Foccacia	Foccacia	Foccacia	Drink
Grain	Vegetable	Fruit	—	Ingredients	Jam & Vegetable Panini	Jam & Vegetable Panini	Bread	Casserole	Casserole	Fruit Smoothie
Grain	Vegetable	Oil	—	Ingredients	Vegetable Panini	Vegetable Panini	Foccacia	Foccacia	Foccacia	Vegetable Smoothie
Grain	Fruit	Oil	—	Ingredients	Sandwich	Sandwich	Foccacia	Foccacia	Foccacia	Fruit Smoothie
Grain	Vegetable	Fruit	Oil	Ingredients	Leftovers	Pureed Leftovers	Vegetable Fruit Foccacia	Vegetable Fruit Foccacia	Vegetable Fruit Foccacia	Smoothie
Liquid	—	—	—	Drink	Drink	Drink	Drink	Drink	Drink	Drink
Liquid	Dairy	—	—	Ingredients	Drink	Drink	Bowl of Soup	Bowl of Soup	Bowl of Soup	Smoothie
Liquid	Grain	—	—	Ingredients	Raw Dough	Raw Dough	Bread	Bread	Bread	Power Smoothie
Liquid	Vegetable	—	—	Ingredients	Veggies & Dip	Gazpacho	Stew	Casserole	Casserole	Veggie Smoothie
Liquid	Fruit	—	—	Ingredients	Glazed Fruit	Smoothie	Fruit Compote	Fruit Compote	Smoothie	Fruit Smoothie
Liquid	Oil	—	—	Ingredients	Bowl of Soup	Power Smoothie	Bowl of Soup	Bowl of Soup	Bowl of Soup	Power Smoothie
Liquid	Dairy	Grain	—	Ingredients	Dough	Dough	Bread	Bread	Bread	Drink
Liquid	Dairy	Vegetable	—	Ingredients	Vegetable Soup	Vegetable Soup	Vegetable Soup	Vegetable Soup	Vegetable Soup	Drink
Liquid	Dairy	Fruit	—	Ingredients	Fruit Soup	Fruit Shake	Parfait	Parfait	Fruit Shake	Fruit Shake
Liquid	Dairy	Oil	—	Ingredients	Creamy Soup	Creamy Soup	Creamy Soup	Creamy Soup	Creamy Soup	Drink
Liquid	Grain	Vegetable	—	Ingredients	Veggie Dough	Veggie Dough	Veggie Bread	Veggie Bread	Veggie Bread	Veggie Power Shake
Liquid	Grain	Fruit	—	Ingredients	Fruit Dough	Fruit Dough	Fruity Bread	Fruity Bread	Fruity Bread	Fruity Power Shake
Liquid	Grain	Oil	—	Ingredients	Dough	Dough	Foccacia	Foccacia	Foccacia	Power Shake
Liquid	Vegetable	Fruit	—	Ingredients	Gazpacho	Veggie-Fruitspacho	Soup	Casserole	Casserole	Drink
Liquid	Vegetable	Oil	—	Ingredients	Salad	Salad	Salad	Salad	Salad	Salad-in-a-Cup
Liquid	Fruit	Oil	—	Ingredients	Fruit Salad	Smoothie	Fruit Soup	Fruit Soup	Fruit Soup	Smoothie
Liquid	Dairy	Grain	Vegetable	Ingredients	Sandwich	Sandwich	Dumpling Stew	Veggie Bread	Veggie Burrito	Veggie Shake
Liquid	Dairy	Grain	Fruit	Ingredients	Sandwich	Sandwich	Soup	Fruit Bread	Fruit Bread	Fruit Shake
Liquid	Dairy	Grain	Oil	Ingredients	Panini	Panini	Soup	Foccacia	Foccacia	Smoothie
Liquid	Dairy	Vegetable	Fruit	Ingredients	Salad	Soup	Salad	Salad	Soup	Smoothie
Liquid	Dairy	Vegetable	Oil	Ingredients	Salad	Veggie Smoothie	Salad	Salad	Soup	Veggie Smoothie
Liquid	Dairy	Fruit	Oil	Ingredients	Soup	Fruit Smoothie	Soup	Soup	Fruit Smoothie	Fruit Smoothie
Liquid	Grain	Vegetable	Fruit	Ingredients	Veggie Sandwich	Veggie Sandwich	Soup & Bread	Vegetables and Fruit Sauce	Casserole	Smoothie
Liquid	Grain	Vegetable	Oil	Ingredients	Panini	Panini	Soup & Bread	Bruschetta	Veggie Burrito	Veggie Smoothie
Liquid	Grain	Fruit	Oil	Ingredients	Jam Sandwich	Jam Sandwich	Soup & Bread	Fruit in Pastry	Fruit Compote	Fruit Shake
Liquid	Vegetable	Fruit	Oil	Ingredients	Salad	Smoothie	Soup	Vegetables with Fruit Sauce	Soup	Fruit Shake
Meat	—	—	—	Ingredients	Carpaccio	Tartar	Roast	Sliced Roast	Meatloaf	Slurry
Meat	Liquid	—	—	Ingredients	Carpaccio	Carpaccio Soup	Braised Roast	Braised Roast	Burrito	Drink
Meat	Dairy	—	—	Ingredients	Carpaccio	Carpaccio Soup	Roast	Roast	Burrito	Drink
Meat	Grain	—	—	Ingredients	Sloppy Joe	Sloppy Joe	Calzone	Open-Faced Sandwich	Burrito	Smoothie
Meat	Vegetable	—	—	Ingredients	Carpaccio	Tartar	Roast & Veggies	Stir-Fry	Meatloaf	Slurry
Meat	Fruit	—	—	Ingredients	Ceviche	Tartar	Barbeque	Barbeque	Barbeque	Slurry
Meat	Oil	—	—	Ingredients	Carpaccio	Smoothie	Seared Roast	Seared, Sliced Roast	Soup	Slurry
Meat	Liquid	Dairy	—	Ingredients	Marinated Carpaccio	Tartar	Soup	Soup	Soup	Slurry
Meat	Liquid	Grain	—	Ingredients	Sandwich	Sandwich	Soup	Soup	Casserole	Power Meat Smoothie
Meat	Liquid	Vegetable	—	Ingredients	Shabu-Shabu	Soup	Roast	Roast & Veggies	Casserole	Dinner-in-a-Cup
Meat	Liquid	Fruit	—	Ingredients	Carpaccio with Fruit Sauce	Fruity Stew	Roast	Roast & Fruit Sauce	Casserole	Leftover Puree

Ingredient 1	Ingredient 2	Ingredient 3	Ingredient 4	Raw	Counter Complete	Food Processor Complete	Stove Complete (No Prep)	Counter Prep and Stove Complete	Food Processor Prep and Stove Complete	Blender Complete
Meat	Liquid	Oil	—	Ingredients	Marinated Carpaccio	Tartar	Seared Roast	Seared, Sliced Roast	Casserole	Shake
Meat	Dairy	Grain	—	Ingredients	Sandwich	Sandwich	Dumpling Stew	Pizza	Casserole	Power Smoothie
Meat	Dairy	Vegetable	—	Ingredients	Sandwich	Sandwich	Roast & Veggies	Roast & Veggies	Burrito	Smoothie
Meat	Dairy	Fruit	—	Ingredients	Carpaccio with Fruit Sauce	Shake	Roast with Fruit Sauce	Roast with Fruit Sauce	Meaty-Fruity Soup	Sweet Shake
Meat	Dairy	Oil	—	Ingredients	Marinated Carpaccio	Shake	Roast	Sliced Roast	Soup	Slurry
Meat	Grain	Vegetable	—	Ingredients	Sandwich	Sandwich	Roast	Kebabs	Burrito	Power Slurry
Meat	Grain	Fruit	—	Ingredients	Sandwich	Sandwich	Roast	Sliced Roast	Casserole	Slurry
Meat	Grain	Oil	—	Ingredients	Panini	Panini	Wellington Roast	Sliced Wellington	Casserole	Slurry
Meat	Vegetable	Fruit	—	Ingredients	Hors D'Oeuvres	Ceviche Salsa	Roast & Veggies	Kebabs	Casserole	Sweet Slurry
Meat	Vegetable	Oil	—	Ingredients	Hors D'Oeuvres	Ceviche Salsa	Roast	Sliced Roast	Casserole	Slurry
Meat	Fruit	Oil	—	Ingredients	Ceviche	Ceviche Puree	Roast	Casserole	Casserole	Sweet Slurry
Meat	Liquid	Dairy	Grain	Ingredients	Sandwich	Sandwich	Toasted Sandwich	Pizza	Burrito	Slurry
Meat	Liquid	Dairy	Vegetable	Ingredients	Chef Salad	Stew	Stew	Stew	Casserole	Slurry
Meat	Liquid	Dairy	Fruit	Ingredients	Leftovers	Soup	Soup	Roast with Fruit Sauce	Casserole	Slurry
Meat	Liquid	Dairy	Oil	Ingredients	Soup	Soup	Soup	Soup	Soup	Slurry
Meat	Liquid	Grain	Vegetable	Ingredients	Sandwich	Sandwich	Roast	Sliced Roast	Burrito	Slurry
Meat	Liquid	Grain	Fruit	Ingredients	Sandwich	Sandwich	Roast	Sliced Roast	Casserole	Slurry
Meat	Liquid	Grain	Oil	Ingredients	Panini	Panini	Wellington Roast	Sliced Wellington	Lasagna	Slurry
Meat	Liquid	Vegetable	Fruit	Ingredients	Soup	Soup	Roast	Sliced Roast	Casserole	Sweet Slurry
Meat	Liquid	Vegetable	Oil	Ingredients	Chef Salad	Bowl of Soup	Roast	Kebabs	Casserole	Slurry
Meat	Liquid	Fruit	Oil	Ingredients	Leftovers	Bowl of Soup	Roast	Sliced Roast	Casserole	Slurry
Meat	Dairy	Grain	Vegetable	Ingredients	Chef Salad	Sandwich	Combo Pizza	Combo Pizza	Lasagna	Slurry
Meat	Dairy	Grain	Fruit	Ingredients	Sandwich	Sandwich	Hawaiian Pizza	Hawaiian Pizza	Hawaiian Pizza	Slurry
Meat	Dairy	Grain	Oil	Ingredients	Panini	Panini	Pizza	Pizza	Pizza	Slurry
Meat	Dairy	Vegetable	Fruit	Ingredients	Chef Salad	Pureed Leftovers	Roast	Casserole	Casserole	Slurry
Meat	Dairy	Vegetable	Oil	Ingredients	Chef Salad	Pureed Leftovers	Roast	Sliced Roast	Casserole	Slurry
Meat	Dairy	Fruit	Oil	Ingredients	Leftovers	Pureed Leftovers	Roast	Sliced Roast	Soup	Slurry
Meat	Grain	Vegetable	Fruit	Ingredients	Sandwich	Sandwich	Cheeseless Pizza	Cheeseless Pizza	Cheeseless Pizza	Slurry
Meat	Grain	Vegetable	Oil	Ingredients	Panini	Panini	Roast & Veggies	Pizza	Casserole	Slurry
Meat	Grain	Fruit	Oil	Ingredients	Panini	Panini	Roast & Fruit Sauce	Pizza	Casserole	Slurry
Meat	Vegetable	Fruit	Oil	Ingredients	Salad	Pureed Leftovers	Roast	Sliced Roast	Casserole	Slurry
Oil	—	—	—	Oil	Oil	Frothy Oil	Oil	Oil	Frothy Oil	Frothy Oil
Vegetable	—	—	—	Ingredients	Crudités	Slaw	Roast	Veggie Stir-Fry	Vegetable Soup	Juice
Vegetable	Fruit	—	—	Ingredients	Salad	Salad	Sweet Vegetable Soup	Sweet Vegetable Soup	Sweet Vegetable Soup	Shake
Vegetable	Oil	—	—	Ingredients	Salad	Salad	Warm Salad	Grilled Vegetable Salad	Salad	Salad-in-a-Cup
Vegetable	Fruit	Oil	—	Ingredients	Salad	Salad	Salad	Salad	Salad	Vegetable Smoothie

Making Pet Food at Home

Sure, your Sims could spend their hard-earned cash on expensive dog and cat food, but isn't it more satisfying to make it yourself?

Any plate of prepped, cooked, or served food can be put in the food processor to make a supply of pet food.

Every serving of Sim food makes three servings of pet food. The quality and form (wet or dry) of the resulting pet food depends on the Hunger satisfaction of the original food and the form it's in when placed in the processor (a bowl of Sim food makes wet food).

The higher the Hunger satisfaction of the original food, the better the quality and, therefore, more Hunger satisfaction the homemade pet food will possess.

Leftovers (served, uneaten plates of food) make only one serving of pet food.

Homemade pet food is added to your Sims' family inventory as if it were purchased from the Pet Emporium.

Chapter 23

UNLOCKABLES SUMMARY

There are many powerful and interesting things to unlock in *The Sims 2 Pets*. This chapter summarizes how to get each for your quick reference.

Pet Point Unlocks

Console Unlocks	Unlock Order	Pet Points Required
Pink Cat Bandana	1	115
Green Dog Shirt	2	597
Pink Cat Glasses	3	1,137
Green Dog Cowboy Hat	4	1,318
Orange Cat Hat	5	1,386
Pink Dog Bandana	6	1,794
Orange Dog Collar	7	2,369
Red Cat Fur Color	8	2,630
Pink Dog Marking Color	9	2,675
Green Dog Fur Color	10	3,000
Pink Cat Marking Color	11	3,585
Orange Cat Shirt	12	3,931
Green Cat Bandana	13	3,979
Blue Cat Fur Color	14	4,220
Green Dog Catseye Glasses	15	4,788
Blue Cat Glasses	16	5,216
Purple Dog Marking Color	17	5,294
Red Dog Fur Color	18	5,457
Purple Cat Marking Color	19	5,984
Green Cat Collar	20	6,483
Pink Dog Fur Color	21	6,613
Green Dog Bandana	22	6,713
Pink Dog Aviator Glasses	23	7,178

Console Unlocks	Unlock Order	Pet Points Required
Green Cat Glasses	24	7,730
Green Dog Collar	25	7,930
Red Dog Marking Color	26	7,989
Blue Cat Marking Color	27	8,377
Purple Cat Fur Color	28	8,958
Red Cat Marking Color	29	9,240
Blue Cat Hat	30	9,283
Green Dog Marking Color	31	9,586
Blue Dog Fur Color	32	10,170
Purple Dog Glasses	33	10,537
Green Cat Marking Color	34	10,590
Orange Cat Collar	35	10,810
Green Cat Shirt	36	11,371
Orange Dog Shirt	37	11,818
Pink Cat Fur Color	38	11,906
Pink Dog Golf Hat	39	12,052
Blue Dog Marking Color	40	12,566
Green Cat Fur Color	41	13,079
Panda Cat Marking	42	13,226
Zebra Dog Marking	43	13,314
Purple Dog Fur Color	44	13,761
Star Dog Marking	45	14,321
Bandit Mask Cat Marking	46	14,542

Townie Unlocks

As you accumulate Aspiration points for satisfying Sim Wants on every lot, certain point totals will add one or more new families of townies to the neighborhood population:

- 100 Aspiration Points: Prescott, Boyle
- 1,000 Aspiration Points: Seville, Mellon
- 10,000 Aspiration Points: Lambert, Lester
- 100,000 Aspiration Points: Wong, Pickens
- 1,000,000 Aspiration Points: Howard

Town Square Store Unlocks

Business	Pet Points Required to Upgrade to Good Level	Pet Points Required to Upgrade to Awesome Level	Upgrade Effect
Pet Bakery	360	400	More objects to buy
Pet Emporium	600	667	More objects to buy
Pet Purveyors	450	500	Larger selection of pets
Pet Salon	200	222	More Pet Accessories and Create-A-Pet options
Pet Toy Store	300	333	More objects to buy

Cart	Revealed by Spending Collective Pet Points	Pet Points Required to Upgrade to Good Level	Pet Points Required to Upgrade to Awesome Level
Coffee	Initially revealed	156	222
Ice Cream	200	345	345
Smoothie	400	385	385

Other Town Square Unlocks

When 80 percent of the stores and carts are at the second (or "Good") level, the fountain, the statue, and the kennel upgrade to Good.

When 40 percent of the stores and carts are Good and 60 percent of the buildings are at Awesome—the highest upgrade level—the fountain, statue, and kennel upgrade to Awesome.

> **note**
> Upgrades to the kennel reduce the per day cost of boarding a pet.

Obedience Trainer NPC

The Obedience Trainer NPC appears on the Town Square once four or more stores or carts are upgraded to Good.

Alien Pet Treat

If a Sim is abducted by aliens (by using a telescope at night), there's a chance he or she will return with some alien pet treats in inventory.

Any pet that eats one of these extraterrestrial delicacies will be temporarily but profoundly changed:

- Hunger, Energy, and Bladder Motives are set to maximum and their bars glow green.
- Pet Want changes to a Want to go to the Town Square.
- Pet behaves like a Hyper pet regardless of its actual Personality.
- The pet glows green.
- Pet's relationship with the Sim who gave it the treat dramatically rises.

Chapter 24

BUILD YOUR OWN ABODE

Whether you're building from scratch or modifying an existing lot, it pays to know your way around Build mode.

This section introduces all the tools and objects that make home building and improvement part of the pleasure of controlling your own little virtual people.

Walls and Fences

Walls are the most important part of a building, as they define indoors versus outdoors and delineate one room from the next. Fences are purely decorative, adorning your Sims' lawns or even any indoor space.

Despite their differences, walls and fences are laid out in exactly the same way.

Drag a straight or diagonal wall.

Select the wall or fence you want to use, place the tool where you wish the wall to begin, press the Tool button, and drag in the direction you wish the wall or fence to run. When you reach the end of the desired run, press the Tool button again, and the section is complete.

Diagonal and straight walls can't intersect, but they can meet at corners.

Walls and fences can be run parallel or perpendicular to the street or at 45-degree angles. Diagonal and straight runs, however, can't intersect each other.

You can lay out entire rooms at once by holding the Build Room button and dragging out the shape of the room you envision.

Build an entire room at once with the Build Room button.

Walls or fences to be removed are marked with Xs.

Remove walls and fences by selecting the Remove Wall tool in Build/Buy Catalog. Drag the removal tool along the unwanted wall or fence (red Xs appear over sections to be demolished) and press the Tool button to complete. Holding the Build Room button in the Removal mode enables deletion of entire rooms at once. The cost of removed walls and fences is refunded.

Walls cost §1 per section; fences vary (per section):

◆ Picket Fence: §4   ◆ Japanese Fence: §5
◆ Friendship Arch Fence: §8   ◆ Expensive Fence: §12

Wallpaper

Wallpaper can be applied to any wall segment using the Wallpaper tool. Select the wall covering you desire, place the tool at the end of the wall, and drag the length you wish to cover. At the end, press the Tool button again, and it's covered.

tip
When demolishing covered walls, strip the wallpaper off first, or you won't get the refund for it.

The Fill Room tool makes papering a breeze.

To paper an entire room at once, position the tool inside a room and press the Fill Room button. To do the same outside, position the tool outdoors. This papers every exterior wall, even in noncontiguous buildings.

Remove wall coverings and return the underlying walls to their bare state by entering the Wallpaper section of the Buy Catalog and pressing the Removal Mode button. Drag the Removal tool along the unwanted wallpapered sections (red Xs appear over sections to be stripped) and press the Tool button to complete. Entire rooms can be stripped if you hold the Uncover Room button. The cost of removed wallpaper segments is refunded.

Wallpapers range in cost from §1 to §5 per segment.

tip
The more expensive the wallpaper in a room, the higher the Room score.

Floors

Floors cover the bare grass under your Sims' feet, even in indoor spaces.

Floor coverings can be applied to any indoor or outdoor ground. Select the floor covering you desire and place the tool wherever you want to start placing tile. Press the Tool button once to place a single tile, or hold and drag to place a rectangle of tiles. At the end, release the button to apply the tiles.

Diagonal rooms automatically cut off corners of floor tiles that run outside the walls.

To carpet an entire room at once, position the tool inside a room and press the Fill Room button.

note
When flooring rooms with diagonal walls, it appears that tiles are placed in the corners outside the walls, but this is only the case before you release the Tool button. The finished floor deletes any portion that's outside the walls.

Red Xs mark floor tiles to be removed.

Remove floor tiles and return the underlying ground to its bare state by entering the Floors section of the Buy Catalog and pressing the Removal Mode button. Drag the Removal tool along the unwanted floor tiles (red Xs appear over sections to be demolished) and press the Tool button to complete. Entire rooms can be uncovered if you hold the Uncover Room button. The cost of removed floor tiles is refunded.

Floor coverings range in cost from §1 to §5 per segment.

tip
The more expensive the floor covering in a room, the higher the Room score.

Doors

Doors provide access between indoor and outdoor spaces and between indoor rooms.

Doors can't be hung on diagonal walls.

Doors are hung on empty wall segments and can be rotated for the desired swing. Doors can't be placed along diagonal walls.

Making Diagonal Rooms

To make a room diagonal, there must be some part of it that features straight walls so that doors may be installed.

Build a straight room adjacent to a diagonal room and make their walls meet at the corners.

You may then put doors on any of the nondiagonal walls.

To solve this problem, run a straight wall up to a corner of the diagonal room. Run another straight wall parallel to the first so it lines up with another diagonal corner. Delete any diagonal walls that separate the two spaces, and you have one big room with both diagonal and straight walls and, most importantly, a way to get in and out.

To remove doors, enter the Doors section of the Buy Catalog and press the Grab Mode button. Select the door you wish to delete and sell it.

Doors vary in price:

- Abiding Elegance by Durabliss: §100
- Barred Door: §50
- Boggs Saloon Doors: §100
- Boggs Western Door: §100
- Bulkhead Latch: §75
- Coat-of-Many-Layers Door: §50
- Country Claw Designs Door I: §75
- Country Claw Designs Door II: §75
- Deko Door: §75
- Door with Small Window: §50
- Door, Catalog # 000001: §50
- Embofree Quality Air Lock Plus: §100
- Imprestige Door: §100
- Klassick Repro Multi-Frame Door: §75
- Klassick Repro Ornamental Door: §100
- Knobs & Hinges Door I: §50
- Knobs & Hinges Door II: §50
- Mahogany Leaded Glass Door: §75
- Metal Mentality Door: §50
- Oak Towne Simple Interior Door: §100
- Pet Blockades—Exterior Gate: §50
- Pet Blockades—Interior Gate: §50
- ResistIt Door: §75
- Shojitsu Door: §150
- Shojitsu Screen: §150
- Sliding Glass Door: §100
- Solana Vista Window: §75
- The All New 2005 "Portál": §50
- The Invisidoor: §50
- ValueWood "Just a Door": §50
- Wood-n-Steel Door: §100

Windows

Windows provide light in indoor spaces.

The more windows in a room, the happier the Sims within.

Windows are hung on empty wall segments. They cannot, however, be placed along diagonal walls.

To remove windows, enter the Windows section of the Buy Catalog and press the Grab Mode button.

Select the window you wish to delete and sell it just like you would any object in the Buy Catalog.

>
> ## tip
> More windows mean more light, and that means a higher indoor Room score. Use as many windows as you can afford.

Windows vary in price:

- Four Pane Punch: §50
- Gohji Full Pane Window: §100
- Gohji Half Pane window: §100
- Half Imprestige Window: §100
- Imprestige Window: §100
- Low Rider: §50
- Molotov Pre-Broken Window Set: §50
- Molotov Wild West Window Set: §50
- Peep Hole: §50
- Porthole: §100
- Nautilus Window: §50
- Ocular Home Orifice Alpha: §75
- Ocular Home Orifice Beta: §75
- Old and Glassy: §100

- OmniView Horizontal Half Pane: §75
- OmniView King Admiral: §75
- Paw Portal: §75
- Paws of Pane: §75
- Porthole NextGen: §100
- Practical Window: §50
- Short Pane "Setting Sun" Window: §50
- Super Sill 3000: §75
- Tall Pane "Setting Sun" Window: §100
- "The Four Pane": §50
- Whiskerton Windows Deluxe: §50
- Whiskerton Windows Standard: §50
- Window to the Past: §100
- Window-Rama: §75

Fireplaces

Fireplaces are wonderful decorative items, and they provide Fun in the form of watching the fire. While watching, your Sim can toast marshmallows for a little bit of Hunger satisfaction.

There's nothing quite like roasting marshmallows in front of a roaring hearth.

Fireplaces must be kept clean, or they become a fire hazard. Locate fireplaces along any nondiagonal wall. Be sure, however, to keep flammable objects at least a few feet away from the open flames.

Add and delete them like any Buy Catalog object.

- The Hearty Hearth: §500; Fun 5, Room 1
- Minimal Fireplace: §650; Fun 6, Room 2
- Empire Fireplace: §800; Fun 7, Room 4

Landscaping

Landscaping plants and shrubs are purely decorative items that can be placed outdoors only.

Want shrubbery? Try a two-level effect with a little path running down the middle.

Add and delete shrubs like any Buy Catalog object.

- Black-Eyed Susan: §75
- Cactacaea, aka Cactus: §100
- "Daisies of our Lives": §175
- Gnarly Carly Hardwood: §410
- Green Leafy Cats: §510
- Green Leafy Cats: §560
- Green Leafy Dogs: §510
- Green Leafy Dogs: §560
- Maple Tree: §375
- Ole Timey Climbin' Tree: §1,700

- Pale Birch: §210
- Papaver's Poppies: §210
- Pine Tree: §150
- Red-Faced Larry: §150
- Shrub d'Art: §130
- The Green Tree: §350
- Tip Top Tulips: §95
- Tree Unit Number Seven: §200
- Willow Tree: §150

Blueprint Mode

Blueprint mode allows you see a lot under construction from the advantageous top-down view. Plus, doors are diagrammed with the direction and size of their swing, and wall outlines are highlighted in orange, windows in white, and doorways in blue.

>
> ## tip
> Use your controller's D-pad to precisely move around in blueprint view.

Architectural Tips

- Keep bathrooms and beds near the front of the house to make the before-work routine as close as possible to the street and the carpool.

- A well-functioning house might not really look like a house at all. Do what works best for your strategy, not how you think a house should look.

- Leave plenty of room for Sims to maneuver around each other. A three-tile-wide space is much better than a cramped one- or two-tile-wide hallway.

- To help facilitate smooth movement of Sims, it's a good idea to make sure that there are at least two doors in every room. If you only have one, it is very easy for an autonomous Sim to engage in an activity (like socializing) right in front of the lone door, trapping Sims inside the room.

Chapter 25

THE SIMS 2 PETS FOR PLAYSTATION PORTABLE

For the first time, a handheld version of *The Sims* 2 will provide the full freeform Sims experience. In fact, with a few differences, the PSP version of the game is exactly like the PS2 and Gamecube versions.

This chapter explains these differences so PSP players can also utilize Part II of this guide. Being aware of these differences allows you to know what information in the console part of this guide doesn't apply to you.

Feature Comparison

Only lucky PSP players get the snazzy alien (and robot) pets.

Most major features between the PSP and console versions are the same. This table offers a quick comparison:

Feature	PSP
Alien/Robot Pets	Exclusive. Available in Create a Pet.
Aspirations	Same, but Aspiration points unlock new house templates rather than new townies.
Breeding, Puppies and Kittens	No
Breeds	Fourteen dogs (large only) and fourteen cats
Build Mode	No freeform Build mode. Instead, you may choose from increasingly large and expensive templates. Decor can be chosen from five styles: Modern, Traditional, Country, Atomic
Caged Pets	Same
Careers & Skills	Same
Classic Control	Classic Control is similar. Instead of a cursor, all visible objects appear, sorted by frequency of use and distance to the Sim, in an action list summoned with ⊠.
Create a Pet	Similar but simplified
Create-A-Sim	Simplified
Family Inventory	Simplified.
Fire Code	Same
Food Creation	Simplified: recipes must be unlocked via Cooking skill and reading.
Learned Behavior	Commands and reinforced behaviors
Neighborhood	Four exclusive lots

Feature	PSP
New Service NPCs and Expanded NPC Abilities	Same
Objects	Same but some unique objects
Personality	Same
Pet Motives & Mood	Same
Pet Points	Yes. Pet Points spent at Town Square stores upgrade individual stores.
Pet Point Unlock Codes	No
Pet Sharing Codes	No
Pet Wants	Yes, to earn Pet Points
Renovation Mode	Change houses with renovation templates instead of Build mode. Wall and floor coverings can also be applied to any renovation template.
Social Interactions/ Relationships	Similar. Learn an NPC's zodiac sign by achieving +40 (Friend) relationship and learn their Aspiration by achieving +75 (Best Friend) relationship.
Stray Pets & Running Away	Pets will run away.
Town Square	Yes. Buildings upgrade visually and expand inventory.
Visitation	No uninvited random visitors except the welcome wagon the first time you play a lot.
Weather	Same

Houses have a variety of layouts.

Home Template Unlocks

Satisfying your Sims' Wants earns them Aspiration points. The neighborhood-wide total of Aspiration points unlocks several home templates:

- 1-Bedroom layouts: 1,000 Aspiration points
- 2-Bedroom layouts: 5,000 Aspiration points
- 3-Bedroom layouts: 15,000 Aspiration points

Town Square

The Town Square is the central meeting place for Sims and their pets.

The Town Square in PSP is largely identical to the console version with a few minor changes. Most obviously, when buildings upgrade, they don't increase in size but rather only in appearance. They do, however, expand their selections as they upgrade.

As with console, upgrades are fueled by the number of Pet Points you spend in each store:

Store/Cart	Pet Points Spending Required for Upgrade to Good	Pet Points Spending Required for Upgrade to Awesome
Pet Bakery	200	133
Coffee Cart	86	74
Ice Cream Cart	192	115
Smoothie Cart	213	128
Pet Emporium	333	222
Pet Purveyors	250	167
Pet Salon	111	74
Pet Toy Store	167	111

Food Creation

The food creation system is the same, but several recipes need to be unlocked:

Name	Fridge	Unlocked Via
Burrito	All	Cooking skill level 2
Casserole	Stainless Steel Fridge	Cooking skill level 10
Cheeseless Pizza	All	Cooking skill level 9
Chef Salad	All	Read newspaper
Fruit in Pastry	All	Read book
Fruit Shake	All	Read in bed
Fruit Smoothie	All	Cooking skill level 5
Hors d'Oeuvres	All	Read toilet magazine
Kebabs	All	Cooking skill level 3
Parfait	All	Cooking skill level 4
Roast & Fruit Sauce	Chow Town Eco-Fridge	Chat on computer
Samosas	All	Read book
Sandwich	Default recipe	Default recipe
Sweet Vegetable Soup	Default recipe	Default recipe
Wellington Roast	Stainless Steel Fridge	Cooking skill level 7

Objects

Dozens of objects can be bought from home or the town square stores.

The object selection on the PSP differs somewhat from the console:

- 2Player Sofa
- Atrocity Now!
- Baritone Chair
- Beaumont Double Bed
- Beaumont Twin Bed
- Bed D'Jour
- Big Ernie's Couch for Men
- Built for Two Loveseat
- Captain Eclipto Dining Chair
- Celestial Loveseat
- Clarabelle in Poppies
- Classy Counter
- Club Futura
- Couch Tater
- Countertop Rodeo
- Country Chair Jamboree
- Cuddles N Kisses Loveseat
- Curvilinear End Table
- DeBingo Dining Chair
- Empire Reading Lamp
- End Table—Trojan Series
- Esmeralda Chair
- Eternal Loveseat
- Farmer Ted, Self-Portrait #47
- Flares of VaMule
- Grandma's Barnyard Double
- Higgen-Hog Loveseat
- Hometown Honeymooner
- Infinity Lamp
- Lamponilé
- Moth Ball Inc. Floor Lamp II
- Nebula-Bedula
- Oval Square
- Quantum Lantern
- Rocket Cot
- Simple Pleasures
- Sofa Supreme
- Solo Dining Chair
- Space Escape
- S-Table
- Stellar Sofa by Sputnix Furnishings
- Super Supper Table
- Super-Cyber Sconce
- The Big Sleep
- The Bumpkin Bunk
- The Conn
- The DreamTron 3 Billion
- The Executive
- The Hammock-Chair
- The Knitter's Lamp
- The L7
- The Lightsicle
- The Living End Table
- The McPansy Chair
- The Parlor Sofa
- The Power Counter
- The Ranch Hand Dining Table
- The RecTable
- The Rounded Table
- The Sit-A-Spell
- TruSquare Country Table
- Winner's Bed
- Working Cubes 3.0
- XMD700-DS103
- Ye Ole Countertops
- Zaparoni Table Lamp II